THE CLERICAL PROFESSION

The Clerical Profession

ANTHONY RUSSELL

LONDON

SPCK

First published 1980
Second impression 1981
SPCK
Holy Trinity Church
Marylebone Road
London NW1 4DU

Printed in Great Britain by Billing & Sons Ltd,
Guildford, London and Worcester

ISBN 0 281 03721 3

To Sheila

Contents

Preface

In recent years so much has been written about the ministry of the Church and the historic problems and contemporary dilemmas of its priesthood that any new book would seem to demand an apology. However, this debate has principally been concerned with a theological analysis of the development of the doctrine of the priesthood. This book has been written in the belief that in order to understand many of the contemporary attitudes, both to the Church's ministry itself, and to changes in its modern form, it is necessary to set an historico-sociological account of the development of the clergyman's role alongside the extensive theological literature on the nature of priesthood. Thus, this book seeks to be at one level a monograph on the clerical profession, and as such a contribution both to church history and to the sociology of professions; however, at another level, the book is also a contribution to the contemporary debate about the nature of the Church's ministry.

My debts of gratitude for help in preparing this book are extensive. Among the many people who have assisted me, I am particularly indebted to Dr Bryan Wilson; this book and its author owe very much to his guidance and kindness. I am especially grateful to Canon Leslie Houlden for his encouragement and assistance throughout the preparation of this book. Among many historians, sociologists, and churchmen I owe special thanks to Professor David Martin, Dr John Walsh, and Dr Brian Heeney. I am grateful for the help of the Librarians and staff of the Bodleian Library and for the financial assistance of the J. Arthur Rank Group Charity, which made the completion of this book possible. To Miss Anne Durham who typed the manuscript, I owe a considerable debt of gratitude.

Finally, I have had cause on many occasions to recall the dictum of a former Archbishop that writing a book is a hazardous undertaking for a parochial clergyman. Undoubtedly the book has suffered from the piecemeal fashion in which it has been written amidst the many demands of a clergyman's life. To my parishioners, my colleagues at the Arthur Rank Centre, National Agricultural Centre, and not least my family, I am deeply indebted for their patience and support.

Whitchurch Rectory   ANTHONY RUSSELL
January 1979

PART ONE

The Clergyman's Role and the Professional Ideal

1

Introduction

The Church of England is a notoriously enigmatic institution and scarcely less so is the role of the clergyman which is the subject of this book. 'Clergyman', 'Minister', 'Parson', 'Clerk in Holy Orders', 'Priest' and 'Vicar': this range of designations indicates the variety of ways in which the religious functionary of the Church of England may be regarded. However, a basic and fundamental distinction can be maintained between theologically derived and historico-sociologically derived definitions; that is to say, between the terms 'priest' and 'clergyman'. To call the religious functionary of the Church of England 'a priest' is to use a theological definition grounded in the writings of the New Testament and the subsequent development of the doctrine of ministry and priesthood within the Church. The term 'priest' denotes a theological status within the Church and the criteria for testing the adequacy of such statements are theological criteria. However, the term 'clergyman' denotes an occupational role among the many occupational roles in society. In this case, the role of the religious functionary may, like any other role, be examined and subjected to investigation according to historical and sociological methods and principles. Here the criteria for testing the adequacy of the definition are the criteria of empirical verification.

The fact that the terms 'priest' and 'clergyman' afford a double definition of the religious functionary of the Church of England can create much confusion, particularly when statements based on different sets of criteria are too readily juxtaposed. For instance, it is not uncommon to find statements to the effect that the Church's ministry should not be regarded as a profession because it is a vocation. That the priesthood is a vocation is a statement legitimated by theological criteria, and it is a statement which does not nullify the assertion that the clergyman's role is sufficiently

3

similar to professional roles for it to be included in that ill-defined category of occupations. By the same token, the suggestion that a role is becoming marginal to the main-stream of social life is a sociological statement and of a different order to statements about the need for detachment in the life of a priest. The latter is a statement based not on sociological but on theological legitimation. To suggest (as is suggested in the final chapters) that the clergyman's role is becoming increasingly marginal in contemporary society is to make a sociological observation about the altered social position of an occupational role; to suggest that a priest needs to possess a sense of detachment is to make a wholly different statement. Similarly, to question the effectiveness of the role is not from the theological standpoint a primary and possibly not even a legitimate question. However, from the historico-sociological standpoint, it is a valid question of considerable significance, which may be asked of all social institutions and occupational roles. Thus, the analytical distinction between 'priest' as a theological status and 'clergyman' as an occupational role must be maintained. This book is concerned with the development and con-temporary situation of the clergyman's role and is not a treatise on priesthood.

As Western European society passes through a period of profound turbulence, so the position of many of its ancient and venerable institutions has become increasingly prob-lematic. Even by the standards of contemporary society and the much labouring of the word 'crisis', it does not appear to be an exaggeration to suggest that the Churches have reached a point of deep crisis. Until quite recently, this phenomenon was commonly analysed in ideological terms, and it was suggested that, in an increasingly secular age, religious practice and belief would sharply decline both in incidence and significance and that the Churches would become increasingly anachronistic institutions. However, whilst the decline of the historic Churches has continued to the point where under 3 per cent of the population regularly attend a Sunday service, there is at the same time evidence to suggest that people have not abandoned a religious per-spective. As institutional religion continues to decline, so the practice of religion appears to have become more privatized (as have other activities in contemporary society) and new extra-ecclesial and quasi-religious forms of spirituality enjoy considerable popularity. It is certainly evident that spiritual writing and spiritual leaders arouse widespread public interest. Thus, it might be suggested that it is the Church rather than man's ability to respond to the spiritual that is dying, and that the crisis through which the historic Churches are passing is predominantly institutional and organizational rather than ideological in nature. However, such a distinction is not easy to sustain in the case of religious institutions because in a sense the organization is a symbolic and structural expression of the belief system, or to make the same point in theological terms, the Church is the primary sacrament. Similarly, the priest stands within and is in a sense a part of the mystery which he himself signifies and proclaims.

Thus, in contemporary society the Churches find themselves facing an organizational crisis, and the clergyman's role appears to be the hub around which so many of the problems which face the contemporary Church are located. The depth of the crisis in the Church's ministry may be judged from such objective indices as the progressive contraction in the total number of clergy, the comparatively low levels of recruitment, the predominance of clergy in senior age groups, the number of younger clergy who 'opt out' and leave the parochial ministry, the fact that the academic standards of the clergy appear to be falling relative to other professions, and the way in which the Church has been forced to grapple with severe financial and manpower problems in order to maintain its reduced parochial ministry. These factors, together with the frequently voiced doubts and uncertainties about the clergyman's role in contemporary society and the constant reference by the laity to domineering clericalism, particularly with regard to the limited clerical perspectives within which the contemporary debate about ministry takes place, indicate some measure of the extent and depth of the crisis.

The Church of England accords to its history a considerable significance because so many aspects of its organization cannot be understood without reference to the past; among these the clergyman's role is a pre-eminent example. Although this book is principally concerned to analyse the situation of the clergyman's role in contemporary society, it is necessary to preface this consideration with an account of the development of the clergyman's role during its formative period in the nineteenth century. In this period, the clergy took the emerging professions as their model and reference group, and the role of the clergyman came to be shaped in its recognizably modern form. Indeed, this period may be regarded from the contemporary point of view as the crucial period of change since when there have been only minor modifications.

Thus, this study is centrally concerned with the process by which the clergy, a pre-professional occupational group, acquired certain professional characteristics. Whilst, in the eighteenth century, the clergyman's role may be seen as 'an occupational appendage of gentry status', in the nineteenth century the clergy were anxious to regard themselves and be regarded by society as a professional body with specific functions and duties. However, the clergy did not entirely approximate to the role of a professional man; one of the essential differences being the very diffuse nature of their role. Thus, the clergyman's role today includes many functions which are not legitimated by ordination but which arose in particular from the social position of the clergy in the late-eighteenth-century countryside. Of the typical clergyman of that period, Dean Church wrote:

> He was often much, very much, to society round him. When communication was so difficult and infrequent, he filled a place in the country life of England which no one else could fill. He was often the patriarch of his parish, its ruler, its doctor, its lawyer, its magistrate as well as its teacher before whom vice trembled and rebellion dare not show itself.[1]

The major part of this book is concerned with analysing the changes which the adoption of a new model for the role, namely that of a professional man, brought to these various aspects of the clergyman's role. These elements of the role may be regarded as the role-sectors, and for the purposes of this analysis, the following have been identified: leader of public worship, preacher, celebrant of the sacraments, pastor, catechist, clerk, officer of law and order, almoner, teacher, officer of health, and politician.

It is possible that no profession has more readily available published and manuscript material on the performance of the role of its members than the clerical profession, and in this study only a limited selection of that material has been employed. Two principal sources have been used. First, before theological colleges were founded, the only instruction which a clergyman received was from books specially written for the purpose, and in the late eighteenth century and the early nineteenth century many of these 'handbooks' were published, with such titles as *Hints from a Minister to his Curate for the Management of his Parish; The Clergyman's Instructor; The Clergyman's Obligations Considered;* and *Practical Advice to the Young Parish Priest*. These books provide a valuable source of information on the changes which the clerical profession underwent during the crucial period in which it was moulded into its modern form. If this book has any claim to originality, it lies in the use of approximately a hundred 'handbooks', found in the Bodleian Library, which were published between 1750 and 1875.[2] Most of them were written by busy parish priests whose names are not familiar from the standard histories of the Church. Indeed, so predominant has been the tendency to write the history of the Church as if it were the history of the upper echelons of the institution, the bishops, cathedral dignitaries, and Oxford dons, that there are few published works on the parochial clergy and such as there are tend to be anecdotal rather than analytical. To supplement the 'handbooks', biographical and autobiographical material, in which the Victorian church is particularly rich, has been used to provide a picture of the manner in which the role was actually performed throughout the period. Although literary data are the evidence on which the analysis of the changes in the clergyman's role is based, the book is not in any conventional sense an intellectual history. Whilst the great ideological changes in Christianity which occurred,

especially in the nineteenth century, had profound consequences for the clergyman's role, it is with the detailed
shifts in the conception and implementation of clerical duties
that this study principally concerns itself. The prescriptions
of the Tractarians and Evangelicals about a clergyman's
functions and role are of considerable doctrinal interest, but
in contrast to numerous studies of the intellectual history of
religion in the nineteenth century, this study concerns itself
not so much with doctrinal preferences and assumed consequences in the role of the clergyman as with the actual
changes that can be observed from the literature of the
period concerning the way in which the clergy went about
their work and reflected on it.

Thus, the book seeks to be at one level a monograph on the
clerical profession and a contribution to the sociology of
professions and to nineteenth-century church history.
However, at another level, the book is also a contribution to
the contemporary debate about the nature of the Church's
ministry and the crisis in the priesthood. This crisis has
already produced a wealth of theological literature alongside
which the historico-sociological considerations that arise
from a study of the development of the clergyman's role and
its contemporary situation need to be placed in order that the
bounds of the debate may be fruitfully extended.

2
The Emergence of the Professions in English Society

It is in religious usage that the word 'profession' retains the original meaning of the Latin *profiteri*, 'to declare publicly'. In post-Augustan Latin the term *professor* was applied to the occupant of a teaching post. In contemporary usage, the term 'professional' bears a whole range of meanings, usually as an antonym of unpaid, amateur, or part-time, and this variety of meanings indicates something of the imprecision in the use of the concept of the profession in contemporary society. Carr-Saunders and Wilson, in the first analytical study of professions, found it impossible to better the *Oxford English Dictionary* definition: 'A vocation in which a professed knowledge of some department of learning or science is used in its application to the affairs of others or in the practice of an art founded on it.'[1]

Much of the recent writing on professions has concerned itself with three principal areas of debate: the characteristics of a true profession; the process by which an occupation becomes a profession; and the conflict between the two principal tendencies in industrial society towards the professionalization of roles and the bureaucratization of institutions.[2]

In as much as they may be regarded as a select group of high-prestige occupations, professions have existed in society in various forms from very early stages of development. Indeed, Herbert Spencer traced their origins among primitive people.[3] In the broadest terms an analytical distinction may be maintained between those occupational roles which are based on the practice of a specific skill or craft and those roles which are related to some branch of human knowledge. The sum of knowledge of any society has to be developed, interpreted, applied, and handed on for the good of that society. The professional occupations may broadly be regarded as those occupations based on knowledge which fulfil these functions in society. Their distinctiveness results from their maintaining a monopoly over certain areas of knowledge which have considerable practical application and social usefulness. The professions, as they emerged as distinct groups in society, developed a monopoly sanctioned by the community over certain areas of knowledge and practice such as religion, medicine, pharmacy, teaching, and law – areas which were appropriate to certain individual and social needs. Access to these areas of knowledge became the exclusive privilege of the profession. The professional man became an acknowledged authority in an area of human knowledge which was socially important but of which most people were ignorant.

It is evident that the professions are closely related to the structure of knowledge in society. In a primitive society most knowledge is sacral in character, however secular may be its application, and the religious functionary occupies a role of critical social significance. However, changes in the structure of knowledge such as those that occurred in Western Europe at the time of the Renaissance and the Reformation (and later at the time of the Industrial Revolution) had a profound effect on occupational roles in general (of which there were relatively few) and the clergyman's role in particular. The development of common law and the decline of ecclesiastical law, the encouragement of Greek learning in the universities of Europe by Linacre and his colleagues, and the changes in university teaching precipitated by the new learning of the Renaissance clearly had a direct effect on the way these occupations based on systematic learning were performed in sixteenth- and seventeenth-century Europe. The processes of secularization and the developing scale and compartmentalization of learning provoked a complementary fragmentation of occupational roles. As religion lost its ubiquitous position of presidency in Western European society, so theology lost her role as 'the Queen of Sciences'. Whilst formerly ordination was almost the sole qualification for high-status occupation roles, and whilst the clergy controlled the access to all areas of human learning, in this period the role of the clergy became an occupational role among an increasing number of broadly similar roles.

That knowledge is the basis of the authority and legitimation of a profession is clearly demonstrated by the process of initiation. A professional body may be regarded as a separate sub-culture into which a postulant enters only after selection, training, examination, and certification, culminating in a ritual which has some of the significance of a *rite de passage*. This period of initiation is characterized by instruction in a body of knowledge that has been organized into a coherent system. The initate is required to familiarize himself with the system of abstact propositions that account in general terms for the phenomena comprising the profession's interest. This preoccupation with systematic theory is one of the principal distinguishing marks of a profession and is virtually absent in the training for non-professional roles. Knowledge is the principal resource of the professional body which is corporately concerned to develop, protect, and guard it. [4]

It is not possible to speculate on the early origins of the professions in general or of particular professional groups. However, sociologists have attempted to account for the existence of bodies which may recognizably be termed professions in all advanced societies. Two processes may be identified which have had a mutually reinforcing and interdependent influence on the growth and development of professions. In the first account of the rise of professional bodies, it is the functional needs of society which are regarded as the catalyst. The areas of knowledge and their consequent application over which the professions preside are areas of particular sensitivity in which any abuse or exploitation would result in great harm either to an individual or to society as a whole. The professionalization of certain occupational roles is a process by which, for society's benefit, these roles become hedged about by a complex arrangement of norms, codes, laws, expectations, and sanctions. These arrangements are developed to protect society and its individual members from exploitation and abuse. In this view, professionalization may be regarded as a device generated by the community for guaranteeing the nature and validity of services, and for controlling those who

seek to render them, in areas either of acute personal uncertainty, or in which the individual is at risk of being exploited as a result of his inability to evaluate the quality of
these services.[5]

The other view is in some ways the opposite, having its
starting point not in the needs of the community but in the
desires and aspirations of the occupational role. It is summed
up in the words of George Bernard Shaw: 'All professions
are conspiracies against the laity.'[6]

In this view professionalization may be regarded as the
device by which certain occupational groups have maintained their high social status and comparable standards of
remuneration by means of a protective monopoly on a body
of knowledge of importance to the wider society. It can be
suggested that the insistence on their high standards of
practice, altruistic concern, and ethical obligations merely
serve to disguise the more selfish desire to create an artificial
scarcity and to win the material and non-material advantages
which readily flow from such a situation.[7] A professional
body is able to isolate itself from public scrutiny, and thus
increase its operational autonomy, by developing its esoteric
knowledge, maintaining a homogeneous and coherent
personnel and, increasingly in recent years, by developing a
community language (jargon) which is inaccessible to the
layman. Talcott Parsons considered that in many respects
professional roles which market skills and judgement should
not be differentiated from businessmen who market com-
modities and services. He regarded them as equally concerned with individual success and their apparent altruism as
institutionally expected behaviour restricted to the pro-
fessional-client relationship and thence generalized into a
broad social attitude. The display of sympathy and understanding towards the client is needed for the efficient
performance of the service.[8]

However, professional men have been anxious to point out
in every age that not only is their role based on a different
form of authority and legitimation from that of non-
professional roles but that it is essentially different in type to
other roles. When Adam Smith classed professions as un-
productive labour, he was no doubt acknowledging the fact

that the professions stand outside capitalistic relations and constraints. From the time when sociologists first concerned themselves with the study of professions, they have been anxious to stabilize the meaning of the term and to construct a model of the true profession (an ideal type); this has led to many attempts to provide a definitive list of attributes, or traits. In his Herbert Spencer lecture of 1927, Professor Carr-Saunders defined a profession in terms of specialized skills and training, minimum fees and salaries, formation of a professional association, and a code of ethics governing professional practice.[9] Another list of traits contained four basic elements:

1 Practice is founded upon a base of theoretic esoteric knowledge.
2 The acquisition of knowledge requires a long period of education and socialization.
3 Control is exercised over recruitment, training, certification and standards of practice.
4 The colleague-group is well organized and has disciplinary powers to enforce a code of ethical practice.[10]

A composite model may be constructed and the ideal type of a profession may be understood as an occupational group that has specialist functions; a prolonged training; a monopoly of legitimate performance; self-regulating mechanisms with regard to entry and expulsion; colleague-group solidarity; autonomy of role performance; a fiduciary relationship between practitioner and client; a distinctive professional ethic stressing altruistic service; a reward structure and career pattern; and a research orientation and control of the institution within which the professional role is legitimated.

Models or ideal types are of use not only as a way of deciding just which occupational groups can appropriately be regarded as professions, but perhaps more important, for assessing the degree to which an occupational role approximates the ideal type. It is possible to suggest that there is a continuum between, on the one hand, the completely unorganized occupational categories (non-professional) and the fully professionalized roles, and to assess along this continuum the degree of professionalization of a particular occupation. Professionalization may be regarded as a dynamic process which has affected to a lesser or greater extent all occupations in contemporary society. Clearly the process has affected different roles in different ways and there is no single end-state to which they are progressing; but the widespread existence of this process and its influence on all occupational roles is acknowledged in contemporary society. It is the operation of this process in relation to the role of the clergyman which forms the central theme of this study.

THE PROCESS OF PROFESSIONALIZATION

Those who have studied the professionalization of occupational roles have laid great emphasis on the professional organization or institution as the principal agent in this process. The formation by an occupational role of an institution or central agency which is able to gain rewards and status in society which individuals could not hope to attain is an early development in the process of professionalization.[11] The Church as an institution performed this role for the clergy from an early stage. Wilensky has attempted to establish a natural history of professionalization in which he sees roles passing through four stages: the occupation is followed on a full-time basis; formal training is established; training is provided in a university; local and then national professional associations are established.[12]

Clearly the notion of training is of importance for it is by this process that standards are enforced and maintained, and internal cohesion is reinforced. The aspirant internalizes a system of social values, behavioural norms, and the symbols of his occupational group. An emerging professional group is also particularly anxious to impose both official and unofficial sanctions on role performance with the aim of standardizing behaviour and reducing deviancy.[13] All professions are self-disciplining bodies which seek to exclude the unworthy and those likely to bring the profession into disrepute. It is no coincidence that the Church was much concerned with the twin matters of training and discipline in the nineteenth century.

As occupational groups developed into professional bodies so they became increasingly concerned to identify and maintain boundaries between their specific occupational concern and other neighbouring occupations. The clergy in the nineteenth century were much involved in these processes of role definition as new occupational roles took over aspects of their ancient role. Many of the occupations which are termed professions resulted from the mechanical revolution and the progress in science and technology associated with the Industrial Revolution which gave rise to a demand for specialists to handle the new complex machinery – material, institutional, and bureaucratic. Professionalization, although not exclusively a process of rationalization of highly skilled labour, embraced a considerable degree of rationalization. The impact of rationalization on the clergyman's role was considerable, since as a role it was based on traditional, non-rational assumptions. The degree to which rationalization, as a process by which more effective means might be designed to achieve known and empirical goals, can be applied to a profession the goals of which are at least in part supernatural, is limited.

During the nineteenth century, as occupational roles developed into professions in the recognizably modern sense, so they developed systems of entry, certification, and expulsion, subtle and not so subtle disciplinary powers, and a common language, norms, and standards. Eventually they became distinct sub-cultures with their own symbols, insignia, emblems, language, dress, history, and folklore. It was at this time that the notion of a career, as a self-conscious continuity between jobs, began first to be developed. Allied to all this, the professions continually nurtured the ideals of altruism, community service, and personal dedication.

Professional roles differ from other occupational roles in society in that they minimize the distinction between person and occupational role. This (as will be shown) relates to the early period in their development when professional roles were more closely connected with status than with tasks, and when in consequence the distinction between person and role was not made. This blurring of the boundaries between work and non-work by which a professional man is expected to conform to a particular life-style (as evidenced by the fact that a professional institution regards its members' non-occupational behaviour as a legitimate area for its concern and direction), together with the ancient notion that a professional man is never off duty, is another characteristic feature of the professions. The concept of 'totality' may be borrowed from Goffman's analysis of institution and applied to occupational roles to indicate continuous and complete membership, and this concept is particularly useful in the analysis of the clergyman's role. [14]

HIGH-STATUS OCCUPATIONAL ROLES IN PRE-INDUSTRIAL SOCIETY

Although professionalization is regarded as a phenomenon of advanced industrialized societies, nevertheless it is possible to recognize changes in occupational roles in the eighteenth century which had considerable significance for the later development of the professions. Society, in the eighteenth century, was predominantly seen as a divinely ordered system which rested on the maintenance of a hierarchical social structure in which everyone was required to do his duty in that state of life to which it had pleased God to call him. As in all traditional *gemeinschaftlich* rural societies, occupational roles were less clearly defined, and more ascriptive and closely involved in non-work aspects of life than later became the case. Similarly, the distinction between the various institutional spheres of society (economic, judicial, political, civic, familial, etc.) were less evident than they later became. Furthermore, as in all traditional pre-industrial societies, the numbers of high-status occupational roles were severely limited.

Eighteenth-century society was broadly divided into two unequal parts: those who performed manual tasks, and those who were members of the very small leisured class. The ownership of landed property broke the direct connection between work and income which governed the lives of the vast majority. Land conferred independence, leisure, and freedom from manual labour which were the three hallmarks of the gentry class.[15] Between these two classes, the leisured and the labouring, were a small number of high-status non-manual occupational roles from the ranks of which the professions eventually emerged.

Many factors were responsible for the enhanced status of these occupational groups in the late eighteenth century. The specialist services of the lawyer were in great demand in a society where land was the source of almost all wealth and lay behind the legal, political, and social assumptions of the age. As the purveyor of much highly regarded and socially important technical knowledge with regard to such matters as ownership, succession, rents, and general estate management, the lawyer became indispensable to all landed families. As the institutions of society became more complex, so the role of the lawyer grew in status and significance. By the mid-eighteenth century the tariff system had grown so intricate that merchants were forced to employ lawyers to guide them through it. The lawyers were the first professional group to gain some measure of control over the institutional context of their work. In 1739, the Society of Gentlemen Practitioners in the Courts of Law and Equity was established by an Act of Parliament (2 Geo. II. i. 23) which sought among other things to regularize entry into the legal profession by requiring a five-year apprenticeship followed by an examination by a judge. Like all emerging professional groups, the lawyers were compelled to conduct a long battle against unqualified practitioners, for in an age when book learning was rare, any literate person might readily take on legal business for his neighbours.[16] In this way the lawyers as an occupational group developed some of the aspects of professionalization at a time when, because of the increasing scale and complexity of society, there was a developing need for their skills.

Another factor in the development of high-status occupational roles, which particularly affected the clergy, was the changes that took place in rural society in the eighteenth century. The progressive inflation, and the enclosures and the development of the large estates which were such a notable feature of rural life at this time, left many of the lesser gentry in reduced and parlous financial circumstances. As in all traditional societies, the family was the basic economic unit and sons. of such families expected 'a competence' – a sufficient income to live as a gentleman. The provision of this came either from land or from the patronage to which the family had access.[17] For these families the changes in the countryside were such that it was increasingly to a place in a government office, a commission in the army, or a living in the Church that they looked for the provision of a competence for their sons. By the mid-eighteenth century, sons of such families (particularly younger sons) were increasingly found among the ranks of the clergy and army officers (who had previously been either militia or mercenary).

However, in a pre-industrial society, there were few high-status occupations and these groups were small in size (except the clergy who alone were numbered in four figures by the end of the eighteenth century) and heavily concentrated in London and the other major cities. For instance, the Royal College of Physicians, in 1745, had 52 fellows, 3 candidates, and 23 licentiates; in the period 1771–1833, only 168 fellows were admitted.[18] At that time medical knowledge was at a rudimentary stage and the outcome of most medical procedures was at best uncertain. The expansion and professionalization of the medical profession took place in the nineteenth century as a result of the great advances in medical knowledge which conferred on the doctor's role a greater social status in recognition of its increased social utility and significance. The military professions had only recently become full-time occupations, and, since the Peace of Utrecht, the Army and Navy had been maintained at a low level. In the second half of the eighteenth century there was a considerable expansion, and, whereas in 1739 there were only 367 lieutenants in the Navy, the number had risen to 1349 by 1783.[19]

In the mid-eighteenth century there did not exist the large number of administrative and bureaucratic posts which changes in the scale, complexity, and nature of society eventually brought into being. In 1745, the complete establishment of the Treasury (including housekeeper, doorkeeper, and messenger) was 23; the Secretary of State's Office was 26. On the eve of the period of Imperial expansion, there were 13 clerks in the War Office, 10 at the Board of Trade, and 8 at the Admiralty. Even at the close of the Napoleonic Wars, the entire clerical staff of the Treasury was 86, the Home Office 19, and the Foreign Office 23.[20] All these appointments, as well as cadetships in the East India Company which were keenly sought after and well paid, were in private patronage. All appointments were made by this system and membership of a landed family gave direct access to the patronage system. Significantly, patronage was least important in the legal profession where skill was readily recognizable. However, as in most professions, expensive backing was the indispensable foundation for a career and a device for preserving the group's exclusiveness. It was in the Church that patronage was of the greatest significance and to be ordained without any prospects was to be condemned to live as a 'journeyman' clergyman, accepting the best curacies that an incumbent offered. Among the high-status occupational groups in the latter part of the eighteenth century, the clergy were by far the most numerous, and possibly larger than all the other professions put together.

The entrance to all professions was through the university and it has been said of the eighteenth-century universities that they had more to do with socialization and lifestyle than with learning.[21] The examination of candidates prior to their admission to the professional bodies was not so much concerned with evidence of knowledge and expertise as with the candidate's possession of characteristics appropriate to his claim to be accepted into an exclusive professional body. Candidates for ordination were only required to give evidence of a classical education with all the connotations of status and accepted values that this carried in eighteenth-century society.

Certainly, in this early period, professional work was not sufficiently specialized (with the possible exception of the law) to be regarded as the routine application of a particular expertise to a certain set of problems. The ability to perform professional functions seems to have been a less important aspect of high-status occupational roles at this period than the ability to live a suitably leisured and cultured lifestyle. It is noticeable in the Army that those regiments connected with specific expertise, engineers and artillery, were accorded lesser status than other regiments, and commissions in these two corps were never bought or sold.[22]

Thus, by the late eighteenth century, the high-status occupational groups were beginning to establish themselves between the leisured and the labouring classes. They achieved this by becoming occupational appendages of the gentry status in society. However, work for remuneration remained incompatible with high social status; Dr Johnson remarked of someone that he did not care to speak ill behind the man's back but he believed the gentleman to be an attorney.[23] The particularly high status accorded to the clergy and to Army officers at the time appears to derive in part from the fact that their roles were connected with no specialist expertise or craft, and partly from the fact that the service of God and the Crown were both an ancient aristocratic function.[24] Clearly, in the latter part of the eighteenth century, these two roles had as much to do with the distribution of status in English society as with the division of specific work tasks.

THE DEVELOPMENT OF THE PROFESSIONS IN VICTORIAN ENGLAND

'The importance of the professions and the professional classes can hardly be overrated, they form the head of the great English middle class, maintaining its tone of independence, keep up to the mark its standard of morality and direct its intelligence,' wrote H. Byerley Thomas in *The Choice of a Profession*, published in 1857.[25] The professions developed into their recognizably modern form as England was transformed into a predominantly industrial and advanced society as a result of the Industrial Revolution and the great growth in the scale and complexity of social life in the nineteenth century. The processes of social change in the early decades of the nineteenth century which transformed English life from that of a basically rural and traditional to an increasingly urban and industrial society, included the development of a higher level of institutional differentiation which caused all occupational roles to become not only more skilled and technical, but also more specific and focused around the central functions which gave them legitimation in an increasingly rational and pragmatic social system. The scientific and technological developments associated with the Industrial Revolution gave rise to a whole new range of high-status occupational roles, concerned not only with these new developments but also with the new financial institutions and bureaucratic structures of advanced society. The process of institutional differentiation caused the fragmentation of some of the old high-status occupational roles and a consequent contraction in the range of their functions. The roles of the clergyman and the lawyer were particularly affected by this process. The latter had been known in the eighteenth century by the landed gentry as 'my man of business', but, by the late nineteenth century, his role had become much more specific and new professional bodies (land agents, surveyors, architects, estate managers, accountants, quantity surveyors, and estate agents) had emerged to take over elements of the formerly diffuse lawyer's role as the specialism of a new profession. This process of fragmentation and increased specificity of roles was an important aspect of the development of the nineteenth-century professions.

The new urban middle classes aspired to needs which had formerly been restricted to the leisured class. The men who met these needs, who were recruited from the urban middle class in large numbers, were no longer members of small socially prescribed cliques but large professional associations competing for status with groups of near equals.[26] The new middle classes, drawing on the recently created sources of industrial wealth, exercised powerful pressure on the occupational system for changes to accommodate their needs.

The great expansion of industry and the commercial life of the nation in the nineteenth century represented a considerable threat to the old high-status occupational roles. As English society became more advanced, power, particularly financial power, was passing away from the traditional status hierarchy to the entrepreneurs and businessmen of the cities. The emergence of the ideology of professionalism may be seen in some aspects as the response of the high-status occupational roles to the challenge and threat of this fundamental shift in power in Victorian society. Professionalization was a means by which the prestigious occupational roles retained their status and authority in the face of the growing economic power of the business and commercial world. The professional associations which were formed to represent the interests of professional men, made it their task to protect and develop the socially important knowledge and skills which the professions possessed. They called the business world to recognize its limitations and its dependence on the services of professional men. The emphasis on the service ethic, on 'duty' and 'principles', gave the professions a moral superiority over the profit motive of the commercial world which they exploited to the full. The entrepreneur or businessman was a new figure in English society, and the objections to trade and business only weakened slightly in the Victorian period. The social dominance of the middle classes and their culture which is so pre-eminently associated with the Victorian era was created in large measure by the professions, who emerged as a strong, confident, coherent high-status group with an ethic which was elaborated in part in opposition to the growth of industrialism and commercialism.

It was the professional man, gentlemanly but highly skilled, cultured but technically capable, conscious of the service ethic yet making a good livelihood, standing or falling by his own skill or judgement, who was the quintessential self-made man, and who became the cultural hero of late-nineteenth-century English society.[27] The archetypal Victorian men – the doctor, the clergyman, the lawyer, the civil servant, the colonial administrator, the engineer, the architect, the army officer, the schoolmaster, were all professional men, and it was these men who had such a profound influence on the shaping of Victorian society and a significant influence on national affairs. Whereas, in the eighteenth century, the professions had been small high-status élites, they rapidly developed in the nineteenth century into large organizations whose members were numbered in thousands rather than hundreds. By 1881 there were 17,400 barristers and solicitors; 15,100 surgeons, physicians and doctors; 3600 dentists; and 15,000 army and naval officers on home station alone.[28]

In the emergence of the professions the professional associations played a decisive role. The formation of these associations among which were the Law Society founded (in its modern form) in 1825; the Royal Institute of British Architects, 1834; the Royal College of Veterinary Surgeons, 1844; the Institute of Mechanical Engineers, 1847; the British Medical Association, 1856; the Surveyors Institute, 1868; the National Union of Teachers, 1870; and the Institute of Chartered·Accountants, 1880, marked a crucial stage in the development of professionalization.[29] The associations were particularly concerned to raise the status and emolument of their profession; to define its role and relations with society, possibly by Act of Parliament; to set up minimum standards of entry and professional practice; to establish a disciplinary procedure; to develop and extend the profession's theoretical knowledge and practical skill; and to fight off encroachments by other professions. In a society which increasingly accorded status and prestige to competent skill and socially useful expertise, all associations had a particular concern for developing and extending the theoretical knowledge on which their practice was based. The publication of professional journals, the encouragement of learned societies, the sponsoring of meetings and lectures, and the establishment of university chairs were a prominent part of the activity of the professional associations. The interrelation of knowledge and prestige was demonstrated in the case of the medical profession, the position of which remained that of comparatively low status until the major medical advances of the mid and late nineteenth century. So weak was the position of medicine in the 1830s that in the Poor Law Amendment Act of 1834, considerable cuts were proposed in medical provision on account of the uncertainty of most curative medicine at that time. The Annual Register of 1832 records: 'The cholera left medical men as it found them – confirmed in most opposite opinions, or in total ignorance as to its nature, its cure and the cure of its origins if endemic or the mode of transmission if infectious.'[30] Such was the attitude towards medicine in the first half of the nineteenth century that it was not until 1845 that naval surgeons were commissioned.[31]

In the mid-nineteenth century occupational roles, particularly those that were influenced by the process of professionalization, sought their legitimation and authority no longer primarily in terms of status but rather in terms of the social utility of their knowledge and skill. The performers of occupational roles became particularly concerned with technical competence and skill, for clearly no occupational role could now be seen as a refuge for the unqualified and incompetent. The old system of patronage and pupillage had worked when the professions were small coherent organizations, but the utilitarian spirit of the early nineteenth century and the considerable expansion in the size of the professions, demanded the establishment of new procedures of training and certification. The Apothecaries Act of 1815 gave the Company (a City of London Livery Company) the duty of examining and certificating pharmacists throughout the country. The East India Company's College, established at Haileybury in 1806, was the first residential institution, but this example was followed by other professions, including the Church, which established colleges in considerable numbers from the 1840s. Entry to almost all professions was by qualifying examination. These examinations were established for the Ordnance Survey in 1825, for attorneys in 1836, and for solicitors in 1837. The Public Health Act of 1848 set up examinations for the engineering inspectorate, and the Medical Act of 1858 established the General Council of Medical Education and Registration.[32]

The effects of establishing standards of entry and practice were wider than the mere improvement of professional skills, for they conferred on the professions a new sense of coherence, corporate identity, and loyalty which had not formerly existed. This was particularly the case in the Army and the Navy, the teaching and the medical professions, and the Church, where residential training became increasingly the norm. In these institutions, the prospective member of a profession learned the values and standards of the profession, and came to see the profession as a coherent body of men engaged in the same task. Social control was internalized by the assumption of these standards and of the professional ethic, and this was particularly necessary where the amount of external control that could be exercised over individual professional practice was minimal and the opportunities for exploitation and abuse (and the consequent discrediting of the professional body) were manifold.

Clearly no account of the development of the professions in the nineteenth century would be complete without reference to the public schools, since they were of more significance than any other institution in developing the professional ideology of public service, 'duty', and high ethical standards, 'principles', which underpinned Victorian public life. The public schools, the majority of which were founded in this period, symbolized the fundamental changes in the structure of wealth, class, and status which resulted from the Industrial Revolution. Increasingly the competitive examinations for such institutions as Woolwich, Sandhurst, and the Imperial Services College came to influence the education which these schools provided, and which had hitherto been entirely classical in content. Edward Thring, headmaster of Uppingham, was the first to respond to the pressure of parents and include 'modern studies' in the timetable, in other words those subjects, such as languages, natural sciences, and technical drawing, which were needed for the competitive and qualifying examinations. But the greater significance of the public schools lay in their imparting of the professional ethic, the notion of 'duty' and 'principles', to those aspiring to the professions. By the late nineteenth century, they had succeeded in transforming the professions into a coherent body of occupational roles, sharing common norms, standards, and behaviour patterns as well as common social and educational experiences. It is difficult to overestimate the mutually reinforcing relationship which existed between the public schools and the professions, and their significance for English life and society at this time.

A further element in the change in nineteenth-century

society which resulted from, and facilitated, the professionalization of high-status roles was the development of
systems of appointment which were not based solely on
patronage. When occupational roles were restricted, as in
traditional society, to serving the landed aristocracy,
patronage was a means of maintaining control in their
hands. However, in an advanced industrial society in which
skills, merit, and technical competence were at a premium,
the system of patronage was no way of guaranteeing the
appropriateness of appointments. The Northcote–Trevelyan
Report on the permanent Civil Service of 1854 advocated a
system of open competition for the Home Civil Service such
as had already been introduced for the Indian Civil Service
by an act of the previous year.[33] Slowly all appointments and
posts were made on the basis of merit and ability, and, in
1871, the purchasing of commissions in the Army was ended.
By the end of that year only the Royal Navy and the Foreign
Office retained a system of nomination together with
examination. The old era of patronage, purchase, nepotism,
and interest was finally closed in English public life with the
single exception of the Church, where the ancient system of
patronage remained.[34]

Thus, the professions emerged in the Victorian period and
took on their recognizably modern form. The professional
man, working on his own in private practice, with a high
sense of duty and principles, marketing his skills, and
standing or falling by his own judgement, became one of the
most important figures in late-nineteenth-century public life.
By this time the professions were seen predominantly as
occupational roles in society concerned with specific work-
tasks and the application of knowledge and skill to particular
problems. However, the older conception of the professional
man which dated from the pre-industrial period had by no
means died and some of the professions remained important
as means of conferring or achieving high social status.
There is little doubt that, in 1870, when Anthony Trollope
recorded Miss Marrable's views on the subject, he intended
to convey that they were old-fashioned; none the less there
would have been many then (and there are probably not a
few now) who would have shared her views:

'She always addressed an attorney by letter as Mister, raising up her eyebrows when appealed to on the matter, and explaining that an attorney is not an esquire. She had an idea that the son of a gentleman, if he intended to maintain his rank as a gentleman should earn his income as a clergyman, or a barrister, or a soldier, or a sailor. These were the professions intended for gentlemen. She would not absolutely say that a physician was not a gentleman or even a surgeon; but she would never allow to physic the same absolute privilege which, in her eyes, belonged to Law and the Church. There might also possibly be a doubt about the Civil Service and Civil Engineering, but she had no doubt whatever that when a man touched trade or commerce in any way he was doing that which was not the work of a gentleman. He might be very respectable and it might be very interesting that he should do it, but brewers, bankers, and merchants were not gentlemen, and the world, according to Miss Marrable's theory, was going astray, because people were forgetting their landmarks.'[35]

3

The Clergyman's Role and Professionalization

The clergy in the pre-Reformation Church formed a separate estate in society. To those who were beneficed the tithe and the freehold gave a legal independence and security unique among occupational roles at that time. They were a means of using landed property to facilitate what may be readily recognized as a professional role in a social system which had not as yet evolved specialized professional roles in the modern sense. The clergyman's role received its authority from the Church, from the institutional and routinized charisma of the religious institution. This was the typical form of authority in traditional pre-industrial societies in which religion had presidency over all other institutions. The role of the clergyman was legitimated in terms of the total society and was one of considerable power and authority. Indeed, as religion was the supreme legitimating and authorizing agency in traditional society, so the clergyman was, in a real sense, the legitimator of all other roles, inasmuch as the values he disseminated established the worth of all activities in such a society.

The English Reformation was much more than the establishment of national independence from Rome in ecclesiastical matters; it was also a reaction against the poor quality and abuses of the medieval clergy and the assertion of secular authority over the ecclesiastical corporation. In terms of the clergyman's role, it represented a challenge by the laity to the clerical estate of the medieval church. Its effect was to deprofessionalize a role which had developed some aspects of professionalization in a traditional society, particularly as a result of the influence of the monasteries. By means of the ecclesiastical courts and the operation of the patronage system in the medieval church, the clergy had developed a high level of autonomy for the performance of their role, an

28

autonomy against which Luther had particularly protested. The Reformation made the King in Chancery (the Court of Delegates) the highest ecclesiastical court and saw the transference of a large proportion of ecclesiastical patronage into lay hands as a result of the dissolution of the monasteries. Elizabeth I, like her father, had manipulated the Church to pursue secular objectives and had both participated in and connived at the large-scale depreciation of clerical living. This 'plunder' of the Church was carried out by means of the impropriation of livings, whereby the lay rector received the benefice income and was required to pay the vicar's stipend. This had taken place in 4000 of the 9284 livings by 1603. In practice, the lay rectors took the lion's share; at Hornchurch in Essex at this time the benefice income amounted to £800 and the vicar's stipend was £55. At Hogsthorpe in Lincolnshire the benefice income was £90 and the vicar received £10. Ruefully, an early seventeenth-century vicar remarked that the clergy got 'leavings not livings'. Impropriation led directly to non-residence, absenteeism, pluralism, unqualified and otherwise unsatisfactory clergy, and the general demoralization of the Church in the seventeenth and early eighteenth centuries.[1]

Before the Reformation the Church was a major element in the institutions of government and the clergy formed an absolute majority in the House of Lords. By the early eighteenth century, after 200 years of change and conflict and the lowering of the constitutional status of the Church by the Act of Toleration, the Church was left even more dependent on the State at every level. The once powerful ecclesiastical courts were devoid of independent coercive power, and Convocation had been prorogued in May 1717 following a confrontation with the State over the question of ecclesiastical authority, and was not to meet to conduct business again until 1852. At the parochial level the clergy were subservient to the landed interest which had been so firmly re-established by the Glorious Revolution. When Viscount Scudamore in 1671 built a rectory for the previously homeless vicar of Hempsted in Gloucestershire, the second occupant caused this Te Deum to be carved:

Whoe'er doth dwell within this door
Thank God for Viscount Scudamore.

Furthermore, the seventeenth and early eighteenth centuries witnessed a sharp decline in religious practice. With the exception of a few years at the beginning of the eighteenth century, the period from 1689 to 1740 had seen Whig governments who suspected the Church of Tory and Jacobite sympathies and were not disposed to view the rise of religious apathy with any concern. This, together with the relaxation of the sanctions against irreligion formerly operated by the ecclesiastical courts, led to a situation where clergy in 1738 replying to Bishop Secker's Primary Visitation inquiries regularly reported habitual non-attendance among 'the lowest ranks'. One of the most striking aspects of these reports was the implication that religious practice had fallen off alarmingly within the lifetime of incumbents still alive in the 1730s.[2] There is a tendency to overlook the fact that the alienation from the Church of the urban working classes in the nineteenth century had its origins in the practice of rural communities in the previous two. centuries; habits of indifference stretched back over several generations and corresponding attitudes towards the Church had become embedded in the local culture.

The clergy, during the first half of the eighteenth century, have been generally portrayed by historians as enjoying comparatively low social status on account of their humble social origins, lack of education, the poverty of their benefices, and the rusticity of their lifestyle, and particularly the socially degrading tasks they were forced to embrace in order to supplement their stipends. The curate of Lastingham in the early eighteenth century had thirteen children to support on a stipend of £20. His wife kept a public house and he was able to convince the archdeacon that his indirect clerical management (and his fiddle-playing) caused the parishioners to be 'imperceptibly led along the paths of piety and morality'.[3] In 1704, the establishment of Queen Anne's Bounty was a means by which some of the Church revenue was used to create a fund for the relief of the ill-housed and poor clergy. This gesture followed a survey which had revealed that half the benefices were worth less than £80 a year and many of the curacies less than £12 a year. All generalizations, especially those made by the Victorians concerning the parochial clergy of the eighteenth century, need to be approached with some caution, but even those who were sympathetic tended to damn by the faintness of their praise. However, it is a part of the paradox of eighteenth-century religious life that although what was practised and preached by many of the clergy was uninspiring and undemanding, none the less, few periods of English history have been so prolific in serious thought about the fundamental nature and justification of the whole system of Christianity and especially the Established Church itself.[4]

The clergy of the early eighteenth century, like many occupations of that period, were divided between 'masters' and 'journeymen'. The poor, usually unbeneficed, clergy were rustic in manner, primitive in outlook, and ranked in society along with the tradesmen and upper servants of the great houses. John Clare observed that the poor clergy who lived, worked, and prayed with their flocks and who went out when pauperism and enclosures came in, were affectionately remembered by country people.[5] This distinction between the higher and the inferior clergy was justified by William Paley in 1782 as a means by which the Church could minister to a highly stratified society.[6]

It was the Agrarian Revolution, the Enclosure Movement, and the steady rise in the price of grain throughout the eighteenth century that had a profound influence on the development of the clergyman's role. Substantial farmers agreed that the only way to maximize profits was by enclosure and this process considerably increased the clergy's income. W. R. Ward estimates that, of the 3128 Enclosure Acts between 1757 and 1835, in 2220 instances the tithe was commuted and, in the overwhelming majority of cases, commuted for land. The conditions of commutation were remarkably generous to the clergy and it was usually calculated that the tithe, for the purposes of commutation, was worth at least one-seventh to one-eighth of the parish land.[7] However, the very processes that made the clergy richer pressed hard upon the rural community and the agricultural labourers in particular.

By the late eighteenth century a marked change was taking place in the social status of the clergy, for both individually and as an occupational group they were experiencing a steady, upward social mobility. At a time when respectability was gauged in acres and the owners of the soil derived from it wealth, high social status, and the right to govern, the clerical profession made a rapid advance in every respect.[8] The new wealth of benefices attracted entrants of a higher social status, particularly the sons of the lesser squires who were severely hit by the inflation of the eighteenth century and the development of the large estates; this further reinforced the growing respectability of the clergy.[9] In 1756, Lord Chesterfield wrote to one such man: 'I entirely agree with you in your resolution of breeding up all your sons to some profession or other.' He went on to suggest 'general rules by which I would point out to them, the professions which I should generally wish them to apply to: I recommend the Army or the Navy to a boy of warm constitution, strong animal spirits, and a cold genius, to one of quick lively and distinguished parts – the law; to a good dull and decent boy the Church . . .'[10]

Furthermore, at this time the property-owning classes, deeply shocked by the events of the French Revolution, came to regard religion and the clergy as an important bulwark against revolution and Jacobinism, and as making a significant contribution to maintaining the stability of the social structure. The local gentry no longer regarded the parochial clergy as a threat corporately or individually and the alliance between them was steadily strengthened. Slowly, during the later part of the eighteenth century, the clergy began to be aligned with the gentry status group in society. The new wealth provided for the clergy by the commutation of tithes (in the form of rent from land similar to that of the gentry) allowed them to build parsonages, which more closely resembled the hall than the farmhouse, and to adopt modes of dress and recreation suitable to their new status.[11] However, these changes should be seen in the context of a process of social differentiation which affected all eighteenth-century society, and which made the farmer less likely to house and feed the farm labourers in his own home. [12] The high box pews of the eighteenth-century church in a sense symbolized the new concern for social differentiation. By no means all the clergy were able to attain this new status and a significant number remained poor and socially degraded, as unbeneficed 'journeymen' clergy. But increasingly, in this period, the role of the clergyman was regarded as one of gentleman status, and this was only to be expected in a society where the notion of gentility was based almost exclusively on the ideal of the country squire. Thus, as G. F. Best has shown, a new version of the theory of ecclesiastical establishment was developed which emphasized the social affinity and mutual interdependence of the clergy and the gentry. [13]

A clergyman of the last quarter of the eighteenth century, unless he had been affected by the Evangelical Movement, could partake in the interests and recreations of the gentry to a degree that made it difficult for contemporaries to regard the clergy as a distinct body. Benjamin Newton, in the early nineteenth century, combined the duties of rector with the interests and occupations of a moderately well-to-do gentleman. He hunted with all the neighbouring packs; he shot over the manor of which he had the deputation of sporting rights; he fished; he kept greyhounds; and he attended the race meetings at Richmond and Catterick, as well as the local balls. He farmed on a considerable scale his own glebe and rented land; he bred horses; he sat on the County Bench and visited and entertained his friends in a constant round of hospitality. An entry in his diary on 6 February 1817 betrays the new class consciousness of the age:

> Went hunting with Mr. Bell's hounds, had tolerable sport, these hounds please me much as they are attended by gentlemen only, no farmers. [14]

There is evidence to suggest that not all the clergy welcomed these developments in their role and particularly its growing involvement in aspects of that of the country gentleman. William Jones wrote of some of his neighbouring clergy at about the same time:

As to the fine gentlemen themselves, they are far more anxious to attain the fame of being 'excellent shots', giving the 'view halloo' well mounted in the field and being 'in at the death', than raising their voices in the desk and pulpit or feeding the flock which they are eager to fleece.[15]

John Skinner wrote of the Revd Mr Gunning of Farmborough who called on him:

He seems an open-hearted man, but I do not think exactly calculated for a clergyman, as he keeps his hounds, and having no other pursuits, thinks more of a hare than he does of hunting out what may benefit his parishioners.[16]

William Canning may be taken as providing a good example of the career of a well-connected gentleman clergyman of this period. Between ordination and becoming incumbent of Heslerton (Yorkshire) in 1817 at the age of thirty-seven, he had been tutor for two years to a young man who, in the view of his uncle Lord Cremorne, needed a 'guiding and restraining hand'. He spent three years in Persia (as chaplain to the British Minister, Sir Gore Ouseley) and then in India. He was curate at Clewer for two years. Clearly this did not provide him with a livelihood but gave him a pleasant position in which to wait for suitable patronage. This was a long time coming, but in 1817 he moved to Heslerton. His mother noted after his initial visit:

He met the curate, a good kind of elderly man half farmer, half parson who had resided many years at the Rectory a very miserable shabby house much out of repair. The late Encumbent [*sic*] never resided there, he was Chaplain to Lord Carlisle and his Agent which we suppose excused his non-residence.

Canning remained at Heslerton and was later presented to a canonry at Windsor. Preferment in each case came directly from family connections.[17]

By the end of the eighteenth century, particularly in the less desirable and accessible parts of the country, there was still a significant number of 'journeyman' clergy who served two or three curacies for stipends often calculated at the rate of half a guinea per Sunday. Charles Blomfield, later Bishop of London, made constant reference to the miserable state these men were forced to live in, and the adverse effect that this had on the status of the profession.[18] When the beneficed clergy of the late eighteenth century are compared with the Caroline clergy, they can readily be seen as an occupational group which had advanced considerably in wealth, education, and status. Those clergy, who lived in their parishes, and who did not entertain exalted notions concerning the dignity of the priesthood, nor were affected by the Evangelical Movement, lived lives which were for the most part indistinguishable from those of the surrounding gentry. It is these clergy who are represented so accurately in the pages of Jane Austen's novels; she herself was both the daughter and the sister of a clergyman.

The fact that the Church and its clergy were in a precarious situation at the end of the eighteenth century is more evident in retrospect than it was at the time. The Church's principal weakness lay in its unpreparedness for the degree of social and economic change that was about to transform English life. The Hanoverian church was dependent at both the parochial and the national level on the patronage, wealth, and political support of the landed interest. But the influence of the landed interest, so all-embracing in the eighteenth century, was much diminished in the political and economic turbulence of the nineteenth century, and the squire and the parson came to be regarded as men with vested interests in preserving as much as possible of the attitudes and social relations of the pre-industrial period. It is ironic, as A. D. Gilbert has observed, that whilst the Church was strong enough to resist early Methodism, its strength lay in precisely those social structures and cultural values which inhibited its easy adjustment to the religious needs of an emerging industrial society.[19] But the changes of this era were not confined in the industrial and urban areas, for the countryside also saw, in a relatively short time, the overthrow of the traditional agrarian economy which fundamentally altered the patterns of settlement, land tenure, and class relations. Furthermore, the unsettled times gave rise to a popular radicalism which resented hereditary privilege, unrepresentative government, the political hegemony of the landed interest, and the whole prescriptive basis of traditional society. William Cobbett was an observer of the dislocation of rural society in the early period of the nineteenth century, and after completing his tour of Hampshire, Berkshire, Surrey, and Sussex in 1823, he wrote: 'I cannot conclude my remarks on this Rural Ride without noticing the new sort of language I hear everywhere made use of with regard to the parsons, but which language I do not care to repeat.'[20]

This mounting wave of agitation broke heavily on all ancient institutions and they were subjected to every sort of attack including physical violence. The unreformed Hanoverian church found itself assaulted on every side in an age which would no longer tolerate the abuses and privileges which it harboured. It was widely agreed that a sizeable proportion of the national wealth should no longer be set aside for the maintenance of the clergy simply as an appendage of the gentry. The Ecclesiastical Commission, established by Peel in 1835, was the means by which it was hoped by laymen and progressive churchmen alike that the so obviously archaic structure of the Church of England could be remodelled so that it could more effectively discharge its pastoral duties. But the Church proved a difficult institution to reform, not least because of its localism and because its functions could not be subjected to the customary utilitarian criteria, and in consequence the achievements of the Commission were principally to improve the administration and the utilization of resources.

At the same time a number of Parliamentary Acts sought to achieve the same goals by altering the context in which the clergyman performed his role and by laying certain statutory obligations upon him. Acts of 1795 and 1813 sought to enforce the employment of properly paid curates when the incumbent did not reside, thus making non-residence expensive. An Act of 1817 was a more elaborate attempt to stimulate higher professional standards. It limited the amount of land a clergyman could farm and sought to prevent his engaging in trade; it attempted to impose further restraints on non-residence, and it required the clergyman to keep the parsonage in repair. Furthermore, it gave the bishop the right to appoint a curate to serve a parish where by reason of age or infirmity the incumbent was unable to carry out his duties. Like all reforms this Act was regarded by many clergy as a gross infringement of personal liberty, but it demonstrated most clearly that society would no longer tolerate the abuses and laxity which had previously prevailed. It is hard to gauge how effective this Act was in achieving higher standards; certainly by 1827 only 4413 of the 10,533 benefices had resident incumbents. In the next two decades there was a number of further Acts which sought to reform abuses and encourage higher standards. Among these the most significant were the Act of 1826 concerning residence and parsonage houses; the Clergy Resignation Bond Act of 1828 (which ended an abuse of patronage by which a living was 'kept warm' for a minor); the Pluralities Act of 1836; and the Clergy Discipline Act of the same year. The effect of some of these Acts can be gauged from the doubling in the number of assistant curates between 1835 and 1841. In the latter year it was 2032 and rose to 3437 in 1853. By 1850 only 9.5 per cent of all beneficed clergy were non-resident (and some no doubt only in a technical sense).[21]

The congruity of the clergyman's role with traditional society made it particularly vulnerable to the changes which industrialization and urbanization brought to society. The Parliamentary reforms, which were desired as much by energetic clergy as by reforming Parliamentarians represented a step along the way towards establishing higher standards of role performance, which was in itself a small movement towards professionalization. However, more significant advances in this direction were to result from movements which had their origin within the Church. The Evangelical Movement in the Church of England, and more particularly the Tractarian Movement, in some of their aspects were responses by the Church to the broad movements of social change which occurred in English society in the eighteenth and early nineteenth centuries. Both movements were attempts to redefine the Church and by implication the clergyman's role in society. Both had the effect of moving the clergyman's role in the direction of professionalization and both drew in different ways on theology as the central skill and expertise of the Church.[22]

The changes in the scope, structure, and functions of occupational roles which resulted from the growing industrialization and urbanization of an advanced society affected the clergyman's role in a fundamental way. In the first place there emerged a number of roles in society whose specific function included elements which had formerly belonged to the diffuse role of the clergyman as it had been enacted in traditional society. The Poor Law administrator (and other civil servants), the political agent, the teacher, the registrar, the doctor, the policeman, and even the sanitary engineer, all these new or developing occupational roles came to administer functions which the clergyman had been content to perform in an essentially amateur capacity. Also, the clergyman was affected by the general movement of institutional and role differentiation which was such a prominent feature of nineteenth-century society. Like other occupational roles that of the clergyman became more sharply defined, less diffuse in its functions, and focused on those 'charter' elements authorized by the Ordinal. A mid-nineteenth-century layman wrote of the increasing specificity of the clergyman's role:

> Undoubtedly, an educated and intelligent Christian gentleman may undertake any of the ordinary duties of life which pertain to his class; but a Christian minister has, it is supposed, devoted himself to a special calling and one of so holy a character, that anything tending to interfere with or mar its purpose, ought not to be sought or encouraged . . .[23]

This change in the role of the clergyman resulted in large part from the disintegration of the old structure of traditional authority and the gradual perception by the Church that the nature of its legitimation in an advanced society could no longer be the mixed feudal and aristocratic assumptions which had previously sustained it.

The Evangelicals differed markedly from the majority of

late eighteenth- and early nineteenth-century clergy, particularly in claiming authority for their role from the Bible and from personal inspiration; sources of value which unlike status or social utility are internal to the religious institution and not necessarily shared by the wider society. The Evangelicals on the whole did not have a conception of the Church as a divine institution but they paved the way for this later development by their insistence on the spiritual nature and authority of the clergyman's office.[24] The Hanoverians were shocked at the idea of an authority which was inherent in the Church and not derived from the secular power. With the long shadows of the Laudians and of the Civil War still falling in the eighteenth century, they quickly condemned any ecclesiastical pretensions as 'priestcraft'.

The Tractarians were certainly aware of what they saw as the need for the Church to establish its autonomy and to underline its distinctive nature and values, and this awareness gave the movement much of its impetus. The Tractarian protest was a product of the *de facto* relegation of the Church to a subordinate position brought about by the trend towards structural differentiation and increasing institutional plurality in society.[25] Newman wrote in the first tract:

> Should the Government and Country so far forget their God as to cast off the Church to deprive it of its temporal honours and substance, on what will you rest the claim of respect and attention which you make upon your flocks? Hitherto you have been upheld by your birth, your education, your wealth, and your connections . . .

The authors of the tracts took their stand on the doctrine of Apostolic Succession, the classic example of routinized charisma. The enthusiasm with which some of the clergy received the Oxford tracts, and the progress their viewpoint made throughout the Church of England, bore witness to the response of the Church to the changes in legitimation which occurred at this time. These changes had the greatest influence on the performance of the clergyman's role, for their authority for role performance was now internal to the institution and not necessarily (and in fact decreasingly) acknowledged outside. This change was symptomatic of the growing fragmentation and compartmentalization of Victorian society, but it also facilitated the increased professionalization of the clergyman's role. The consequences of these processes of change for the clergyman were manifold but most significant were the changes in his functions (a consideration of which forms the central part of this book), and the changes in his lifestyle.

In the eighteenth century, the clergyman's role had included many elements which derived from his status and position in rural society rather than from his ordination. Many were magistrates (the accolade of country gentry status), many became active in politics and as officers of law and order, others assumed the functions of almoner, doctor, teacher, and civil servant within their parishes, but, in the nineteenth century, the clergyman's role became markedly less diffuse in the range of its functions. As the role ceased to be primarily legitimated by its association with the gentry status so those elements which derived their authority from that quarter played a diminishing part in the functions of the role. By the later part of the nineteenth century the clergy were notably less anxious to be selected as magistrates and the Lords Lieutenant less likely to include their names on the list. The clergy found that activity in such essentially secular matters as politics and in the administration of the Poor Laws detracted from their increasingly spiritual and sacerdotal conception of their role. At the same time the clergy were sensitive to the new specialists who began to perform functions which had once been merely aspects of the clergyman's diffuse role obligations. As a result of these processes, the clergy of the mid-nineteenth century were disposed to accord greater significance to that central and irreducible religious function of the priestly role, the leadership of public worship. In this element of his role at least the clergyman had a monopoly of legitimate function. In an age which came to accord high status to those who possessed socially useful technical knowledge, the clergy, by their emphasis on liturgical studies, attempted to become the technologists of the sanctuary. Certainly the increasing frequency and significance of the celebration of Holy

Communion which was such a prominent feature of the Oxford Movement and a major instance of the growing emphasis on the sacerdotal aspects of the clergyman's role marked a further step in the development of professionalization among the clergy. The vast amount of church restoration work undertaken at this time and the concern with the minutiae of worship and liturgy which was such a feature of Victorian church life witnessed to the new understanding of many clergy that the sanctuary of the Church was the centre and focus of their work. On 9 October 1870, when B. J. Armstrong recalled in his diary twenty years of work in his Norfolk parish of East Dereham, the record he outlined was entirely composed of liturgical changes and structural improvements undertaken within the church. [26]

Perhaps even more evident than the changes in the clergyman's functions in the nineteenth century was the adoption by the clergy of a distinctive lifestyle which tended to mark out the clergyman and separate him from the gentry status group; the development of what may be called 'the rectory culture'. The widespread wearing of a distinctive occupational dress, and the abandonment of their hitherto close involvement in the recreations of the gentry, are both significant indicators of the way in which the clergy of the mid-nineteenth century came to conceive their role.

The Evangelical 'handbooks', with their strong insistence on the importance of the clergyman's spiritual function, attempted to show the clergy that their role was distinct and had particular and demanding functions. Because of their ideological viewpoint, and commonly, the poverty of their benefices, the Evangelical clergy tended not to be accepted as social equals by the gentry. [27] This too helped them to establish the particular nature of their role. The Tractarians, in a sense, followed the Evangelicals in their insistence on the distinctiveness, independence, and autonomy of the clerical profession, though they based their prescriptions on an increasingly sacerdotal understanding and a desire to revive aspects of a vanished past. Bishop Kaye of Lincoln wrote in his Charge of 1846:

The most powerful argument against a civil establishment of religion is that its tendency is to produce secularity in the clergy; to assimilate them to the laity in their habits, their studies, their amusements, to cause them to cherish no higher aim than that of becoming useful members of civil society, to forget their character as ambassadors of Christ, to merge the ministry of reconciliation in the citizen.[28]

The new independence of the clerical role and the emphasis on its spiritual functions, can be gauged from the caution of one 'handbook':

The young lady will scarcely care to recognise as her proper spiritual guide and friend her partner at last week's ball: and the dancing priest may well find it difficult to assume at once his ministerial character towards those with whom he has shared the small-talk and trifling things of a cricket or archery club ball . . .[29]

Perhaps one of the most significant indications of the growth of professionalism and professional self-consciousness among the clergy was the increasing frequency with which they met together to discuss matters of common interest and concern, and so developed the notion of themselves as a distinct occupational body. At the end of the eighteenth century, few clergy met together for anything other than social reasons and of these clerical meetings and societies the majority were organized by Evangelicals. They, conscious of their position as a minority group with a distinctive conception of their role, met together frequently for mutual support and assistance. In 1767, Henry Venn presided over a group which met in his Huddersfield vicarage, later known as the Elland Clerical Society. Other meetings were established by Stillingfleet at Hotham, and Samuel Walker at Truro, and by the end of the century there were Evangelical clerical societies established at York, Bristol, Creaton, Rauceby, and Islington, together with the famous Eclectic Society which met in London from 1783.[30] Stonhouse's advice is typical of that of Evangelical handbooks: 'Endeavour to live on friendly terms with the neighbouring clergy and to cultivate a particular acquaintance and friendship with such as are serious . . .'[31]

In the first quarter of the nineteenth century, Evangelical clerical societies were established in many parts of the country. Henry Moule describes such a society in Dorset: 'Its members selected not by any narrow party test but by a law of spiritual sympathy, were Evangelical churchmen, incumbents, and curates who arranged to meet monthly, if I remember right, at the house of some one of the number.'[32] In the late eighteenth century, the lack of any distinctive professional self-consciousness among the majority of the clergy was exemplified by their lack of any agencies by which this aspect of professionalization could be promoted.

A conspicuous feature of the revival of the Church was the development among the majority of the clergy of such agencies, and, throughout the nineteenth century, clergy became, as David Newsome has observed, 'intensely assembly conscious'. The handbooks of the mid-nineteenth century warmly recommended the clergy to meet together for mutual support and assistance: 'No men', wrote C. J. Vaughan, 'have so much to say and to hear, in meeting with members of their own profession, as we have . . .'[33] Certainly the clerical meetings which sprang up everywhere were an important means by which the clergy became aware of themselves as members of a distinct profession. Nowhere is this more clearly articulated than in the introduction to the account of the proceedings of the Alcester clerical meeting (1842 to 1860). Richard Seymour commented on

. . . the importance of cherishing a proper professional feeling among the clergy. Other learned professions have their own opportunities for conference, their own informal tribunals which determine the conduct and behaviour of their members. None stand so much aloof from one another as the clergy: though none perhaps needs, so much as they, the support of counsel and example in the details of their common work . . . Unprepared in general by distinct training for their office, stimulated by no hope of temporal reward to gain a thorough mastery of all that belongs to their calling, the clergy are tempted to consider a decent performance of needful pastoral ministrations the beginning and end of their work.[34]

Whilst the clerical meetings were essentially informal associations, the clergy also developed formal organs for the expression of opinion and the exchange of views. The reviving authority of the bishops in diocesan affairs was illustrated by their re-establishment of the office of rural dean, and later, the ruri-decanal chapters. Contemporary sources suggest that it was the publication of W. Dansey's book *Hora Decanicae Rurales*, in 1835, that was largely responsible for the re-establishment of rural deaneries. By the second publication of the book in 1844, nineteen dioceses had rural deaneries and two had deanery chapters; by 1863, seventeen dioceses had deanery chapters.

The mid-nineteenth century saw considerable activity at the diocesan level in the formation of societies and associations to promote church affairs. The most famous of these are the diocesan church building societies and the boards of education, but there were also a large number of missionary associations (diocesan branches of national organizations) and the numerous 'defence' associations or *ad hoc* meetings which sent petitions to London on such subjects as the Gorham judgement, the ritualistic imprisonments, the Colenso affair, and other matters of widespread concern. The railways and the new roads made meeting easier and the old isolation of the clergy was broken down as they became conscious of their membership of a distinct occupational group. The 'business' of the mid-nineteenth-century clergyman is illustrated in a letter in which Samuel Wilberforce, then a parochial clergyman on the Isle of Wight, surveying the previous week, explained that he had no time to make progress with his father's biography, as he '. . . had been to a Church Building Society meeting in Winchester, a dinner engagement with the Archdeacon, a meeting at Southampton, and four church meetings in Newport'.[35]

At the national level the clergy had been without an organ for the expression of a distinctive clerical opinion since 1717.

In the early decades of the nineteenth century, there was a real sense in which the large national church associations, particularly the National Society, performed this function. The eventual revival of Convocation (a legacy from the estate system of the Middle Ages), proved less successful than was hoped in the role of a central policy-making organ, because in the early years it was dominated by the ritualist controversies. However, although no single body could claim to be an expression of total clerical opinion, the large number of national organizations such as the English Church Union, the Church Association, and Church Congress testify to the developing institutional self-consciousness of the Church and the clergy.

Another indication may be found in the number of ecclesiastical journals and periodicals which enjoyed a large circulation at this time.[36] Although the clergy did not have a professional publication which compared with *The Lancet*, none the less *The Ecclesiastical Gazette* (1839) and *The Clerical Journal* (1853) fulfilled broadly similar functions. It is a moot point whether such publications reflect or create distinct interest groups, but they provided another means whereby the clergyman could become aware of the developing identity of his profession. The same may be said of clerical directories which first made their appearance in the early nineteenth century. *The Clerical Guide* (first edition 1817) and *The Clergy List* (first edition 1841) were both superseded by *The Clerical Directory* (first edition 1858) which, as *Crockford's Clerical Directory*, became an annual publication in 1876.

It has already been noted in the previous chapter that the development of residential training institutions greatly accelerated the development of professionalization in high-status occupational roles. By the mid-nineteenth century, the Army, the Navy, the East India Company, the medical and teaching professions, and, to a lesser extent, the legal profession, had such institutions. The Church regarded its clergy as receiving their training at the universities (principally Oxford and Cambridge), and the ordaining bishop through his examining chaplain was required to satisfy himself that the candidate was 'learned in the Latin tongue and sufficiently instructed in the Scriptures'. By the 1840s, a course of lectures was established at Oxford given by the five Divinity professors and the Hebrew professor, after which candidates could sit an examination and receive a *testamur*. Contemporary sources indicate that few attended the lectures and few bishops actually required the *testamur* before ordination.[37] This was but a first step.

Whilst, in general terms, the establishment of the theological colleges in the mid-nineteenth century arose from the desire of the Church to train its clergy in a way which approximated more closely to the training of other professional men and to provide training for the increasing number of ordinands who had not been at Oxford or Cambridge, the actual establishment of the colleges owed more to the urgent needs of the cathedrals to defend their wealth from the Ecclesiastical Commission. For this reason most of the early colleges were established in cathedral closes and cathedrals came to fulfil again an ancient function. The 'cathedral' colleges included Durham College (later University) 1831, Chichester 1839, Wells 1840, Lichfield 1856, Canterbury 1860, Salisbury and Exeter 1861, Gloucester 1868, Lincoln 1874, and Ely 1876. The founding by Bishop Samuel Wilberforce of a theological college across the road from his rural palace at Cuddesdon in 1854 was of considerable significance, for this was the first college to have a common life based, if only distantly, on the Catholic seminaries and monasteries of Europe. The adoption of this ethos and mode of training came to have a considerable influence on the development of the clergyman's role, as many other colleges tended to follow this example. However, it was not until after the First World War that at least a year's residence at a theological college was required of all ordinands (previously Oxford and Cambridge graduates had been excused this requirement).[38]

Thus, the early decades of the nineteenth century saw both the beginning of the eclipse of the social theory and practice of the traditional regime, of which the established Church was an integral part, and also the development of professionalsim. These developments precipitated a transformation in the status, function, and self-conception of the clergyman. Bishop Blomfield's biographer wrote:

> In character, habits, attainment, social position, and general reputation the ordinary clergyman of 1860 is a very different being from the clergyman in 1810 . . . Speaking generally, the remark of Mr. Thomas Grenville, who died in 1846 at the age of 91, may be taken as true, that no change which has taken place in his lifetime was so great as the change in the clergy of the Church of England. [39]

Sydney Smith, in speaking to Gladstone of the transformation in the character and conduct of the clergy, made the same point in different terms when he remarked: 'Whenever you meet a clergyman of my age, you may be sure he is a bad clergyman.' [40]

The contradiction in the range of clerical functions, the increased autonomy of the professional body, the desire to re-establish representative organs, the proliferation of clerical journals and periodicals, the anxiety to exclude unworthy persons and the concern at maintaining high standards, and the establishment of the theological college may all be regarded as demonstrative of the growing acceptance by the clergy of the professions as a new reference point for the development of their role. In 1839, in his book *Parochial Ministration*, the Revd S. Best wrote: 'Without discipline, without system, see what are the results: what might they not be, were the Church organised as other professions are.' [41]

However, it would be simplistic to suggest that the late-nineteenth-century clergyman had merely substituted the professional man for the country gentleman as the model for the performance of his role. Such transformations are only gradually made. Many assumptions that belonged to traditional society continued to be made long after the widespread urbanization of English society. Indeed, they continue to influence contemporary practice. Certainly, the notion of gentleman status, which was closely bound up with the professional ideal, continued to be of significance to the clergy. Bishop Samuel Wilberforce stated in his presidential address to the Oxford Diocesan Society on 25 Nov. 1866:

I maintain this, that the ministry of the Church of England has been hitherto and is at this time, filled by gentlemen of the nation of England, by men who have had a gentle education, who have come often – yea, and in most numerous cases of gentle, and even of the highest blood of this land and who have entered the Church with all that distinctive formation of character which comes from such an education and such an inheritance . . .[42]

He argued that this could not continue if the clergy were not paid more, for by the last quarter of the nineteenth century, with the declining returns from land, the long downward spiral in the relative value of clergy incomes had already begun. Particularly after 1873 the endowments of rural livings began to lose their value, and by the first decade of the present century almost every second parish in England was obliged to augment its parochial endowment with a voluntary Easter offering.[43] This was one of the reasons why, by the end of the century, as Wilberforce implied, the clerical profession was becoming significantly less attractive; the other principal reasons lay in the many alternative opportunities which the Empire afforded.

The surrogate terminology of the clergyman's role, (pastor, flock, shepherd, parish, parson) witnessed to the shaping of the role by the prescriptions of traditional rural *gemeinschaftlich* society. In the nineteenth century the clergy were forced to reassess the traditional understanding of their role in order to perform it within the context of an increasingly urban and advanced society. The embracing of the professional ideal by the clergy and the consequent changes in their role may be seen as the means by which the clergy adapted to the impress of social change. This adaptation made possible not only the continued performance of their role but also, in part, the considerable expansion of the Church in Victorian England. However, it also brought consequences which this expansion, together with the high social status of the clergy at that time, served to mask and obscure. It is a part of the paradox of the nineteenth century that by its close the nation was both more secular and more religious: in the sense that a higher proportion of the population went to church at the end of the century than had done in the 1830s. However, it was not until the middle decades of the twentieth century, with the sharp decline in the Church's social support and significance which followed both world wars, that the extent and nature of these dilemmas came to be acknowledged. In a later chapter this connection between the marginality of the Church and the professionalization of its clergy will be more fully explored.

PART TWO

The Professionalization of the Clergyman's Role in the Late Eighteenth and the Nineteenth Century

4

Leader of Public Worship
– Sunday Worship

THE SUNDAY AND WEEKDAY SERVICES

The function which is particularly associated with the priest as opposed to other religious leaders, such as the prophet and the shaman, is that of leading public worship. It is for the priest the irreducible, almost the defining, religious function which lies at the centre of his role, as Bishop Mant wrote in his handbook: 'The prominent object for which a clergyman is invested with the ministerial character, is the Public Celebration of Divine Worship.'[1]

The Church of England clergyman's charter role derived from the Ordinal in the Book of Common Prayer, which may be regarded as 'the foundation charter' of his role, envisaged him as leading the worshipping community by performing the public services of the Book of Common Prayer in church at the stated times or when occasion demanded. The Church of England clergyman had the monopoly of legitimate performance as the leader of public worship, and anyone who infringed this monopoly was liable to punishment under civil law. The rubrics make it clear that the function of the clergyman in public worship is to lead and direct. Sanctions are enforceable in canon law against a clergyman who fails to perform this function adequately, and complete neglect of public worship constitutes one of the few crimes for which an incumbent can be ejected from his benefice despite his freehold. Later in the period the reading of Morning and Evening Prayer on Sundays became a statutory obligation.[2]

This irreducible function was the only clerical activity of some eighteenth-century clergymen and became known as 'the duty'. J. J. Blunt wrote:

There was a period and almost within my own memory when a notion prevailed that the duties of the clergy were the duties of the Sunday and little more; that their sphere lay pretty exclusively in the due performance of the public services of the Church. That was, I need not say, a very imperfect view of clerical obligations. [3]

In the main it is true to say of that period that the public conceived the clergyman's role in terms only of the performance of public worship. Bishop Blomfield wrote of this time:

A decent and regular performance of Divine Service on Sunday was almost all that anyone looked for in a clergyman, if this were found, most people were satisfied. The clergyman might be non-resident, a sportsman, a farmer, a bon-vivant, or a courtier; but if he performed in person, or by deputy, that which now usurps the name of his duty, that was enough. [4]

It is an assumption of all the handbooks that the conscientious clergyman read both Morning and Evening Prayer on Sundays. Practices differed, but, as a general rule in the eighteenth century, the morning service started at 10 a.m. and comprised Morning Prayer; Litany; Ante-Communion; and a sermon. The evening service was at 3 p.m., so the people could return home before dark, and comprised Evening Prayer and a sermon, though with the exception of large urban churches, a second sermon was rare in the eighteenth century. The two-hour interval between the services was filled with performing baptisms, churchings, marriages, and burials. Therefore the clergyman would be in church from before 10 a.m. to some time after 4 p.m., and if non-resident would often eat his lunch in the vestry. [5]

Throughout the eighteenth century the amount of Sunday duty performed by the clergy had been steadily declining and by the last quarter of the century and during the early years of the next century, there was a large number of churches which did not have double duty (i.e. Morning and Evening Prayer). In the Forest Deanery of Gloucester in 1750, of the 35 churches, 23 had single duty. [6] From the Visitation Register of 1783 it appears that in those parishes under the jurisdiction of the Bishop of Oxford (excluding Oxford city) double duty was performed in 118 (67 per cent), and single duty in 58 (33 per cent), and duty only on alternate Sundays in 4 parishes.[7] The trend towards single duty continued in the 1820s when in the returns drawn up for the Privy Council 1818–25 it was found that the number of churches with single duty had increased to 75 (40 per cent).[8] So common had this practice become that the words 'twice every Lord's Day' were omitted from the 1821 queries of the Bishop of Exeter, for by then it had come to be accepted that the normal practice was one service with a sermon on Sundays.[9] James Woodforde, although he was constantly resident, had only single duty and even this occasionally had to be cancelled when the church was being cleaned, or the weather was bad, or Woodforde being ill or away was unable to find a substitute.[10]

As a result of non-residence and the inability of sick and aged incumbents to retire,[11] a large portion of the ordinary Sunday duty was done by curates or other neighbouring clergy. It seems that the fee for single duty in this period was half a guinea and thus the curates were forced to serve several churches on the same day.[12] These curates became known as the 'gallopers', frequently living in market towns and serving the surrounding countryside. The curates leaving the city over Magdalen Bridge on a Saturday afternoon were considered one of the sights of Oxford in the eighteenth century. On 9 December 1775, James Woodforde recorded that the snow stopped the curates leaving the city. The various effects of this system were that single duty became the rule, that the curate was forced to hurry through the services,[13] and that the Sunday service was at no fixed time. Charlotte Yonge recalled that at Otterbourne at the end of the eighteenth century there was only one service, and that the bells were rung when the curate could be seen riding towards the church.[14] These practices not only affected the quantity of Sunday duty but also the quality. Numerous anecdotes point to the careless performance of the services, and they bear witness to what must have been common experience. Dr George Horne (later Bishop of Norwich) wrote, in 1787, of his visit to a country church. Having described the dilapidated state of the church and graveyard, he continued:

The Minister of this noble edifice was answerable to it in dress and manners. Having entered the church, he made the best of his way to the chancel where he changed his wig; put on a dirty iron moulded ragged surplice; and after a short angry dialogue with the clerk, entered his desk and began immediately without looking into the book. He read as if he had ten other churches to serve that day, at as many miles distance from each other. The clerk sang a melancholy solo – neither tune nor words of which I ever heard before.[15]

An important, though not unexpected, result of these practices was a decline in the number of people who attended the Sunday services of the Church. Since 1750 penal coercion to attend church had almost disappeared; the Diocesan Correction Books for the reigns of William and Mary, Anne, and George I include a few cases of presentment of non-worshippers and non-communicants, but they contain no record of any actions having been taken. The clergy themselves, finding the procedure fruitless, gave up the prosecution of habitual non-attenders. One of the last references to attempts to exercise ecclesiastical discipline of this nature occurred in 1778. The neglect of church attendance had caused concern before the last quarter of the eighteenth century, but there seems little doubt that it had now reached much larger proportions. John Butler, shortly after his translation from Oxford to Hereford in 1788, sent out visitation queries and compared the results with the diocesan survey last made in 1747. The decline in church attendance was so distressing that he was unwilling to divulge the figures. The church attendance figures had been by no means high in 1747, and, when the increase in population was also considered, the results were even more alarming.[16] The Report of a group of clergymen in Lincolnshire published in 1800 revealed that in seventy-nine parishes with a population of 15,042 (11,282 adults over fourteen years of age) the average number of congregations was 4933. 'So that the ordinary number of attendants on Divine service does not amount to a third part of the number of inhabitants.'[17] Edward Stanley recorded that when he took over the family living in 1805, the established practice was for the clerk on a Sunday morning to stand in the churchyard and call the vicar only if someone came to church.[18]

The practice of abandoning the second service had a much more serious effect upon church attendance than the clergy imagined. John Napleton realized its effect when he wrote in his handbook:

> The consequence of having no evening service is [that] . . . it entirely frustrates and ultimately prevents, the religious distribution of domestic business, by which they who are detained at home one part of the day may attend divine service at the other; so that in many families there are servants who can attend at neither.[19]

In the Cheshire Article of Inquiry of 1789 a curate of the village of Tattenhall wrote that half the people never attended any place of worship: 'Prevalence of dairying and cheesemaking requiring some Sunday work . . .' Domestic servants and persons connected with livestock were in many instances prevented from attending Morning Service, and therefore the afternoon service was in some respects the servants' service.[20] There can be little doubt that the failure of the Church of England to provide an afternoon (or evening) service on Sundays in the latter half of the eighteenth century considerably assisted the spread of dissent. It is often forgotten that the alienation of the urban working classes from the Church, about which so much was written in the early years of Queen Victoria's reign, had its origins in the slow alienation of the rural working classes throughout the second half of the eighteenth century and the first two decades of the nineteenth century.

'The French Revolution', wrote Canon Smyth, 'illustrated the connection between good morals and the order and peace of society more than all the eloquence of the pulpit and the disquisitions of moral philosophers had done for many centuries.'[21] It is difficult to overestimate the effect of this event upon the Church of England. Laymen, especially those of the upper ranks, hearing of the events in France, were alarmed at the prospect of irreligious doctrines spreading through the English working classes. The clergy, witnessing the arrival of the exiled French priests, looked with a new concern to their own position. Everywhere religion was put forward as the bulwark against revolution; a Royal Proclamation was issued for paying a decent and due regard to Sundays and the churches were again well attended. Gladstone as a young man heard 'persons of great weight and authority . . . ascribe the beginning of a reviving seriousness in the upper classes of lay society to a reaction against the horrors and impieties of the first French Revolution in its later stages.'[22]

But the French Revolution was neither the first nor the only cause of a movement among the clergy to set higher standards for the performance of their duties. The Evangelicals in the Church of England were always only a small proportion of the clergy and in this period their numbers were very few. However, their influence on the manner in which the clergy came to perform their role was very much greater than their numbers might suggest. With their new spiritual conception of the role they set out to perform what they saw as their duties with a zeal and a parochial strategy which immediately marked them off from their clerical neighbours. The Evangelical clergy insisted on two services on Sundays, and in many cases established a third evening service, specifically to compete with the dissenters. Cadogan at Reading instituted a service in the evening rather than at 3 p.m. when 'all heavy'.[23] John Venn at Clapham established a Sunday evening service described as 'a great novelty';[24] and Daniel Wilson at Islington established, in 1824, a Sunday evening service at which all seats were free.[25]

The majority of clergy who lacked the Evangelicals' new conception of their role were slower to see the need to increase services. However, by the third decade of the nineteenth century new standards were beginning to be demanded of the clergy with respect to Sunday duty. Bishop Mant wrote in his handbook of 1830: 'In many churches of the kingdom only a single Sunday service is performed . . . a clergyman ought not hastily to acquiesce in the notion of the impracticability of two services.'[26] Between 1818 and 1838, in the diocese of Oxford, the percentage of churches with single duty had declined from 40 per cent to 19 per cent. [27] There are many examples of individual clergymen increasing the number of services; Richard Seymour, incumbent of Kinwarton, considerably increased the services when he arrived in 1834; [28] Julius Hare established a second Sunday service on 2 June 1830. [29] Even clergymen renowned for non-clerical activities managed to increase the number of services; Parson Jack Russell of Swimbridge had four services every Sunday when his predecessor had had only one. [30] An interesting example of the lengths to which clergy were willing to go is afforded by Charles Blomfield (later Bishop of London), who found the observance of Easter Sunday impossible in a village on the main road to Newmarket, where the Spring Race Meeting started the next day. 'More than forty pairs of horses have sometimes been changed there on Easter Day,' he wrote, 'a great proportion of them, while I was celebrating Divine Service.' Eventually Blomfield with the aid of some powerful laymen had the start of the Newmarket Spring Meeting changed to a Tuesday. [31]

When G. A. Selwyn returned to England in 1855, he said in the course of a sermon at Cambridge: 'A great and visible change has taken place in the thirteen years since I left England. It is now a rare thing to see a careless clergyman, a neglected parish, or a desecrated church.' [32] Although there is evidence to suggest that Selwyn's view was tinged with the euphoria of the missionary on furlough, there is no doubt that a greater diligence and a higher standard were required by public opinion and demanded by the bishops. Residence was now strictly enforced and the majority of parishes, even in rural areas, had a resident clergyman and double duty on Sundays. Bishop Wilberforce in particular had taken a strong line over single duty, and in the county of Oxfordshire (excluding Oxford city), in 1866, only nine churches had single duty (4 per cent of the total). [33] The clergy influenced by the Oxford Movement were particularly active in the multiplication of services and at St Peter's, London Docks, there were eight Sunday services during the 1860s. [34]

The growth of statistical data in the early years of the nineteenth century and especially the decennial census provided data which, when compared with diocesan and parochial figures, indicated the wide gap which existed between the population and the church facilities. The decade 1840–50 saw efforts in church building unparalleled in the history of the Church of England, and the clergy were continually exhorted to provide more services. The publication in 1854 of Horace Mann's religious census data confirmed in statistical terms what many of the clergy already suspected: that these policies were not achieving the goals at which they were aimed. In every element of the clergyman's role, the middle decades of the nineteenth century saw new strategies being developed to extend the outreach of the Church. In terms of the Sunday services, there were three principal forms of experiment: (1) the division of the Sunday morning services; (2) the introduction of new forms of services; and (3) experimentation with new places of worship.

Long before this period there had been agitation for breaking up the long Sunday morning marathon of Morning Prayer, Litany, Holy Communion and a sermon. By the 1850s action of this nature was considered essential by some clergymen in order to make churchgoing more attractive, although it was not until the Act of Uniformity Amendment, in 1872, that this became legal. However, Ashley Oxenden records that early attempts to shorten the Morning Service met with great opposition.[35] J. C. Miller, the Evangelical incumbent of St Martin's, Birmingham, was one of the first clergymen to actually separate the three services in the late 1840s.[36] A committee of the ruri-decanal chapter of Leeds, appointed in September 1851, consisting of the vicar and six other clergy to consider the best means of reclaiming the lost portion of the poor, recommended as their first point the division of the Sunday morning service and an increase in the number of services.[37] It would appear that this action was principally taken in urban churches – those particularly sensitive to the large numbers of the working classes alienated from the life of the church.

A practice which commanded a much greater following among the clergy was the policy of attempting to attract congregations with new types of services. The ritualist experiments in employing Catholic ceremonial are probably the best known. However, a much less controversial and more widely adopted plan was that of providing choral services. Most eighteenth-century congregations heard little music and if there was any, it was probably a small village band accompanying the singing of the Tate and Brady version of the metric psalms (known as the 'singing psalms'). The Methodists had discovered that congregations enjoyed singing hymns, and the more widespread introduction of various types of organ allowed many clergy to experiment with choral services (especially with a choral afternoon or evening service). Gatty noted, in 1853, that together with Morning Service, and, at 3 p.m. Evensong, he also had a 'Choral Service and a sermon' at 6 p.m.[38] In June 1865, William Butler wrote in the Wantage parish journal that there was parochial disquiet about the choral service which he had recently introduced every Sunday; henceforth he intended to have it monthly.[39] Jones, in his handbook of 1866, counselled against choral services if they were badly done, and suggested staying their introduction until congregations were ready for them.[40] In this as in other matters of parochial strategy, the clergy showed their willingness to learn from the non-conformist tradition.

The third experiment, which was almost the hallmark of a zealous urban clergyman by the decade 1860–70, was the practice of holding services outside churches. There are various traditional and legal reasons why, before 1850, and indeed long after it, this policy was viewed with the deepest suspicion by the majority of the clergy. However, regular Sunday worship had for some time been undertaken outside churches. Benjamin Newton mentioned an example in 1818 when the people of Redcar, having no church nearer than three miles, met in a schoolroom on Sundays. When they applied to the Archbishop of York to consecrate the room, he declined but applauded the practice and recommended its continuance.[41] Needless to say, it was principally in the large towns and cities where such expedients were considered necessary. In the early 1830s in London, Blomfield was very reluctant to allow services in unconsecrated rented rooms; he softened his high-church resentment with the knowledge that more permanent consecrated facilities would eventually be provided for a new lower class congregation, which might not have existed otherwise. After the publication of the 1851 religious census figures, which showed that many of the new churches (such as those in Bethnal Green) were poorly attended, Blomfield was compelled to comply with the demands of his more zealous Evangelical clergy for more latitude in establishing missions. Their work, which always involved services in unconsecrated buildings by such organizations as the London City Mission and the Home Missionary Society, was distrusted by the vast majority of the clergy.[42] Shaftesbury, a supporter of such methods, met with opposition from A. G. Edouart, the incumbent in whose West End parish he attempted to hold services. But, in 1855, Shaftesbury succeeded in having the law amended that had prohibited the meeting for religious worship of more than twenty people except in a church or licensed dissenting chapel.[43] This led to the immense gatherings for public worship in Exeter Hall in 1856. This policy, pioneered by the Evangelicals, was slowly taken up by the rest of the clergy, and, by the mid-1870s, services were regularly held in theatres, railway stations, factories, tents, and in the open air. In 1866, an Evangelical author wrote: 'Open air services have been largely blessed. It is cause for thankfulness that in all parts of the country the clergy have adopted this plan to reach with the blessed sound of the Gospel the masses of men.'[44] However, the vast majority of clergy, whilst willing to hear of anything that would increase the outreach of the Church, would not countenance the performance of Sunday worship anywhere but in a parish church or licensed chapel.

In conclusion, it may be seen that when the practices of the mid-nineteenth century are compared with those of the mid-eighteenth century, there had been a considerable change and improvement in the standards of the clergy in this element of their role. The clergy, particularly after the French Revolution, responded to the temper of the times which demanded a more conscious performance of the clergyman's central religious function. At the same time, the new conception of the role and the demand for higher standards encouraged the clergy to seek more effective means of discharging their duty.

WEEKDAY SERVICES

The weekday services of the Book of Common Prayer may be divided between: (1) The Saint's day services and services performed on days of obligation (Ash Wednesday, Good Friday, Holy Week, Ascension Day, and Christmas Day); (2) the services for special days (services commemorating the Martyrdom of Charles I, Restoration of Charles II and the Gunpowder Plot, which were deleted from the Prayer Book in 1859, and days of national fasting decreed by Parliament); (3) the daily services of Morning and Evening Prayer (the Litany being added on Wednesdays and Fridays). There can be no doubt that the charter role of the Church of England clergyman envisaged him as saying the Saint's day and other special services publicly in church as the rubrics of the Book of Common Prayer directed. The rubric concerning the daily services was contained in the introductory section, *Concerning the Service of the Church*, and stated:

And all Priests and Deacons are to say daily the Morning and Evening Prayer either privately or openly, not being let by sickness or some other urgent cause. And the curate that ministereth in every Parish-Church or Chapel, being at home, and not being otherwise reasonably hindered, shall say the same in the Parish-Church or Chapel where he ministereth and shall cause a bell to be tolled there-unto a convenient time before he begins, that the people may come to hear God's Word and to pray with him.

It is clear that the rubric required every clergyman to say Morning and Evening Prayer daily, and those who were responsible for a cure of souls were to say it in their church. The ambiguity lies in what constitutes 'some other urgent cause' or 'not being otherwise reasonably hindered'. In the eighteenth century these phrases were allowed the widest interpretation, and the public performance of daily services was restricted to a very few city churches.

Sykes showed in his analysis of Archbishop Herring's Visitation Returns of 1743 that of the 836 parishes, 253 had some form of weekday services, 80 had Holy Day, Wednesday and Friday services, and 24 had daily prayers.[45] The decline in the incidence of these services can be seen in the rural deanery of Holsworthy in Devon. In the Visitation of 1744 the parish church at Holsworthy alone had regular Wednesday and Friday services. Two other clergy said they had Holy Day services, when they could get a congregation. Twenty years later the only mention of Holy Day services is by Holsworthy, and by 1799, all reference to weekday or Holy Day services had completely disappeared. In Bishop Carey's Primary Visitation of 1821, the question was significantly amended to apply only to Sundays.[46]

In the county of Oxford there was no parish which had regular daily services at the end of the eighteenth century. It appears that a number of the towns, Witney, Bicester, and three villages, had some form of Saint's day services in 1793, and a few more had them in Lent, Whit Week, and Holy Week. However, as McClatchey concluded, in the majority of cases apart from Christmas and Good Friday, the officially declared Public Fasts and Thanksgivings, the position is summed up by the incumbent of Great Rollright who wrote in 1793: 'No prayers on Holy Days on account of the non-attendance of the people.'[47] There can be little doubt that weekday services in the vast majority of parishes had ceased to be performed. James Woodforde had services only on Christmas Day, Ash Wednesday, and Good Friday. William Cole had services on Saints' days when he could get a congregation, but this was by no means always. On 15 July 1767 he wrote in his diary, 'St. James. No one at Matins so I came away.' However, he did have Holy Week services, unless bad weather forced him to cancel them.[48]

The failure of the clergy to give sufficient attention to this element of their role was one of the persistent criticisms of the Evangelicals. However, although they were passionately concerned to increase the number of opportunities for prayer, they did not set about this by re-establishing the Prayer Book services of Morning and Evening Prayer. They preferred to turn their own private family prayer meetings into parochial prayer meetings, where the laity could worship, and also learn to conduct their own household devotions. This practice was the hallmark of the Evangelical clergy. Grimshaw of Haworth went on monthly visitations around the hamlets of his parish borrowing a farm kitchen and summoning seven or eight families at a time. 'If you will not come to church to hear me,' he told them grimly, 'you shall hear me at home; and if you do perish, you shall perish with the sound of the gospel in your ears.'[49] Berridge of Everton admitted 'the serious people of the parish to his vicarage on Saturday evenings'.[50] Henry Crooke of Leeds had a meeting every Thursday night in 1755 for thirty to forty 'awakened' colliers, another meeting on a Friday, and a service on Saturdays. In 1757, he had services on Wednesday, Thursday, Friday, and Saturday, either morning or evening.[51] John Newton's weekly timetable involved eleven weekday services or meetings for particular people.[52] Conyers of Helmsley erected a room adjoining the parsonage which was every morning and evening open to all who thought it proper to be present at his domestic religious exercises.[53] Cadogan of Reading invited his parishioners to join in his family prayers on Tuesday evenings, only to find that they availed themselves in such numbers that it became necessary to adjourn to the chancel of St Giles's Church.[54] Thomas Scott of Aston Sandford had prayers every morning, of which his grandson wrote: 'Family prayers at Aston Rectory were formidable, particularly to a child. They lasted a full hour, several persons from the village usually attending.'[55]

However, whilst the Evangelical clergy regarded these weekday services as an essential part of the ministry, they were looked upon with varying degrees of distrust by the majority of the clergy, who considered the line between such meetings and the prophesyings of the dissenters to be at best thin. Certainly, this practice encouraged dissent, and trained potential dissenting ministers in the performance of this section of the clergyman's role. Undoubtedly some of these meetings were illegal, for the Conventicle Act and the laws which superseded it, prevented the meeting together of more than twenty persons for an act of worship outside a church or licensed chapel. But, although the fervent prayer meetings of the early Evangelical clergy slowly gave way to the more regulated cottage and schoolroom meetings of the later period, at the same time by degrees the majority of clergy began to realize the importance of providing some form of public worship over and above Sunday duty.

The policy of multiplying services which was so widely adopted between 1830 and 1850 was more dramatically illustrated by the increase of weekday worship. The clergy, who had almost totally neglected this element in their role in the preceding decades, managed in a short space of time to re-establish weekday worship. By the 1860s, it was expected of the active clergyman that he would keep the Saint's day and have either daily prayer or a system of cottage meetings and schoolroom lectures; many had both. The re-establishment of Saint's day services and daily services will be considered first. McClatchey recorded for the county of Oxford that between 1793 and 1821 to 1825 there was no real change in the situation; six towns had Wednesday and/or Friday services. However, the picture in 1866 is a very different one. There were seventeen instances of daily Morning and/or Evening Prayer, including a number of villages and newly formed parishes. There were services once or twice a week in twenty-six other villages, in addition to the observance of the Holy Days and special seasons.[56] A pamphlet of 1824 called for more provision for weekday worship and gave details of the situation at that time. In some London churches the bells were still rung for Morning Prayer, but, 'on entering the church, you are met and indecently acquainted that though the bell is tolling there will be no service, as no congregation is expected.' Of the fifteen churches in Canterbury, other than the Cathedral, none had services on weekdays or Saints' days.[57] But, by the 1840s, the handbooks regularly mentioned daily prayers. Sandford wrote in 1845: 'The revival of daily public prayer is a subject which must be interesting to pious churchmen.' His own practice at Dunchurch for more than three years was to have Morning Prayer at 7.30 in the summer and winter; the largest attendance was 64, the smallest 36, the average 40.[58] The revival in regular weekday services in church and in particular the daily service, was in the main confined to those influenced by Tractarian views. John Keble started daily Morning Prayer at Otterbourne in 1838.[59] Samuel Wilberforce, soon after he arrived at Checkendon, in 1829, had instituted special services on Saints' days, and when he moved to Alverstock, in 1841, he had daily prayers.[60] Hamilton, whilst he was incumbent of St Peter's in the East, Oxford, started daily services at which Newman attended.[61] Suckling had a daily service,[62] and Butler established daily service at Wantage in 1846, 'at once attending by some old men and women with regularity'. By 1849, Butler not only had a course of Holy Week addresses but a series of Lenten services.[63] Hook had much the same system with special Wednesday morning services in Lent, and daily during Holy Week. Bennett had daily services at St Barnabas, Pimlico from 1847, and St George's Mission had both services at 8 a.m. and 8 p.m. in 1856.[64] When Samuel Wilberforce appointed Randall to the living of Graffham cum Lavington of which he was the patron in 1851, Randall found that daily prayer was already well established by Manning and Laprimaudaye. In Lent the service was at 6 a.m. on Fridays for the benefit of early workers. He made a great point of the observance of Ash Wednesday and Ascension Day. When he arrived only Samuel Wilberforce, as squire, gave a holiday to his workers on Ascension Day; the other farmers did not. By 1855, all the farmers save one gave a holiday.[65]

However, even by 1855, the daily service in church would have been a considerable exception to the general rule and enough to mark off a clergyman as sympathizing with Tractarian views. A more common and more widely adopted strategy for the provision of weekday worship was the holding of schoolroom 'lectures' and cottage meetings. The schoolroom 'lecture' was, despite its name, a service – usually no more than a hymn, a prayer, a reading from Scripture, and an address. It was called a 'lecture' principally because if it had been called a service it would have been more obviously illegal. The cottage meeting in some cases was clearly related to the class meeting of the Methodists, but was more usually seen by the clergy, anxious not to appear in any way irregular, as an extension of the private services of the Visitation of the Sick. The schoolroom 'lecture' will be considered first. Bishop Law, whilst Bishop of Chester from 1812 to 1824, had sanctioned only with the greatest reluctance a Sunday evening lecture. His successor Blomfield set his face sternly against the Wednesday evening lecture; 'and thought that where there were two full services on Sundays such weekday services were not required'.[66] This attitude was not that of his successor, J. B. Sumner, who became a great innovator and encouraged his clergy in any measure which might result in the enlarging of the ministry of the Church. In his Charge of 1838, J. B. Sumner suggested that as the poor would not mix with the rich, schoolrooms and lecture halls should be used where the poor would not be ashamed to attend. However, Sumner was exceptional in countenancing such measures, and it took many years for the majority of the clergy to realize that expedients of this nature were both necessary and safe. In the mid-1830s, a clergyman at Sandgate had opened his school for such a service which had proved successful in attracting the fishermen, but it was suppressed by the bishop.[67] In 1845, the Bishop of Salisbury prosecuted one of his clergy for 'having aided and abetted' a mission service in his schoolroom.[68] However, despite a reluctance on the part of the majority of the bishops to sanction this innovation, 'lectures' were widely introduced. H. C. Ridley had a regular schoolroom meeting in 1829.[69] Hook, whilst at Whippingham from 1821 to 1826, used a sail loft in which he had evening services attended by sailors, fishermen, and other poor people.[70] Ashley Oxenden, whilst at Barnham, had a Wednesday evening schoolroom service.[71] Andrews, the Evangelical incumbent of Ketteringham, had meetings in his schoolroom.[72] Julius Hare started Saint's day services in the school in 1839; Augustus Hare recorded: 'attended by one old woman and ourselves'.[73]

On the other hand, the cottage meeting was possibly of the two the more popular expedient. The clergy found that some people who were sick or infirm and those who had the care of small children, whilst being unable to attend church, would come to small gatherings in a neighbour's cottage. Samuel Wilberforce, whilst at Checkendon, established a cottage service in the house of an infirm woman;[74] he used the Prayer

Book service, 'The Visitation of the Sick'. Evans, in his handbook of 1842, discussed such services as a way of reaching the poor:

> The simplest kind is that for which you call a few neighbours into a sick room, if the sick can bear it; or to the cottage of an infirm person who is unable to attend church; or give notice a day or two previously that you will lecture at such and such a place.[75]

However, despite some opposition (a correspondent in the *British Magazine* in 1838 felt sure that such policies would lead to a neglect of the Church and schism),[76] there can be little doubt that by the mid-1840s among the active clergy cottage meetings were an established part of parochial strategy. Beachcroft had established cottage meetings in each hamlet of his large parish by the late 1820s.[77] Henry Moule at Fordington had established a number of cottage meetings by 1829.[78] H. C. Ridley had cottage meetings in five different cottages around his parish.[79] G. S. Bull of Byerley, in 1826, 'held regular house meetings in different localities. On Sunday evenings he lectured at various places round the parish and every Monday in Widow Riley's house at East Bowling'.[80] The curate at Culmstock, in the 1830s, took prayers with an exposition of the Scripture in each household in the parish, unless the householder declined to admit him for such a purpose.[81] After Samuel Wilberforce had been at Brighstone for three months he had established three weekly cottage meetings.[82]

The schoolroom 'lecture' and the cottage meeting were both considerable innovations for the Church of England in the early years of Queen Victoria's reign. Although many clergy no doubt found them useful in enlarging the opportunities for weekday worship, by the early 1860s they were increasingly viewed with disfavour. John Burgon wrote in his handbook of 1864: 'The quasi-irregularities of cottage lectures and the fancy services in the school-room we altogether deprecate and dislike.'[83] The handbooks of this period regarded the re-establishment of the daily service as the most important objective. Edward Monro, who wrote very extensively about daily prayer, considered it to be the centrepiece of pastoral strategy,[84] and its importance was stressed by J. H. Blunt and J. J. Blunt.[85] However, the handbook writers were concerned not just that the daily services should be said, but that they should be performed at such a time as would give the working man an opportunity of attending. It was widely observed that by having Morning and Evening Prayer at the usual time (10 a.m. and 3 p.m.) only the retired and the leisured could possibly attend. A letter in the *British Magazine* of April 1841 observed that daily Evening Prayer in London was never later than 5 p.m., and sometimes much earlier. The correspondent considered that it should be between 7 and 9 p.m. to give working men the opportunity of attending.[86] The problem particularly exercised Monro:

> Whilst gambling houses and gin palaces, public houses and taverns, stand doors wide open to entrap the passing artisan and wearly herdsman in their evening walk, why should the church alone be dark and her doors alone closed, when she too might entice men who pass by to hear words which might warn them of the nearness of eternity and the awefulness of judgement.[87]

Monro considered that in an agricultural parish daily prayer should be at 7 p.m. in winter; 8 p.m. in summer; and 9 p.m. in harvest. A practice which must have been comparatively rare was the adoption of daily choral evening prayers. Armstrong of East Dereham had a choral daily service in 1855.[88] Dean Hole recalled: 'For many years I educated six boys and maintained a daily choir at a cost of 2/6d. per week.'[89] St Peter's, London Docks, had a choral evening service at 8 p.m. in the 1860s.[90]

The revival of the daily service had a greater importance than the mere addition of another weapon to the clergyman's armoury for parochial evangelism. It is significant that when the Alcester Clerical Association met to discuss the daily service, having talked about it in relation to parochial evangelism, the two clergymen who had had some experience of the daily service thought it should be considered primarily in relation to the clergy themselves.[91] During this period, it became apparent to some of the clergy that their claim to professional status, indeed their claim to any sort of public recognition, bore some relationship to the manner in which they performed this central and distinguishing element of the clergyman's role. Gradually the daily service came to be seen not from the point of view of the parish and parochial strategy, but from the point of view of the clergyman and the invigoration of his ministry. The rediscovery of continental Catholic spirituality had a considerable influence and many clergy imbued the bishop's question at the ordination service: 'Will you be diligent in prayers . . . ?' with a new significance. It was the clergyman's life of prayer which gave purpose, structure, and significance to all his other duties. James Russell Woodforde said in his ordination lectures at Cuddesdon College in 1861: 'The grand object of this perpetual repetition of the sacred offices is to create and maintain a higher spiritual life and a distinctive professional character in the clergy.'[92] Monro was particularly concerned that the clergyman should not fritter away his time: 'Of all arrangements to meet this end, none can be more beautiful than the institution and keeping of Catholic hours.'[93]

THE CONDUCT OF THE SERVICE

As the clergy sought to emphasize the spiritual and professional character of their role, they were particularly concerned to improve the standards of public worship and to assert their authority over everything that happened in the church building. The handbooks contain extensive advice on the performance of the services and on elocution. There is much evidence to suggest that standards rose rapidly, and that the clergy approached their work with a new zeal and enthusiasm. However, in an eighteenth-century church, the clergyman was not solely responsible for the conduct of the services, for the clerk, the singers, the bandsmen, and the ringers all contributed distinctive elements to public worship. The rustic activities of these men were frequently sited by the clergy as the principal obstacles to the achievement of higher standards. The reforms of the nineteenth century, and particularly the widespread adoption of the organ or harmonium, as they became cheaply available, considerably altered the conduct and ethos of the services. The dominant nineteenth-century attitude is illustrated by J. H. Blunt, who wrote in his handbook of 1864: '. . . let the clergyman be advised always to maintain his authority as director of Divine Service.'[94]

The parish clerk, whose liturgical functions customarily included leading the responses, reading the notices and briefs, and reading over the psalm before it was sung by the congregation, was appointed in a variety of ways, either by the incumbent, or more commonly by the vestry, or in some cases it was an hereditary office. The office was freehold, and, owing to the difficulty of dismissing a clerk, it was not unusual to appoint to the office a gentleman or farmer who nominated a deputy to do the work. There is evidence to suggest that, in the latter part of the eighteenth century, it was a common practice to give the office to a pauper so that he could earn an income and relieve the parish of his main-tenance. By whatever means he was appointed, the clerk was often a source of considerable mirth and irreverence in the eighteenth-century parish church, being on occasions quite unequal to his duties. Woodforde recorded in his diary on 14 April 1791: 'Poor old John Smith my clerk made a shocking hand of it singing this afternoon in church much laughed at.'[95] With increased literacy, there was no longer a need for the clerk to lead the congregation. The three-decker pulpit itself was an object of scorn to Victorian church restorers, and with its removal went the office of the occupant of the lower seat.

In the eighteenth-century church, the singers and band were usually installed in the west gallery above, and out of sight of, the congregation. They performed during the singing of the psalm, and in the more ambitious churches there was also an anthem, during both of which it was common practice for the congregation to turn round to face the gallery (hence the expression 'to turn and face the music'). The musicians had a considerable reputation for independent action and were liable to meet any interference by the clergyman with a demonstration of their disapproval, often during the service. A large number of clergy had 'trouble with the musicians' (as Woodforde noted on several occasions). At the same time, the standard of their performance was often very low. Oxenden wrote of the Barnham musicians: '. . . the singing was almost ludicrous, provoking laughter rather than an expression of praise.'[96]

The late 1850s and early 1860s saw major changes in the form of worship in many parishes. Hymns, which had not been common in the 1840s, were widely introduced, and the old musicians were often incapable of the new demands made upon them. In many parishes the musicians had to make way for a new harmonium and a choir of the children from the parish school, both placed in the chancel and under the clergyman's eye and direction. Implementing these reforms was not easy, and they were often undertaken against a background of bitter opposition from the displaced musicians. T. T. Carter described the removal of the gallery and breakup of the choir at Clewer as 'a terrible grievance'.[97] Thomas Hardy, in his novel *Under the Greenwood Tree*, described the last days of the gallery musicians and singers in a Dorset village and the introduction in the chancel of an organ, played by the schoolmistress. He wrote in the Preface:

> Under the old plan, from half a dozen to ten full-grown players, in addition to the numerous more or less grownup singers, were officially occupied with the Sunday routine, and concerned in trying their best to make it an artistic outcome of the combined musical taste of the parish. With a musical executive limited, as it mostly is limited now, to the parson's wife or daughter and the schoolchildren, or to the schoolteacher and the children, an important union of interests has disappeared.[98]

But, despite the difficulties, the clergy were determined to achieve higher standards and a greater sense of decorum in the services and their attitude to church music is reflected in the handbook of J. H. Blunt:

> But though a clergyman may be able neither to build an organ nor to perform upon it when built, his general authority over everything that is to be done or used in divine service imposes upon him the duty of supervising organs and organists as well as other things and persons.[99]

The same attitude was taken with the other people involved in the services of the Church. During the eighteenth century, there were considerable advances in the art and popularity of bell-ringing. The bells were used not only to call worshippers to church, but whenever the ringers decided to mark a national or local event. The ringers usually rang the bells when anyone of importance passed through the parish, or for departures and arrivals at the big houses, expecting some remuneration from those so honoured. In the nineteenth century, the clergy frequently complained of the conduct of the ringers both on account of drunkenness and non-attendance at the services for which they rang, and the clergy looked for opportunities to assert their authority. Armstrong wrote in 1864: 'The recasting of one of the church bells seemed to me to be a good opportunity of putting the Company of Ringers on a better footing. I drew up some rules and induced them to meet the churchwardens and myself in the vestry. The rules were agreed upon.'[100]

Some churches retained a number of minor officials such as beadles, pew openers, 'sluggard wakers', and dog whippers; of these it is sufficient to say that the mid-nineteenth-century clergy sought to curtail and restrain the disputative activities of these officials during the services which could be so fatal to the sense of dignity and decorum that was such a feature of Victorian church life.

With the coming of the railways, and the breakup of the old isolation, the clergy even in remote rural areas became increasingly conscious of what was happening in the large city churches and in the cathedrals. The eighteenth-century pattern of worship, which involved a number of the villagers and which was in many respects a communal undertaking, gave way to church practices and a form of service completely controlled by the clergyman. In short, by the late nineteenth century the service had in many respects become 'the parson's show', in which the parishioners could take their place only as members of the congregation.

In the decades which followed the close of the Napoleonic Wars, a new spirit can be observed among the clergy. In part, it resulted from their being thrust forward as the preservers of the peace of the nation. In part, the new spirit of invigoration arose from the clergy themselves, who saw that new times demanded new standards. In part, it resulted from the new conception of the role which the Evangelicals and the Tractarians set before the Church. If the single Sunday duty of the mid-eighteenth-century Church is compared with the extensive endeavours of the mid-Victorian clergy, it is possible to trace both a considerable improvement in the manner in which the clergy performed this element of their role, and a marked increase in the significance they accorded to it. Everywhere the number of services was increased, churches were extended and rebuilt, and the last quarter of the nineteenth century was to witness the high-water mark of churchgoing as a popular activity in this country.

5

Leader of Public Worship – Surplice Duties

One of the important functions of religion in any society is to solemnize the life-cycle, and the clergyman as the leader of public worship performed this function by conducting the appropriate *rites de passage*. By the middle of the eighteenth century, the surplice duties (Churchings of Women, Marriages and Burials; Baptism is included in chapter 7) were generally performed on a Sunday (with the occasional exception of burials which, in cases of contagious disease, had to be performed immediately after death). The adoption of this practice was no doubt dictated by the demands of people's work, and the widespread practice of clerical non-residence. However, it appears that even resident clergy performed these services on a Sunday, and Benjamin Newton carefully recorded in his diary that he did duty in the parish church on Sundays, marrying and burying his parishioners.[1] By the mid-nineteenth century, there was an increasing preference among the clergy for performing the surplice duties during the week. This must have resulted in part from the multiplication of Sunday services and the addition of a Sunday school in many parishes. However, Evangelical sabbatarianism frowned upon burials and marriages taking place on a Sunday, presumably on account of the attendant festivities.

The surplice duties were important to the clergy, particularly the poorly paid curates, as a source of income. Woodforde's first curacy at Newton Purcell gave him the annual sum of £28 together with the surplice fees.[2] Although these fees would have been modest in a small country parish, in a large town parish they could amount to a substantial sum. In many urban parishes after the period of the Industrial Revolution, many assistant clergy were largely paid for by these fees.

The evidence on the manner in which the clergy performed this element of their role is not readily accessible; the services were treated at this time as essentially family and private occasions. However, such evidence as there is allows certain assertions to be made: first, about the structural problems of the Church of England which arose from the urbanization that was associated with the Industrial Revolution; and second, concerning the way in which the clergy began to restrict the services of the Church as a means of discipline.

THE MARRIAGE SERVICE

By the eleventh century the Church claimed exclusive jurisdiction over matters relating to marriage. The Reformation in England did not alter this and it was Lord Hardwick's Marriage Act of 1753 that first forced a breach between civil and canon law. By this legislation clandestine marriages (those celebrated without banns or licence) were considered void in secular law; although according to canon law they were considered as irregular but valid. This legislation was repealed in 1823, when the Marriage Act of that year declared clandestine marriages valid, but the officiating minister a felon. The important effect of the 1823 legislation was to make marriages by licence more widely available. The clergy had the legal right to act as reigstrars and to solemnize marriages but there is some evidence that they abused this right and some, including the incumbent of Fledborough in the 1740s, did a regular trade in performing clandestine marriages.[3] This practice did not altogether cease in the nineteenth century, and at a meeting of the Alcester Clerical Association, it was decided that a letter should be sent to the Rural Dean of Birmingham complaining that clandestine marriages of local people were being performed in his area.[4] Bishop Phillpotts of Exeter said, in his charge of 1833, that marriages were not infrequently celebrated by banns in parishes where neither of the parties had been resident: 'This is a serious evil.' There were other reasons why the clergy felt uneasy about some of the practices associated with marriage in the eighteenth century. Under the 1733 Bastardy Act, if a woman swore before a magistrate that a man had given her a child, the Justice could order the

Overseer of the Poor to apprehend and imprison the man unless he gave security to indemnify the parish. Marriage was the only alternative to imprisonment for a poor man. It appears that many marriages resulted from the enforcement of this Act. Woodforde performed the ceremony, with uneasiness, for such a case on 25 January 1787: 'The man was a long time before he could be prevailed on to marry her when in the churchyard and at the altar behaved very unbecoming. It is a cruel thing that any person should be compelled by law to marry.'[5]

By the middle of the nineteenth century there is some evidence that the clergy were willing to use the withholding of the ceremony as a weapon in their battle against immorality. A correspondent of the *British Magazine* wrote to say that he had refused to marry two persons who had been living 'in open sin'.[6] There was widespread concern about the propriety of marriages in which brides already had, in the words of Archdeacon Hope's Charge of 1841, 'the offspring of unhallowed lust lying beneath their bosoms'.[7] The clergy also tried to stop persons marrying at the solemn seasons of the year. In 1857, George Gorham, incumbent of Walkeringham, tried to stop a wedding in Holy Week. Finally, he allowed the ceremony, but refused to have the bells rung.[8] (However, in 1852, the Prince of Wales married Princess Alexandra of Denmark in Lent.)

The whole situation was radically altered by the twin Acts of Marriage and Registration of 1836. By this legislation superintendent registrars could issue licences for marriage in the office of the registrar or at a nonconformist place of worship (but not according to the rite of the Church of England or in any church or chapel belonging to it). This legislation had the effect of setting up civil marriage as an alternative to what had formerly been the monopoly of the Church of England. There is a great deal of evidence to suggest that the clergy deeply resented the breaking of their monopoly. Of the large number of articles and letters which appeared in clerical journals of this period, it is sufficient to quote one example. When the clergyman referred to above published his letter recording his refusal to marry two persons living 'in open sin', there was in the next issue of the

British Magazine a strong letter stressing the importance of encouraging people to marry in ·church and not throwing them into the arms of the registrar for a civil marriage. Although, throughout the nineteenth century, the number of marriages in Anglican churches continued to increase (1844 – 120,009; 1847 – 150,819; 1904 – 165,519), the proportion of Anglican marriages fell sharply. There was a steady rise in the number of civil ceremonies in proportion to the total number. (Total civil marriages in 1844 were 3446; 1864 – 14,671; 1874 – 21,256; 1884 – 26,786; 1894 – 33,550; and 1904 – 46,247.) Marriages in Roman Catholic chapels rose sharply after the great period of Irish immigration, and the number of nonconformist marriages also showed a steady increase. By the end of the nineteenth century, the number of Church of England marriages had fallen to 642 per 1000, from 907 per 1000 in 1844; conversely the number of civil ceremonies had risen from 26 to 179 per 1000, and those performed by the nonconformist ministers from 49 to 131 per 1000. These figures illustrate most clearly the altered situation of the Church of England at the end of the nineteenth century, and the growing religious pluralism of English society.[9]

THE BURIAL SERVICE

In this service the clergyman presided at a *rite de passage* in which an important part of the life-cycle is solemnized. By the 68th Canon, no clergyman could refuse to bury a corpse that is brought into the church or churchyard, 'convenient warning being given him thereof before', in such manner and form as is prescribed in the Book of Common Prayer, except the deceased were denounced *excommunicate majori excommunicatione*. In effect this meant that all (except suicides) living within the parish were buried in the churchyard, including dissenters. Cremation was almost unknown in the eighteenth century, and was only revived in the nineteenth century in free-thinking circles. The evidence suggests that, as in other elements of their role, the eighteenth-century clergy were lax in attending to their duties and that this stemmed in part from the widespread practice of non-residence, but also in some cases the fear of contracting infectious diseases. William Cole on 20 March 1766 had to perform the service in the neighbouring parish of West Bletchley, because the clergyman resident there refused to conduct the service, the man having died of smallpox.[10] A common eighteenth-century practice was that of performing only the graveside part of the service over a poor man. Clubbe in his handbook of 1770 warned: 'Carry not a rich man into the church and read over him the whole burial service and huddle a poor man into his grave with a small portion of it.'[11] Hook found this practice in operation at Moseley and immediately abolished all fees (at a personal sacrifice of £20 per annum), to do away with this distinction.[12]

The first rubric in the Burial Service states: 'Here is to be noted, that the Office ensuing is not to be used for any that die unbaptized or excommunicate, or have laid violent hands on themselves.' In the eighteenth century it would seem that all except suicides were buried in the churchyard, but in the nineteenth century there arose a concern for the enforcement of spiritual discipline. Samuel Walker of Truro refused to bury a drunkard and raised a considerable controversy.[13] Robert Gregory wrote in the 1850s: 'I am anxious to check this by refusing to bury unbaptized children and in all cases to require proof that a child has been baptized before allowing it to be buried with the rite of the Church.'[14] In 1857, George Gorham of Walkeringham refused to allow a Methodist-baptized person to be buried and he recorded that many adult baptisms followed.[15] Bryan King of St George's in the East would not bury the unbaptized.[16] Burgon advised the clergy not to bury excommunicants.[17]

As with marriage, there is much evidence that the clergy deeply resented the inroad made on their monopoly by the Acts of 1836. The legislation required that clergy could not exercise their function of burying a person without first having a death certificate issued by the registrar. A clergyman who performed a burial without a certificate had seven days to report the burial to the registrar, otherwise he was liable to a £10 fine. It was this notion of a penalty which particularly annoyed the clergy. Yet despite the further legislation of 1852, 1853, and 1870 which allowed for greater provision of cemeteries, both municipal and denominational, in most villages the Church of England burial ground remained the only one and most people were buried there.

THE CHURCHING OF WOMEN

This service is one of thanksgiving in which a woman publicly thanks God for deliverance from the dangers of childbirth and for the birth and gift of her child. However, the service had traditionally been imbued with other overtones which imply that a woman is impure until she has undergone a prescribed ritual, and in many areas a woman recently having given birth would not leave her house until the service had been performed. The rubric implies that the service should take place on a Sunday, and definitely states that the woman 'shall come into the church'. However, it was common practice at this time for baptism and churching to be performed at the same time and not infrequently at the house of the family. On Tuesday, 2 January 1827, Skinner was asked to baptize and church in a house for his clerical neighbour: 'Mr. Hammond (the incumbent at Priston) I think is wrong in admitting this innovation. The rubric mentions Sundays and Holy Days for these ceremonies. We cannot be too exact now in keeping to the old regulations.'[18]

Evidence in the administering of this essentially private service is not easily found, but it can be suggested that, in the early nineteenth century, although the clergy became more zealous in their pastoral work, they also were inclined to take a higher view of the administration of this service. They were increasingly inclined not to perform it in a private house, and to exclude those who gave birth to illegitimate children. Benjamin Newton refused such a woman on 6 September 1818, and wrote in his journal: 'This ceremony is not used in the south when women are brought to bed of illegitimate children and I think it very clear that our church never intended this form of prayer to be used for them.'[19] H. R. Moody acknowledged that 'it is a common custom' to refuse it to those who were unmarried and 'generally acquiesced in', but he doubted the clergyman's legal position if he did so.[20] A correspondent of the *British Magazine* counselled that women delivered of illegitimate children should not be churched.[21] The author of *Pastoral Recollections* took this view as 'a necessary means of discipline', and claimed in a manufacturing district of 3000 people to have reduced the annual illegitimacy rate from twelve to three or four per annum.[22] Randall refused to church publicly in cases of illegitimacy. In this way the clergy were able to express their disapproval and forward the campaign against immorality in their parishes.[23]

The urban parishes in the early decades of the nineteenth century faced an acute problem. The parochial system developed within the constraints of a traditional and predominantly agrarian society was not adaptable with any speed to the sudden change in the scale and complexity of English society. Large manufacturing towns remained as single parishes, which consequently placed a great strain on the clergy as they endeavoured to perform the surplice duties. Hook, Vicar of Leeds, constantly made this point as he argued for the subdivision of his enormous parish. In 1844, the population was 88,741, and, although a considerable number of churches had been built in Leeds, the majority were 'curacies without care of souls'; that is, churches within the city parish. With the exception of three areas, the surplice duties for the whole of Leeds had to be performed in the parish church and by its staff of three. They baptized and 'churched' twice every day. Burials were performed twice a day in winter, and three times in summer. Hook tabulated the statistics for 1842 and 1843:[24]

	1842	1843
Marriages	1004	1163
Baptisms	1812	1810
Burials	1339	1320

It was evident that, as Gregory of Vauxhall remarked, '. . . in some areas the routine of marrying, burying, churching occupies a good deal of time.'[25] Clearly this situation could be multiplied many times. The parish church at Manchester, which had a population of 25,000 in 1750, served a population of about 500,000 in the 1850s, and, although it was a collegiate body, the work of performing the surplice duties for this vast city fell to two chaplains and a clerk. The indecorum and the registrarial difficulties which attended the performance of the surplice duties for such a vast population became something of a national scandal.[26]

The inability of the Church of England to respond to the rapid and dramatic changes in its environment during the early decades of the nineteenth century is well known. Apart from the problems of inadequate endowment, non-residence, and pluralism, the parochial system, which was shaped within the constraints of a rural and agrarian society, was unable to meet the challenges of urbanization and industrialization and the growing scale and complexity of English society. (The population rose from 5.5 million in 1740 to 7.2 million in 1751; 10.6 million in 1811; and 13.2 million in 1831.) The occasional churchman saw the need for reforms and reorganization to improve clerical effectiveness, but it was much more common for an appeal to be made for stricter residence legislation and a more diligent performance of pastoral duties. The rise of Methodism, the spoken and unspoken criticisms of the Evangelicals within the Established Church, and the persistent rumbling of anti-Church feeling in the country were regarded as more significant issues than the migration of people to the cities and their consequent growth.

The strategy of 'church extension' was itself a conservative answer to the problem, and its success was limited. Blomfield consecrated nearly 200 new churches in London during his long tenure, but the situation was only marginally improved. The effect of the rise in the number of Church of England clergy from 10,718 in 1831, to 17,621 in 1851, was of the same order. The somewhat belated legislation of 1843, which allowed for the subdivision of parishes, went some way to alleviating the situation in the worst areas. But, clearly, before these partial remedies were applied, the Church had been unable to perform the surplice duties, or any part of its ministrations, with the attention and decorum which people necessarily demanded at these most significant moments in their lives. This may be regarded as one reason why, when the Church did revive in the mid-nineteenth century, it had lost significant sections of the population. The abuses of the eighteenth century, together with the social and cultural changes associated with the early decades of the nineteenth century, left a significant proportion of the working population, especially those in urban areas, outside the life of the Church. Thus, it was in this element of their role that the clergy of the nineteenth century were first made aware of the pluralism, denominationalism, and secularism of modern society.

6

Preacher

The sermon is, for many, if not the characteristic activity of the clergyman, then certainly the most conspicuous element of his role. It is an element in the charter role of the clergyman and prominently emphasized in the Ordinal. Unlike other elements of the role, which depend predominantly on untrained abilities, this element of the clergyman's role is one where learned technique and acquired skills are most explicitly employed. The handbooks, therefore, devote large sections to this element of the role and the lengthy programmes of reading, which were enjoined on the young clergyman, were principally designed to equip him for this task. In every generation, the clergy have been aware that it is their performance in the pulpit on which many tend to form their opinion of the clergyman's all-round competence and abilities. Certainly, up until the widespread abolition of pew rents, many urban clergy were dependent for part of their income on their abilities in the pulpit to attract a congregation.

In a largely illiterate society in which the ability to read and write anything more than a personal letter was restricted to a few, the facility to preach before the assembled congregation Sunday by Sunday conferred on the clerical profession and the individual clergyman a particular power. He formed the link between the villagers and the political and social life of the nation beyond the parish boundaries. The sermon provided him with a weekly opportunity to disseminate news, flavoured by his own opinions, with the sanction of divine authority, from the platform of the pulpit. The power of the sermon had been widely acknowledged in previous centuries. One of Elizabeth I's first acts had been to forbid the clergy to preach except by a special licence, and in 1576 there were only fifty-seven qualified preachers in the vast Lincoln diocese. At the same time the clergy were

commanded to read a number of Parliamentary procla-
mations from the pulpit on appointed days: that against
perjury a week before the Assizes; that on the observation of
the Lord's Day on the second Sunday in May; that against
drunkenness on the first Sunday in Advent; that against
blasphemy, swearing, and cursing on the second Sunday in
Lent; and that against adultery and fornication on the fourth
Sunday in Lent. On these Sundays the clergyman was expected to preach on the proclamation he had just read.

Certainly the role of the sermon as a principal vehicle of
communication in a pre-literate society was already
diminishing in the second half of the eighteenth century, at a
time when rural communities were less isolated and slightly
more literate, and when the importance of newspapers,
handbills, popular orators, and other channels for the
communication of ideas were increasing in significance.
None the less, even into this century, the sermon remained a
significant means of disseminating information and opinion
within a local community (a situation which was radically
altered by the widespread availability of the wireless).
Despite the vast numbers of published volumes of sermons,
it is not the aim of this chapter to comment extensively on
their content or relative quality, but rather to consider the
place of preaching within the clergyman's role.

The handbooks in the mid and late eighteenth century
generally assumed that the sermon was the most important
single event of the clergyman's week, one which called for his
greatest efforts and a considerable degree of preparation.
However, those ordained in the Church of England during
this period received no training other than the writing of
disputations at university which fitted them for preaching a
sermon. Thus, many clergy were forced to resort to the
common practice of the day, that of reading printed sermons. William Jesse lamented this fact and added, '. . . I
conceive there are many clergymen who would compose their
own sermons, if they knew how to do it.'[1] The handbooks,
therefore, had an important duty to perform in helping the
young clergyman acquire the necessary professional skills.
To this end, the handbooks recommended that the young
clergyman should embark on a course of theological reading

and study. An analysis of these lists of recommended reading would make a rewarding study, but in the context of present concerns, it may be said that the recommendations usually included, with varying degrees of emphasis, the Scriptures in Greek and Hebrew, with a variety of commentaries; the Reformation documents; the writings of the Caroline Divines, and a selection from patristic sources. In addition, the handbooks emphasized that the clergyman should be sufficiently acquainted with his parishioners to make his sermons comprehensible to them.[2] Whilst the handbook authors allow that the young clergyman might initially resort to preaching other people's sermons, this is clearly regarded as a substitute. With only a few exceptions, extempore preaching was condemned.

In the eighteenth century the sermon commonly took precedence over all other clerical activities, as an anonymous handbook of 1722 states. '. . . publick preaching is the best, the most generous, and likely method of winning souls to God.'[3] The arrangement of the seats in the church emphasized this point, and the best seats were nearest to the pulpit. In St Paul's Cathedral, in 1804, the pulpit was moved from where Sir Christopher Wren had placed it to a position in front of and completely obscuring the altar. The church had become an auditory for the hearing of a sermon rather than a setting for the performance of a liturgical ceremony. The evidence suggests that it was the common practice in the late eighteenth century to preach once a Sunday (whether there were one or two services). The sermon came at the end of the service, and what has previously been said about the infrequency and lax performance of Sunday worship naturally applies also to preaching. The widespread practice of plurality and non-residence together with the employment of itinerant curates led to the perfunctory performance of this duty. It is beyond doubt that the practice of reading printed sermons or those of someone else was widespread. The newspapers included sermons which the clergy could use and printed sermons by well-known preachers enjoyed enormous sales. In 1771, the ingenious Dr Trusler established a business in abridging the sermons of eminent divines and reprinting them in copperplate, so that if the pulpit was overlooked by a gallery, the occupants of the gallery would think the clergyman was reading his own composition.[4] It is a constant feature of later attacks on the clergy that they were content to read from the pulpit sermons they had not written.

Preaching in the eighteenth century was dominated by the example of Archbishop Tillotson. His sermon 'His Commandments are not grievous' typified an age in which the doctrine of the Divine Wisdom and God's beneficence achieved pre-eminence. Tillotson established a school of preaching which was markedly different from the medieval school. His preaching was centrally concerned with morality and made its appeal to reason and common sense rather than to divine revelation.[5] There were many reasons why the eighteenth-century pulpit was not concerned with doctrinal preaching. No doubt the doctrinal bigotry of the previous century had produced a reaction and the shadows of that period extended will into the eighteenth century. Certainly, at a time when the common people were unable to influence the circumstances of their lives, it was not inappropriate that the clergy should be preaching serenity, contentment, and obedience to lawful authority. Thus, the sermons of the period extended well into the eighteenth century. Certainly, moral questions rather than doctrinal disputations. 'Morality', a handbook author of 1741 wrote, 'is the best subject you can possibly make choice of upon many accounts.'[6] However, such preaching provoked its own reaction, and, in 1748, Bishop Lavington of Exeter began his Charge with an attack on moral preaching.[7] William Cole did not approve of the sermons he heard preached: '. . . the name of Christ is scarce ever heard, nor any of the characteristic doctrines of his holy religion. The watchword or catchword . . . is "Morality".'[8] But it seems that this type of preaching, with the notable exception of the Evangelical school, held sway in the English pulpit until well into the nineteenth century.

In the eighteenth century it was inevitable that the educated clergyman, who took pains to express himself as a scholar, in carefully composed literary exercises, spoke only to the educated members of the congregation. The clergyman who took the university disputations as his model, who composed, with the aid of references from the Greek and Hebrew texts, a sermon which occupied him for a considerable part of the week and took more than an hour to read, or the clergyman who simply read his father's or grandfather's compositions, or who dealt with Dr Trusler, would have had some difficulty in holding the attention of a country congregation. For the rest the sermon could often have had little meaning, particularly when clergymen like the Revd John Coleridge of Ottery St Mary introduced lengthy Hebrew quotations into his parochial sermons, since he regarded Hebrew as 'the immediate language of the Holy Ghost'.[9] Clearly Hogarth's cartoon of the sleeping congregation recorded an experience with which many could identify. It has frequently been observed that a large part of the appeal of nonconformity lay in the more energetic and colloquial preaching of ministers whose social and educational situation more closely approximated that of their congregations.

The Evangelicals' conception of the role of the Church of England clergyman caused them to view preaching in a way which contrasted sharply with the Latitudinarian clergy. If the leading of public worship characterized the priestly interpretation of the role, then preaching characterized the prophetic interpretation embraced by the Evangelicals. From the earliest period the Evangelicals endeavoured to maximize the opportunities for preaching. Grimshaw, in 1747, expressed his admiration for the Methodists and became a field preacher. He had two circuits, and in two weeks he preached between twenty-four and thirty times.[10] But the later Evangelicals, adhering more closely to the traditional patent of the clergyman's role, set about increasing the number of preaching opportunities in the parish church. In particular, they insisted on two sermons every Sunday. Henry Venn, speaking of his clerical neighbours at Yelling, said: 'My name is sufficient to disgust them and, if not, the preaching twice of a Sabbath is.'[11] Not only did the Evangelicals have two Sunday sermons, but they pioneered the weekday lecture. Job Orton wrote of Dr Stonhouse: 'He preaches during his residence, twice every Sunday and has a lecture on

Wednesday evenings.'[12] Venn had a Thursday evening lecture and preached eight to ten sermons per week in private houses or in the open.[13] Cadogan had a Tuesday evening lecture in Chelsea, and a Thursday evening lecture in Reading.[14] The Evangelical societies, such as the Bible Society, operated by obtaining pulpits in areas and sending preachers on tour; this allowed the development of a new form of itinerancy. However, the majority of clergy disapproved of this new development of weekday preaching, and, when Archbishop Vernon Harcourt spoke against it in 1813, he echoed their sentiments. But perhaps the most obvious difference between the Latitudinarian and Evangelical clergy was in the style and content of their sermons. In particular the Evangelicals hurled abuse at the Pelagianism of Tillotson and at moral preaching. As Jones of Southwark wrote: 'We have preached morality so long that we have hardly any morality left; and this moral preaching has made us so very immoral that there are no lengths of wickedness which they are not afraid of running into.'[15] The preaching of the Evangelicals was plainer, more energetic, and more easily understood by the congregation. In all these aspects there can be little doubt that the Evangelicals had learned much from the Methodist preachers.

Apart from the manifest function of propagating the faith, there were other purposes for which the clergyman could use the platform of the pulpit in the eighteenth century. In particular, in a small isolated village community where every person was known, it was open to the clergyman to use the fear of public exposure as an agent of social control. A resident clergyman by subtle allusion could make his opinion on events or individuals publicly known before the whole village or at least a large part of it. Some clergymen were more direct; Grimshaw made public any irregularity of conduct which he discovered or even suspected.[16] Robert Nicholls, Dean of Middleham, passed a public censure from the pulpit on two attorneys' clerks who had previously incurred his displeasure.[17] However, an example of the subtle use of the sermon to this end is provided by Benjamin Newton, who wrote in his diary on 17 October 1818:

Was much pleased to hear that Mrs. Askwith with her husband's permission invited Mr. and Mrs. Dawson to their ball which is to be given on Wednesday and felt very severe pleasure in the idea that what I glided into my last Sunday's sermon purposely to touch Mr. Askwith had some effect. [18]

The influence of the French Revolution on English religious life, as has been mentioned already, was of a deep and lasting nature. The propertied classes demanded that the poor should be reassured that the inequalities of rank, wealth, and power were part of the grand design to maximize human happiness, or at least they should be made to understand that socially disruptive behaviour would precipitate both earthly retribution and eternal punishment. [19] As the clergy were the principal agents, and the sermon the principal means of disseminating this doctrine, preaching in the early part of the nineteenth century was exalted to a position of the greatest significance. The events in France particularly stimulated the Evangelicals to renewed endeavours, for the connection between infidelity and civil disorder provided an object lesson in the doctrine of human depravity.

The handbooks of the period, particularly those of Charles Bridges and Henry Thompson give a considerable amount of space to helping the young clergyman gain the necessary technical skills. [20] The evidence suggests that in the early nineteenth century the active clergyman rarely missed the opportunity to address his parishioners. At all the many additional Sunday and weekday services the clergyman either preached a sermon or gave a short scriptural exposition or address. [21] In the late 1820s Beachcroft had established a weekday lecture. Samuel Wilberforce, between 1828 and 1830, gave simply Sunday afternoon lectures on the Gospels, and, when he moved to Brighstone in 1830, he immediately added a second Sunday sermon. [22] Whately instituted the practice of weekday lectures. [23] H. C. Ridley described the lectures he gave four times a week: 'The clergyman rings the bell himself and on entering the room a short prayer is offered up. 10 to 30 verses of Scripture read, paraphrased, duties pointed out. Lord's Prayer. Final Prayer.' [24] Alfred

Suckling wrote of his work at Bussage: '. . . not knowing how to reach the people I hired a cottage in which I preached extempore once a week having a collect or two before and after the sermon. I saw no other way of reaching the people and they came to Church better for it.'[25] An energetic Evangelical clergyman like Andrews of Ketteringham would preach in almost any circumstances. He preached on a journey to a wagonload of thirteen people, and on another occasion he engaged in wayside preaching on his way home from a clerical meeting.[26] At the beginning of the 1850s both Seymour at Kinwarton and Hook at Leeds preached short sermons on every day of Holy Week.[27]

However, towards the end of this period, as the influence of the Oxford Movement was felt more widely in the Church, preaching came to be viewed in a changed light. The new emphasis on the worship of the altar caused many to see preaching as occupying an over-prominent place in public worship which obscured all else. Charles Bridges wrote: 'The public ministry of the Word is the most responsible part of our work – the most extensive engine of Ministerial operation . . . preaching is indeed the grand momentum of Divine agency.'[28] But by contrast, the author of Tract 89 wrote (somewhat surprisingly): 'We would not be thought entirely to deprecate preaching as a means of doing good. It may be necessary in a weak and languishing state; but it is an instrument which Scripture to say the least has never recommended.' Many others saw that preaching had hitherto occupied so great a position of prominence in the Church that it had obscured other aspects of public worship which were now considered by those influenced by Tractarian theology to be more important. Monro wrote:

> Men will appreciate and seek for sacramental power in the instruments of religion; and if they are deprived of the right and proper Sacraments of the Church, they will invest preaching with sacramental energy and raise an inferior instrument to the place of the first ordinance of religion . . . preaching has been as much exalted as Holy Communion has been depressed and it has been looked to as an actual channel of grace instead of being but a guide to that which is so.[29]

It is of interest to compare the prominent place that preaching had in the deliberations of the Evangelical Eclectic Society compared with the very sparse attention given to it by the rather high-church Alcester Clerical Meeting. Of 129 topics discussed between 1842 and 1860 at Alcester, preaching came under discussion only five times. But the disposition to make the sermon less prominent was only a relative matter, for there was a considerable absolute rise in the amount of preaching, and most clergymen of the period still regarded the sermon as the main weapon in the fight against infidelity. Church accommodation was reckoned in terms of 'sittings', and as an article in the *British Magazine* commented: '. . . the great aim has been to provide for the accommodation of the greatest number of hearers in the smallest space, so that room in many cases has scarcely been allowed for the purposes of devotion . . .'[30] Certainly the Evangelicals were in no doubt about the primacy of the pulpit; J. C. Miller wrote: '. . . if we fail in our pulpit, it is fatal to our ministry. For all else is subordinate to this – Preach the Word.'[31]

The style of sermons in this period still owed more to the old ways than to the new more colloquial style pioneered by such preachers as Charles Kingsley. The practice of preaching written or printed sermons was still widespread and continued to be recommended by handbooks for the younger clergyman. However, the handbook authors increasingly favoured a clergyman writing his own sermons, and they suggested that the clergy might have more success in capturing the attention of their congregations if they made their sermons more local. John Skinner preached sermons on the death of parishioners, and on the impending fate of two young women dying of consumption.[32] The last edition of the *Homilies* of the English reformation, published for reading in church, appeared in 1859; in changing times a different type of sermon was required.

Thus, during the early decades of the nineteenth century, the sermon was regarded as the chief weapon with which the clergy set out to recommend Christianity to their parishes. The complete dominance which the sermon had had in the clergyman's role in the eighteenth century was now challenged by the rise in importance of other elements of the role, particularly those of the celebrant of the sacraments, the leader of public worship, and pastoral duties. This process was encouraged by the Tractarians, many of whom felt that the prominence of preaching had tended to obscure other, and in their opinion more important, elements of the role.

The census of 1851 had served to demonstrate to the clergy in statistical terms the degree of separation between the Church and the working classes. Thus the clergy sought new ways of reaching those alienated from the Church, both by addressing them where they could be found, either at their place of work, or in the streets, and by preaching in a style which they could more readily understand. Preaching outside the church building was considered by the majority of the Church of England clergymen as undesirable, irregular, and illegal. In 1837, Bishop Samuel Butler had written: 'If the inhabitants will not take the trouble to come to hear your sermons . . . I am sure they do not deserve to have them brought to their doors.'[33] The Evangelical clergyman, J. C. Miller, is usually credited with having been responsible for reviving this practice, and he saw it as a direct response to the situation which the 1851 census revealed. He wrote: 'Prejudice is overwhelmed beneath the appalling facts and statistics which press themselves upon us . . .'[34] In December 1856 the *Christian Observer* wrote: 'Within a few years, open-air preaching, previously used almost exclusively by the followers of Mr. Wesley has been employed very extensively and under new conditions in the Church of England.'[35]

At the same time theatres and halls were used, particularly in London, where services with sermons by popular preachers were frequently held. In 1855, Lord Shaftesbury managed to have modified the law which had previously prohibited the meeting together outside a church of more than twenty people for religious worship. This led to the vast popular services at Exeter Hall. These services, of which the sermon was much the most important part, were disliked by many clergy and the incumbent in whose parish Exeter Hall was – A. G. Edouart – proceeded against the services. But

A. C. Tait (Bishop of London) approved of them and after a time they were restarted. [36]

Open-air preaching was recommended in 1851 by the committee of the ruri-decanal chapter of Leeds under Hook, who suggested the possibility of a movable tent. [37] Moule preached in the open air on Sunday afternoons in 1854. [38] Although Evangelicals were responsible for the early development of this pastoral technique, its practice was not eventually restricted to them. In the early 1870s, Lowder preached in a street on the site of the accidental death of a sewer man. [39] On Ascension Day 1871, Butler found a large body of idle men on an iron bridge making rude remarks at passers-by. Having reprimanded them, he took out his Prayer Book, read the gospel and preached an extempore sermon. [40] This type of outdoor preaching received the blessing of Bishop Tait, who scandalized many of his friends by preaching in the open air during the spring and summer of 1857. To quote his biographer:

> His diary shows him going off from the House of Lords to speak to a shipload of emigrants in the docks, from the Convocation discussions on Church Discipline to address the Ragged School children in Golden Lane, or the omnibus drivers in their great yard at Islington. He preached to the costermongers in Covent Garden Market; to railway porters from the platform of a locomotive; to a colony of gipsies upon the common at Shepherd's Bush. [41]

Tait was particularly anxious to utilize outdoor preaching in a systematized way and to commend it to the parochial clergy. Within a year of becoming Bishop of London, he put forward plans for a Diocesan Home Mission 'for distinctly evangelistic or aggressive work in crowded districts'. The Mission, together with a number of other organizations, sponsored 'preaching weeks' in areas where they considered there to be a need. [42] Such activities were the beginning of the 'parish mission' movement which had received considerable encouragement when Bishop Wilberforce organized missions in the Oxford diocese.

Despite the marked lack of enthusiasm for some Evangelistic activities among a number of the clergy, the fact remains that the quantity of preaching undertaken by the active clergy continued to increase markedly, and on some it began to impose considerable strains. In 1864, John Burgon wrote:

> Those who are most severe in condemning the reproduction of old sermons must be reminded that a parish priest who undertakes to provide two perhaps three addresses on Sunday; a weekday lecture; and it may be a sermon at the workhouse, that this man cannot compose discourses fast enough to meet such constantly recurring needs.[43]

But it was not only changes in place and frequency which marked off the preaching of this period from that which had gone before; the clergy were increasingly conscious that the old styles of address would no longer meet the demands of a changing society. As Best wrote:

> It is one of the extraordinary disadvantages of an age of boasted enlightenment, that we are in very many instances speaking in an unknown tongue. Our language has undergone a change and education has not kept pace with it. It is difficult for an educated mind not familiarised through parochial ministrations with the language and ideas of the people to realise to itself our true position.[44]

In 1844, Charles Kingsley had been criticized by Bishop Sumner for preaching sermons which were 'too colloquial'. However, this had enabled him not only to fill his church, but also to reach the working man. In this period the clergy on all sides set about developing a style of address which would recommend their discourses more readily to working men. They aimed at preaching in 'plain and dignified language' a sermon which was readily apprehensible, and whose principal points were easily remembered. The clergy were urged to forget the academic congregations of the university cities and seek to be understood by the unlettered shepherd, the carter, and the ploughboy. J. W. Burgon's instructions to those preaching to a class of children bore little relation to the sophisticated and cultured preaching of the previous century: 'He may strike the table with his clenched fist if he can procure attention in no more scientific way, while he points out before them some plain truths about Death and Judgement, Heaven and Hell, in the most idiomatic English he can command.'[45] Above all, the handbooks of the period encourage the young clergyman to abandon the reading of sermons, and to adopt the practice of preaching them from notes, or ideally, to address the congregations extempore. As Monro wrote:

And in speaking of preaching I must be understood to mean a preaching of an earnest and if possible extemporary kind: nothing will affect our people like this style of address; there is an apparent unreality in a written sermon which prevents it so reaching the heart, the poor find it hard owning to want of acuteness and quickness of perception, to follow out ideas which are rapidly enunciated and to enable them to do it they need the impressiveness and earnestness of extempore delivery.[46]

In order that the clergyman might develop this freer mode of address, visiting was insisted upon as part of the preparatory work for the writing of a sermon so that he should know the problems of the poor and be able to address them in language that they would readily understand. The sermons of the period were typically shorter than those of the previous period. Oxenden favoured between twenty-five and forty-five minutes depending on style; Jones said that a preacher should never run over twenty minutes, whilst Burgon specified half an hour.[47] Published sermons continued to sell in great numbers, but increasingly it was the books of 'plain', 'village', or 'parochial' sermons which attracted most attention. In all this there can be little doubt that the Church of England, as in much else, had learned a great deal from the nonconformist tradition.

Whilst the clergy's principal thrust was aimed at the urban working classes who were perceived to be almost wholly outside the Church, at the time there arose a concern that in other areas the rising level of education and access to the public political and intellectual world among the middle classes was placing new demands on the ability and competence of the preacher. One agitated clergyman wrote, in

1866, that he felt quite overwhelmed when he mounted the pulpit to see pews full of 'hard-headed, brain-working men' before him.[48] By the 1860s, the handbooks indicate a growing concern for the educated élite, who were now also regarded as drifting beyond the compass of the Church. The new professional training and the theological colleges themselves were designed to equip the clergyman to hold his place in a world of intellectual unsettlement. However, as Brian Heeney has observed, it seems that much of the parochial preaching of this period was innocent of any serious awareness of the major movements of social change that were taking place in English society, and in particular of any attempt to grapple with the problems of biblical criticism and theological reinterpretation, which received such prominence in the mid-decades of the nineteenth century.[49] The evidence suggests that the clergy were increasingly discounted by the educated public as leaders of thought and opinion, and that the sermon gradually lost its position in the latter half of the nineteenth century as a principal source of explanation and interpretation. In an increasing plural society educated people turned to other sources and were affected by the rising level of scepticism and infidelity. As Burgon remarked: '. . . it is to be observed that the temper of the age is such, that we have no alternative but to bestir ourselves. We cannot slumber in the pulpit even if we had the desire. A censorious spirit is abroad.'[50]

'The Country Parson preacheth constantly, the pulpit is his joy and his throne,' wrote George Herbert.[51] Certainly preaching occupied a prominent place in the clergyman's role, not only as the most conspicuous element of his work but also as that part of it which required a definite professional skill and the development and refinement of particular techniques. During the eighteenth century, the prominence of preaching resulted from the fact that it was for many clergy the principal and most time-consuming element of their role. In the nineteenth century, despite the marked absolute increase in the amount of preaching, as the clergy seized every opportunity to press home the truths of the gospel, there was a relative decline in its significance. This relative decline in the significance of preaching resulted in part from the new pastoral orientation of the clergyman's role, and in part from the new sacramentalism, as a result of which the altar rather than the pulpit became the architectural focus of the church of the late nineteenth century.

7

Celebrant of the Sacraments

The Articles of Religion state that there are two sacraments, Holy Communion and Baptism, which are to be understood as 'effectual signs of grace'. From a theological standpoint, a sacrament is a divinely ordained means by which God saves and sanctifies his people, or in the words of the Catechism, '. . . an outward and visible sign of an inward and spiritual grace given unto us, ordained by Christ himself, as a means whereby we receive the same and a pledge to assure us thereof'. These effectual signs are encapsulated within rites which may be traced back through Christian history to the pages of the New Testament. Christians have differed frequently and fundamentally about the interpretation and theological significance of these rites, and this debate was particularly prominent in the Church of England in the nineteenth century. In this period, many came to see the Church and the ministry itself in increasingly sacramental and sacerdotal terms, as a means by which Christ was mediated to the world. On the other hand, there were others who stood in the tradition of the Reformers, whose initial criticisms of the sacramental tradition had centred on 'the sacrifice of the Mass', and the doctrine of transubstantiation, who regarded the sacramental interpretation as fundamentally at variance with the true nature of the rite, and the New Testament evidence. It is part of the charter role of the Church of England clergyman that he should be the celebrant of these rites. These two services are considered separately, the former being a part of the public worship of the Church, and the latter a *rite de passage* and similar from a sociological standpoint to the marriage and burial services.

HOLY COMMUNION

In the seventeenth and eighteenth centuries, the service of Holy Communion held a significance over and above its religious importance, for in a society where religious and secular institutions were closely intertwined, periodic attendance at Holy Communion was regarded as a symbol of political and social conformity. Indeed, until the Toleration Act of 1689, which was in the words of its title 'an act to exempt their majesties' Protestant subjects dissenting from the Church of England for the penalties of certain laws', non-attendance at Holy Communion was a punishable offence. Through the operation of the Test and Corporation Acts, no person at this time could hold a public office who was not an attender at this service. These acts were repealed in 1828 in the face of a sustained campaign by nonconformists for equality.

In the eighteenth century, although the first part of the Communion service, Ante Communion (sometimes called 'Holy Communion without celebration'), formed the third element of the long Sunday morning service, celebrations at which bread and wine were consecrated were much rarer occurrences. The Book of Common Prayer of 1549 and the 21st Canon of 1604 had recommended a minimum frequency of three celebrations per year. What was recommended as the minimum in fact became the norm. Holy Communion was customarily celebrated only at the three great festivals of the Church, Christmas, Easter, and Whitsun, though more frequent celebrations were constantly recommended to the clergy, particularly in episcopal Charges. In the parish of Barrington (Cambridge), during the lengthy non-resident incumbency of the Revd R. W. Finch at the end of the eighteenth century, there were no celebrations of Communion for twenty-five years.[1] Bishop Secker, in his Charge of 1741, pleaded for more frequent celebrations and suggested: 'One thing might be done in all your parishes; a sacrament might be interposed in that long interval between Whitsunday and Christmas.'[2] The evidence suggests that in the last quarter of the eighteenth century four celebrations were increasingly the rule, with the extra celebration either at Michaelmas or else on some convenient Sunday after the completion of the harvest. McClatchey recorded that in the 156 Oxfordshire parishes in 1778 (excluding Oxford City), forty parishes had three celebrations per year, fifty-six parishes had four, and only six parishes had a monthly celebration.[3] The comparable figures for Devon in 1799 were: three celebrations in eleven churches; four or five celebrations in 343 churches; six to eight celebrations in seventy-one churches; twelve or more celebrations in forty-one churches.[4] Benjamin Newton at Wrath had four celebrations each year between 1816 and 1818, as recorded in his diary.[5]

The handbooks of the period are strangely silent on the subject of Holy Communion, but in part this was because they were written for the newly ordained deacon, who did not celebrate this rite.

There is little doubt that many in this period, in particular those of the lower classes, never attended Holy Communion. Confirmation services were rare owing to the difficulties of travelling, and the age and infirmity of many eighteenth-century bishops. Even among those who had been confirmed, many did not subsequently take communion. An old man in Thomas Keble's parish is recorded as having said: 'I was confirmed when I was a boy but of course I never took communion. That was for the quality.'[6] In Secker's Charge of 1741, he found it necessary to comment that: 'Some imagine the sacrament belongs only to persons of advanced years or great leisure or high attainment in religion, and is a very dangerous thing for common persons to venture on.'[7]

It was against such attitudes as these, and against the prevalent neglect of Holy Communion, that the Evangelicals set their face. John Wesley had been anxious to increase the frequency of communion, and the Oxford Methodists bound themselves by a rule to receive communion weekly.[8] Grimshaw had monthly celebrations, which formed the climax of the month's devotions in his church, which was filled with about a thousand people.[9] Thomas Jones of Creaton had a celebration every six weeks;[10] and Richard Conyers of Helmsley is recorded as having had 1800 communicants.[11] Daniel Wilson at Islington was the first clergyman to establish an early celebration at 8 a.m., particularly to attract the poorer people, who were unable to attend the morning celebration on account of the rented pew system.[12] Leigh Richmond established a monthly communion in 1806.[13] No doubt the interpretation placed on the rite by the Evangelicals was at times at variance with that of other churchmen, but it is noteworthy that the practice of more frequent celebration of the service of Holy Communion was initially restored by the Evangelicals in the Church of England.

As has been noted, following the period of the French Revolution and the European war, the clergy made a considerable effort to increase the opportunities for public worship. Four celebrations were now considered to be the minimum, though many churches had celebration of Holy Communion at greater frequency. In Oxfordshire, in 1838, only five parishes had three celebrations; the majority had four, but a number had more: seven parishes had five celebrations; ten had six celebrations; five had seven celebrations; two had nine celebrations; and nine parishes had monthly celebrations.[14] A handbook author writing in 1834 acknowledged that four celebrations per year was the common practice, but continued: '. . . these are not sufficient, even in small parishes'.[15] H. C. Ridley at Hambledon had seven or eight celebrations per year and ran classes of instruction for communicants on the Sunday before a celebration.[16] This was also the practice of Julius Hare in 1831.[17] Mant, conscious of the difficulties of cottagers with children or livestock to look after on Sundays, applauded the practice of a clergyman who celebrated eight times a year, but on four pairs of consecutive Sundays, so that all adults could go on either one Sunday or the other.[18] Bishop Sumner of Chester was greatly concerned by the falling-off of communicants, but was able to announce in his Charge of 1832 that numbers had risen by a seventh in the preceding three years. However, this increase in frequency and numbers of communicants was not universal, and many parishes, as late as the early 1840s, still had only four celebrations, while many retained the old pattern of three. It was particularly difficult to increase the number of celebrations in a parish where the clerical work was done by a curate who was a deacon, and, therefore, had to procure the services of a priest. The only way Edward Boys Ellman could get a celebration for the Sussex village of Berwick on Easter

Day 1839 was by swapping duty with another clergyman.[19]

The great increase in the frequency of celebration in the 1840s and 1850s was principally the result of the influence of the Oxford Movement. No doubt, a part of the cause of the former infrequency of celebration lay in the tradition (of late medieval origins) of communicating only once a year. Certainly, the temper of the eighteenth century, which favoured reason above all else and was deeply suspicious of mysticism and the emotions, was against any form of sacramentalism. Yet, in the face of the broad movement from reason to feeling which occurred in the early years of the nineteenth century, together with the rediscovery of the historical perspective, it was only natural that people came to reassess the sacramental and mystical elements in religion as G. M. Young has commented:

> In a generation enchanted by Scott it was obvious that the corporate and sacramental aspects of the Church should re-emerge and that religion would have to find a place for the leanings of beauty, antiquity, and mystery which the ruling theology had dismissed or ignored as worldly or unprofitable or profane.'[20]

The Tractarians had learned from the Evangelicals not to be afraid of their feelings and they sought to present Christianity in such a way that sympathetic hearts could at once perceive the history, the beauty, the mystery, and the poetry of the faith.

In this way, the general temper of the times predisposed many to hear with approval what the Tractarian authors had to say. But the clergy had a particular reason which inclined them, or at least many of them, to listen with sympathetic interest to the new opinions which flowed from Oxford. Throughout the 1820s, the Church had found itself standing against a broad flood of anti-clericalism and anti-Church propaganda. New and more moderate voices joined its traditional attackers, the radical politicians, the dissenters, and tithe-payers, in the demand that the Church be reformed. But the Church was unwilling and unable to reform itself. In February 1833, Parliament proposed a moderate reform of the very costly Church in Ireland which, among other things, involved the reduction of the number of Irish sees from twenty-two to twelve. From this Bill, English churchmen deduced that Parliament was poised for a drastic and far-reaching reform of the Church of England. The proposed legislation provoked John Keble to preach a political sermon to the Assize judges in Oxford on 14 July 1833; the event which Newman later regarded as the beginning of the Oxford Movement. Above all else the Tractarians sought to establish the autonomy of the Church in contra-distinction to the Erastianism of previous decades. At the centre of their understanding was a more spiritual conception of the Church and a more sacerdotal conception of its ministry. This new understanding of the role contained an obvious appeal for a group developing a new corporate self-consciousness, and seeking an authority which could not be challenged by an increasingly hostile State. At the centre of this new interpretation of the clergyman's role, and at the apex of the system of sacramental theology, lay the clergyman's function as celebrant of the sacraments.

Those who had been influenced by the Tractarian writers, and departed early from Oxford for parochial duties, at once sought to make the Holy Communion the centre of parochial worship. Pusey wrote to T. T. Carter in 1844 suggesting that he should have weekly communions at an early hour.[21] Samuel Wilberforce at Alverstoke had three celebrations per month.[22] Robert Suckling who saw the weekly communion at the centre of all his work, wrote: 'And regarding the point of weekly communion itself I feel it is imperatively our duty to offer the sacrifice every Sunday.'[23] Butler, though he kept initially to the old pattern of monthly communions at Wantage, regarded the service in the highest light and undertook a heavy programme of preparation for it, taking twelve classes of different types of parishioners in every week preceding a communion. His early communions on Ascension Day were at 4.45 a.m., and on New Year's Day 1849 he celebrated at 4 a.m.[24] *A Clergyman's Companion to the Celebration of Divine Service*, published in 1847, assumed that there would be a weekly celebration.[25] Dean Hole, writing somewhat later, concluded that increasing the number of celebrations from three to fifty-four per year was the most important effect of the Oxford Movement.[26]

By the late 1850s and early 1860s monthly communion had become the norm and this pattern was taken up by most clergy irrespective of churchmanship. In the 156 Oxfordshire parishes McClatchey recorded that, in 1866, only ten had four communions per year, and twenty-one had five or six whereas twelve villages now had weekly celebrations, and another twenty had three-weekly or fortnightly celebrations. (Cowley had a daily celebration.) The majority had monthly communions which represented a considerable change from the practices of earlier decades. In 1855, of the 556 parishes in the diocese of Salisbury, 181 had monthly celebrations, and five had weekly celebrations. By 1867, the frequency of communion had markedly increased; 292 parishes now had monthly celebrations, ten had celebrations every week.[28] At this time Pusey celebrated every morning in Oxford often at 4 a.m., and although a daily celebration was extremely rare, some followed his example.[29] G. R. Prynne at St Peter's, Plymouth, started a daily celebration during the cholera visitation of 1850, and the same cause established this practice at St Saviour's, Leeds.[30] St Peter's, London Docks, in the late 1860s, had two daily celebrations at 5.45 a.m. and 8 a.m.[31] The invalid James Skinner at Newland near Malvern increased the frequency of celebrations in the first six years of his ministry from seven times per year in 1861, to daily in 1867.[32] However, daily communion was certainly exceptional in this period, and a weekly communion was rare enough to be considered as a party-badge and to mark off the celebrant as a sympathizer with the Tractarians. For the main, monthly celebrations were the norm, but this represented a considerable increase in the frequency of celebration.

The Holy Communion, being the third of the Sunday morning services, was traditionally celebrated at about midday. The Evangelicals had been the first to start early celebrations, on account of the poor being unable to attend the main service at which all the seats were appropriated.[33] The clergy influenced by the Oxford Movement who were anxious to establish a more catholic ethos in their parishes also encouraged early communions when the sacrament could more readily be received fasting. There were also practical reasons in favour of the practice in that the earlier time was more convenient for servants and labourers who had the care of children or livestock. At the same time an experiment which was tried with the particular aim of reaching the poorer classes in urban areas was the practice of evening communion. The ruri-decanal chapter of Leeds in 1857 recommended 'celebrations of Holy Communion at a greater variety of hours', and as a result Hook introduced an evening communion on such holy days and Saints' Days as did not fall on a Sunday. Edward Jackson of St James's, Leeds, went further and introduced evening communion on every Saint's day and Sunday.[34] The practice was independently started in Birmingham. J. C. Miller introduced afternoon communions in December 1851, and by July 1852 had incorporated evening celebrations into his schedule of services. He found it suited the habits of the poor and on 1 January 1860 he recorded that there were thirty-two communicants at the early celebration, 121 at mid-day, and 179 at the evening celebration.[35]

Initially the practice was slow to recommend itself to many other incumbents. High-churchmen considered it against the teaching and practice of the early Church and were particularly disquieted by the fact that communicants did not take the sacrament fasting. Samuel Wilberforce wrote in his Charge of 1860: 'Imagine a worthy squire rising from the wine after dinner to attend Holy Communion in his parish church. We forbear to dwell on the picture.' After the criticism of Wilberforce and Liddon the practice of evening communion was confined to the Evangelical clergy. However, the clergy were willing to experiment with any expedient which might extend the outreach of the Church. Many came to realize that in a country no longer populated by 'worthy squires', but by the urban working masses whose opportunity for churchgoing was limited, it was necessary to hold services at a greater variety of times. Thus, the practice of evening communion steadily increased in popularity, and whereas in London there were only sixty churches with evening communion in 1860, in 1867 there were sixty-five; in 1874, there were 179; and by 1879, 262.[36]

A further way in which the clergy sought to enhance the significance of this element of their role was by elaborating the ceremonial contained in and associated with the service of Holy Communion. Many reasons lay behind the renewal of interest among the clergy in ceremonial but among them was the desire to extend the outreach of the Church by appealing to the eye and the sense of mystery and beauty. The clergy in the poor areas of large cities were particularly conscious that a visual presentation, rather than oral instruction, was required to bring home to the masses the nature and the solemnity of the Communion service. Bishop Blomfield was reluctant to take action against the ritualist clergy because their numbers included some of the most conspicuously successful Evangelists and hardworking pastors in the most unprepossessing areas of his diocese.[37] In Oxford, Newman had used altar lights and the mixed chalice. Full eucharistic vestments were used for the first time in 1849 at Wilmcote in Warwickshire.[38] By the 1850s, nine or ten London churches used vestments and four had introduced the use of incense.[39] The ritualist controversies which these innovations provoked caused an internecine war between the English Church Union and the Church Association, which reached its climax in the trial of Bishop Edward King of Lincoln before Archbishop Benson on seven ritualistic charges. But the more extreme innovations were confined to a few churches and some London chapels which drew eclectic congregations. The majority of the clergy did not emulate the early ritualists; many opposed them and all they stood for. However, there arose throughout the Church of England as a whole a new concern for reverence in worship and for order, beauty, and colour in the sanctuary, which the Tractarians and the ritualists did much to inspire.

The enthusiasm of the clergy for liturgical science and the minutiae of ceremonial and sanctuary design, which was such a characteristic feature of church life in the late nineteenth century, can be related in some degree to the changes that occurred in professional roles in this period. The functions and scope of the clergyman's role were at that time contracting, and occupational roles in general became more clearly defined around a central specialism. The rise of sacramentalism and the interest in liturgical science can be seen as a means by which the clergy, in the face of a changing relationship between roles in English society sought to reinterpret their role and to centre it around a new specialist technology. It has been argued by Bryan Wilson that there is a tendency for religious leaders who are conscious that they are losing social influence and privileges to reinterpret the character and mission of their institution in such a way as to emphasize the more traditional preoccupations of the religious specialist and to assert their distinctive competence.[40] The Oxford Movement may be seen as exemplifying this process in so far as it sought to reinterpret the character of the Church in spiritual, sacramental, and communal terms, and to assert the sacerdotal and priestly nature of the clergyman's role. As its Oxford origins imply, the movement was essentially clerical, intellectual, and conservative. It sought to redefine the Church and to reinterpret the clergyman's role by reference back to the medieval and patristic periods, as seen through Victorian eyes. Central to this reinterpretation of the clergyman's role was his function as the celebrant of the sacraments. This was his irreducible priestly function; this was the element of his role in which his indispensability was most clearly demonstrated. When many clergymen regarded the Church as under the imminent threat of reform from a hostile House of Commons, the writings of the Tractarians with their emphasis on the catholic nature and spiritual autonomy of the Church had a powerful and compelling appeal, and provided the Church with a source of authority less precarious than its establishment. If the number of clergy who closely identified themselves with the movement was never large, its influence may be detected everywhere as the clergy reinterpreted the character and nature of their role.

Thus the development of sacramentalism and the new sacerdotal concept of the Church of England clergyman's role were an important aspect of its professionalization in the nineteenth century. Faced with a contraction in the range of their functions, and a loss of social significance, the clergy tended to reinterpret their role in terms of a more sacramental understanding, and to conceive their role in terms of its irreducible priestly functions. It has been observed that in the eighteenth century no one quite knew what to do with the chancels of parish churches. They were sometimes used as stores for cleaning utensils, or for the coats of worshippers; sometimes they were used as a school or were allowed to fall into ruin.[41] But, by the middle of the nineteenth century, the altar was viewed by many clergymen as the centre of the church and the parish on which the great sacrament of the Christian faith was celebrated at frequent intervals. They did all that was possible to make the chancel a sanctuary conveying the feelings of mystery and tradition which they associated with the sacrament. By the end of the period processions, vestments, and incense were still regarded with suspicion by the vast majority of the clergy, but imperceptibly there developed a taste for beauty and reverence in public worship. At the same time the new sacramental theology contained the means by which the clergy could appeal to a new source of authority which invested their role with a greater significance than any appeal to social position or social utility could give.

BAPTISM

The celebration of baptism is an element of the clergyman's charter role, but it differs from other elements in that the clergyman does not have the monopoly of legitimate performance. Although it was desirable that the ceremony should be performed by a clergyman, it was valid if performed by any lay person in a case of imminent death so long as the correct Trinitarian formula was employed. In the eighteenth century, baptism was regarded much as any other surplice duty, and performed together with weddings, churchings, and burials in the period of about three hours between morning and evening prayer. The service had two essentially separate functions. First, it was the initiation rite of the religious institution, and second, it was the act of civil registration. Baptism at this time conferred on a child not only membership of the Church, but also legal existence.

Two practices were common in the eighteenth century with regard to baptism. In the first place, the ceremony was often delayed for a considerable length of time, and second, it was not infrequently performed in a private house, instead of in church as the rubrics of the Book of Common Prayer direct. In fact, so common was the second practice that one hand-book gives appropriate instructions for a domestic bap-tism.[42] Despite this, the evidence suggests that the clergy were conscientious in performing the rite, and Woodforde seemed genuinely shocked, when, on 28 October 1781, a child died without having been presented to the Church: 'I privately named it in January last. It was never brought to church to be presented. I am sorry for it. A great negligence in the parents of it, I think.'[43]

As a result of the Evangelicals' differing conceptions of what constituted church membership, they tended to em-brace a more sectarian attitude towards initiation, and, whilst in no way abandoning the rite of baptism, regarded conversion as the most significant moment in an in-dividual's religious career. It is the opinion of Dr Walsh that the early Evangelicals were not afraid of the sacramental language about baptism in the Book of Common Prayer. However, Berridge wrote: 'I do not much prize our church catechism, it begins so very ill, calling baptism our new birth and making us thereby new members of Christ, children of God and heirs of the kingdom of God.'[44] But Berridge's view increasingly became that of the Evangelical element among the Church of England clergy, who, as Newman observed, did not believe in baptismal regeneration.[45] This ideological clash reached the national stage in the conflict between Gorham and Bishop Phillpotts of Exeter.

Two events gave baptism, as a religious rite, a greater significance for the nineteenth-century clergyman than it had held in the century before. First, the process of institutional differentiation at work in the first half of the nineteenth century caused more distinct boundaries to be placed bet-ween secular and religious institutions. In the legislation of 1836 baptism was separated from civil registration. This, together with the new spiritualized conception of their role, made the clergy anxious to stress the religious and sacramental nature of baptism. Monro observed: 'Anyone used to the ways of the poor will at once recognize their remarkable ignorance on the nature of holy baptism, their inclination to mistake it for parish registration or some other merely civil arrangement.'[46] J. H. Blunt wrote, in 1864, 'I have actually found old women [nurses and midwives] confuse baptism and vaccination.'[47] At the same time, when the implications of denominational plurality were beginning to be more widely felt, the Church of England became more concerned with defining the exact limits of church membership. It became a matter of some importance that a man could prove he was a member of the Church of England. The clergy increasingly drew a line between members of the Church of England and non-members. Robert Gregory refused to bury unbaptized children and in all cases required proof that a child had been baptized before allowing it to be buried with the rites of the Church of England.[48] In 1857, George Gorham of Walkeringham refused to bury a person baptized by a Methodist minister,[49] and J. H. Blunt remarked that most burial clubs made it a rule not to pay the burial money for those who had not been baptized.[50]

One way in which the same clergy sought to extend their influence in the village community and connect themselves with the family life of their parishioners was by standing as godparents to their children. John Burgon wrote in 1864:

A very near kinsman of mine is Godfather to about 300 children in his village . . . were the pastor of the flock, for instance, to accept the sponsorial office to his little lambs, consider the great advantages which would follow, the increased foothold it would give him in a family perhaps indisposed to the Church's administrations; the control he would inevitably acquire in the further matter of education.[51]

Apart from general exhortations that the clergy should seek out unbaptized children and bring them to the font, the handbooks do not contain much guidance as to the performance of this duty or any indications of a change in its relative importance. However, there is little doubt that the increasing sacramental understanding of the rite in the middle decades of the nineteenth century invested it for many clergy with a significance which it did not formerly possess.

8

Pastor

The diffuse functions and heterogeneous nature of the clergyman's role are particularly evident in this its most generalized element. Although the term 'pastor' is sometimes used to describe the totality of the role, it may also be used to describe certain functions which form a distinctive and separate element. Certainly, in the mid-nineteenth century, the clergy would have regarded pastoral duties as different in kind from liturgical, educational, and other functions. The authority for this element of the role lay in the Book of Common Prayer containing the clergyman's promise '. . . to use . . . private monitions and exhortations, as well to the sick as to the whole . . .' The example of Jesus and of the apostles provided additional authority, and an illustration of the way the New Testament was used to legitimate the performance of this element of the role is provided by Gerard: 'It is our business to instruct (2 Tim. 2.25), to convince, to exhort (Titus 1.9), to charge (1 Tim. 4.17 and 2.14), to intreat (1 Tim. 5.1), to reprove, and to rebuke (1 Tim. 5.20 and 2 Tim. 4.2) others.'[1] For the purposes of analysis the functions of this aspect of the clergyman's role are divided into four parts: general or house-to-house visiting; the co-ordination of lay agencies; the visitation of the sick; and counselling.

GENERAL OR HOUSE-TO-HOUSE VISITING

The paying of a periodic visit to every parishioner has long been regarded as a part of the clergyman's role, and was an appropriate duty for the officer of a church which regarded every person as a member. George Herbert recommended that the country parson '. . . upon the afternoons in the weekdays, takes occasion sometimes to visit in person, now one quarter of his parish now another.'[2] Many of the handbooks of the eighteenth century insist on the duty of the

clergyman to visit his flock, but there is considerable
evidence to suggest that this advice was largely ignored.
Tindal Hart comments that, in the eighteenth century,
house-to-house visitation was neither practised or desired.[3]
Certainly it was not the practice of William Cole or James
Woodforde, and when the latter wrote in his diary: 'I am
heartily weary of visiting so much as I have but if I did not it
would be taken amiss by some', he is referring not to
pastoral visiting but to the social exchange of visits among
the gentry which was so prominent a part of eighteenth-
century social life in the countryside.[4] As has been noted
earlier, the expectations of the clergyman's role in the
eighteenth century were largely confined to leading public
worship and preaching, and the lack of an extensive programme of weekday pastoral activities contrasts sharply
with the expectations of the mid-nineteenth century. Of this
early period William Paley wrote: 'I have repeatedly said
that if there be any principal objection to the life
of a clergyman . . . it is this – that it does not supply
sufficient engagements to the time and thoughts of an active
mind.'[5]

The major exceptions to this norm were the Evangelical
clergy who set a new standard of pastoral efficiency by their
constant house-to-house visiting offering spiritual assistance
to those who wanted it. Grimshaw was an indefatigable
visitor unhindered by disease or bad weather in his constant
round.[6] Henry Crooke of Leeds in 1757 set aside Monday
and Tuesday for visiting.[7] Miles Atkinson, who was vicar of
Kippax in 1784, and later perpetual curate of St Paul's,
Leeds, spent between five and six hours each day visiting in
his parish.[8] Cadogan at Reading spent two hours every
afternoon visiting on horseback the outlying hamlets, and
then after dinner he visited in the town.[9] A common factor in
all Evangelical handbooks is their insistence on the importance of general visiting. William Jesse wrote:

> Very few of the clergy seem to have any idea of the
> necessity and importance of parochial visitations, that is
> of going from house to house to inquire particularly into
> the state of the people's souls, to teach and press upon

their conscience truths which have been delivered from the pulpit in a more general way. [10]

A speaker at the Eclectic Society meeting on 4 June 1804 stressed a point which the Evangelicals considered of great importance, that it was necessary to visit in order to know how to preach more meaningfully to a congregation. He commented: '. . . the neglect and decay of pastoral duty is one of the crying sins of the present time.' [11] A visit from an Evangelical clergyman to an illiterate labourer, unused to seeing a clergyman except in church, must have been a frightening occasion; certainly if Stonhouse's advice to a young clergyman was followed.

> At your first visit to the inferior families after the customary civilities, the following questions may be asked. What books have you? . . . Do you read some part of the Scripture daily? . . . Do you meditate on what you read? . . . Do you pray to God in secret? . . . Do you examine yourself as to the state of your soul? . . . Have you any family prayers? . . . Do you attend public worship? . . . Do you take your Bible to church with you? . . . Do you show the text to the absent? . . . Do you learn it by heart and frequently think on it in the following week? . . . [12]

There were three principal reasons why the majority of the eighteenth-century clergy did not visit their parishioners. In the first place, the non-residence or absenteeism of so many incumbents in the eighteenth century made even the most perfunctory attempts at pastoral work impossible. The itinerant curates, who substituted for the absentee incumbents, confined themselves to the liturgical functions. Second, it may be assumed that, where the clergyman was resident, the communal nature of the small isolated rural community did not make it necessary for him to visit the homes of his people to be acquainted with them. In such communities, where churchgoing was still a majority practice and where all, including the clergyman, were involved in the agricultural processes, it was not necessary for the clergyman to visit to exercise some measure of pastoral oversight. There can be little doubt that one of the reasons for the increasing emphasis on general visiting in the second and third decades of the nineteenth century was the growing pace of urbanization, and the consequent breakdown of the traditional community structure. In the new cities and suburban areas it was necessary for the clergyman to visit in order to have any direct contact with his people. Third, it may be suggested that when the legitimation of the role was based on social position, it was not necessary for the clergy to justify their considerable rewards of office by extensive pastoral work as later became the case. Public expectation in this period did not require of the clergyman more pastoral work than was involved in the visitation of the sick.

However, such social factors were not the only reasons for the considerable increase in general visiting in the early decades of the nineteenth century. As has been shown on page 57, one ramification of the French Revolution was to raise the public expectation of the clergyman's role, and to demand that he should be more energetic, particularly in combating irreligion and vice. The legislation that followed at the turn of the century which affected the clergyman's role (limiting the size of farms, preventing clergy engaging in trade, requiring the parsonage house to be repaired, and pre-eminently the residence legislation) was all aimed at ensuring closer attention to pastoral duties. Sydney Smith was made to reside in his parish where no clergyman had lived for 150 years. At the same time, such surveys as that in the Lincoln diocese in 1800 demonstrated to the clergy that large numbers now lived beyond the reach of the preacher. The only way to reach such people was by visiting them in their homes. When the clergy were under attack from many quarters and the test of utility was becoming an increasingly important criterion, it befitted the clergy to apply themselves to their pastoral duties.

It was the considerable diligence of the mid-nineteenth-century clergy in visiting their parishioners which marked them off so distinctly from their perfunctory predecessors. The handbooks of the period abound with exhortations to the clergyman to visit every parishioner in his home, and the biographies of the period portray the active clergyman as giving much time to the work of visiting. W. R. W. Stephens wrote of Richard Durnford, incumbent of Middleton in the late 1830s (and later Bishop of Chichester):

> No person probably ever was more thoroughly persuaded of the absolute necessity of regular visiting among his poorer neighbours. Without undervaluing the importance of church services or school instruction, he was firmly persuaded that the first duty of the Pastor in Parochia was to know his people and if they were to be known, they must be known at home. [13]

The refinement of administrative techniques in other fields had its effect on the clergyman's role, and increasingly at this time he was expected to maintain accurate records of all his parishioners, and the visits he paid. The handbooks of the period frequently suggested that a register should be kept. When Robert Gregory arrived as curate to Thomas Keble in 1843, and Edward Boys Ellman arrived at Wartling, both regarded it as their first duty to draw up a register of every inhabitant in the parish. [14] During this period special pocket books were published which allowed the clergyman to enter details of all his parishioners. Among the more popular was *The Clergyman's Private Register* (1838). This pocket book allowed four pages for each family, and had space for entries under 'General Character'; 'What books read'; 'What clubs belonged to'; and a large section for weekly accounts. *Speculum Parochiale* (1859) had, apart from the above, a space for sanitation details which reflected the interest of a later generation of clergy. It was in this period that the traditional threefold division of the clergyman's day became firmly established. The morning was spent in the study, the afternoon in visiting in the parish, and the evening with family or friends, though increasingly it was occupied by various recreational and educational activities.

During the 1850s and 1860s, house-to-house visiting lost none of its popularity among the clergy and was advocated on all sides. William Butler wrote: 'Our only hope, humanly speaking and considering the unpopularity of the side which we advocate is in gentleness, resolution, demonstrative self-denial, and hard work in visiting. We must honestly and conscientiously devote at least three and a half or four hours daily to visiting work.'[15] However, there can be little doubt that, gradually, house-to-house visiting played a lesser part in the clergyman's role. In the first place, there was a growing feeling that all the energy thrown into this work in the previous decades had failed to produce tangible results. In 1866, Harry Jones, a keen advocate of general visiting, showed his awareness of its critics when he wrote: 'I know that some clerical cynics say "What is the good of visiting at all? House-to-house visiting has produced no results".' And later he acknowledged that 'many a man pays pastoral visits with an uncomfortable suspicion that he produces nothing but entries in his journal.'[16]

Second, house-to-house visiting suffered in this period in terms of relative importance from the increasing part played by other elements of the clergyman's role, particularly that of celebrating the sacraments. Some high-churchmen developed a noticeable coolness towards house-to-house visiting as they saw others promote it to being the most important element. When, in 1850, Edward Monro wrote of visiting, he did not use the unqualified terms of approval that had been common twenty years earlier.

> Another part of the parochial system is that of cottage visiting and visiting house to house. Though this has been by some far too much dwelt upon and that to the exclusion of the higher and holier portions of the parish ministrations and more than this has been often allowed to transgress the bounds of reverence and due reserve by encouraging promiscuous religious conversation at unfit times, still, of course, it cannot be safely omitted.[17]

The third reason lay in the sheer size of the task and the increasing business of the clergy. From the 1830s, especially in urban areas, the clergy realized that they could not possibly undertake general visitations of their parishes in view of the many demands on their time and energy. Increasingly the clergyman became the administrator and co-ordinator of the activities of a number of lay agencies and did not engage in actual visiting himself, except in special cases which the district visitors brought to his attention.

THE CO-ORDINATION OF LAY AGENCIES

During the eighteenth century, such visiting that was done which was not of a purely social nature was more likely to be done by the lady of the manor or the rectory, usually for the purpose of delivering food or other articles to the poor at times of illness or childbirth. Such visiting did not necessarily command the unqualified praise which it would have elicited a few decades later. However, the Methodists had always been visitors of the poor, and their Benevolent or Strangers' Friend Society, founded in 1785, visited and relieved the sick and poor in London and its vicinity. This society was gradually taken over by the Church of England Evangelicals, and was one of the first examples of the systematic application of the principle of district visiting. This example was followed by the Society for Bettering the Condition and Increasing the Comforts of the Poor, founded in 1794, and the Ladies' Royal Benevolent Society of 1812. The Evangelical clergy employed the method in their parishes, led by Venn, who divided Clapham into four districts and had a number of visitors in each. The use of the laity was advocated by Charles Simeon and district visiting societies were discussed with approval by the Eclectic Society on 13 July 1807.[18]

After the war ended in 1815, there was increased activity in this direction by the laity, particularly Evangelical ladies, and the district visiting movement began to assume a national character. In 1828, the General Society for the Promotion of District Visiting was established, and, by 1832, London had been divided into 866 districts where 573 visitors, regularly employed by twenty-five local societies, made 163,695 visits.[19] J. B. Sumner commended it to his clergy in his Charge of 1829 on the model of Chalmers's organization in Glasgow. By 1830, Bishop Blomfield had overcome his suspicions and cautiously recommended the practice, but it was not until 1843 that he was prepared to accept the presidency of the Metropolitan Visiting and Relief Association. District visitors were not the only lay agents, and the enterprising urban clergyman also employed Scripture readers, Bible women, city missioners, mission collectors, and parochial mission-women. In 1847, Blomfield approached Archbishop Howley to officially endorse the practice of Scripture readers; he told the Archbishop that there was no longer any question that 'earnest laymen' were of 'the greatest assistance in Church extension'.[20]

The early decades of the nineteenth century were characterized by the general desire of clergy and laity to extend the Church's ministry by whatever means were available. Despite the fact that the use of the laity, particularly as district visitors, was an expedient which the clergy were cautious in accepting, by the mid-1830s the movement had reached wide proportions. Visiting societies were recommended (with a variety of conditions) by the majority of handbooks of this period as being of the greatest use. Samuel Best gave a clear statement of the aims of a visiting society:

> In the largest parishes with the aid of a visiting society properly organized, a complete but not officious surveillance may be effected and by sections judiciously arranged, the most perfect order may be established, while the ministrations of the clergy, called in only when circumstances may require it, may be rendered far more efficient than it were otherwise possible in a large parish.[21]

Some of the clergy regarded the activities of these lay agents as a potential threat to their role, and, certainly, many were suspicious of the ladies of the district visiting society. A typical letter of 1829 referred to such a lady as 'a female spiritual quack'.[22] However, such was the temper of the times, and the influence of Evangelical piety, that there is little doubt that many such ladies would have taken it upon themselves to visit the homes of the poor with or without the incumbent's sanction. For the clergyman it was better if he overcame his suspicions of visiting societies and enrolled such women as members, rather than have them working independently in his parish. The clergy, with their new conceptions of their role and its importance, were anxious to remain at the head of such activities, and thereby limit some of the excesses of their lay assistants. Like other professions, the clergy were worried about the encroachment of assistants into their area of professional competence. Whately wrote: '. . . visitors do not, of course, assume any of what are strictly clerical offices, nor encroach on or interfere with the rights and duties of the parish minister; but aid and facilitate his labours.'[23]

The widespread employment of district visitors and other lay agents brought about a change in the mid-nineteenth-century clergyman's role, as Charles Bridges wrote: 'A minister can't undertake everything . . . he must be the centre to a hundred hands and minds moving around him.'[24] The clergyman became increasingly the controller and co-ordinator of the efforts of others in the field of general visiting, and went himself only in cases of sickness or some other particular necessity which a visitor might report to him. Simpkinson wrote of London incumbents: 'There is a tradition . . . that it is out of the question for them to attempt visiting on any system; theirs is a work of supervision and general government.'[25]

The handbooks were largely concerned with the manifest functions of general visiting; the extension of the influence of the Church; and the building-up of a sympathetic relationship between parishioners and clergyman. However, some handbook authors also mentioned the important latent function of social control, which played a part in justifying the role in the eyes of the nation and particularly Parliament during this period. Most people were willing to agree that by general visiting the energetic clergyman contributed to the maintenance of law and order in the countryside, for among other things he possessed an intimate knowledge of the local community which the formal agencies of law and order could make use of. R. W. Evans wrote: 'The possession of this knowledge, which is so essential in a spiritual sense, is also most useful in a civil. In building up spiritual society, he also by the way builds up civil and becomes a must useful source of information to the ruling power.'[26]

THE VISITATION OF THE SICK

The 67th Canon of 1604 required that 'when any person is dangerously sick in any parish the minister or curate, having knowledge thereof, shall resort unto him or her to instruct and comfort them in their distress . . .' It would seem that the clergy in all periods have considered this duty as a serious obligation, and that despite the perfunctory performance of the eighteenth-century clergy in many aspects of their role, there is evidence to suggest that they did not entirely neglect the visitation of the sick. The early handbooks all insist on the clergyman's duty to visit the sick. The Evangelical clergy were by no means the first religious specialists to realize that sickness presented special opportunities. They were particularly diligent in sick visiting, and both Fletcher and Grimshaw lost their lives through contracting disease whilst visiting. One handbook author directed the clergyman to '. . . watch for the hour of sickness or sorrow; seasons which are directed by a gracious Providence to soften the stony heart and to give us an opportunity of making some impression.'[27]

In the nineteenth century the visitation of the sick continued to play an important part in the clergyman's role, especially among the Tractarian clergy, who were influenced by the example of the devotion of the continental clergy (and religious) in attending the sick and the dying. Whereas there had been some reluctance to visit in cases of contagious illness, the clergy of the late 1830s and early 1840s not only visited and prayed at the bedside of the many victims of the various waves of cholera in those two decades, but sometimes even moved their lodgings to be nearer the stricken slum areas. It was largely the fearless sick visiting of such men as W. J. E. Bennett in 1849 in Oxford, which allowed the early Tractarians to win the confidence of their parishioners.[28]

During the nineteenth century, although there is the isolated example to the contrary, such as Edward Stanley's predecessor whose boast it was that he had never seen a sick person in his life,[29] the overall impression is that the clergy conscientiously discharged this element of their role. The visitation of the sick has always been a central part of the clergyman's role and it is possible that in relative terms it increased in importance during the nineteenth century, when the clergyman was forced to hand over much general visiting to lay agencies. As J. J. Blunt wrote: '. . . in populous places (it) will be almost the only visit he can find time to pay.'[30]

COUNSELLING

The Book of Common Prayer directed the clergyman to give 'private monitions' to his parishioners. However, this part of his role as pastor was essentially a voluntary element in that its performance largely depended on the parishioner's being willing to accept the offices of his clergyman as a counsellor or spiritual director. The evidence of the eighteenth century indicated that the clergy rarely acted in this relationship and that their services as spiritual directors were not customarily required or expected by their parishioners. However, the Evangelicals with their spiritual conception of the clergyman's role encouraged the practice. During Henry Venn's ministry at Leeds, those who were 'awakened' were encouraged to call at the vicarage for comfort and advice, and a continual stream of people came, often in deep distress. Dr Walsh considered that of the Evangelical clergy Henry Venn was unequalled as a spiritual general practitioner capable of tempering his advice to Christians of all sorts and in all stages of the spiritual life.[31] Gerard considered it the clergyman's duty to give '. . . people advice in cases of conscience which they may propose to their minister'.[32]

At the end of the eighteenth century and early in the nineteenth, English society was faced with the possibility of a breakdown in the means of social control. The rapid social changes of the period rendered the old forms of control of little effect, particularly in the new urban areas. The internalization of the norms of social behaviour by which the conscience became the guarantor of high moral integrity, replaced the old external social sanctions as the principal means of maintaining social control in Victorian society. This was particularly important in the new factories and business houses where the close supervision of the work force, possible in an agricultural community, was no longer feasible. In this broad movement from external to internal forms of social control, the Evangelicals played a large part by demonstrating the supernatural sanctions which lay behind the promptings of the conscience.

The clergyman affected by the Oxford Movement favoured the reintroduction of the old external means of social control in the form of sacramental confession. However, confession in a small isolated agricultural community where most social acts were common knowledge, and confession as practised in the eclectic ritualist congregation in London and other cities, fulfilled differing functions. In the last analysis there was little practical difference between the Evangelical clergyman treating a case of conscience and a nineteenth-century Tractarian clergyman hearing a confession; both placed themselves in the role of spiritual director.

Sacramental confession was first practised by the clergy. Among early examples were G. D. Ryder, who asked John Keble to become his spiritual director in 1843, and William Butler, who made a general confession to Dr Pusey in March 1846.[33] At the Alcester Clerical Meeting a clergyman talked of the difficulty of getting private conversation with some individuals, and mentioned cases in which clergymen had succeeded in bringing many of their parishioners to the practice of periodically laying open to them their minds and seeking private counsel.[34] J. H. Blunt wrote: 'It would be a great advantage to many persons to be able to go to their clergyman to seek his guidance on doubtful points respecting their Christian duty in the common affairs of life . . .'[35] Many high-churchmen found themselves in Faber's position of being confronted with an unruly and irreligious parish, but prevented from supplying what they considered to be a remedial spiritual discipline. T. W. Allies wrote in his journal:

> This is the true bond between the pastor and his flock: the true maintainer of discipline and instrument of restoration. Accordingly in Catholic countries we see the priest truly respected, cherished, and obeyed by his flock, however much he may earn the dislike and suspicion of the world and unconverted.[36]

It was a prominent feature of the handbooks of the 1850s and 1860s that they laid considerable stress on the development of a personal relationship between the clergyman and his parishioners. This is particularly marked in Edward Monro's *Parochial Work*, where he suggests that in an agricultural parish a clergyman should give three hours on three evenings a week to this work of seeing people individually.

> The fact is, in everyone there is such a yearning after mention of sins and troubles which weigh on the soul, that the poor will come gladly to do this the moment the restraint is broken through; which the great alienation of the classes of society has created between the clergyman and his people.[37]

None of the handbooks suggested systematic sacrament confession. Monro, despite his sympathy with Tractarian theology, was strongly against it.[38] The average Englishman viewed such things with the greatest suspicion, particularly when they involved women. It was the teaching about confession which made the ritualists and particularly the Society of the Holy Cross so very unpopular.[39] When Keble urged that he could not know what was in the minds of his Hursley parishioners without confession, Heathcote, his sympathetic patron, told him frankly that if he could not understand 400 souls without confession he could never understand them with it.[40] The Evangelicals were considerably stronger in their criticism. Dr Hugh McNeile advocated capital punishment (arguing that transportation would only remove the evil from one part of the world to another).[41] However, although Pusey wrote to *The Times* in 1866 reporting that he received confession from persons of every rank, age, and profession, outside a few eclectic ritualist congregations confession was extremely rare.[42]

Three principal reasons may be suggested for the considerable increase in counselling as an element in the clergyman's role in the nineteenth century. First, it is not unreasonable to suggest that the clergy, anxious to model themselves on other professional groups, encouraged the development of a relationship between client and practitioner in which personal matters (matters beyond legitimate public concern) were openly discussed. Second, at a time when the numbers in urban parishes were increasing to such a level that general visiting by the clergyman became an almost impossible task, counselling a few parishioners in some depth became the way in which the clergy fulfilled their function as pastors. Third, the processes of social change at this period which caused the breakup of the old agricultural community, together with the increasing fragmentation of social life, favoured the development of pastoral practices and techniques primarily concerned with individuals rather than with groups. Increasingly the clergyman found himself dealing with the casualties of these processes of social change. In the pre-industrial village communities, all social action was in a sense public. The urbanization and industrialization of society in the early Victorian era, with its attendant social isolation, permitted the development of private life. In this situation tensions and problems were made manifest which had not formerly existed, and the clergyman's activity in counselling became a system of personal therapy for the people, who were deprived of the solidarity of the traditional village and the extended family.

Thus, the clergy began to treat the pathological aspect of the growth of private life, and this element became of considerable importance in their role. In the pre-industrial village, the clergyman's functions were essentially communal, and it was the public character of his role which dominated his relations with his parishioners. The ideological viewpoint of the Evangelicals, with its strong emphasis on the individual and his responsibilities, and their concern with the personal rather than the societal elements of theology, emphasized the private functions of the clergyman's role. By the mid-nineteenth century, both in response to the increased social atomization which accompanied the changes in society, and in response to the size of many urban parishes, the clergy became progressively concerned to develop a close personal relationship with certain members of the parish, rather than attempt to encompass the whole parish as a public character. Monro was an ardent promoter of this new style of ministry: '. . . men must be worked upon individually; it is impossible to operate very efficiently on the mass; whether in a town population or an agricultural.'[43] In this shift of emphasis, the clergy, particularly in urban areas, further acknowledged the changes which had taken place in the Church's position in the social structure. At the same time it was an acknowledgement of the self-selection of the 'faithful' among parishioners and the increased voluntarism and individualism of mid-Victorian religious life, a combination so successfully exploited by the non-conformists.

The energetic pastoral work of the mid-Victorian clergy is sharply contrasted with the perfunctory discharge of this element of their role by their eighteenth-century predecessors. Clearly, the mid-Victorian clergy were influenced among other things by the altruism of the age and the ideology of public service, which was a central characteristic of the professional ethic. The word 'duty' conveyed to an eighteenth-century clergyman simply the performing of the Sunday services; for the mid-Victorian clergyman it had a depth of meaning which encompassed a whole range of new expectations.

One of the distinguishing features of the clergyman's role, as opposed to other professional roles, is that of the varying levels of relationship which exist between the professional man and his client. In most professions there is essentially only one level of professional relationship based on the client's desire for the expertise of the professional man. The clergyman, by contrast, stands in a relationship with his parishioners which is much more complex and contains divergent, and not easily reconcilable, strands. For instance, he may be regarded as standing in an authoritarian position as the guardian of morality, as moral exemplar, and as censor, whilst at the same time he may be looked upon as pastor, friend, and counsellor. Clearly, various clergy at different times have sought to place the emphasis on differing elements of this complex relationship. Although it is hard to speculate on the nature of this relationship at any particular time, it is difficult to avoid the conclusion that, in rural areas throughout much of the period under consideration, this relationship was dominated by the clergyman's identification with the gentry class, his position as magistrate, and as owner of the glebe, and recipient of the tithe. Certainly, the latter factors dominated the clergyman's relationship with the farmers. If he was resident and attempted to take his tithe in hand, relationships could deteriorate to such a point that skirmishes took place in the fields. Farmer Skuse's men fought what amounted to a pitched battle with the Revd John Skinner's tithemen as they attempted to remove corn from the fields.[44] Another farmer, determined to pay his tithe at the most inconvenient time, drove the tithe lambs through the rectory gates just as Bishop Sumner arrived.[45] If the clergyman farmed his glebe, he laid himself open to involvement in village quarrels about strayed animals, damaged crops, and other sources of friction in agricultural communities. Where the clergyman was non-resident, he had no use for tithes (nor did many resident clergymen welcome tithes in kind, as they lacked the means of coping with the additional stock and grain). There is no evidence that the farmers were happier to pay money than see the corn removed from their fields. The later commutation of the tithe removed the clergy from direct involvement in agriculture, but, by making the clergy dependent on rents for their income, it further identified them with the landed proprietors. It is not difficult to imagine that the mid-nineteenth-century clergy had some difficulty in establishing pastoral relations with the farmers in the wake of the long legacy of animosities which the tithe system had created. Commutation reduced friction with the farmers, but it helped to further alienate the rural working classes, who saw the clergy as part of the landed interest they blamed for the consequences of the Enclosure Movement, which included the loss of common rights, and for the oppression of the agricultural workforce during the 'high farming' period of the 1860s and 1870s. Considering the workings of the tithe system, the fact that there was relatively little anti-clericalism in the English countryside was a tribute to the pastoral good sense with which most clergy approached this problematic arrangement.

As for the relation between the clergy and their people as a whole, in urban areas the labouring man had become a member of a new urban proletarian sub-culture, which, despite all the efforts of Church extension, was almost completely alienated from the Church and the clergy. In the countryside contact was much more readily made and sustained, but the evidence indicates that the clergy approached their people with an authoritarian and magisterial air. As McClatchey has observed, the relationship between the clergyman and his poor parishioners was characterized by his approach to the village as if it were his own property. Palmer of Finmere considered that it was as a landlord that he was best placed to pursue his pastoral work. An anonymous handbook author wrote: '. . . and when the diligent country parson walks or drives about his parish, not without a decided feeling of authority and ownership . . .'[46] One of Samuel Wilberforce's first acts at Brighstone was an attempt to purchase land in the parish, for he believed that this would set the tone of his pastoral work. Even when he was Bishop of Oxford, he loved to refer to himself as a Sussex squire by virtue of the estate he owned at Lavington.[47]

By the mid-nineteenth century it was clearly seen that the maintenance of such a degree of social distance prohibited the development of pastoral relations of the character we would recognize today. In short, much advice under this head in the later handbooks was aimed at helping the clergy 'get alongside' working men. Monro wrote in 1850:

> . . . the visits of a clergyman to his poor must lose very much force unless he lays aside the magisterial air, so very commonly used. He has no right to cross the poor man's threshold with a covered head, nor in any degree to demean himself as a superior within the walls of the cottage.[48]

And J. H. Blunt observed:

> Among operatives there is a disposition to think that their clergyman looks down upon them from a lofty height of 'aristocratic' pretension and with this idea in their minds they take pains to assert their own independence, by holding aloof from the parson's advances, and by sometimes treating him with surliness and disrespect.[49]

9

Catechist

The 59th Canon of 1604 stated:

> Every person, vicar or curate, upon every Sunday and
> holy day before evening prayer shall for half an hour, or
> more, examine and instruct the youth and ignorant
> persons of his parish, in the ten commandments, the
> articles of the belief, and in the Lord's Prayer; and shall
> diligently hear and instruct and teach them the catechism
> set forth in the Book of Common Prayer.

Catechizing is an element of the charter role of the Church of
England clergyman and was authorized both by the Book of
Common Prayer and the example of Jesus as recorded in the
New Testament. At his ordination the clergyman promised
'to instruct and teach' the people committed to his charge,
and this function he fulfilled both by preaching to the
assembled congregation and by catechizing the children.
Catechizing was regarded as of great importance in the
period after the Reformation, when there was strong insistence on the duty of religious instruction. The Church of
England catechism was included by the compilers of the
Book of Common Prayer and consisted of a series of
questions and answers, after the Socratic method, concerning the Baptismal covenant, the Apostles' Creed, the
Decalogue, and the Lord's Prayer, together with a section on
the sacraments of Baptism and Eucharist. Among the final
rubrics was one which stated that, 'the curate of every parish
shall diligently upon Sundays and holy days after the second
lesson at evening prayer, openly in the church instruct and
examine, so many children of his parish sent unto him as he
shall think convenient in some part of the catechism.'
    In this element of his role the clergyman acted as the
Church's agent of socialization in that he prepared the
juvenile members by a form of dogmatic instruction for their

role as adult members of the institution. The catechism may be regarded as a prescribed course of formal socialization to which the candidate had to submit before being presented to the bishop for confirmation and full membership of the Church. But catechism had a wider significance in a pre-literate traditional society. The stability of any social system depends on the acceptance of a pattern of constraints which serves to minimize potentially disruptive behaviour and is indispensable for the maintenance of social order. Invariably in traditional societies these constraints were couched in religious terms and consisted of the promise of rewards and the threat of sanctions based on supernatural authority. Religious leaders in such societies possessed important functions in communicating the values, norms, and opinions of that society on which its order and coherence essentially depended. In the largely pre-literate society of eighteenth-century England, the clergy as catechizers and preachers were the principal communicators of these values, and there is evidence to suggest that their performance of this function was widely acknowledged by contemporaries.

Catechizing was advocated in all the early handbooks as an important element of the clergyman's work, and an integral part of his Sunday duty. An account of its nature and significance was given by George Herbert and was frequently quoted in subsequent works:

> The Country Parson values catechising highly; for there being three points of his duty, the one, to infuse a competent knowledge of salvation in every one of his flock; the other to multiply and build up this knowledge to a Spiritual Temple; the third to inflame this knowledge, to press and direct it to practise, turning it to reformation of life, by pithe and lively exhortations . . . He requires all to be present at Catechising: First, for the authority of the work; second, that Parents and Masters as they hear the answers prove, may when they come home, either reward or punish. Third, that those of the elder sort, who are not well grounded, may then by an honourable way take occasion of better instruction. [1]

The rubric instructed that the catechism should be taught

by the clergyman in church on every Sunday and holy day, and the 59th Canon laid down that this duty should be performed after the second lesson at evening prayer. The handbooks indicate that in the early and middle eighteenth century catechizing was frequently only a seasonal activity, often confined to Lent. Secker wrote in his Charge of 1741: '. . . I observe that in many (parishes) it is practised only during Lent. Now I should apprehend that the summer season would in general be much more convenient both to the minister and the congregation.'[2]

It has been generally suggested that in the eighteenth century catechizing was most infrequent. Overton and Relton stated that 'the practice by degrees was dropped except in Lent and then altogether'.[3] Warne's examination of the Exeter diocesan returns of this period led him to conclude that 'in the rural parishes generally the rubric which insisted on this being a regular Sunday afternoon activity was no longer observed'.[4] On the basis of his examination of the Cheshire Articles of Inquiry Walker concludes that catechizing was at best limited to Lent, or the few Sundays prior to confirmation.[5] However, McClatchey is inclined to think that the general picture is 'too gloomy' and to believe Bishop Secker when he wrote: 'There are very few places in the diocese where catechising is omitted.' After an examination of the Oxford diocesan returns McClatchey concluded that catechizing held its place as a function of the parochial clergy and was one to which a number devoted thought as well as time.[6] However, James Woodforde, although he was resident in his parish and heard his bishop's Charge on this duty on 19 July 1799, makes no mention in his diary of ever having catechized the children of the parish.[7] But the practice was followed by William Cole, who catechized the children at the evening service in Lent.[8] Lawrence Sterne, at Sutton-on-the-Forest, instructed the parish children in the vicarage on Sunday evenings in Lent.[9]

Certainly, the circumstances of eighteenth-century church practice did not encourage catechizing. In the first place, as has been mentioned on page 55, many churches had only one service and that in the morning. Catechizing, as the 59th Canon stated, was an element of evening prayer, and therefore the abandoning of the evening service naturally led to the abandoning of catechizing. Archbishop Synge in his Charge of 1742 said that catechizing was unpopular because it prolonged the afternoon service by an additional half-hour.[10] Also, the widespread practice of non-residence and the consigning of Sunday duty to itinerant curates made it impossible for the officiating clergyman to catechize in any of the several churches which he served on that day. Secker himself blamed non-residence for the neglect of catechizing; and William Jesse afforded an example: 'The great distance I have been obliged to live from my cure has in some degree prevented an exact discharge of this parochial duty.'

The role of the eighteenth-century bishop stressed his political function as a member of the House of Lords, which required him to reside in London for the greater part of the year. This factor, together with the difficulties of transport, and the extreme age and infirmity of many eighteenth-century bishops, made confirmation a service which was performed infrequently. As a general rule, the bishop confirmed in the market towns of the diocese once every three years (at the time of his visitation). In fact, not even this frequency was maintained. When Archbishop Herring went on a confirmation tour in that diocese in July 1743, he had to confirm the arrears of twelve years of neglect.[11] Towards the end of the century, matters had not substantially improved; there is no record of any of James Woodforde's parishioners having received confirmation. On one occasion Woodforde saw the bishop and talked with him about 'the confirmation at Foulsham next Wednesday being near ten miles from Weston'. Woodforde may well have been complaining that there was no nearer confirmation, for such a distance was sufficient to prevent the children of the poor in remote country villages from attending the service.[12] Furthermore, the confirmation services of this period were notorious for their disorder and lack of reverence, on account of the large congregations involved. They provided an assembly of people that only an election could rival for size. William Jesse wrote: 'Multitudes are dragged together from various parts of the country to be bishop'd as they call it, regarding confirmation as an idle ceremony, or as a charm, the assembly looks more like a riotous meeting than a religious congregation of devout people.'[13]

The duty of catechizing, so widely neglected by the majority of the clergy, was taken up by the Evangelical clergy, who showed a particular interest in children and a sensitivity to the pastoral opportunities of youth (though it is certain that they did not always use the Catechism as the basis of their instruction). The Protestant heritage demands that every individual should be capable of affirming to the truths of the faith for himself from within the pages of the Bible, and the Evangelicals mounted a vigorous attack on the ignorance which they observed on all sides. Among the early Evangelicals, Haweis, Crooke, and Conyers included catechizing as part of their regular weekly parochial duties.[14] Henry Venn took particular care with the children of his parish, catechizing for an hour once a fortnight, and touring the parish catechizing the children before a confirmation.[15] James Stonhouse did much to popularize this duty, and in his publications he recommended that the clergyman should either catechize before and after the service in the vestry or publicly during the service.[16] Job Orton in his handbook advised the clergyman to divide the children into two classes and catechize each for an hour.[17] Cadogan at Chelsea delivered extempore catechetical lectures on Wednesdays and Fridays.[18] The Eclectic Society discussed the problem of instructing children on 22 January 1798 and during the discussion the importance of catechizing was frequently underlined.[19] However, the most significant contribution made by the Evangelicals to the development of catechetical instruction was the introduction of a new institution, the Sunday School. (These schools are discussed more fully in chapter 13.) Originally such schools were institutions for the teaching of reading in order that the scholars could learn to read the Bible for themselves, rather than catechetical schools. In some of the schools catechizing was performed, whilst in others the schoolchildren sat in their allotted places during the afternoon service, which might or might not include catechizing.

The Sunday School, in the modern sense of the term, whose principal function is to give denominated teaching, dates from after 1870, when the Forster Education Act established the board school in which no teaching of this nature was permitted to be given. Robert Raikes's school in Gloucester, about which he wrote a pamphlet in 1783, was regarded as the *terminus a quo* of the Sunday School movement, although it is certain that some schools preceded that of Raikes. By the end of that year Fletcher at Madeley had started six schools, and Wilson had established one at Slaithwaite. In 1784, Cornelius Bayley had started a school in his Manchester parish, as had Atkinson at Leeds.[20] The progress of the Sunday School movement and the renewal of interest in catechizing may be seen as marks of the Evangelical clergy's pastoral concern for children, and their belief, common to so many minority groups, that if they could only make limited progress within their own generation, at least they were preparing a rich harvest in the next.

In the third and fourth decades of the nineteenth century the clergy sought new weapons to take up in their fight to extend the Church and its influence over the hearts and minds of Englishmen. Catechizing was among the expedients which were used by the clergy towards this end. As early as 1800 it had been among the 'remedies' suggested by the group of clergy who surveyed the neglected state of church life in the Lincoln diocese.[21] The handbooks of the first half of the nineteenth century contain many exhortations to the clergy to perform this duty each Sunday afternoon in the church. Some handbooks dealt solely with this function,[22] and in one such handbook the Hon and Revd Samuel Best spoke of the practice of catechizing as a principal weapon in the Church's armoury against rural ignorance; for the doctrinal system of the Church was '. . . brought home, in the most inviting manner, to the hearts of many who may have heard with indifference the most eloquent sermon, from their incapacity to follow out the argument.'[23] In the course of 1846 the *British Magazine* carried a series of articles by Best advocating catechizing and tracing its progress from patristic times, together with a Sunday-by-Sunday plan of catechizing for the year.[24] John Sandford wrote in his handbook:

> . . . it may be questioned whether instructions . . . can ever be so effective as those delivered in the face of the congregation in the presence of friends and relations, and when the exercise is regarded as part of the public service, and consequently duly prepared for by both catechist and catechumen. [25]

In the early decades of the nineteenth century, catechizing established itself as a part of the regular Sunday duty of the active clergyman. Archdeacon Bather, finding he could make no headway in his parish, introduced catechizing in 1804, and during the week brought the children of the two dame schools to church and catechized them also. John Skinner, in 1823, heard a group of children repeat their catechism prior to confirmation, but was dissatisfied with their performance and only one child received a ticket. [26] (A system of tickets was widely used at confirmations to prevent children who had not passed a catechetical examination from attending.) It is recorded of the Evangelical clergyman Beachcroft that he catechized the children after the afternoon service every Sunday. [27] Hamilton in the late 1830s at St Peter's in the East, Oxford, started Sunday-afternoon catechizing, which was attended by many university men, and Newman also attracted a similar congregation at his catechizing at Littlemore. [28] Samuel Wilberforce, when he moved to Alverstoke in 1841, started catechizing on Wednesdays and Sundays. [29] Hook regarded catechizing as being of the greatest importance as an element of parochial strategy. He had 1200 children under instruction at Coventry in 1836, and when he moved to Leeds he attempted to continue the practice there. In the early 1840s he was invited to stay with Archbishop Vernon Harcourt, but as the proposed visit included a Sunday, he refused. He wrote to the Archbishop:

> I catechise upwards of 1,000 children every Sunday afternoon and I have succeeded in making the duty interesting to a large congregation. I am pursuing a course of catechetical instructions; so that I could not delegate the duty to another, and any interruption in the course, until the custom is fully established, would be injurious. [30]

On Good Friday 1844 Richard Seymour wrote in his diary: 'I catechised the children on the events of the day after the second lesson and having made a beginning I hope, please God . . . to go on with this practice, which I have long desired to begin.'[31]

However, it would seem that although catechizing enjoyed something of a revival, it was still a minority practice. In his Primary Charge (1833) to the diocese of Exeter, Henry Phillpotts commented that on the basis of the returns he had received it appeared that this duty was rarely discharged. Edward Boys Ellman wrote of this period:

> Archdeacon Hare tried to revive the Rubric for catechising before the congregation. The only instance of it having been within my memory was in Southover church by Rev. J. Scobell but I did not think it very edifying. I, however, tried to act at the Archdeacon's call but grievously failed. The children were nervous and seemed as if they could not answer before the congregation.[32]

By the early 1840s the rapid development of the day school movement allowed the clergy, who, like Boys Ellman, found public catechizing impossible, to fulfil the spirit of the Prayer Book rubrics by catechizing in the schools. The evidence does not allow anything more than a general comment, but it seems that as more children attended the schools in the parish, it became common practice for the clergy to catechize in the schools or to assemble the schools in the church for catechizing during the week. The public catechizing 'after the second lesson' at evening prayer appears to have gradually given place to this new method.

The service of confirmation, previously so neglected, became, during the middle decades of the nineteenth century, a solemn rite for which a long period of preparation was necessary. In part this was due to the increased emphasis on sacramental worship by many clergymen. The coming of the railways and the improvement in road transport made assembly for any purpose easier and allowed bishops to confirm with greater frequency in a larger number of centres. Many of the handbooks indicated that there was a new seriousness associated with the preparation of candidates for confirmation. Peter Young, a curate of John Keble's, wrote of his preparation of candidates, and this was made famous through the later writings of one of his candidates, Charlotte Yonge:

> He took great pains in preparing the young people for confirmation. His usual course was to go through in order, first the Baptism service, then the Catechism, and lastly the Office of Holy Communion. He took a certain proportion each time making perhaps 20–30 lessons on the whole.'[33]

However, as with catechizing, the new standards were not uniformly attained. In 1840, the Revd Francis Goddard walked to a neighbouring clergyman's house and found the drawing room full of girls being instructed for confirmation. He wrote: 'It is a fact that I never before heard of classes of instruction for confirmation: the only mode adopted by me and others was a sort of house-to-house visit to those we could pick up after their work was done.'[34] The new concern for matters of liturgy and ceremonial meant that the confirmation service was performed with a reverence and orderliness which had been notably absent from the practice of the previous century. The clergyman and his wife accompanied their handful of carefully prepared candidates to the service and back home (so that none should end the day in a public house).

Throughout the third quarter of the nineteenth century, the practice of public catechizing on Sunday in the church was advocated as a salutary discipline for parishioner and clergyman, and as an important element in the parochial strategy. C. J. Vaughan wrote: 'The public catechising, especially in village churches, has a most important office not only towards the young. Many parents and friends of the young can gain almost more by learning thus with and besides their children than they can gain from sermons.'[35] Many other handbooks also contained recommendations that the clergy should catechize frequently, and J. C. Miller wrote of the desirability of a 'universal revival' of public catechizing.[36] However, the evidence suggests that in the second half of the nineteenth century with a few exceptions such as the church of St Barnabas, Pimlico, the traditional mode of catechizing, by oral questioning of the children in church before the congregation, had given place to new forms.[37] In particular the clergy, who were active in the schools, performed this duty in the classroom as a part of the routine of the school. John Keble taught in the village school at Hursley from 9 a.m. to 10 a.m. every day.[38] Armstrong on 5 October 1855 recorded examining 'fifty chubby little children' in their catechism at Etling Green School.[39] Regular catechizing in the school was a feature of the ministry of Randall, as curate of Graffham cum Lavington from 1851.[40] Edward Monro suggested that catechizing should be a regular feature of the village night school.[41] There can be little doubt that many clergymen followed the advice of J. H. Blunt, that after taking morning prayers the clergyman should 'keep on his surplice . . . and catechise then and there daily . . .'[42]

Second, there arose a movement to substitute, in the place of catechizing, a children's service in the afternoon. Even the most ardent advocates of catechizing had always been disturbed by the fact that the children of middle-class parents never attended the service. Also, the increasing literacy of the children and the ideological difficulties which some Evangelicals had always entertained over the sacramental teaching of the catechism, made the children's service a feature of Sunday worship, which quickly recommended itself to many incumbents. As with other innovations in parochial strategy, J. C. Miller, the Evangelical incumbent of St Martin's, Birmingham, was credited with having started this practice. Initially Miller had a service once a month for children, 'the addresses at which are characterised by something of the catechetical element'.[43] In London, at St George's in the East, not only were there special children's services on Sunday afternoons, but also the clergy gave simple catechetical addresses from the steps of the church.[44]

The third alternative, which it might be suggested many clergy followed, was to concentrate on giving extensive private instruction to the candidates before confirmation (and after). Oxenden was particularly anxious that six months' notice should be given before a confirmation in order that a course of detailed instruction could be initiated by the clergyman.[45] Edward Monro gave a considerable amount of thought to confirmation and to the course of preparation which should precede it. He was particularly concerned that confirmation should come at a time when the parish youth, having left the school, were beyond the control of the clergy and confirmation preparation was considerably more difficult than it would have been if the rite were performed for younger children.[46] The nature of confirmation instruction, given in small groups in the clergyman's study, as opposed to public catechism, is a further example of the impact of privatization on the clergyman's role.

The elevation of catechizing (in its various forms) and the service of confirmation to an importance which they did not possess in the eighteenth century, may be regarded as indicative of a number of changes taking place in the wider society. In the eighteenth century, the Church saw itself, in the manner of Hooker, as conterminous with the State; it was not concerned with its own boundaries for everyone was regarded as a member of the Church (though the notion of 'membership' is not one they would have used). However, in the considerably changed circumstances of the mid-nineteenth century, when birthright membership of the Church could no longer be so readily assumed, the Church became conscious of its boundaries, its membership, and its need to recruit in a positive manner. The increasing significance which the clergy attached to the process of socialization was in some sense an acknowledgement of these changed social circumstances, and, in particular, of the implications of denominational pluralism in Victorian England.

Both in absolute and relative terms, catechizing greatly increased in significance within the clergyman's role. His involvement with children, which was in most instances slight in the eighteenth century, increased until, in the twentieth century, aspects of the role which were connected with children (Sunday schools, youth clubs, the choir and servers, leadership of uniformed youth movements, confirmation classes, teaching in schools, parish outings, family and mother and child services), came in some instances to dominate the clergyman's parochial activities. This shift in emphasis has been regarded by some observers as indicative of the growing marginality of an institution which came to involve itself principally, though by no means exclusively, with women and children; that is, with the familial and private experience of society as opposed to its central and public concerns.

10
Clerk

'Clerk' was the general term applied to both the clergy (clerks in Holy Orders) and all literate men in the medieval period, when for the most part the two categories broadly coincided. The clergy of the eighteenth century inherited from previous centuries certain functions of an administrative nature which had their origins in the fact that the clergyman was the only locally available literate man or 'man of public character'. The presence of this element in the clergyman's role further witnessed to the close intertwining of secular and religious functions. The incumbent of a parish was by law the registrar for that area, and births, marriages, and deaths were a legal fact only when they had been entered in the parish register, upon the evidence of which many cases, particularly those concerning legacies, depended. The principal functions of the clergyman in this element of his role involved keeping the parish register up to date and preserving the old registers, which by law had to be kept in a chest in the church. The clergyman was obliged to make the necessary entries in the register (though it appears that this was often done by the parish clerk), and annually to send a copy of the register to the office of the diocesan registrar. The clergyman was also required to give copies of entries in the register to those who wanted them for legal purposes. William Cole gave three such certificates on a single day in August 1766.[1]

To these legal requirements others were added when, in 1783, the Stamp Tax was introduced; this levied a tax on every entry in the parish register. This requirement placed the clergyman in the invidious position of a tax-gatherer, and as it provided so unpopular a method of raising money, the legislation was replaced in 1794. The clergyman, as a man of public character, was used by the State for administering official business, particularly where the matter depended upon local knowledge such as the identification of a person. Parson Woodforde recorded the enactment of legislation in 1792 for preventing frauds and abuses in the payment of seamen's wages, and which also provided for the execution of seamen's wills. Under this legislation various duties were laid upon the clergyman, including testifying to the identity of the executor if resident in his parish, swearing him as such, and declaring the bona-fides of witnesses. The clergyman's signature was in constant demand on the papers of emigrants, sailors, soldiers, clergymen's widows, pensioners, lunatics, and persons wanting to keep a public house.[2]

Although there is some evidence that the clergy were willing to take pains to keep their registers correctly – a notice in the *Norwich Mercury* of 17 August 1776 offered twenty-five guineas for information about a break into a parish chest and the removal of several pages of the register – much of the evidence suggests that the registers were not maintained with the care that was required.[3] The legislation of 1812 compelled the clergy to send copies to the diocesan registrar, but even in 1833 a quarter of the parishes in England and Wales made no return. A Northampton rector's daughter was found to have used the old registers of one parish as lace parchment.[4] Archdeacon Musgrave in his Charge of May 1865 mentions that he spent much time chasing up missing registers all around the country.[5] Sabine Baring Gould recalled a Cornish parish where only male names were entered, as certificates were needed for work at the local government dockyards, and women were not employed.[6]

The twin acts of Marriage and Registration were passed in 1836 and had a profound effect on this element of the clergyman's role. The Marriage Act allowed marriages by licence from the registrar which could be performed either as a civil marriage or in a nonconformist place of worship. The clergyman continued to act as registrar for marriages in the parish church, and special books were now provided, copies of which had to be sent to the Registrar General's office under penalty. It seems that many of the clergy resented the new legislation and a number were implacably opposed to it.

The Poor Law had created an official in every area and his duties were now extended to include the registration of births and deaths. No longer was the clergyman the registrar of births in the parish, and this had the effect of making baptism a voluntary rite rather than the ceremony which confirmed legal existence upon the child. As a correspondent of the *British Magazine* wrote in November 1836: 'The long and short of the act, as it affects baptism, is simply this, that the child shall not be compelled to receive Christian baptism in order to have its birth and existence recognised by the civil authority.'[7] Many clergy thought they had been robbed of an essential element of their role and were very much afraid that baptism might now be widely disregarded by the people. John Burgon considered it necessary in his handbook to tell the clergyman that he should explain 'that the Divine Sacrament has not been superseded by the act of registration'.[8] The burial legislation also angered the clergy as it imposed upon them a £10 fine if they buried a corpse without a death certificate from the registrar.

The other aspect of the clergyman's role as clerk, that of countersigning official documents, usually as evidence of identification, became something of a burden for the busy mid-nineteenth-century incumbent of an urban parish. W. W. Champneys complained of this, as did Robert Gregory, and one London incumbent found it necessary to hold open levee in his vestry on Wednesday mornings for two hours.[9] Edward Spooner wrote:

> Few people know how many things come upon a town clergyman, because of his being the only public character in the parish. There are hosts of certificates of identity for pensioners, for depositors of money in savings banks, in sick clubs, etc., which require the signature of either a clergyman or a magistrate; but who knows the residence of a magistrate in London? and whom therefore can they come to but the clergyman.[10]

The size and complexity of early Victorian society could no longer tolerate an administration based on the irregular efforts of unpaid amateurs. The new bureaucratic methods demanded by a more numerous and complex society concentrated administration in the hands of a few specifically trained government officials. The Marriage and Registration Acts effectively brought to a close the era in which the clergy had been responsible for these administrative functions, and even in such responsibilities as remained to them, they were subject to the registrar. In this sector of his role, as elsewhere, the mid-nineteenth-century clergyman experienced a contraction of his functions, as, in response to the demands of an industrialized and more populous country, the new administrative professions developed and established themselves. The clergyman's administrative role was increasingly within the church, but at this time there was little to foreshadow the heavy administrative burdens which many clergymen have to shoulder in the twentieth century, and the new significance which would be accorded to the term 'clerk', not in the service of the State, but in that of the Church.

11

Officer of Law and Order

The maintenance of cohesion and order in society presents a constant and fundamental organizational problem, and the survival and persistence of any particular society depends upon the construction of a pattern of constraint, which enforces conformity and minimizes deviant and potentially disruptive behaviour. In traditional societies, social order was authorized in terms of supernatural authority and was based on a shared conception of transcendental order. In short, society was seen as both divine in character and immutable in nature. Furthermore, in traditional societies, the maintenance of social order was essentially a local rather than a societal function and was achieved by the mobilization of local sanctions, controls, and personnel. In such societies social order was achieved by the regulation of personal relationships rather than by the legal provisions, technical devices, and bureaucratic procedures which characterize the maintenance of social order in an advanced society. It may be observed that much of the ethical teaching of the Bible and the Church is about the regulation of personal relationships in the face-to-face situations of a family and local community, rather than the impersonal role relationships of a more advanced social system. The pre-eminent significance accorded to religion in traditional societies resulted in large measure from the role which religion played in shaping and controlling inter-personal relationships and personal dispositions.

In traditional societies the religious leaders were seen as the guardians of the common history and traditions, in terms of which notions of prosperity, wisdom, morality, decency, and a sense of order were formulated. The basic moral values and social conventions were sanctioned in religious terms, and the acceptance of them was symbolized by allegiance to the Church. In such societies, political dissent often took a religious form. The sacral nature of social order in traditional societies may be gauged from the fact that, in such societies, a distinction was not customarily made between sin and crime. The religious leader in a traditional society was the mediator and communicator of its values and norms and had an important function in terms of maintaining and enforcing the order and coherence of that society. The structure and prescriptions of feudal society were among other functions shaped as a means of maintaining social control, and stressed, on the one hand, authoritative paternalism, and on the other, dependence and deference. The highly localized and communal nature of society permitted this system to work effectively. A society based on personal (invariably face-to-face) relationships was meanable to the influence of religion. [1]

The changes that affected English society in the late eighteenth and early nineteenth centuries caused a breakdown (gradual for the most part, but dramatic in the new industrial urban areas) in the traditional means of social control. The breakdown of community, increased mobility, and the growing impersonal nature of relations within society precipitated the attrition of those social arrangements which had previously guaranteed the stability, coherence, and integration of society. At the same time there arose sections of the population who were no longer disposed to accept the constraints of the dependency system, and in many areas the gentry and the aristocracy slowly withdrew from their traditional functions of social control. Thus, there was a period between the onset of the gradual breakdown of the old communal means of social control, and the development of modern societal systems of social control, dependent on specialized personnel, technical devices, legal provisions, and bureaucratic procedures, when it seemed to many contemporary observers that a complete breakdown in social order was imminent. There were major outbreaks of popular disorder in 1795–6, 1800–1801, 1810–13, and 1816–18, and the fear of popular disturbance, and even revolution, was a persistent factor in English life right up until the Paris Commune and the shooting of the Archbishop in 1871.

In the eighteenth century, at a time of small armies and no police, the State played almost no part in the maintenance of law and order at the local level. This was the duty of the Lord Lieutenant, aided by the Justices, and in extremes, by the yeomanry. As the century progressed, and particularly in the last years after the revolution in France, the Church and the clergy found themselves pushed forward as the principal bulwark against civil disorder and revolution. In one sense this was not a wholly inappropriate function for a national Church. Certainly, any description of the developing role of the clergyman would be defective without our taking into account the extensive part the clergy played as officers of law and order. At this time Bishop Watson wrote:

> The safety of every civil government is fundamentally dependent on the hopes and fears of another world which are entertained by its members; and the safety of every Christian civil government is brought into the most imminent danger, when infidelity is making a rapid progress in the minds of the people . . . It may be difficult to find a full remedy for this evil, but the residence of a respectable clergyman in every parish and hamlet in which there is a place of established worship, appears to me to be more fitted than any other for that purpose.[2]

This element of the Church of England clergyman's role may seem to have no place among the sacral and spiritual functions of his charter role. However, it is explicitly referred to in the Ordinal and the clergyman before he is ordained is required to answer the question: 'Will you maintain and set forward, as much as lieth in you quietness, peace, and love, among all Christian people and specially among them that are or shall be committed to your charge?' Bishop Gibson in his *Directions given to the Clergy of the Diocese of London* in 1724 quoted this section of the service as authority for the clergyman to act in this way.[3] The contribution made by the clergy to the maintenance of law and order can be divided between their participation in the formal system of social control, the secular and ecclesiastical courts; and their informal activities as agents of social control in the local community.

The church courts of the eighteenth century were in almost every respect similar to those established by William I. He had separated the ecclesiastical from the Hundred courts, on the principle that cases touching souls should not be dealt with in the secular courts. The reformation had left the ecclesiastical courts unaltered, with the exception that final appeal could be made to the King in Chancery (the Court of Delegates). However, in the intervening period the church courts had become weak and corrupt; their spiritual censures lacked moral weight; their excessive fees, their delays, and vexatious procedure further weakened their authority. During the late seventeenth and early eighteenth centuries the number of cases concerning disciplinary charges against the laity progressively declined, and the archdeacon's court, whose function it was to hear such cases, tended to fall into abeyance. The church courts in the mid-eighteenth century still possessed jurisdiction over such matters as the collection of the church rate, testamentary cases, matters of probate, matrimonial cases, and those concerning usury, defamation, and slander, brawling in church or churchyard, and sexual immorality, together with jurisdiction over clergy, lay church officers, and church property.

The manner in which the Church contributed to the enforcing of public order is apparent from the requirements of the visitations of the eighteenth century which demanded that the churchwardens should bring to the discipline of the church courts, those of the laity who were suspected of adultery, fornication, or incest, and those who were 'common swearers or blasphemers of God's Holy Name', as well as 'unclean and filthy talkers and sowers of sedition, faction, and discord among their neighbours'. Those who failed to attend divine service at church or chapel, those who compelled their servants to work on Sundays, and publicans who opened their doors at service time were also to be presented in court. There is no doubt that a resident incumbent backed by the parish officers, by means of presentation to the church courts, could have constituted an effective means of social control.[5] However, the prevalence of non-residence, and low public regard for the church courts, undermined their effectiveness and the evidence suggests that bastardy and fornication (together with slander and defamation concerning these offences) were the most common cases heard in the church courts. For these offences public penance was usually required and failure to comply with the court's directions could result in excommunication for contumacy; an offender risked imprisonment if he remained excommunicate for forty days.

Woodforde wrote in his diary on 3 February 1768: 'Sarah Gore came to me this morning and brought me an instrument from the Court at Wells to perform publick penance next Sunday at Castle Cary church for having a child.'[6] (Public penance involved standing in a white sheet and holding a lighted taper in church at service time while reading a confession of guilt.) John Burgon (writing in 1864) regretted the disappearance of this discipline, and noted that two people did penance in his church in 1789.[7] William Wordsworth recorded that he saw a woman doing penance in church in a white sheet, sometime before the death of his mother in 1778.[8] G. R. Balleine suggests that John Pugh, vicar of Rauceby, 1771–99, was the last person to insist on offenders doing public penance.[9] Although there was an instance of a man being imprisoned for refusing to perform penance as late as 1830,[10] by the end of the eighteenth century the discipline of the church courts played little part in the maintenance of law and order. In the mid-eighteenth century brawling and slander had become civil offences. In the legislation of 1857, matrimonial and testamentary matters were transferred to the civil courts. By the nature of the functions left to ecclesiastical courts they were reduced from national institutions to professional institutions concerned primarily with the discipline of the clergymen and some lay church officials, and with church property.

The diminishing part played by the clergy in maintaining public order by means of ecclesiastical discipline was balanced, at this time, by their increasing involvement in the administration of the civil law. The close involvement and interdependence of religious and secular institutions was reinforced in the second half of the eighteenth century as the clergy, who had previously only rarely served as magistrates, increasingly found their names on the Lord Lieutenant's

Commission of the Peace. In a sense it was natural that a group of men whose increasing wealth and social status qualified them to be considered as country gentlemen, should accept what amounted to an important element of the country gentleman's role, for service as a magistrate was regarded as an obligation which all competent country gentlemen were obliged to undertake. The Justices, under the Lord Lieutenant of the county, were the formal agents for the upholding of the King's peace. Their duties included holding Petty and Quarter Sessions; supervising weights and measures; repairing roads and bridges; supervising the police, gaols, houses of correction, and local markets; licensing higglers, drovers, and ale-houses; and the administration of the Poor Law. It is hard to exaggerate the extent of the executive and judicial authority which the magistrates had accumulated in this period, much of it without statutory warrant.[11]

In the last quarter of the eighteenth century two circumstances combined to place many clergymen on the Commissions of the Peace. In the first instance, it was widely believed that the parish machinery and the resident incumbent were the best possible means of countering the insidious influence of 'profane ideas' and the principles of the French Revolution. Second, the changes in agrarian society bore heavily upon the smaller squires and gentry, many of whom were forced to sell their properties. The development of the large estates in many counties based on mercantile wealth inevitably resulted in a shrinking in the number of people qualified to serve. Particularly where the new landlords of the large estates were for significant parts of the year resident elsewhere, the clergy provided the only source of suitable available and qualified candidates.[12]

The appointment of the clergy as Justices was important to the clerical profession for two reasons. First, it was the final acknowledgement that the members of the profession could be regarded in some degree as equal to the country gentlemen; that the clergy were to be regarded as 'gentlemen by profession', if not 'gentlemen by birth'. Second, in a profession with no career structure, the possibility of being appointed a Justice offered to the ambitious clergyman the possibility of achieving advancement, which might lead to other appointments some of which were honorary, some lucrative. McClatchey has recorded the figures for the county of Oxford (excluding the city of Oxford):[13]

Date of Commission	Lay Justices	Percentage	Clerical Justices	Percentage
1775	166	67.0	75	31.0
1797	172	71.7	68	28.3
1816	110	63.2	64	36.8

However, it appears that among the Justices the clergy were particularly active and made a large contribution to the work of the Bench. McClatchey gives the details for the county of Oxford of convictions recorded at Quarter Sessions:

Year	Number bearing signatures of clerical Justices	Percentage	Number bearing signatures of lay Justices
1780	19	82.6	3
1790	19	85.7	2
1800	9	75.0	3

The diary of Benjamin Newton revealed that he was an active Justice not only in his attendance at Petty and Quarter Sessions, but also in the smaller matters of a magistrate's duty in the local community.[14] Blomfield, when at Dunton, wrote in June 1813:

> . . . my time will be somewhat more occupied than formerly as I am now a commissioner of Turnpikes and a Justice of the Peace: and the county business will never get on without me. I must study Burn with diligence before I can indifferently minister justice . . . I shall moreover probably be a commissioner of the Property Tax, all of which offices will a little interfere with Greek.[15]

However, the clergy were by no means unanimous in applauding this addition of the magisterial to the ministerial character, and as early as 1764, an anonymous handbook author considered it 'absolutely a mistake' to believe that a clergyman could gain respect by adding the office of a Justice to that which he already possessed.[16] Simeon disapproved of clerical magistrates 'unless in very peculiar cases'.[17] William Jones of Broxbourne observed: 'Many clergymen are magistrates – but the office seems to me unsuitable for any Minister of the Gospel; it must consume much time and create many enemies.'[18] Despite such opinions the evidence suggests that many clergymen were active as Justices and that a number were conspicuous for the diligence with which they discharged their magisterial duties.

In a society which was by nature local, the influence of the clergy particularly as agents of social control arose more from their dispersal and situation than from any other factor. William Cobbett wrote in May 1802:

> . . . the clergy are less powerful from their rank and industry than from their locality. They are, from necessity, everywhere, and their aggregate influence is astonishingly great. When, from the top of any high hill, one looks around the country and sees the multitude of regularly distributed spires, one not only ceases to wonder that order and religion are maintained, but one is astonished that anything as disaffection and irreligion should prevail. It is the equal distribution of the clergy, their being in every corner of the kingdom, that makes them a powerful and formidable corps.[19]

It was the essential local power of the clergyman which was recognized by churchmen and politicians to be such a powerful agent of social control. The risk of provoking the disapproval of the man who controlled the local school, the local charities, and much else in village life, was a strong sanction in itself against disruptive behaviour. Thomas Percy, Dean of Carlisle, remarked to Dr Johnson: 'It might be observed whether or no there was a clergyman resident in the parish by the civil or savage manner of the people.'[20] Some of the early handbooks acknowledged the clergyman's duties in this respect; George Herbert suggested that sin should be punished by 'withdrawing bounty and courtesie', and then by private and public reproval.[21] The clergy were described by one handbook author in 1764 as 'teachers of religion and overseers of the morals of the people'.[22] Bishop Watson wrote:

> Let us as ministers of the gospel of peace, co-operate in our proper stations with our superiors, in promoting harmony and good order in society, in preserving a due respect to authority and a proper confidence in the ability and integrity of those who are set over us.[23]

In the absence of any formal agents of policing in the local community, the clergy took upon themselves the maintenance of law and order. On 17 December 1769, when James Woodforde was suspicious that prowlers were in the village, he took it upon himself to make sure all was quiet. 'Brother Heighes, Jack and myself, all armed, took a walk at twelve this evening around the parish to see if we could meet any idle folk . . .'[24] However, it was largely in less dramatic ways that the clergyman contributed to the maintenance of public order by keeping general pastoral surveillance over the community, and by using the authority of his role to reprimand those whose conduct was the cause of local disquiet. Woodforde was consulted by the churchwardens on 17 July 1781 about a man who was causing trouble in the parish and he advised them to secure a warrant for the man's arrest.[25] Skinner frequently complained to the parish constable that he was failing in his duty.[26] The clergy had particular authority with regard to public houses, for a prospective licensee needed a reference from the incumbent of the parish when applying for a licence and its subsequent renewal. Woodforde refused to give his consent to a proposed new licensee who was a man of notoriously bad character.[27] In the relatively stable social conditions of the mid-eighteenth century, particularly in the small isolated rural communities with their powerful local mechanisms of social control, the maintenance of public order was not a factor of over-riding importance in the role of the clergyman. When industrialization and urbanization, together with new political philosophies, changed this stable situation, the old agencies of social control were weakened. Though this loosening of the fabric of society was mainly an urban or suburban phenomenon, none the less the groundswell of these movements was felt even in the most isolated villages.

During the last quarter of the eighteenth century there was widespread public concern about the maintence of law and order. The week of terror in London occasioned by the Gordon Riots in May 1780, in which seventy houses and four gaols were burnt down, proved the inadequacy of the law-enforcement agencies.[28] The revolution in France and the threatened invasion of England, the spread of revolutionary literature and in particular the works of Tom Paine, the formation of 'Revolution Clubs', the mobbing of the King in 1795, and the mutiny of the Fleet at the Naze in 1797, together with the widespread civil unrest occasioned by inflation and the high wartime price of food, all combined to make the preservation of social stability a matter of the most immediate concern, particularly for the propertied classes. The upper classes increasingly realized the importance of cementing their alliance with the clergy in the face of political radicalism and social unrest, and the Established Church was regarded as a bulwark against enthusiasm and levelling tendencies. The French Revolution and the enthusiastic interest in it so widely shown at first in England conclusively sealed that alliance between the upper orders of Church and State already well in being before the revolution began.[29]

The social status of the clergy rose perceptibly at this time as they assumed the position of front-line officers in the battle against atheism, infidelity, and regicide. The number of clerical magistrates increased sharply in the early years of the nineteenth century. Meetings of the nobility, gentry, and clergy were summoned to raise subscriptions for local defence requirements, both against the French and from threat from within. Bishop Samuel Horsley, whose reaction to the French Revolution was particularly extreme, considered that the clergy should be mobilized as an armed militia for the final defence of the nation.[30] An anonymous clergyman in Kent, by his own account, was responsible for the organization of a defence unit: 'Should the French make good a landing on the Kentish coast . . . the name of each man among you is set down on a list in my hands, with the respective part that each is most willing and thought most fit to take on such an emergency.'[31]

The clergy as a body had particular reasons for their intimate involvement in the preservation of social stability. The anti-clericalism of the French Revolution, and the reception in England of the exiled French priests, made the clergy regard their own situation in a new light, particularly as the abolition of tithes was a popular and conspicuous element in the platform of radical groups in this country. Thus the clergy, with great energy, in pulpit, parish, or school, proclaimed the certainty of an after-life in which divine rewards and punishments would be meted out, and continually taught the lessons of social subordination and obedience to lawful authority. John Napleton wrote in his handbook of 1801 that it was the duty of the clergy '. . . to promote . . . affection and submission to constitution and government; to advance all these purposes within your parish, by your improving knowledge of men and things; and some of them (if you should become a magistrate) in your parish and neighbourhood by your authority.'[32] The Evangelicals showed themselves particularly energetic in defending law and order; the tracts of Hannah More (her tracts sold over two million copies in 1795 alone), the Royal Proclamation of 1787 against vice, the Society for the Reformation of Manners, and the revival of sabbatarianism, were all instances of their activity at this time.

The social unrest which had been such a prominent feature of the last decades of the eighteenth century continued during the first three decades of the nineteenth century, and the period after the close of the Napoleonic Wars was one of considerable unsettlement and alarm. The new cheap popular press fanned the flames, and with the breakdown of the old external forms of control the forces of coercion were often unable to contain manifestations of discontent. In the urban areas, particularly in the north, every period of distress seemed to convince the popular mind that it was the newly installed machines that were robbing the working man of a living wage; and that such small wage increases as there were were nullified by the high cost of food. The Luddite riots during the war were followed by agricultural riots caused, in part, by the high cost of food, and in part, by the widespread under-employment. The desperation of the agricultural labourers was vented against the threshing machines, which took away the little winter work that was available. Although these riots were never serious and were largely confined to East Anglia, they caused widespread alarms, and the Justices, among whom the clergy were conspicuous, suppressed them vigorously. But the agitation was not confined to the countryside and meetings were common in urban areas advocating the need for parliamentary reform.

In the year 1830, the growing social unrest, particularly in the southern counties, manifested itself in rioting, machine-breaking, rick-burning, cattle maiming, and infringements of the game laws. As before, the amount of damage to property and the numbers injured bore no relationship to the amount of fear and disquiet that reports of these outbreaks caused. The early outbreaks coincided both with the elections in this country and the 'July Revolution' in France. As the events in France took on ominous proportions, so the politicians readily imagined what inspired the labourers to threaten the farmers. The rioting, led by the ubiquitous 'Captain Swing', was directed in every county against the substantial farmers and the clergy, particularly if they were magistrates. Accounts of the outbreaks betray the degree of alarm which these events generated. Charles Anderson wrote to Samuel Wilberforce with hair-raising accounts of incendiarism in the north. Even in Lavington it was rumoured that they wanted 'the parson's head', and the barns were watched and social visiting ceased.[33] Augustus Hare took part in the defence of the property of the chief farmer at Alton Barnes, which was threatened by the mob, and, at neighbouring Herstmonceux, four wheat ricks and four barns were set on fire in June 1831.[34] When these events were coupled with the Reform Bill agitation, propertied people, whose lives had been spent in an atmosphere of war, revolution, and social instability were haunted by fears of a major social upheaval, for which there was such a woeful precedent.

The failure of the reforms of the fourth decade of the nineteenth century, and in particular the disillusionment of the poor, especially in urban areas with the workings of the

Poor Law, precipitated a further period of unrest. The charter of Place and Lovett became a rallying point for discontent, and although the sporadic attempts at armed rebellion (particularly that of Frost in November 1837 in South Wales) were easily put down, much alarm was generated and fears that had existed at the beginning of the decade were again widely expressed. Many people were convinced that their fearful premonitions were about to be realized. The clergy were particularly sensitive to the socialist and chartist spokesmen, who bluntly condemned the Established Church as plundering and selfish, and totally unconcerned with the plight of the working people. Their followers invaded churches, verbally assaulting the clergy and people. The Revd C. K. Prescot, Rector of Stockport, was a frequent target, for it was hard to bridge the gap between the Rector with his £2500 per annum and the mass of cotton operatives starving on an average income of 1/4$\frac{3}{4}$d per week.[35]

Country life in the early nineteenth century was ubiquitously boorish and uncultured, and could often be wild, savage, and brutal. It must have appeared even more so to men who left the seclusion of Oxford to take up a family or college living and found themselves in the midst of a community at best indifferent, but frequently openly hostile, to its clergyman. In a letter of 1828, the incumbent at Checkendon advised Samuel Wilberforce, his successor, not to allow his man to sleep in the village. He said it was his practice to have his man on guard at night carrying a gun loaded with ball and a swordstick.[36] The whole period was pervaded by the atmosphere of war, revolution, and social instability and in such circumstances the minds of the propertied classes were naturally much occupied with the problem of maintaining public order.

The clerical magistrates, who were singled out for special attention by the rioters of 1816–17 and 1830–31, were particularly active in suppressing the various outbursts of lawlessness. In the East Anglian riots of 1816, the Revd Henry Law was the magistrates' spokesman, and he appealed to the Home Secretary for the use of troops on a number of occasions. He and a fellow magistrate, the Revd

Henry Bate Dudley, rode to Ely on 24 May 1816 with the 42nd Royston Volunteer Cavalry. The next day they proceeded to Littleport, where Bate Dudley found the rioters in The George inn and commanded them to surrender. In the ensuing *mêlée* three people were killed.[37] At the Spa Field assembly of 17 August 1819 two of the magistrates who summoned the troops were clergymen, and one of the clerical magistrates read the Riot Act. The working classes were slow to forget such actions, and the clerical magistrate was for a long time a prominent anti-establishment symbol.

The period of the Swing riots of 1830–31 was one of great activity among clerical magistrates, whose numbers, it is estimated, rose to 1354 in 1832. At this time, about one clergyman in eight was also a magistrate. During these riots the clergy were not only active as magistrates but also organized local defence units. H. C. G. Moule described the riots of 1831 as '. . . almost nightly alarms . . . my Father [the rector] organised patrols and served on them.'[38] Troops were no use against sporadic rioting over a wide area, and, in the absence of any other law-enforcement agency, the clergy in some instances mobilized local defence units. In his evidence to the Select Committee on the Sale of Beer, Robert Wright, incumbent of Itchen Abbas, a magistrate of twenty-six years' standing and chairman of the Quarter Sessions, stated:

> . . . ever since the riots have commenced, I have had a kind of petty system of police at my own expense which has every week gone regularly round the village so that I have had correct information of everything that has proceeded in those [beer] houses.[39]

It appears that the rector was placed in command of the Duke of Buckingham's tenantry. When the rioters from Winchester came into the district, the Rector, with a force of a hundred men, met them in an action which resulted in forty to fifty prisoners being taken.[40] In Berkshire the riots lasted for several days in November 1830, with a mob advancing through the countryside. At Colthrop, near Thatcham, they destroyed the machinery in a paper mill. However, that afternoon at Brimpton Common, they met their match in the shape of a resolute magistrate, the Revd E. Cove, Vicar of Brimpton, who had collected a large body of tradesmen and constables to meet them. The Riot Act was read and a battle ensued at the end of which eleven rioters were arrested and taken to Reading gaol.[41] The activity of magistrates in the courts in punishing outbreaks of rioting with great severity did not make it easy for the poor to regard the clerical magistrate as their pastor and friend, when their natural sympathies lay with those who were transported.

In Warwickshire in 1830, twenty-one of the fifty-four active magistrates were clergymen. Such a figure was not exceptionally high for the English and Welsh counties, in eight of which there was a majority of clerical magistrates. The clerical magistrates were particularly active in the industrial and mining areas of north Warwickshire: in 1827, for instance, the most active in the industrial suburbs of Coventry were the Revd T. C. Adams, the Revd F. D. Perkins, and the Revd T. C. Roberts, all with livings in the area.[42] The activity of the clergy as magistrates can be clearly correlated to the gradual abdication of this responsibility by the aristocracy and gentry. In Warwickshire, for instance, although ten peers had country seats, only Lord Aylesford was willing to serve. By contrast in counties nearer London, the numbers of clerical magistrates were low: in Kent only two, in Sussex nine.

By the beginning of the 1840s, the opposition to the union of the ministerial and magisterial character, which had always been loud and vocal among the ranks of dissenters and radical politicians, was increasingly heard among the clergy. The arguments in favour of this union lost ground in the face of the new emphasis on the consecrated character of the clergyman and the spiritual nature of his role. It became improper for a pastor, as Brian Heeney has observed, 'to mediate both the forgiveness of God and the punishment of the State'.[43] The clergy who remained on the Bench (and a number did, as appointment was for life), did so in the face of increasing opposition, both from radical politicians and from within the Church. These men tended to be older clergy, who brought to mid-nineteenth-century problems assumptions about human nature and social harmony which they had learned in the previous century. Many clergy were discouraged from becoming magistrates by the knowledge that the office of a Justice would jeopardize the pastoral relationship which should exist between the incumbent and his parishioners. In the eighteenth century, when this relationship was characterized by the ownership of land and by kinship with the local gentry, the addition of the magisterial office did not effect a substantial change. However, the magisterial office was incompatible with the type of pastoral relationship which some clergy were attempting to develop in the 1840s, with its emphasis on the clergyman's functions as pastor, friend, and counsellor. R. W. Evans wrote in his handbook of 1842:

> Let us suppose an instance; a clerical magistrate quells a disturbance; but is he obeyed from any deference to his spiritual character? Be that high as it may, does it present itself to the eyes of the people? Assuredly not: it is quite hidden under his temporal, which as it bears the sword engrosses all attention. The evil consequence results that they have contemplated him in a merely temporal view, and will never afterwards be sufficiently alive to his spiritual attributes.[44]

Charles Jerram, Rector of Witney from 1834 to 1853, explained in his memoirs both the considerations which at an early stage in his career had led him to serve as a Justice, and why later he declined to serve. Despite the fact that service on the Bench had enabled him to tackle social evils connected with the administration of public houses, Sunday observance, and the Poor Law, the net result he felt had been injurious to himself and his standing with his parishioners.[45] A further fact which must have influenced many was that the new demands made upon the clergyman's role did not leave sufficient time for attending to the considerably increased work of a magistrate. Blomfield, himself once a magistrate, came to disapprove of clergy being magistrates largely on the grounds that it took up too much time.[46] However, despite growing opposition, perhaps the majority of the clergy would still have endorsed Sir Eardley Wilmot's enthusiasm for clerical magistrates as expressed in

the House of Commons on 10 February 1837, for among
other functions it allowed the clergy 'to act as friends of the
poor and heal disputes as arbitrators and referees'.[47] But the
poor themselves saw the clerical magistrate not as a friend,
but as a symbol of an authoritarian class, which oppressed
the rural population. The game laws, which punished
poaching with particular severity, came to be seen as the
symbol of class privilege in a society which was increasingly
less willing to accept such harsh and uneven constraints. It
was a commonplace of radical politicians that the clergy
were simply an instrument in the hands of the government
for the oppression of the people.[48]

In the early nineteenth century, the parish and the resident
clergyman were widely regarded as the main instrument for
preserving the stability of the social structure. The legislation
in the early decades of the nineteenth century concerning
non-residence, pluralities, the employment of curates,
clerical farming, together with the money voted by
Parliament for church building, and the creation and endowment of new parishes by the Ecclesiastical Commissioners (known as the Peelite parishes), were in part
manifestations of the anxiety of some church leaders to clear
away abuses and anomalies, and the desire of Parliament
and the nation that the clergy should do their duty. However,
it was not as Justices or organizers of local police units that
the clergy made their most significant contribution to the
maintenance of law and order, but rather in the numerous
informal ways in which, in the course of their parochial
work, they were able to encourage appropriate patterns of
social conduct. The schools inevitably played a large part in
this, for in them the young were brought up to honour the
Victorian virtues of thrift, sobriety, self-help, hard work,
and respect for the class hierarchy. Blomfield told the House
of Lords that religious education, given by teachers of
religion, was 'the cheapest, as well as the most effective
measure of police which our Government can adopt'.[49] The
clergyman, as the almoner of the parish, had in his hands a
powerful weapon of social control, particularly in the harsh
times after the reform of the Poor Laws, and was able to
sanction the correct pattern of behaviour by denying coal,

soup, bedding, clothes, medicines, and other vicarage gifts to those who incurred his displeasure.

Public houses were regarded by the clergy as particularly obnoxious and as harbouring all that was profane and vicious. The clergy, by way of recommendations for licences, had some power over public houses, and the evidence suggests that they used their authority to the full, checking frequently that the doors were shut at the appointed hour, that there was no rowdyism within, and, if there was, summoning the constable to do his duty. The Report of the Select Committee on the Sale of Beer (1833) contained the evidence of many clergymen who testified to the fact that the beerhouses had been the headquarters of the rioters in the recent disturbances. The history of the temperance movement, and the part the clergy played in it, lies beyond the scope of this book, but there is little doubt that most parochial clergy, whether they approved of total abstinence or not, did everything in their power to provide counter-attractions to the public house and to reduce the level of rural drunkenness which was the chronic social disease of the countryside at this time. The many evening and night schools, the penny readings, the lectures and talks illustrated with a magic lantern, were in part introduced to provide a rival attraction. A parochial reading room was in effect a public house without alcoholic drink, and these were established in many parishes. A shop or cottage was rented by the committee, equipped with comfortable furniture, well heated and lighted. The newspapers and selected magazines were taken; books were available, as were table games, such as draughts and chess; and tea was served.[50] Here the working man was encouraged to spend his evenings. A parochial lending library and a series of lectures or readings were found in many parishes at this time.

A further way in which the clergy attacked the problems of social disorder was by attempting to regularize the village festivals and the hiring fairs, which were notorious for the accompanying drunkenness and immorality. Most villages enjoyed a week's holiday after the harvest which frequently coincided with the Martinmas hiring fairs. The service of harvest festival with its accompanying processions and feast was an attempt by the clergy to establish their authority over proceedings. However, it would seem that despite the cricket matches, concerts, lectures, readings, and feasts organized by the vicarage, the villagers often preferred the public house with its dance tent. The clergy also organized feasts and entertainments to mark both local and national occasions, such as the births and deaths at the manor, the church festivals, and the various victories which marked the expansion of the British Empire. Doubtless the clergy were happy to take a hand in organizing these occasions for their entertainment and leisure value (concepts which were growing in significance in Victorian society), but the latent functions of social control and order were never far from their minds. It was the clergy to whom, in the words of John Sandford, 'the State looks, to be the conservators of public morals and the guardians of public peace'.[51]

In the third quarter of the nineteenth century, the changed conception of the clergyman's role with its stronger emphasis on his sacral and spiritual duties made many clergy cautious of accepting the Lord Lieutenant's invitation. As one handbook author wrote: '. . . but if he deliberately accepts a commission to be a Justice and divider over the people, then good-bye to his priestly influence.'[52] Another reason for the relative decline in clerical Justices lay in the increasing demands which public expectation made of the clergyman's (and the Justice's) role at this time. Armstrong had to appear before the Justices in a dispute over some rectorial glebe:

> Two of the magistrates, well known to me, were clergymen. I could not help thinking they had mistaken their vocation. They were not distinguished by any clerical dress and here they were discussing sewers with the keenest and liveliest interest while one of them has a large parish and no school, and the other two parishes with only one Sunday service in each although having a curate.[53]

In the third quarter of the nineteenth century, a number of factors made the clergy less willing to serve as magistrates and the Lord Lieutenants less likely to ask them. First, a campaign of considerable strength was waged in the popular press against clerical magistrates, which reached its height in

May 1873, when two clerical magistrates at Chipping Norton convicted sixteen women for intimidating blackleg labour. The sentences, which varied from seven to ten days' imprisonment, caused a national outcry. A Bill was introduced in the House of Commons seeking to disqualify the clergy from being magistrates, but it failed.[54] Second, the expectations of the clergyman's role (which increasingly centred on his sacral and spiritual functions) entertained by the clergy and the nation at large found the conjoining of the ministerial and magisterial office increasingly repugnant.

In Warwickshire in the early 1830s, 40 per cent of the magistrates were clergy. However, in 1837, Sir J. E. Eardley-Wilmot, Chairman of the County Quarter Sessions, declared himself in principle against their appointment, but conceded that in some areas it was a necessity in the absence of other candidates. His successor, the Earl of Warwick, was equally opposed to their appointment, and by 1868, the clergy constituted only 7 per cent of the Warwickshire Bench.[55] Country doctors were often selected to replace the clergy on the Bench.

In 1856, the County and Borough Police Act extended the police, who had previously been organized only in urban centres, to the whole country. Although initially their numbers were small and their effect was limited, there was no longer a need for the clergy to assume responsibility for such matters. But the clergy continued to act as moral 'policemen' in the local community and were particularly harsh against 'vice'. Lee Warner, incumbent of Tarrant Gunville in the 1870s, said that girls who so disgraced themselves could not expect mercy or pity. He would not 'church' them and he enlisted the aid of the squire to evict the chronically immoral.[56]

In the 1860s and 1870s, the clergyman devoted an increasing proportion of his time to promoting the large number of parochial organizations and societies and the local branches of supra-parochial institutions, which were found in many parishes. The importance attached to these organizations can be seen by the number of village halls which were erected in this period to provide suitable accommodation for the meetings of the societies, penny readings, lectures, shows, talks, and concerts. The increase in leisure time and the moral seriousness of the period combined to place the clergyman at the head of a wide variety of activities which had both an educational and a recreational dimension. Many of these activities were no doubt organized for the pleasure and instruction they gave, but there is little doubt that the clergyman's enthusiasm for penny readings, magic lantern shows, libraries, concerts, 'bright hours', lectures, evening schools, and allotments was not unrelated to his concern for the maintenance of stability and order in a countryside where drunkenness and brutality were still chronic social diseases.

A concern with class and the possibility of an impending class conflict was a distinctive element of much of the social philosophy of this period. The classic Marxist documents were written in this country at this time. Unlike the separately educated and celibate Roman Catholic clergy, who were to a degree set apart from the class structure, the clergy of the Church of England have at all times been intimately involved in the social hierarchy on the basis of family connections, property, and education. However, in the second half of the nineteenth century, there was a tendency among the clergy to stress the importance of the reconciling and mediating role of the clergy between the different classes of society. Some clergymen had stressed this function before. J. B. Sumner wrote in 1820:

> Take away the minister of the gospel and who will remain to stand between the employer and his labourer, between the magistrate and the offender . . . the minister forms the connecting link between the different ranks and degrees of society, the cornerstone of our political and social fabric.[57]

It was particularly among those clergy influenced by the Tractarian Movement that there arose a belief that the clergy should be outside the social hierarchy, and free to mediate between the rich and the poor. Harry Jones observed that the clergyman must abandon authority based on social position in favour of spiritual authority, if he were to mediate between the duke and the ploughboy. 'This right, however, is restricted or denied, and wisely, too, to those who desert their proper standing ground and affect an influence akin to the country gentleman rather than the parish priest.'[58] It is hard to believe that the poor regarded the clergy in any other light than as an element of the country gentry, and that they were willing to lay disputed matters before their incumbent. The agricultural labourer of this period was more inclined to look to the new trade unions for help in his struggle with the farmer. In many respects the notion of the clergy, as social mediators, was part of the nostalgic longing for the un-corrupted harmonious countryside with its idyllic social relationships which occupied the minds of many clergy in the second half of the nineteenth century as they grappled with the impact of urbanization.

In traditional societies, the maintenance of order and control is invariably the function of religious leaders, yet it was a particular configuration of circumstances which made this function of such significance for the role of the clergy in the late eighteenth century and the nineteenth. Between the gradual breakup of the traditional rural communal society with its strong paternalistic authoritarianism, and the emergence of modern forms of social control, there existed a period when the clergy found themselves pushed forward as the bastion against widespread civil disorder and even possible revolution. In the late eighteenth century, as the role of the clergyman progressively approximated that of the country gentleman, it was natural that the clergy should accept this duty. It is hard to underestimate the significance of the joining of the magisterial and ministerial roles in the early decades of the nineteenth century for the development of the clergyman's role and its place in society. In the tense air of 1833 the *Quarterly Review* warned those landowners who were inclined towards resentment of the tithes that for all its imperfections, the Church had one great virtue: 'It maintains order.'[59]

The changes which occurred in the middle decades of the nineteenth century in the clergyman's role sought to emphasize its consecrated and spiritual character, its distinctive tasks, skills and lifestyle, and as a result the clergy's attitude to this element of their role underwent considerable change.

However, it is clear that old attitudes persisted among many of the clergy. J. H. Blunt wrote in 1864: 'Wise politicians set a high value upon the clergy of the Church of England, as the most effective national police that exists, but for which crime would extend enormously.'[60] But many clergy now clearly saw that their role was of a different nature. James Russell Woodforde, when addressing students at Cuddesdon, said: 'We repudiate the notion that the clergyman is a State's officer of morality and assert him to be the keybearer of eternity, the minister of Christ, the steward of the mysteries of God.'[61] And Charles Kingsley, when addressing a meeting of clergy, said:

> It is our fault, our great fault, that you should sneer, sneer at the only news that ought to be your glory and your strength. It is our fault. We have used the Bible as if it were the special constable's handbook – an opium dose for keeping beasts of burden patient while they are being overloaded – a mere book to keep the poor in order.[62]

By the last quarter of the nineteenth century, English society had begun to take on a recognizably modern form, and the old constraints of its feudal and pre-industrial past were gradually losing their significance. As English society was transformed from an agglomeration of local communities, in the decades after the Industrial Revolution, into an increasingly urban society, so the old forms and personnel of social control slowly gave place to the technical devices, the statistical and bureaucratic procedures, the legal provisions, and the appropriate professional personnel, which are the means of social control in an advanced society.

12

Almoner

The Christian tradition has always regarded the poor as
having a particular claim on the Church's sympathy and
assistance. In the Ordering of Deacons it states:

> And furthermore, it is his office, where provision is so
> made, to search for the sick, poor, and impotent people in
> the parish, to intimate their estates, names, and places
> where they dwell unto the Curate, that by his exhortation
> they may be relieved with the alms of the Parishioners, or
> others.

In the eighteenth century there were three principal sources
from which the needs of the poor were met and the clergy
played a prominent part in all three. Under the Elizabethan
poor laws, a rate was levied in every parish according to the
decision of the Vestry, of which the clergyman was chairman. The money was made available, through the overseers
of the poor, for those who had a settlement in that parish,
either by means of outdoor relief, or by lodgement in a
poorhouse or workhouse. Second, there was the informal
system of charitable relief. This came either from endowments or from charitable trusts, usually administered by
the incumbent and churchwardens. Third, the poor could
always resort to making personal pleas to the beneficence of
the local gentry. Owing to the parsimony of local vestries and
the maladministration of local charities, the beneficence of
the local gentry played an important part in the lives of the
poor, particularly during the winter months. It was part of
the expectation of the role of the country gentleman that he
should protect the people who lived in the village from the
worst privations of disease, cold weather, bad housing, and
inadequate food. As the role of the clergyman progressively
approximated to that of the country gentleman in the
eighteenth century, and as men of higher birth and wider

means were ordained, it was expected that the clergy should also provide doles of food, soup, blankets, and clothes. By the second half of the eighteenth century it had clearly become a part of the public expectation of the clergyman's role that he should act in this way. It was recognized in the handbooks of the early period that relieving the poor was an appropriate duty for the clergyman, but, at a time of slender clerical incomes, it was not suggested that he should do this himself. George Herbert placed the emphasis on employment, and suggested that the clergyman should take care that 'there be not a beggar or idle person in his parish but that all be in a competent way of getting their living'.[1] Gilbert Burnet wrote: '. . . inquire into its [the parish's] necessities if they seem very poor, so that those to whom that care belongs may be put in mind to see how they may be relieved'.[2] The advice of the early handbooks was summed up by Gerard: 'It is incumbent on a minister to search out the poor and indigent in his parish and to contrive means of supplying them.'[3]

The Elizabethan poor laws were the foundation of the legal and social administrative systems of the country in the eighteenth century, and were the formal system for relieving the necessities of the poor. They placed great reliance on the parish as the unit of local government, and the parish officers as amateur unpaid administrators. The system was controlled by the Justices, and administered by the churchwardens, overseers of the poor, masters and mistresses of the workhouse, and the constables. In effect it meant that the problems of the poor and the unemployed were consigned to the hands of local interest and the parochial jealousy of the Vestry. The chief concern of the Vestry was to keep the poor rate as low as possible and to drive out of the parish anyone who might become a burden on the rates. Consequently, landowners were cautious about building or improving cottages in case more people gained a settlement (a year's residence), and subsequently became a burden on the poor rate of that parish. It was for this reason that, although a labourer might work for a single employer for his whole life, if he lived outside the parish he was dismissed and hired anew each Michaelmas, so that he never gained a settlement in his employer's parish.

Although the legislation of 1722–3 had permitted groups of parishes to build workhouses and apply what was known as the workhouse test, throughout the middle decades of the eighteenth century parishes found it easier and cheaper to give outdoor relief to the sick and aged, and to find work for the able-bodied within the parish. The underlying motive of the Elizabethan legislation was stability, with its emphasis on the parish as the unit responsible for its own people. The settlement system made it almost impossible for a man to leave the place of his birth, whatever the conditions. The system worked within the limitations of its amateur administrators throughout the greater part of the century, but was not adaptable to the new conditions which arose in its last decades, and in the early years of the nineteenth century, as a result of the rise in population, the movement to the towns, and the progressive inflation caused by the Napoleonic Wars. Pauperism rose at a steep rate during the war years (1783 to 1815), and correspondingly there was a sharp increase in poor rate expenses, from £1½ million in 1776; £2 million in 1786; £4 million in 1803; to over £6 million in 1812.[4] An attempt to meet the problem of under-employment, particularly in rural areas, was a system known as the Speenhamland policy (which was started in Berkshire in 1795, and eventually extended to most of southern England), whereby a labourer's wages were made up to a certain fixed minimum. It resulted in the farmers employing their labour force at a very low rate and at the same time receiving high wartime prices for their produce. This period was one of considerable prosperity for the farmers, and also for the clergy as glebe and tithe owners.

In this the formal system of relief, the clergyman as the chairman of the Vestry, the principal organ of local administration, was able to play an important part in ameliorating the lot of the poor, by using his authority to direct as best he could their decisions, and by attending the paying out of the dole. Gisborne wrote in 1795:

Abuses which take place in the administration of particular affairs may frequently be corrected by the prudent interposition of the clergyman; and by his influence with those who are either not interested in their continuance or are obstinately averse to co-operate in redressing them.[5]

An example of the clergyman mediating between the parish authorities and the poor is provided by Benjamin Newton, who heard from a man with a complaint against the parish overseer that he had not received the relief due to him. Next day the overseer came with his book to prove his innocence.[6] James Woodforde helped a man who had escaped from a workhouse where he was barely kept alive.[7] Although documented examples of such action on the part of the clergy are few, there can be little doubt that they were in a position to assist the poor by influencing the parochial administration in their favour.

The first element of the informal system of relieving the poor, the parochial charities, can be divided into two parts: the sacrament money (money collected at the service of Holy Communion), and the trust funds and other charitable endowments. Gisborne recommended that the clergyman should make sure that the sacrament money was distributed appropriately.[8] On 4 January 1818 Newton rode around his parish distributing the sacrament money together with some charity money, so that every poor family had fifteen shillings.[9] When T. T. Carter arrived at Clewer, the sacrament money was distributed by the churchwardens at the end of the service to the poor who attended, which had the effect of preventing the poor from attending for fear of appearing as beggars.[10] With regard to the parochial charities, Bishop Secker wrote in his Charge of 1753: '. . . I hope you . . . will think yourselves bound, if not in law, yet in conscience, to take joint care with the churchwardens, of the parochial charities.'[11]

The majority of the parishes had some form of charitable endowment which the original donor had intended for the poor. McClatchey recorded that of 160 answers to Bishop Smallwell's parochial inquiries between 1793 and 1799, only fifty-five recorded that there were no parochial charities. In a large number the incumbent of the parish had been nominated as sole or joint trustee or executor. The general impression is that although some of these charities were well husbanded and used in accordance with the intentions of the donor, some were diverted to other purposes and many lapsed altogether. [12] This was the result of the widespread non-residence of incumbents, and the apathy of curates, together with their inability to fight expensive legal battles with the executors on behalf of the poor. However, the poor of some parishes were particularly well served by their endowments. In South Moulton, for instance, forty penny loaves were distributed every Sunday. [13] The general impression that the eighteenth-century clergy were lax in their administration of parochial charities was confirmed by the Charity Commissioners' reports of the early nineteenth century, which instanced many examples of charities that had gone into abeyance through the neglect of the clergy.

The principal part of the informal system of providing for the poor in the second half of the eighteenth century was the charitable gifts and doles which they received from the country gentry. The public expectation of the role of the country gentleman was that he should be prepared to support the villagers in particularly harsh times and always be ready to help in individual cases of hardship or misfortune. The constant feature of the life of James Woodforde was his readiness to meet cases of ill-health or misfortune with an appropriate gift of money, food, or other supplies. Although it would be misleading to take Woodforde as in any way typical (he was both single and wealthy, with an annual income of approximately £300), yet it seems that the clergy as gentlemen *ex officio* recognized the obligation to dispense charitable gifts according to their means. However, early Evangelical clergy were often men of slender means, and thus their ability to dispense charity was limited. But the charitable activities of the second and third generation of Evangelicals has been well recognized, for many consigned large proportions of their income to charitable projects. Conyers of Helmsley married John Thornton's widow and together they distributed food, clothing, and medicine to the poor, and in years of bad harvest they bought in large stocks of corn against the winter. [14] Cadogan, at Reading, went about on Saturdays with his pockets full of silver, and supplied the poor with meat and broth in winter. [15] In his two

Leicestershire parishes Henry Ryder, the Evangelical Dean of Wells, ran a soup kitchen and periodically distributed clothes.[16] But among the Evangelicals there was a distinct preference for performing this duty through the new associations and societies for visiting and relieving the poor. These agencies, with the employment of full-time lay district visitors, recognized the limited effect of random acts of personal charity, and brought in the first elements of rationalism and professionalism. The development of visiting societies was an appropriate response in the face of increasing urbanization, as the societies provided a means by which the gifts of the gentry, mainly living in rural areas, could reach the working-class urban areas.

The manifest function of this section of the clergyman's role was generally understood to be the relief of the sufferings of fellow human beings as an expression of Christian charity. The disinterested giving of alms has always been regarded as an important element in the Christian spiritual life. However, charity has certain social effects. By relieving the sufferings of the poor before they embarked on socially disruptive behaviour, charity had the latent function of maintaining the stability of the social order. Certainly, at the time of the French Revolution, there was a greater sensitivity among the upper classes to the distress of the poor, together with more serious attempts to alleviate widespread suffering. The periods of most severe hardship gave rise to Sir Thomas Bernard's Society for Bettering the Condition of the Poor, founded in 1796, and the Association for the Relief of the Manufacturing and Labouring Poor, founded in 1811.[17] It is important not to impute motive, for certainly Evangelical piety and humanitarian concern played their full part, but the evidence suggests that some contemporaries were fully aware of the social effects of charity.

The Poor Law system of the eighteenth century continued into the earlier part of the nineteenth century, with the single modification that, in 1819, the Select Vestry Act permitted those who paid the highest rates to gain administrative control, but only one-fifth of the parishes adopted this practice. However, the circumstances of the second and third decades of the nineteenth century were different from those that had prevailed before the Napoleonic Wars. The agricultural boom that had accompanied the war years was followed by a slump, and much of the marginal land into which capital had been extravagantly sunk became unprofitable, and reverted to heath or moor. The rising population, and the drift towards the urban areas, helped to create social problems with which the old Poor Law system was inadequate to deal. Pauperism increased at a considerable rate, particularly in the depressed rural areas of the southern counties, where the whole labour force was underemployed. The difficulties were accentuated by the currency derangements of the period, which provoked the collapse of many small banks in country towns as well as continuing inflation. On all sides it was agreed that there was something wrong with a system of relief which was so inordinately expensive, and often administered by illiterate farmers and self-interested publicans.[18] A village in Buckinghamshire, in 1822, spent eight times what the administration of the Poor Law had cost in 1795.[19] Between 1792 and 1831, Poor Law expenditure in the county of Dorset increased by 214 per cent compared with a 40 per cent rise in the population.[20]

The reform of the Poor Law system by Edwin Chadwick and the commissioners forms a classic example of the impact of bureaucratic methods upon social administration caused by the increasing scale and complexity of English society and the use of professional standards, practice, and personnel. Chadwick replaced the old locally based system with a new hierarchical system accountable to the commissioners in London, and manned by trained professional full-time government agents. Before the commissioners' first term of office expired in 1839, the new system of union of parishes under Boards of Guardians elected by ratepayers had been extended to 95 per cent of England and Wales. The principle of the system was simple; by the establishment of workhouses, which were in theory self-supporting, and the abolition of outdoor relief, the relief of the poor could be carried out at the minimum of expense to ratepayers. From 1834, the pauper was confronted with the simple dilemma of starving in his own home or entering the workhouse and facing the inevitable breakup of his family. However, a series of good harvests after 1834, and some small wage increases, made matters easier in the early years of the new system. For the present purpose it is not necessary to chart the effect of this legislation in any detail, but merely to state that the cessation of outdoor relief made the new Poor Law system unworkable in urban areas, and it met with the strongest opposition from all sections of the working classes. It also provided additional material for the chartist campaigners. Moreover, local magistrates in northern counties steadfastly refused to co-operate, and many others were reluctant to press such inflammatory measures. By the 1840s a large proportion of the relief given was still in the form of outdoor payments.[21]

The clergy, through the 1834 legislation, were robbed of the central position which they had hitherto held in the formal system of relieving the poor. They could stand as candidates for the Board of Governors (whose actual powers were very limited), and a number did. However, many considered the new Poor Law unjust in theory and harsh and unworkable in practice. Also they regretted that the traditional function of obtaining relief for the poor had been alienated from the Church. None the less, some were willing to stand as Guardians; Richard Seymour wrote in his journal on 4 April 1843: 'I attended the Board – did not like some of the proceedings which seemed harsh.'[22] The new conception of the clergyman's role which was gaining ground at this time made the clergy less anxious to be involved in the administration of the new system. Richard Durnford was typical of the new generation of clergy; he constantly refused approaches to have him elected to the Board.[23] Also there can be no doubt that, at a time when the clergy came to be more dependent upon the good will of the people, many clergy had no wish to be involved in matters so certain to give rise to local animosity. However, some were willing to face this. Julius Hare was a guardian in Sussex, though 'there was the most ceaseless ferment and outcry against him'.[24] But in the main, the duty of relieving the needs of the poor in its formal aspect passed from the clergy to a professional government official.

It was the very harshness of the new formal system which

gave the clergyman's position in the informal system of relief a new importance. The parochial clergyman in the 1840s and 1850s found himself as the only charitable agent between the pauper and the workhouse. Thus, the typical clergyman put himself at the head of a wide variety of provident institutions and clubs all designed to help the labourer to help himself, and keep him from the workhouse. The institutions which the clergy so actively established had their roots in the work of such eighteenth-century philanthropists as Mrs Trimmer of Brentford and Hannah More at Cheddar. These pioneers established the forerunners of a vast number of provident and saving organizations which grew up in response to the situation created by the new Poor Law system. They arose in the first place because public opinion had turned away from doles and charity in favour of self-help. The withdrawal of outdoor parish relief had been a product of the new social philosophy which considered that such relief, together with the generosity of the gentry, had actually encouraged pauperism.

The clergy of the middle years of the nineteenth century gave a great deal of their time to establishing and organizing these institutions. No parish organization would have been considered complete without its Penny or Savings Bank, Provident Society, Coal Club, Blanket Lending Society, Rent and Shoe Club, and some form of Clothing Club. It is not necessary for the details of these clubs to be outlined here. Almost all were designed to be run personally by the clergyman or his family; the members paid in sums over the year and interest was paid (with money collected from the gentry or given by the clergyman). At certain times of the year the incumbent made goods available to subscribers at substantially reduced prices. These institutions formed an essential part of the work of a clergyman in the eyes of contemporaries and much effort was expended in their administration. The aim of the clergy in organizing these institutions was stated by Sandford:

> His object will be to confer the greatest amount of benefit, in the best way and for the longest time. He will aim not at the relief which is merely superficial but at supplying, if

possible, a radical and lasting remedy for the social ills under which he sees the poor to labour. His aim will be, to ameliorate their social and physical condition and to raise them, as much as possible, in the scale of humanity; and with this view, he will labour to secure them the friendly offices of their richer brethren and above all to help them to help themselves. [25]

However, the friendly societies were conceived within the terms of, and in the spirit of, the old order, and these essentially mid-nineteenth-century institutions owe much to the social philosophy of the last years of the eighteenth century. Often they were administered with condescension, the conditions were sometimes humiliating, and there was frequently strict censorship of purchases. Above all, at a time when it was believed by many people who were neither stupid nor inhumane that in the last resort a man must live by his own efforts and final responsibility must not be removed from him, the policy exaggerated the degree to which the poor were capable of helping themselves. Doubtless the parochial institutions helped many, particularly at times of illness or misfortune, but there remained a degree of abject poverty at the bottom of society which was untouched by such a policy. [26]

As has been noted above, there is considerable evidence to suggest that contemporary clergy were fully aware of the powerful position in which circumstances had placed them in the middle years of the nineteenth century. The labourers found themselves in a real sense dependent upon the provident institutions and the clergy were able, as administrators of these organizations, to sanction irreligious or disrespectful behaviour. The picture of the managing clergyman and his formidable wife ruling the local community dates from this period. Behaviour of which the incumbent or his wife disapproved could be punished by the withdrawal of charities or expulsion from the provident societies with the subsequent forfeiting of money already deposited. Joseph Arch recalled the effect of his mother's disobedience of the vicar's wife (which in part accounted for the strong anti-clericalism which characterized Arch's work to improve the lot of the agricultural workforce): '. . . from that time my parents never received a farthing's worth of charity in the way of soup, coals, or the like which were given regularly as a matter of course from the rectory to nearly every person in the village.'[27] The Hon and Revd S. Best gives three examples of the social control exercised by the provident society in his parish. A young woman, who was called as a witness before a magistrate, admitted being out after dark in a beer shop with 'loose' company. She was censured and warned that a similar offence would precipitate expulsion from the provident society. A copy of the censure was sent to her parents and fixed up in a public place. In the second instance, cockfighting was started in a village and a public warning was issued that anyone involved would be expelled from the provident society. The cockfighting soon ceased. In the third case, a petty felon was expelled and her money was forfeited to the general fund.[28]

Allotments typified the assistance which the clergy gave to their parishioners. By letting out their glebes at moderate rents the clergy were able to provide the labourer with the means of helping himself. Many clergy used this means of promoting 'self-help'. Allotments were regarded as important, for they attached the labourer to the soil and taught him to respect the rights of property, in which he could now feel a personal interest. They were frequently allocated in such a way as to encourage a pattern of approved behaviour and were withheld as a punishment. As Best writes:

> As a privilege it may be made dependent on the performance of duties of a higher nature, and the school list, the sacrament list, and even the provident society may be looked through to determine who shall have the offer of the next vacant allotment.[29]

It was reported to the commissioners inquiring into the Poor Laws in 1834 that the practice of letting small plots of land to labourers 'has become almost universal in Northamptonshire, the clergyman being in general the person who has the thing on foot'.[30] Certainly, the dream of solving the social problems of the country by converting a large section of the poor into smallholders living happy moral lives upon the produce of spade husbandry, has a long history.

The question of whether the clergy should be involved in the distribution of the formal Poor Law relief or indeed any form of relief was one which divided their ranks at this time. Many regretted that the central position in the Poor Law system had been taken from the clergyman and was occupied by a professional government officer. Such men looked particularly to Dr Chalmers's achievements in Glasgow and his evidence before the Select Committee on the Irish Poor Law (1830). Others looked, if somewhat romantically, to the system of relief which had operated in medieval Europe, to almshouses, to Sisters of Charity and to the re-establishment of the diaconate. But the majority, whilst anxious to promote provident institutions, were against the involvement of the clergy in any free distribution of doles or charity whether in the formal or the informal system, and were pleased to have been relieved from compulsory involvement in administering the Poor Laws. The clergy became particularly anxious to be regarded exclusively as ministers of the gospel by their parishioners, and were concerned that there should be no confusion in the eyes of their parishioners between their spiritual functions and the mundane functions of the relieving officer. A report of the Alcester Clerical Meeting stated: 'As to the personal ministry of Almsgiving it was strongly felt by some that injury had resulted from the popular idea entertained of him as the mere dispenser of charity. This confusion between the priest and the almoner was much to be deprecated.'[31] Evans warned in his handbook against 'the vulgar and cheaply earned reputation of giving much to the poor', as did Bishop Kaye in his Charge of 1846.[32]

So the clergy who had formerly so often relieved the needs of their poor parishioners from their own pockets, now in the main ceased to hand out personal gifts and dole for fear that such activities would excite expectations in their parishioners that detracted from the spiritual nature of the clergyman's role. However, the clergy remained intimately involved in the problems of the poor, and worked with great zeal to promote provident institutions. Certainly, when the

Church needed to defend itself in the eyes of the nation, one of the platforms in its argument was the social utility of its role as the almoner of the poor. An anonymous author of a pamphlet defending the Church of England in 1835 wrote:

How many a needy supplicant has had his wants relieved, his necessaries administered to by the clergyman of his parish. How many a drooping family verging on starvation has been raised from the earth and placed in a state of comparative comfort by the timely aid afforded by the minister of the Church of England. [33]

The many provident societies and clubs which had formed such a conspicuous part of the activities of the clergy in the third and fourth decades of the nineteenth century continued to play an integral part in the organization of a well-run parish through the following decades and even into the early years of the twentieth century. Armstrong recorded that on 8 September 1857 he attended a meeting of the savings bank and heard that £4100 had been deposited in three years in his parish. On 11 December 1861 he drew up the report of the Clothing Club and, recorded that, in the year, 362 poor contributors had saved £109.15s. [34]

At the same time, the tendency noted above to abandon indiscriminate almsgiving and to give assistance only in the form of providing 'self-help' institutions, or when it was directly related to the performance of 'duties', gathered more strength in the mid-decades of the nineteenth century. J. C. Miller wrote in his handbook sentiments which would have amazed the clergy of the late eighteenth century: 'Our indiscriminate almsgiving and many of our parish doles have wrought great social mischief in pauperizing our people.' [35] In this period it became axiomatic that to give charity without knowing the circumstances of the case was to encourage pauperism and mendacity. Clothing Clubs and allotments were increasingly tied to the performance of 'duties'. The informal system of relieving the poor was now almost wholly comprised of self-help agencies, and very little direct relief was now given. The spirit of the times was summed up in the Hon Mrs J. C. Talbot's instructions to parochial mission women: '. . . endeavour to benefit those lowest poor *not* by almsgiving but by leading them to feel that they are able still to help and raise themselves.'[36] Among the efforts to this end the most outstanding was that of Robert Gregory, incumbent of St Peter's, Vauxhall, an extremely poor area in the 1860s. Discerning a high level of unemployment among the women, he formed a needlework society and took out government contracts. In his first year, 1862, 13,000 shirts were made; in 1865 he delivered 60,000, and by the end of the decade was making 100,000 shirts and several thousand greatcoats a year.[37] The collapse of cottage industries in the middle of the century, particularly lace-making, left many young women and widows without the means of providing for themselves. The many sewing meetings and the needlework societies were in part a response by the vicarage to this need.

There is evidence to suggest that, during the nineteenth century, the clergy were anxious to win back the charitable trusts and parochial endowments which had previously been lost. However, these were no longer given out as doles at the church door after the service, in the manner of the previous century. On 16 December 1854 Armstrong of East Dereham caused a considerable stir by breaking the long-hallowed local tradition of giving out 400 charity loaves in church on St Thomas's Day, when the church was crammed and many 'undeserving' people received the dole. Armstrong rode round the parish the day before, making the distribution to those whom he considered deserved it.[38] When Vaughan Thomas, Vicar of Yarnton, drew up a schedule for the Alderman Fletcher Charity in January 1855 the last section read: 'To conclude; it is recommended that in making out the lists of the year, all persons whose conduct during the past year has been wicked, should be dropped out of the charity lists.'[39]

An important development in the middle decades of the nineteenth century was the increasing realization by the clergy that any activity associated with relieving the poor tended to undermine the spiritual role by associating the clergyman primarily with matters of relief rather than the preaching of the gospel. It was natural that the clergy should be anxious to be received by their parishioners in their own

right rather than as almoners and relieving officers, and they
increasingly followed the advice that Robert Simpson had
given some years earlier: 'In visiting the sick poor, it is better
not to administer temporal relief at that time but rather to
direct the district visitor to call and relieve them. The
minister's visit should not be looked for from any desire for
pecuniary assistance.'[40] W. W. Champneys advised the
clergyman to leave matters of relief entirely in the hands of
district visitors. 'It enables him to go more purely as the
spiritual teacher, as the man of God when he is not expected
as the almoner.'[41] And John Burgon's opinion was very
similar: 'There is the danger of sinking the Priestly office in
that of the relieving officer and encouraging the poor in
habits of dependence and covetousness.'[42] Thus the clergy
progressively abandoned direct involvement in matters of
relief when it was clear that it damaged and undermined
what they now came to see as the essential and central part
of the clergyman's professional role. Exhorted by the
Evangelicals and the Tractarians in the pursuit of holiness,
they turned their back on all sections of their former role
which might detract from this end. Above all they did not
want their parishioners to tolerate their spiritual message
merely for the sake of gifts and charity which they might
receive. At the same time doubts were expressed about one of
the basic assumptions of earlier pastoral strategy that the
sympathies of the poor could be engaged by appropriate
charities. Oxenden wrote in 1857: 'Many suppose that a
clergyman's influence for good is in proportion to his means
of giving and that silver and gold pave the way to the heart.
There is no greater fallacy than this.'[43]

13
Teacher

Analytically at least, if not always in practice, it is possible to distinguish between the teaching of non-religious subjects and religious instruction. This chapter is concerned with the clergyman as a teacher of non-religious subjects. The chapters entitled 'Catechist' and 'Preacher' have recorded the work of the clergy as religious instructors. In traditional societies it was common for such formal instruction as the children received to be given by the religious leader, and for all teaching to have a sacred character. An element in the secularization of society is the division of teaching material into sacred and secular categories, and the development of a separate body of teachers who make these latter subjects their particular concern. The movement of institutional differentiation manifested itself in the slow separation of religion from formal involvement in educational institutions. A part of this process can be seen at work in the nineteenth century when the direct involvement of the Church and its agents in the process and matter of education progressively diminished.

In the mid-eighteenth century no man could work as a schoolteacher without the licence of the diocesan bishop (the canon was not widely enforced, but a judgement of 1795 upheld the bishop's right to license teachers). No school could be established in a parish without the permission of the Ordinary (and by contrast this right was insisted on). University fellows and the masters of public and grammar schools were almost all clergymen of the Established Church. However, by the 1870s, the principle of secular non-denominational education had been incorporated into legislation by Parliament; university fellows and school-masters were no longer required to be clergymen; and the teaching profession had established itself as a separate professional body.

Despite the fact that the historic connection between education and the Christian Church, as the institution primarily concerned with literacy, had existed for centuries, and that teaching was a traditional and widely recognized function of religious leaders, this element of the clergyman's role was not a part of the charter role. In the Ordination service the clergyman promised to teach the people out of the Bible; this function he performed as a catechist and preacher. This element of the role, as some nineteenth-century handbooks were at pains to point out, though it receives quasi-legitimation through traditional usage, was not performed on the basis of the authority of the Ordinal. This chapter is not a history of the Church's extensive contribution to education in the eighteenth and nineteenth centuries, but rather an analysis of the relative importance of this function in the development of the clergyman's role throughout the period.

It is helpful to divide the work of the clergy in this element of their role between their involvement in the education of the sons of the wealthy, upon which many clergy were dependent for a significant proportion of their income, and their participation in parochial education, which in the eighteenth century consisted almost entirely of charity schools and such parochial schools as were run by individual clergymen. The most common form of secondary education for the sons of substantial farmers and the gentry, before the widespread popularity of the public schools in the second half of the nineteenth century, was to reside for a few years in the house of a clergyman, who for a fee undertook to prepare a number of young men for the university. For this reason a clergyman considered a living with a large and suitable rectory to be a particularly favourable piece of preferment. Thomas Twining recorded that, until 1755, he was under the charge of the Revd Palmer Smythies who prepared him for Cambridge.[1] In the late eighteenth century the Revd Dr Robinson ran a school in Westmorland which numbered twenty clergymen among its old boys.[2] In 1756, the churchwardens of Cullompton proceeded against the vicar for his consistent breach of Canon 41 (non-residence). The vicar ran a school for 'noblemen and gentlemen's sons' in Hampstead. His defence was that as the Earl of Strathmore's domestic chaplain, he was exempt from residence. However, the prosecution were able to produce an advertisement for the school, which declared that the vicar 'devoted the greatest part of his time to their service'. Having lost the case the vicar resigned his living in favour of the school.[3] Frequently the Evangelical clergy were forced to accept the poorer parishes and they used this sytem of private education to great effect, both as a means of making up their small stipends, and of evangelizing. Among the most famous of these establishments was that of the Revd Rawson at Seaforth at which Gladstone and Dean Stanley were pupils; that of the Revd Newcome at Hackney, which Stratford Canning and Mr Creevy attended; and the Revd Reston's school at Little Shelford where T. B. Macaulay was educated.[4]

The sons of the nobility and gentry, who did not attend these establishments, had private tutors who prepared them at home for university, accompanied them there, and on the grand tour of Europe. The bond between the tutor and his pupils' family was often strong, and many tutors, when their years of usefulness were over, received handsome preferment at the hand of their former pupil. For a young clergyman to attach himself to an aristocratic family was a widely recognized and much used means of obtaining preferment, often in later life beyond the rank of a beneficed clergyman.[5]

The poor stipends of eighteenth-century curacies, customarily no more than half a guinea per Sunday, forced those who could not gain preferment to look elsewhere for remuneration. Canon law permitted the clergy to teach for profit, and many curates chose to supplement their slender income by becoming ushers at the local grammar school. The headmastership of the grammar schools was usually held by an incumbent (an office which, at the time, constituted a sufficient reason for non-residence), and the ushers lived at the school, travelling on Saturdays to their churches. At Hull the Evangelical Joseph Milner was headmaster of a famous grammar school which had forty-six pupils at his death in 1706, and counted among its alumni William Wilberforce, John Venn, and George Hammond.[6]

In the eighteenth century parochial education consisted

mainly of dame schools, which were probably little more than child-minding devices, and such teaching as was done by retired soldiers, or clerks, or craftsmen as a secondary employment. George Crabbe recorded in his poem *The Borough* (1810) a description of Reuben Dixon, a shoemaker, who ran a small school. James Woodforde agreed with the village schoolmaster to have his servants taught to read and write for 4s 6d a quarter.[7] Despite the fact that Canon 78 gave the curate of a parish preference in setting up a school, there is little evidence that the clergy of this period undertook the labour of teaching the children of the parish. An exception was Robert Walker in the Lake District, who taught for five and a half days each week in the church, using the communion table as a desk and spinning wool at the same time.[8]

In terms of education it was the charity or endowed schools which made the most significant contribution to the education of those who could not afford private schooling. Although these schools were mainly confined to urban areas, and the number of children so educated was a relatively small proportion of the whole, they did provide an education for some children of the artisan and working classes. The clergy were invariably concerned with the running of these schools, both as trustees of the endowment, and as teachers. The handbooks of the period exhorted the clergy to maintain their influence over such establishments:

> It will be advisable for you to go to the school and see how the children learn and speak to and encourage them and to direct the mistress privately how to discharge her duty and excite her to it. The presence of the minister of the parish now and then, will quicken both teacher and learner and have a good effect.[9]

The encouragement of the rich to establish a charity school was seen by one handbook author as a duty of the clergyman,[10] but although the establishment of such schools may be seen as a monument to the philanthropy of the age, the numbers educated were relatively small and in many areas of the country there were only limited educational facilities at the end of the eighteenth century.

There can be little doubt that in the main the clergy agreed with the dominant lay view of education which, stressing the stability of the social hierarchy, considered that those born to daily labour had nothing to gain from an education. The duty of the poor was considered to be that of labouring, and the education of such people could only jeopardize such a system. The Bishop of Norwich said, at the annual meeting of the London and Westminster Charity Schools in May 1755:

> There must be drudges of labour (hewers of wood and drawers of water as Scripture calls them) as well as Counsellors to direct and Rulers to preside . . . To which of these classes we belong, especially the inferior ones, our birth determines . . . These children are born to be daily labourers, for the most part to earn their daily bread by the sweat of their brows. It is evident that if such children are, by charity, brought up in such a manner that it is only proper to qualify them for a rank to which they ought not to aspire, such a child would be injurious to the community.[11]

The scriptural protestantism of the Evangelical clergy demanded that every person should be capable of affirming the truths of their religion from the pages of the Bible. The early Evangelicals had been supporters of the charity schools, but the widespread employment of children in agriculture and industry, together with the fees charged by most schools, had made it difficult for the children of the poor to receive any education. The development of the Sunday school, as the principal institution for the education of the poor, provided a cheap solution to this problem. Whilst religious instruction was certainly given in the Sunday schools, it is clear that their manifest objective was to teach people to read. Sunday schools had existed in some places throughout the second half of the eighteenth century, but it was the publication, in 1783, of a pamphlet by Robert Raikes, describing his school in Gloucester, which provided a model that was copied throughout the country. In 1783 Fletcher started six schools at Madeley and Wilson one at Slaithwaite. In 1784 Cornelius Bayley had established a school in his Manchester parish.[12]

Miles Atkinson had organized a system of twenty-eight schools in Leeds by 1785, with fifty-six masters and mistresses, and 2000 scholars, which he personally supervised. By the following year Richardson had established a school in York and other schools were started at Dewsbury, Bradford, and Bingley by Yorkshire Evangelicals.[13] In terms of the clergyman's role the important feature of their early Sunday schools was the high level of the clergyman's involvement in the establishment of these schools, and in the weekly routine of teaching.

The attitude of the majority of the clergy to the early Sunday schools was far from sympathetic. The *Anti-Jacobin Review and Magazine*, supported by many of the Latitudinarian clergy, declared: 'We are no friend to Sunday schools which, we are convinced, have been nurseries of fanaticism . . . We know perfectly well that Sunday schools have in many instances been rendered channels for the diffusion of bad principles, religious and political . . .'[14] Bishop Horsley declared that there was 'much ground for suspicion that sedition and atheism were the real objects of some of these institutions'.[15] Francis Wollaston discovered, and gave considerable publicity to, a Sunday school in operation in his parish, which he considered was run by agents of a Jacobin society.[16] Society at large was shocked to hear that those who were taught to read the Bible in Sunday schools were avidly consuming the works of Tom Paine. In the atmosphere of distrust and suspicion engendered by the events in France, the Latitudinarian clergy, together with other members of the propertied classes, were inclined to regard the illiteracy of the rank and file as an important guarantee of domestic peace.

At the beginning any scheme of parochial education which an incumbent might suggest was liable to meet with the opposition of local farmers, gentry, and neighbouring clergy. But the Sunday schools possessed latent functions, which soon recommended them to the propertied classes. In 1786, Bishop Porteus pointed out that '. . . the extreme depravity and licentiousness which prevails . . . among the lowest orders of the people' could no longer be denied. Their manners and morals had to be reformed else 'our houses cannot secure us from outrage, nor can we rest with safety in our beds.'[17] In her tale called *The Sunday School*, Hannah More pointed out a feature which did not escape the attention of many landowners: 'And it was observed, that as the school filled, not only the fives court and public houses were thinned, but even Sunday gossiping and tea-visiting declined.'[18]

It seems certain that the contribution the Sunday schools made to promoting civil order helped to recommend them to those, who, at first, were inclined to view them with suspicion. The children freed from their work on Sundays constituted a public nuisance, and it was recorded in Painswick, in the 1770s, that farmers were reluctant to leave orchards and buildings unguarded to go to church.[19] The establishment of a Sunday school provided a cheap means of disciplining the children of the poor. Thus, the Sunday school movement soon recommended itself to many outside the ranks of the Evangelical clergy, and in 1787, there were 201 schools affiliated to the Sunday School Society, with 10,232 scholars. By 1797, there were 69,000 scholars in 1082 schools.[20] The report of the clergy of the Lincoln diocese in 1800 stated: '. . . many Sunday schools have been set on foot by the endeavours of the clergy, a great proportion of them at the sole expense of the minister and some taught by themselves.'[21] In 1815, a handbook could speak of Sunday schools as a widespread institution: 'Sunday schools are become so general, that there are, I think, few parishes in the kingdom where they have not been established.'[22]

In the first half of the nineteenth century the clergy continued to act as private tutors to the sons of the wealthy, and to run small private schools in their large rectories. Charles Blomfield (later Bishop of London) was initially famous as a scholar and editor of Greek plays, and educated the sons of the aristocracy for high fees in his rectory.[23] Ashton Oxenden recorded attending such a rectory school.

Mr. Abbott was in some respects a marvellous man. He managed the entire school himself, without the aid of a single usher. He duly flogged us; played at cricket with us; punctually reported us to our parents, and in addition to these unassisted labours, he was actually sole curate of the large parish of St. Lawrence, the mother church of Ramsgate. [24]

Although many instances of 'pupillizing' are to be found in the first half of the nineteenth century (and later), there can be little doubt that the increased value of livings, and the new emphasis on the pastoral element of the clergyman's role, led to a decrease in the number of private schools. At the same time as the public schools were reformed by such head-masters as Arnold, Thring, and Benson, the demand for private education for the sons of the wealthy declined.

The enduring monument to the work of the parochial clergy of the nineteenth century is neither their system of parochial institutions, nor their elaborate restorations of the church, which have not survived subsequent changes in local demand and aesthetic taste. However, the system of parochial primary education which was established largely through their efforts, has in many of its essential features remained unchanged to this day. The primary school, with its separate entrances, its prominent foundation stone (in all probability bearing a date between 1840 and 1870) and the schoolmaster's house attached to it, was considered an essential part of the parochial machinery in the middle of the nineteenth century, and within its walls many incumbents considered much of their most important work was done. In the early decades of the nineteenth century, statesmen, in-dustrialists, property owners, and the clergy were united in the opinion that the education of the children of the lower orders was a question that could no longer be overlooked. The statesman and the property owner realized that the parish machinery, well maintained by a resident clergyman, was one of the cheapest and most efficient agents of social control which the nation possessed. It was clear to many that the parochial school, inculcating the safe principles of con-tentment, thrift, and respect for property, authority, and law, was the clergyman's most effective weapon. Thus, some statesmen would have been willing to adopt the Church of England's system of education for the nation and support it from the rates. At the local level, the substantial property owners were among the most enthusiastic advocates and supporters of village schools. The industrialist and the substantial farmer, whose wealth was dependent upon a well-disciplined work force, with a proper moral sense, which could be relied upon not to 'misuse' leisure, or endanger his heavy capital investment in machinery, acknowledged the contribution that church and chapel could make.[25] At a time when the clergy were beginning to acknowledge that the Church's influence over the nation as a whole was being eroded, the school acted as an agent of evangelism of unparalleled potential, and as a sure means of inculcating church principles into the rising generation. The school, in the mid-nineteenth century, was regarded by the clergy as the single most important element in the parochial machinery. By the 1830s, a parish which did not have a school was universally considered as gravely defective.[26]

Although a systematic plan of national education had been frequently advocated, no such scheme came into being until after 1870. Yet the clergy were conscious of taking part in what amounted to a national movement. For the education movement was complementary to the movement of church extension, and the latter rested in part on the assumption that the lower classes would be educated to worship in the new and expanded church buildings. However, the building of a village school depended upon the initiative and work of the local incumbent. In 1811, the National Society was established for the encouragement and support of church schools. The Society was started as a defensive measure but soon became the Church's principal offensive weapon.[27] The history of the clergy's contribution to primary education is in large measure the history of that society. Between 1811 and 1833, with money raised by public subscription, 7000 schools were built or assisted by the National Society, educating half a million scholars. In 1833 the House of Commons voted grants to the two educational societies for the building of schoolhouses. The number of scholars in schools associated with the National Society had doubled by 1846, and 17,000 new schools were established. In the early 1840s the Committee of the Council for Education claimed the right to inspect schools which received a government grant.

As a reaction to the disquiet of the chartist period a Bill came before Parliament in 1843 which included a section advocating a nationwide system of education supported by the rates, with the parochial clergy. and churchwardens as trustees of the schools. So vehement was dissenting opposition to a Church of England monopoly of education that the portion of the Bill containing these proposals was never passed. The failure of this proposed legislation served to increase the Church's determination to become the educator of the poor, and in the remaining years of the decade, the Church campaigned, as never before, on behalf of the National Society. In 1844, £160,000 was raised to provide schools in populated areas. The last years of the fifth decade were dominated by the division of opinion between those in the National Society, who argued that the Church of England alone should be responsible for education, led by Archdeacon Denison, and supported by many clergy influenced by the Tractarian movement, and those, like W. F. Hook, who argued that the State should take over the schools. Hook was closer to the situation in urban areas, and was convinced that the doctrinaire anti-Erastianism of many clergy, influenced by the Oxford Movement, was a mistake. The Church, he maintained, could never fulfil her pastoral and educational mission without seeking the help of the State.[28]

The establishment and general management of the parochial educational system formed a large section in the handbooks of the first half of the nineteenth century. The authors were united in the opinion that the clergyman who did not concern himself with the education of the poor, and who did not provide schools where there was a deficiency, was seriously failing in his duty. John Sandford subtitled his handbook 'The Church, the School, and the Parish'; J. D. Coleridge considered that the work of a clergyman could be divided between 'the school and the House of God'.[29] The importance accorded to education by the mid-nineteenth-century clergy may be judged from the writing of John Sandford. 'The providing of proper schools for the infant poor is one of a parochial minister's most important duties, and ought to be among the earliest objects of his attention.

Without effective schools his labours can never be extensively or permanently successful.'[30]

In the parishes, during the first half of the nineteenth century, the Sunday schools continued to play an important part, but as they were expanded so the clergy did less of the regular teaching. This was consigned to the growing army of volunteer Sunday school teachers, who undertook the work under the general guidance of the incumbent. However, in the day schools, where, despite the National Society grants and the generosity of the local gentry, the financial position was often difficult, the clergyman (or members of his family) frequently found it necessary to do much of the teaching in order to economize on teachers' salaries. It is difficult to exaggerate the importance which the clergy attached to the school as an instrument of parochial evangelism and as a means of re-establishing their authority in the local community. 'Our work is with the school,' said Alfred Suckling, and he took prayers and taught in his school every day.[31] Thomas Keble held that 'this [the school] was the only way of attaching the children to the church and that through the children was the best avenue of successfully reaching the parents.'[32] The increase in the number of Sunday, day, evening, night, and infant schools at this time was dramatic. John Skinner worked hard to establish a day school in his parish, which would be better than that run by the coalpit managers, but his efforts were plagued by his bad relations with the 'Squiress'.[33] Edward Boys Ellman established six dame-schools as his first act in his parish, in each of which he taught twice a week. He later built a day school.[34] Atkinson had a village school in his remote moorland parish which supported twenty free children and the rest paid according to their educational requirements (3d for reading only; 4d for writing and reading; 5d for the three 'Rs' combined).[35] Robert Wilberforce opened a school for boys and another for girls in his own garden in 1839, and was active in extending the work of the National Society in Yorkshire. He was instrumental in the eventual establishment of a teacher-training college for men at York and for women at Ripon. Nothing conveys better the business of the zealous clergyman than a letter by Samuel Wilberforce's mother in 1831: 'We are rather afraid', she wrote, 'of his overdoing himself on Sundays by going twice a day to the school, besides his two services and his examination of the children after evening service, and he talks of an adult school for boys and young men if he can get it together in order to occupy their evening leisure a little.'[36] Richard Seymour built a school in his own village and another in a neighbouring hamlet was opened in 1839; in that year he was appointed as an examiner of the diocesan board of education. He wrote in his journal on 18 November 1839:

> Went early to the school and stayed from 9 to 12, being very anxious to see things in better order. Miss Howe very excellent and rightminded but wants energy. In the afternoon Fanny [Seymour's wife] went, a boy so unruly that she sent for me and I went and flogged him.[37]

The zeal of the clergy for parochial education can be seen in their efforts to reform the system of employing children in agriculture and industry which prevented them from receiving the benefits of the new schools.[38]

The limiting factor in the expansion of primary education was finance. The clergy often found that their education enterprises did not command the financial support of the middle classes, and that they were dependent on the generosity of the gentry, the children's pence, and such grants as could be obtained. In fact, as the National Society survey in 1847 revealed, the quality of parochial education available in any particular village depended in large measure on the extent to which the incumbent was willing to finance the running of the school.[39] For the village with a comparatively wealthy incumbent, or a squire willing 'to do his duty', the system worked well enough. The Revd Edward Boys Ellman donated almost the whole sum for the building of a school and the schoolmistress's house, in the first year of his marriage.[40] However, at the other end of the scale, the educational work of a poor clergyman was dogged by financial uncertainty. The Revd Robert Lawrence, vicar of Chalgrove from 1832 to 1885, found when he arrived in the village that there was no school and he immediately laid plans to convert two cottages, which belonged to the living.

When his financial position deteriorated, he was no longer able to support the school. He hoped to reopen it with each scholar paying 7s per annum (a richer clergyman would have borne this cost). Unhappily, in 1836, he found that with the alterations in the Poor Law the parents could no longer pay this sum. In consequence, the school was closed within twelve months through lack of funds.[41]

It is not unreasonable to ask why the clergy invested so much of their time, and in many cases a great deal of money, in parochial education. The historian must be cautious about interpreting and simplifying men's motives. Clearly the principal reason for the involvement of the clergy in this work was the belief that ignorance in general, and illiteracy in particular, were the principal obstacles to the working people coming to the church. The schools were used as a means to an end, and that end was in the first instance evangelistic. But as in all matters motives are complex, and there is sufficient evidence to sustain the argument that the clergy also regarded the schools as the most effective means of maintaining social order in the local community at a time when village life was boorish and often brutal. Many clergy have left accounts of the shock they received as they came to terms with the reality of mid-nineteenth-century village life. The handbooks make it plain that this function, so appropriate for a national Church, was understood by contemporaries. Often it was in these terms that the clergy tried to justify their claim to a monopoly of education. Bishop Blomfield declared in the House of Lords that religious education was the most effective police measure a government could adopt.[42] This was a view not shared by the farmers, who were quick to point out that the agricultural riots, and later the unions were frequently led by literate labourers who had received some education in Church Sunday or day schools.[43] The handbooks constantly return to the duty of the school to be an agent of social control and a means of civilizing the parishioners. John Sandford wrote:

> The owners of property will more and more be impressed with the conviction, that the best security for property, as well as life, is the establishment of religion in the hearts of

the people; that the best corrective of chartism is Christianity and the best preventive of socialism Church of England principles.[44]

John Skinner bemoaned the disquiet in his pithead parish and the uncouth nature of his parishioners; 'and it is melancholy to think', he wrote, 'that evil is likely to increase as we have no school to inculcate honest principles.'[45] Simpson emphasized the importance of rescuing the child from the pernicious domestic influence: '. . . if no one interferes on their behalf these poor children will grow up in habits of lying, swearing, and theft, and familiarity with drunkenness, gluttony, and the grossest vice.'[46] In the mid-nineteenth century the schoolhouse came to be the symbol of an orderly and well-managed parish. The building housed not only the day school, but also the night school, the Sunday school, the village lectures, and the meetings of the missionary societies. The schoolroom was the focal point of village life in which the clothing club displayed its wares, the provident societies received contributions, and tickets were handed out for the shoe, coal, and blanket clubs. In the schoolroom, until the later village halls were built, were held the penny readings, lantern shows, musical evenings, harvest suppers, and other festivities which formed the staple of organized parochial leisure activities at this time.

In the twenty years that followed 1850 the enthusiasm of the clergy for parochial education reached its zenith. There can have been few clergymen at that time who were not in some degree involved in the education of the children of the parish. Edward Monro, whose concern with parochial education was as great as any handbook author, wrote of the battle with infidelity: 'Education will be the one great weapon of the contest and if the Church is to do her work, it must be wielding that weapon.'[47] During these years, although there was a slowing-down in the rate of school building, there was an increase in the amount of education given, and money available, both from diocesan and State sources. In the 1850s the government grant was paid on the basis of an inspection of the attendance book, and an examination of the pupils. The 'payment by result' principle was embodied in the Revised Code of 1862 (though in fact it had been in operation for many years before). As with all manifestations of higher authority, it aroused much opposition among the clergy.

In the 1850s most politicians and many churchmen advocated a single system of national education, but the denominational basis of the educational system proved an insurmountable obstacle. The Forster Bill of 1870 established the axiom that secular instruction was secular, and that the instruction given in any school was suitable for the children of parents of any denomination. The denominations were given until the end of that year to complete their system of parochial education; the rate-supported board schools filled the gaps that remained. The Cowper-Temple clause allowed parents to withdraw their children from the religious instruction in denominational schools, and no religious instruction of a denominational type was given in board schools. The clergy continued to work for the establishment of schools in their parishes and to provide the appropriate educational facilities for their people. At St Barnabas's, Pimlico, in 1857, there were six schools, an industrial school for girls, a 'ragged school', and two evening schools.[48] William Butler at Wantage had five schools for girls alone in 1854, and taught arithmetic in his study for an hour every morning to senior girls.[49] In the five years prior to 1852, the number of children in church schools in St Pancras increased from 5996 to 8100.[50] In the old parish of St Matthew's, Bethnal Green, in which Blomfield's ten churches were built, the number of schools was increased from one in 1839 to ten in 1853.[51] Thorold, as a parish clergyman in London, laid great emphasis on his schools, and £16,000 was raised by private subscription for this work.[52] McClatchey recorded that in the Visitation returns of 1855–60, in 85 of the 178 villages in Oxfordshire, the school had either been built, repaired, or enlarged. Edward Elton built the school at Wheatley in the 1850s just below the vicarage garden adjacent to the church. When the Bishop of Oxford's butler, a prominent Wheatley resident, sent his children to Cuddesdon school, Elton raised the matter at a deanery meeting and a rule was made that no school should accept children from another village.[53]

Despite the clergyman's continued and extensive involvement in the provision of educational opportunities for his parishioners, there can be little doubt that slowly the clergy's personal involvement in the work began to decline during the second half of the nineteenth century. There were three principal reasons for this: the new conception of the nature and functions of the clergyman's role which placed increased emphasis on pastoral work; the rise of the teachers as a professional body; and the improved financial position of most village schools, which allowed the employment of a qualified teacher to replace the amateur work of the clergy. Ever since the late eighteenth century some handbooks had warned the clergyman against becoming preoccupied with the schools to the exclusion of other elements of his role. In the second half of the nineteenth century such warnings began to be heard with increased frequence: 'You will remember', wrote J. J. Blunt, 'that you did not promise God, through the Bishop at your ordination, to be a teacher of useful knowledge in your parish.'[54] This problem particularly concerned J. C. Miller. 'One has known clergymen', he wrote, 'who seem to have degenerated into mere school managers or schoolmasters.'[55] He considered that Sunday schools were very much over-rated as agents of spiritual renewal, and that no clergyman should waste his time in them if so doing detracted from his other Sunday duties. He would only permit the clergyman to enter the day school 'if other duties allow it'. Samuel Wilberforce offered this caution to his clergy in 1848: 'Your teaching in the school must be that of the pastor not of the schoolmaster.'[56]

Whereas, in the eighteenth century, the schoolteacher in the village school had often had little or no education himself, in the mid-nineteenth century, the Church established a number of diocesan teacher-training colleges, which attracted entrants of a higher social status than the profession had previously known. Furthermore, there was a government apprenticeship scheme, whereby salaries were paid to 'pupil-teachers' (children who remained at school after the age of thirteen and passed the requisite examinations to train as teachers). The greater availability of trained teachers allowed the clergy to entrust the teaching in their schools to other hands. At the same time the change in the content of education from the proverbial wisdom, characteristic of traditional societies, to the scientific knowledge of an advanced society, called for teachers with a greater range of knowledge, and an acquaintance with educational techniques. This forms another example of a new professional group taking over functions which had previously been performed by the amateur efforts of the clergy.

In conclusion, it is possible to identify three phases in the clergyman's performance of this element of his role. In the first, during the second half of the eighteenth century, teaching was of primary significance to the clergy as an additional source of income, and there was little parochial education. In the second phase, in the early nineteenth century, the education of the children of his parishioners was considered a most important function of the clergyman, and a principal element in the strategy of the Church extension movement. The clergy marshalled extensive voluntary resources for the provision of educational facilities. Mann's census of 1851 indicates that of the 10,595 schools receiving State aid, 8170 were Church of England schools, and they educated 76 per cent of the children.[57] The village school was regarded by the clergy as the chief weapon in their fight to re-establish the position of the Church of England. In the second half of the nineteenth century, in the third phase, the clergy's concern with education became progressively restricted to the management of schools. They were content to allow the new professional body of teachers, which they had done so much to create, to take over the function of teaching within the classroom. The demands of other aspects of his role, particularly his pastoral duties, made it no longer possible for the clergyman to devote that proportion of his time to the school which he had done formerly.

This element of the clergyman's role and the changing attitude of the clergy throughout the various phases may be taken to illustrate a number of significant aspects of professionalization. First, it is clear that as the nineteenth century progressed, the range of clerical functions was significantly narrowed. In the parochial school, the trained schoolmaster, whose salary was paid by grants from outside agencies, taught the lessons that the clergyman had previously given in an amateur way. On several fronts the range of the clergyman's functions contracted in the face of the establishment of new professions such as the schoolmaster, the doctor, the Poor Law administrator and the health inspector. In an increasingly secular age activities such as education, welfare, and entertainment (for the school was used for all of these) acquired autonomy and developed professional personnel and elaborate economic structures. The standards demanded by this new age exceeded the resources and energies of amateurism, for the clergyman, in all but his sacral functions, was becoming an amateur in an increasingly professional age. Second, the clergy's activities as teachers illustrate the way in which the role became progressively dominated by the function of administration. The increasing size of Victorian society made it impossible for the clergy to continue active participation in some elements of their role, and in the later half of the nineteenth century, the clergy increasingly managed and directed the activities of a wide range of volunteers, such as Sunday school teachers, ladies who worked in the infant school, and district visitors (who frequently acted as school attendance officers). Thus the clergyman's role, like other high-status roles in advanced society, became increasingly concerned with the supervision of other personnel and with the administration of resources. Third, it is interesting to note how the clergy in the middle of the nineteenth century progressively became, in many aspects of their work, the local representatives and administrators of supra-parochial organizations. As members of the National Society, and promoters of its ideals, the clergy were inevitably conscious of taking part in a movement which transcended parochial boundaries. In the last quarter of the nineteenth century and in the early twentieth century, an increasing amount of the clergyman's work was concerned with being the local representative or branch organizer of supra-parochial institutions. At the same time the clergy became conscious of the growing power of the diocesan organization, for the system of diocesan inspection of schools was an early manifestation of the developing power of the central diocesan bureaucracy. Thus, despite all its wealth and commercial prosperity, the educational system of this country was principally established by the parochial clergy, who shared the belief which gained universal acceptance in Victorian England that education was the panacea for the ills of society.

14

Officer of Health

The practice of caring for the physical ailments of his parishioners is not a part of the charter role of the Church of England clergyman. The Ordinal states that the deacon shall make the sick his particular care, but the terms of the Ordinal only include spiritual exhortation and the assistance of charity. It is from the New Testament that this element of the clergyman's role derived its authority, in that the healing of the sick played a conspicuous part in the ministry of Christ. The classical handbooks of George Herbert, Richard Baxter, and Gilbert Burnet all recommended that the clergyman or members of his family should act as amateur physicians for the parish in the absence of a professional practitioner. In many religious traditions there is a close proximity between the role of the religious leader and that of the medical practitioner.

The diffuse nature of the clergyman's role in the eighteenth century was exemplified by his involvement in doctoring his parishioners. In almost all the early handbooks it was considered that the clergyman, if he were able, should treat the physical ailments of his parishioners. George Herbert's advice was frequently quoted in handbooks: '. . . if there be any of his flock sick, he is their physician or at least his wife . . .'. In cases where the clergyman was unable to do this, Herbert suggested that 'he keep a young practitioner in his house for the benefit of his parish'.[1] Another handbook author advised the young clergyman, 'You will be the more capable of doing good, if you mix some physick . . . with your other studies.'[2] Gerard was typical of the Evangelical handbook authors, in that he stressed the pastoral opportunities which might arise from doctoring: 'If a clergyman understand medicine, he may practise it in his neighbourhood to a certain degree . . . [it] will multiply his opportunities of addressing people as a minister and render them all disposed to listen to his address on subjects of religion.'[3]

The evidence of the eighteenth-century clerical diaries and journals suggests that much of the work which was later done by a qualified doctor, surgeon, midwife, or nurse was in this early period done by the clergyman (or members of his family). A series of entries in the diary of Benjamin Rogers, who was in correspondence with many eminent doctors, recorded the last days of a parishioner and the clergyman's efforts on his behalf.

> (25 March) Order'd William Allen of Bridgend to be blooded for the Pleurisie. (2 April) Order'd him to be blooded again. The first time about 11 ounces was taken away; the second about 9. (3 April) He was blooded again, 10 ounces being taken away as before. (4 April) He died.[4]

It appears that James Woodforde had a considerable reputation for veterinary work in his early days at Castle Cary, for which he received fees. A horse was sent to him from as far afield as Chippenham, Wiltshire. In his Norfolk diaries he recorded the cases of sickness among his servants and parishioners and the attempts he made to cure them. 'My boy Jack had another touch of ague about noon. I gave him a dram of gin at the beginning of the fit and pushed him headlong into one of my ponds and ordered him to bed immediately.'[5]

Even if such doctoring as they received was unsophisticated, it was still a matter of some consequence to villagers whether their incumbent was resident or nonresident. The efforts of the bishops to enforce the Residence Bill of 1803 had the effect of greatly increasing the amateur medical care available to the poor. Sydney Smith, who had long been non-resident but was forced to live at Foston-le-Clay, spent much of his time doctoring his people. When he moved to Combe Florey, he equipped an apothecary shop in the rectory, from which he dispensed medicines and groceries to his parishioners.[6] Even where the clergyman did not practise medicine himself, it was still to the vicarage that parishioners looked for medical advice and supplies. Benjamin Newton saw a sick parishioner on 13 February 1818, and ordered a doctor to be got, when those attending the sick person had given her up as lost.[7] James Woodforde paid for the inoculation of some children in the village.[8] The physical well-being of his parishioners was also the concern of John Skinner. In the case of an accident he sent his housekeeper to assist and a note to summon the apothecary, and in a case of sudden illness he sent and paid for a doctor for a parishioner.[9]

The clergy performed this element of their role partly because they saw it as their spiritual duty as parochial clergy to help anyone in their parish whom they could assist, and partly because the public expectation of the role of a country gentleman was that he should be prepared to look after the people who lived in his village at times of widespread disease or personal accident. This mixture of spiritual and social compulsions manifested itself in the case of the county hospitals which played an important part in the provision of medical facilities for the seriously ill in rural areas. Certainly the doctrine of the benevolence of God and the philanthropy of the second half of the eighteenth century led many clergymen to subscribe to these hospitals. However, entry to a hospital, except in a case of serious accident, was only on the nomination of a subscriber, who qualified for 'turns' in proportion to the size of his subscription. The clergy were required by public expectation to subscribe, not only as a benevolent act, but in order that the village might have access to hospital beds in times of sickness. For a village to have neither clergyman nor squire who subscribed to the hospital was a matter of considerable consequence. McClatchey has drawn attention to the important part played by the Oxfordshire clergy in the history of the Radcliffe Infirmary as managers, visitors, and subscribers.[10]

In the early decades of the nineteenth century the clergy in many instances continued to provide such medical attention as their parishioners received. In 1820, a pamphlet entitled *Instructions for the Relief of the Sick Poor in some Diseases of Frequent Occurrence, Addressed to the Parochial Clergyman Residing at a Distance from Professional Aid* was published for their guidance by a doctor. Edward Boys Ellman's daughter writes of his work at Wartling in the 1830s.

. . . and soon after he went to Wartling there was a very great deal of illness – scarlet fever, measles, smallpox, and low fever. The people could not afford a doctor and the parish doctor did not trouble himself to look after them much. But their new Vicar had a knowledge of medicine and kept a big medicine chest and won many hearts by so doing.[11]

Most of the treatment given by the clergy was simple and homespun; Andrews of Ketteringham used brandy and salt to treat a woman patient.[12] Benjamin Philpot, incumbent of Little Cressingham and Bodney, used the same prescription and commented: 'Brandy and salt was much given in those days and I used it a great deal.'[13] Jessop recorded curing cholera with twelve grams of calomel, and on another occasion of preventing a suicide by setting a broken bone.[14] The only handbook written for the clergyman's wife in this period directed that she should be ready to assist with 'simple and effectual remedies'.[15] H. C. Ridley, who was particularly enthusiastic about vaccination, wrote:

The clergyman is brought so often in contact with the sickness of his parishioners and has so many opportunities of arresting disease in its first attack or of relieving its acuteness, that it seems to be quite in character with the duties of a parochial clergyman to be able to administer . . . those medicines which a good God has bestowed to heal sickness.[16]

In 1827, Samuel Wilberforce was advised by Hurrell Froude to buy the recent new edition of George Herbert's *Country Parson*. He wrote: 'Among the ideas which it has instilled in me, it has made me determined to learn medicine, which in a parson is quite different from in a doctor . . .'[17]

During the period of the old Poor Law the provision of medical assistance for sick people, particularly labourers in remote villages, was minimal. Such qualified doctors as there were naturally tended to live in, or near, urban centres where they could more readily build up a practice. In country areas the work was mainly done by 'medical men'. These men were unqualified, and learned what they knew as apprentices or assistants to apothecaries. Under the old Poor Law the Vestry was able (though not obliged) to hire such a man to attend all the sick in the parish throughout the year. The office was usually farmed out to the lowest bidder. The incompetence and neglect of these 'parish doctors' was notorious. A contemporary wrote: 'Parish help is . . . very often little better than no help at all.'[18] Some villages had provident and sick clubs which retained a 'medical man', but these parish clubs were particularly unstable and could not be relied upon. It is without doubt that the most important source of medical assistance for the poor in this period was the vicarage or the manor.

However, in the middle decades of the nineteenth century this situation began to change. First, the establishment of many of the provincial medical schools at this time, together with the flow of trained men from Edinburgh and Glasgow, greatly increased the number of qualified doctors, and a number of medical discoveries made their treatments more effective. Second, the old system of social administration based on the parish Vestry was replaced by the operation of the new Poor Law. Although Edwin Chadwick was outspoken in his preference for public health medicine, the new unions were now required by statute to provide medical attention for the paupers. As a principal reason for the Poor Law reform had been to reduce the cost of these services, it was not surprising that the provision of medical relief was in some respects worse under the new system than had prevailed before. The medical officer for the union might in all probability be a fully qualified doctor, but this was little comfort to the poor if the area he was responsible for was so vast and his salary so low, that he could afford neither transport nor medicines. A correspondent of the *British Magazine* quoted the example of the Aylesbury Union, one of the largest in the country, which, between 1835 and 1838, had three changes, every new officer living at a greater distance. The guardians were accused of attempting to obtain the statutory medical facilities at the lowest possible cost.[19] The professionalization of the doctor's role and the reorganization of social administration were forces which reduced the need for the clergyman to engage in doctoring.

As in other aspects of their role, the clergy found that functions which they had been content to perform without training, in an amateur fashion, were taken over and became the monopoly of a new professional body.

Nevertheless, so great were the inadequacies of the provision for medical facilities under the new Poor Law, that some clergy, particularly those in remote rural areas, continued to provide simple cures for their parishioners. The same correspondence in the *British Magazine* continued: 'It is well that there is so often a medicine chest in the parsonage . . . for medicine is hope to the agonizing and comfort to the dying. And many clergy are successful enough in their practice; but human life ought not to be left in the hands of amateurs.' But in urban areas the clergy readily acknowledged the legitimacy of the claim of the medical profession to a monopoly of such matters. However, although clergy ceased to doctor their parishioners, they continued to act in an indirect way by organizing sick clubs and dispensaries in order to bring the expertise of the medical profession within the reach of their parishioners in times of sickness, and to agitate for better provision of facilities.

The development of sick clubs and self-supporting dispensaries paralleled exactly the development of provident associations and self-help societies which were mentioned in Chapter 12. The clergy no longer involved themselves in the direct way of providing charity or medical assistance, but confined their activities to the organization of societies by means of which the poor could provide for themselves. John Sandford wrote concerning self-supporting medical clubs: 'According to the terms of these, on the payment of a stipulated sum, the medical man engages, at his own risk, to furnish to the members the necessary attendance and medicine in the event of sickness.'[20] Samuel Best described in a handbook the details of a sick insurance scheme which he had organized.[21] Robert Wilberforce wrote to his brother Samuel asking for his experience of running a dispensary so that he could establish a similar institution in his parish.[22] Self-supporting village dispensaries were established in the Oxfordshire villages of Deddington and Steeple Aston by the incumbent.[23] Another widespread practice at this time was the lending out of bed linen from the rectory in times of sickness and particularly at childbirth. H. C. Ridley wrote:

> Any poor woman in the parish is allowed the use of a set of child-bed linen for the month of her confinement. She is expected to return it clean. There is in the bundle a paper of groats, a handbell, a bottle of castor-oil, and $\frac{1}{2}$ lb. of soap.[24]

Although the clergy of the mid-nineteenth century had largely surrendered to the medical profession the function of doctoring their parishioners, they retained the closest interest in medical matters, not only as the instigators and organizers of local sick clubs and dispensaries, but as campaigners in the cause of public health and sanitation. As has been noted above, no picture of Victorian England has any relation to accuracy unless it takes into account the fact that in many communities, fatal infectious diseases were constantly lurking, and that any year might produce an epidemic which spared neither class nor generation nor sex, and left a broad swathe of bitter domestic tragedies in its train.[25] In previous decades, the state of medical knowledge had only allowed a fatalistic or stoic approach. But, in the fourth and fifth decades of the nineteenth century, a number of discoveries linked the prevalence of such diseases, particularly typhoid, with lack of sanitary arrangements in many urban areas, and the consequent pollution of the domestic water supplies. The various waves of Asiatic cholera which threatened the country at this time, together with a new concern about the conditions in which the urban poor lived, gave rise to a movement of national concern, aimed at implementing the new-found discoveries of sanitation science. In 1848, Lord Morpeth's Public Health Act established the General Board of Health, modelled on the Poor Law Board of the previous year. But this proved in advance of its time and it was disbanded ten years later. During those ten years the sanitation reform movement made much headway and the parochial clergy were among its most energetic supporters. Charles Kingsley wrote:

It was to be hoped that after the late discoveries of sanitary science, the clergy of all denominations would have felt it a sacred duty to go forth on a crusade against filth, and so to save the lives of thousands not merely during the present cholera but every year . . .[26]

When Charles Blomfield was Bishop of London, his efforts in encouraging others to combat cholera with better sanitation had earned him the praise of Benjamin Ward Richardson, the medical originator of the *Journal of Public Health*. Blomfield was foremost among those who supported the 1839 inquiry into sanitation. In his Charge of 1854, he recommended house-to-house visiting not only for spiritual reasons, but also for the purpose of detecting and removing sources of malignant disease.[27] Charles Kingsley, the most energetic of all clerical supporters of the movement, campaigned in London and throughout the country in his crusade against dirt and bad drainage. From London he wrote to his wife on 24 October 1849:

I was yesterday . . . over the cholera districts of Bermondsey; and, oh God! what I saw! people having no water to drink – hundreds of them – but the water of the common sewer which stagnated full of . . . dead fish, cats, and dogs under their window.

His enthusiasm for improved conditions was without bounds, as C. Kegan Paul recorded:

I was with him once when he visited a sick man suffering from fever; the atmosphere of the little ground floor bedroom was horrible, but before the Rector said a word he ran upstairs and, to the great astonishment of the inhabitants of the cottage, bored, with a large auger he had brought with him, several holes above the bed's head for ventilation.[28]

Kingsley was not alone in his enthusiasm. William Butler was concerned about the drainage system and water supply at Wantage where typhoid outbreaks had been frequent occurrences. He went about with the town surveyor personally inspecting 'nuisances', and was a member of the

Sanitary Committee.[29] Edward Elton, when he went to Wheatley in 1850, found a stream running the length of the main street which took all the village refuse. In the teeth of bitter local opposition he managed to get a proper drainage system constructed.[30] Charles Girdlestone, incumbent of Sedgley, organized the Stourbridge Sanitary Association of whose twenty-three officers six were clergymen.[31] Vaughan Thomas, Rector of Yarnton, was chairman of the Oxford Board of Health. In 1853, he issued *Five Papers of Advice* which dealt with such matters as the use of lime as a disinfectant, warnings against drunkenness and keeping late hours, cautions against eating new fruit, and exhortations to keep footwear dry.[32] On 14 September 1854, Armstrong recorded that he took the chair at the Board of Health which made up reports on all 'nuisances' and agreed to have a Vestry the following week to take into consideration the whole question of effectual drainage and water supply in the town.[33] J. H. Blunt wrote in his handbook, 'Some considerable help is expected from the clergy of these days by sanitary reformers. No one else sees so much of those who need admonition in matters connected with it, except the medical man of the district . . .'[34] The agitation of many clergy less prominent than Charles Kingsley helped to bring sanitary matters before the public. In some senses the movement culminated in the 1870s, when, in the provisions of the Public Health Act of 1872, it was required that a Medical Officer of Health should be appointed in all urban areas. Subsequent legislation in 1875 extended this provision to all areas. In the build-up of the public health movement, the clergy, who saw at close quarters the devastation and misery disease could bring, had been conspicuous for their activity and knowledge.

Many mid-Victorian clergy took an active part in the provision of nursing care for their parishioners, particularly midwifery. They did not need the publicity given to the horrors of the Scutari barracks by *The Times* to alert them to the domestic need. As early as 1847 an article appeared in the *British Magazine* suggesting that nurses were the primary need of sick villagers, and that an institution should be established to train them. The article was signed by seventeen laymen and clergy including F. D. Maurice.[35] John Sandford wrote in 1845 that he considered the best way in which the rich could help the poor in times of sickness was to procure a nurse.[36] Some country squires were eventually persuaded to provide a cottage and a salary for a resident nurse in the village. W. J. E. Bennett showed himself concerned with the low standards of rural nursing in his magazine *The Old Church Bench*. He wrote twenty-four articles of a practical nature designed to assist those who attended the sick.[37] In 1872, Richard Seymour helped to start a nursing institute in his area of Warwickshire.[38] It was natural that continental travellers, including Florence Nightingale, should have been impressed by the high standards of the first professional body of nurses, the nursing orders of the Catholic Church.[39] The serious outbreaks of cholera in 1849 and 1866 provided the opportunity for some clergy to establish Sisters of Mercy in their parishes. These took their place alongside the other lay agencies developed in the Church at this time.

The clergyman's diminishing activity in this element of his role during the late eighteenth and early nineteenth centuries provides a further example of the contraction in the range of functions which the role experienced, and the change in the nature of the clergyman's activity from direct to indirect action. In the eighteenth century, the clergy met cases of sickness or accident by rendering what assistance they could. By the mid-nineteenth century, the legitimacy of the doctor's claim to a monopoly of this function was recognized, and the clergy confined their action to indirect agitation for the provision of better facilities by the appropriate authorities. When Bennett wrote his articles on cottage nursing, he showed how sensitive the clergy had become not to encroach upon the doctor's professional competence: 'Let not my medical friends view me with suspicion. I say at the outset, that I utterly repudiate the idea of interfering with their vocation . . .'[40] In the later decades of the nineteenth century, the changes in the nature and authority of professional roles demanded that any clergyman who wished to practise medicine should possess the appropriate qualifications. McClatchey cites three examples of Oxfordshire clergy who qualified as doctors in the 1870s.[41] Edward Russell of St

Alban's, Holborn, soon after his ordination in 1867, decided to study medicine at St Bartholomew's Hospital, so as to be of use to his parishioners.[42] Thus doctoring ceased to form a part of the diffuse obligations of the parochial clergyman, and became the exclusive prerogative of the medical profession.

15

Politician

This sector of the clergyman's role in the eighteenth and nineteenth centuries finds its origins not in the prescriptions of the charter role, but in the close proximity of religious and secular institutions. It is beyond the scope of this book to examine in any detail the relationship which existed between Church and State in the eighteenth century. It is sufficient to say that religious and secular institutions and roles were woven into a complex whole and that many religious institutions possessed political functions in the wider society. Certainly, in the eighteenth century, the Church was regarded by many as merely a complement to the civil power. Samuel Taylor Coleridge wrote in his influential essay, *On the Constitutions of Church and State according to the Idea of Each*, 'the object of the national Church . . . was to secure and improve that civilisation without which the nation could be neither permanent nor progressive.'[1]

In the early years of the eighteenth century the clergy, as a body, were still suspected of being at least less than enthusiastic in their support of the House of Hanover. Except for a few years under Queen Anne, the period 1689 to 1740 had seen Parliament controlled by the Whigs who regarded the clergy, and indeed the whole religious establishment, as predominantly Tory and Jacobite in sympathy. However, after the 1745 rebellion the loyalty of the clergy was no longer questioned. Secker addressed the clergy of Oxford in his Charge of 1747:

> Your behaviour and that of the whole clergy, on this trying occasion both abounded with such proofs of loyalty and affection to the Government . . . that his Majesty hath declared he shall ever have the strongest sense of what you have done for the support of his throne and gladly show his gratitude by any proper method of extending his royal favour to you and your religion.[2]

The eighteenth century saw the progressive laicization of the Church of England which brought the clergy into close involvement with the dominant secular interests and values of the age. The changing relations between the Crown and Parliament were reflected in the Church. The bishops found themselves abandoning their former role of spiritual counsellors to the monarch, and were drawn into the political struggles in the House of Lords, where their votes were of considerable importance until the creation of the new peers by the younger Pitt. At the same time as the clergy gradually acquired higher social status, so they became an important element in the landed interest. The political and religious institutions which had been split apart by the events of the seventeenth century were rejoined more tightly than ever before under the overall dominance of Parliament. By the onset of this period, the Church had a profoundly political character, and was in a sense 'protected' by the State, in whose defence the clergy were expected to be active in propagating the principles of allegiance and subordination.

Apart from such considerations as these, there were other reasons why individual clergymen in the second half of the eighteenth century not infrequently played an active part in politics. At a time when the county franchise was in the hands of the forty-shilling freeholders, it happened in some areas that the votes of the clergy were the only ones cast. In any area the clerical vote was an important one. Not only was the clerical vote important in itself, but the clergy were able to canvass the votes of other freeholders, and considerations of this nature were often to the fore when patrons of livings had vacancies to fill. At a time when the clerical profession was substantially overpopulated (because of the ease of entry and the effect of pluralism in restricting the number of livings), one way in which a clergyman could attract the attention and the confidence of a patron was by political activity. Political calculations played an important part in ecclesiastical appointments and a candidate for preferment at this time possessed improved chances if he had the appropriate political views. The Earl of Coventry wrote to the Duke of Newcastle on 9 October 1751 about a vacant canonry at Worcester: 'The very unsettled state of the Chapter, as well as the political interest of the county seems to require that a steady Whig be sent down to us.'[3]

The case of Dr Josiah Tucker illustrates the way in which clerical advancement could be secured by political activity. In 1754 he assisted in the election of Robert Nugent at Bristol; Mr Nugent in gratitude solicited the Duke of Newcastle (then Prime Minister), for the recompense of a prebend's stall for the clergyman, 'who had so eminently distinguished himself upon various occasions in the Whig cause and recommended himself beyond any other person whatever by his merits and sufferings to his Majesty's best friends in Bristol'. Tucker was made a prebend in 1756, and two years later, George II gave him the deanery at Gloucester.[4] Such was the excess of unbeneficed clergy over livings that participation in political life with the hope of attracting the attention of a possible patron was a considerable temptation. In a sermon of 1781 John Disney castigated those clergymen who '. . . make themselves the dupes of the low arts of carrying an election or make wreck of integrity and uprightness to preserve and cultivate an interest in a venal borough.'[5] However, the handbooks of the mid-eighteenth century generally made little mention of the attitude which a clergyman would adopt towards politics. When any advice was offered it was to avoid any involvement in such matters. 'I resolve', wrote an anonymous handbook author, 'as little as may be to intermeddle with politics, parties, or any affairs relating to the State except my preaching loyalty to the King and fidelity to the nation at proper times may be called such.'[6]

The political activity of the eighteenth-century clergy can be divided between the more formal action of standing for political offices and supporting candidates, and the informal action of canvassing and tending general support to a particular party. In the first respect some clergy of this period were particularly active. The Revd William Jones was a close supporter of Colonel Rawlins in the Hertford Borough elections of 1806. But the colonel was an erratic character whose election expenses were much more than his pocket could meet. Jones signed a joint bond for £230 in his favour, and lent him £30 in cash from his own pocket. He was encouraged to give orders for ribbons for the election, but this he did not do. Rawlins was running against the local landed interest and was defeated, placing himself over £1000 in debt.[7] The election of clergy to minor posts in local government, particularly in the country towns, was very common in this period. Clergy also comprised (as has been mentioned above) a large proportion of the Bench of Justices, in some areas the majority. Although, strictly speaking, such an appointment was not a political one, none the less at this time the Lords Lieutenant and the public in general regarded it as such. The election of a clergyman as a Member of Parliament occurred in only one instance, when the Revd John Horne Tooke was elected for Old Sarum in 1801. Despite the intermixing of secular and religious institutions at this time, it was still regarded as repugnant that the same man should be both a Member of Parliament and a clergyman. A speech of the Earl Temple in the House of Lords illustrated the strength of feeling which existed. The Revd Horne Tooke retained his seat for that session only, during which legislation was enacted which compelled him to resign on penalty of a fine of £500 per day.[8]

However, it was through the informal activity of canvassing and giving general support to the political parties that the clergy made their most important contribution to the political life of the country. James Woodforde was a Tory of the mildest variety and was not particularly active as a politician, but he habitually attended all election meetings and showed considerable interest in the case of John Wilkes. Clearly his clerical neighbours took a more active interest in politics for on 31 May 1796, two clergymen waited upon him at separate times to solicit his vote in the county elections.[9] The many anecdotes of the political activity of the eighteenth-century clergy may not individually be true, but they bear witness to a generally accepted fact, that the clergy played an important part in local political life. It is sufficient to quote one example in the Ashurst-Sunderland contest in Oxford in 1812. Vice-Admiral Lechmere supported the Blenheim interest, but the rector was for Ashurst. The Admiral's wife and the rector raced to solicit a parishioner's vote, but while the lady knocked at the front door, the rector (with more knowledge of the ways of his parishioners) went straight to the candle factory where he guessed that the man would be working, and secured his vote.[10] There can be little doubt that the clergy, who were predominantly Tory, worked quietly but determinedly for the party interest. Certainly the Whigs thought so, and styled them 'the black recruiting sergeants'. It is difficult to assess the degree of influence which the clergy possessed in political life, but some historians were of the opinion that elections were won by their efforts; particularly the Tory triumph of Lord North in 1770 was 'greatly owing to the exertions of the clergy'.[11]

The early Evangelicals, unlike the majority of Latitudinarian clergy, regarded politics as no proper concern of the clergyman. Job Orton wrote to Thomas Stedman in 1791: 'I shall be sorry to find your neighbour Mr.— exposes himself and his ministry by his politics (an ancient bishop says "What hath an ecclesiastic to do with politics?"). Lend him Palmer's Abridgement of Baxter's Reformed Pastor.'[12] But the second- and third-generation Evangelicals who came increasingly from the middle classes, which were themselves becoming progressively involved in political life, abandoned the essentially sectarian position of their predecessors. They saw that the social changes which their ideology demanded could more quickly be effected by legislation than by any other means. They approached politics, as Dr Best has commented, without enthusiasm, realizing that no party could adopt the rules of gospel Christianity for its own, and that the workings of party implied exaggeration and distortion. Wilberforce and Ashley, who headed the Evangelical group in Westminster for over a century, both found party an obstruction to good works, and preferred to be free to support good men and good causes from wherever they might originate.[13]

There can be no doubt that the Evangelical cause suffered from the persistent attempts of both the Latitudinarian clergy and many politicians to dub the Evangelical ministers socialists, levellers, or democrats. However, any doubts which might formerly have been entertained about the loyalty of the Evangelical ministers were dispelled at the time of the French Revolution, when the Evangelical clergy showed themselves to be just as active as their Latitudinarian colleagues in confronting revolutionary principles and the works of Tom Paine. In the early period, when Evangelicals eschewed politics, Jones of Creaton wrote:

> Politics are Satan's most tempting and alluring baits . . . A Christian observes what God is doing on the earth but he studies politics more as a divine providence than a worldly system. Oh! what little things are these to a candidate for heaven and for a glorious immortality. [14]

But, at the time of the French Revolution the Evangelicals abandoned this attitude and lent their voices to the general defence of the constitution by the clergy. Thomas Robinson of Leicester preached a sermon in support of the government on 9 December 1792, and his curate and biographer Edward Thomas Vaughan quoted the sermon in full, and added (he was writing in 1815–16):

> Nearly all if not all to a man of that considerable body of the clergy which coincide with him for the most part in religious sentiment coincide with him also for the most part in their views of the authority of government . . . I am more forward to introduce this remark, because it has been insinuated that the persons usually designed 'evangelical clergymen' are . . . democratically inclined. [15]

During the period of the French Revolution and the Napoleonic Wars, there was no body of men more active in supporting the established order and repulsing infidelity and revolutionary actions than the clergy. The treatment of the clergy in France impressed the English clergy with the horrors of revolution, and in April 1793 they were authorized by the Crown to make a collection (which eventually totalled £41,314) for the French priests exiled in this country. The clergy regarded Edmund Burke as the true interpreter of the times. He declared, 'At home we behold similar beginnings. We are on our guard against similar conclusions.' [16] Loyalist groups such as the Association for Preserving Liberty and Property against Republicans and Levellers under John Reeves, the Anti-Jacobin Club and the Crown and Anchor clubs found the clergy among their most fervent supporters and campaigners. Many became chaplains to the volunteer and yeomanry regiments levied against the threatened invasion. In particular the clergy threw themselves with great energy into publishing counter-revolutionary literature, making speeches, and preaching political sermons, which were subsequently printed as tracts. Anti-republican literature was sent indiscriminately to all clergymen by John Reeves, who knew that they could be relied upon to distribute it.[17]

In the pulpit there can be no doubt that many clergy followed the example of Bishop Horsley and preached frequently and with vigour against the revolution. Isaac Milner was astonished by the Evangelical Miles Atkinson's preaching. 'He is a worthy creature and yet it was a strange thing to bid his audience "Read the Anti-Jacobin Review", and that I heard him say from the pulpit last summer myself.'[18] In this way the close alliance between the Government and the Church was cemented and reached its high-water mark in the fifteen years of post-war Tory government after 1815. The support was mutual and the Church extension programme was actively backed by the Government; ultimately the Church Building Society had received support to the extent of £6 million. This close and continuing alliance was symbolized for eleven years (1817–28) by the presence of Charles Manners Sutton as Archbishop of Canterbury, and his son, also Charles (and later Viscount Canterbury) as the Speaker of the House of Commons.[19]

The political activities of the clergy in the counties reached their zenith during the constitutional reforms of the second and third decades of the nineteenth century. The clergy regarded the Church as being in imminent danger from a Parliament no longer composed exclusively of Church of England laymen, and bent on drastic and far-reaching reforms. However, in spite of the bitter opposition of the majority of the clergy, the reforms were carried through with remarkably little trouble. The repeal of the Test and Corporation Acts in 1828–9 destroyed the former principle of a Church of England monopoly in offices of State and municipalities. The repeal of this legislation, in the words of Sydney Smith, removed safeguards 'without which no clergyman thinks he could sleep with his accustomed sound-ness'.[20] It had for so long been universally regarded that the constitution derived its particular qualities from the struggle against Catholic aggression under James II and his suc-cessors. That Catholic emancipation should have been granted by those who were supposed to be the Parliamentary representatives of the Established Church left a deep sense of shock and betrayal. It was in part out of these feelings that the Tractarian movement arose, for it was clear that the Church could not look for defence and support where it had been accustomed to find it.[21]

The opposition of the clergy to the Reform Bill itself is notorious; the Church was blind to the ncessary aspects of reform and clung fast to the old order. The clergy saw nothing in the Bill but hostility to the Church and religion, and the handing of greater political strength to the non-conformist and intellectual enemies of the Establishment. The Bill was initially rejected in the House of Lords on 8 October 1831; all the bishops except two (the Whig bishops Maltby and Bathurst) voted against the Bill. The un-popularity of the Church, which had been growing through-out the decade, increased markedly. The Bishop of Bristol's palace was burned down, and clergy were hissed and groaned at in church and outside. A curate in Bristol wrote in the *British Magazine* of his expedition to baptize a dying child in which he was abused by a crowd outside a public house and was afraid of being assaulted.[22]

Throughout the period the clergy attempted to defend the Church against its political adversaries as best they could. In practice this meant giving strong support to the Tory can-didates. At most constituency dinners the local clergy were present and one of their number responded to the ap-propriate toast. In 1832, the Revd Mr Tufnell, Vicar of Wormington, spoke at a post-election dinner, but when the local dissenting newspaper reported the speech, it added that the speaker was drunk at the time. In the ensuing legal action the vicar was awarded £50 damages.[23] In 1838, to celebrate an electoral victory, the Hampshire Conservatives announced their intention of building a church, an action which they regarded to be 'congenial with those Protestant and Christian principles which form the basis of true Conservatism'.[24]

But among many of the clergy there was a growing ambivalence towards such a close involvement in the activities of local political parties. Samuel Wilberforce wrote, when he was an incumbent in the Isle of Wight:

> All today I have been there [Newport] upon the hustings the greater part of the day. I was asked to second Mr. Ward's nomination for the county. He comes forward . . . upon the strictly Conservative side. This, however, I declined, thinking it was not the post for a parson. For the same reason I declined to speak there, though I think that I might have done some service. However, this afternoon after the nomination, when Mr. Ward's friends mustered in the Eagle Inn about 100 strong after drinking 'The Church' there was a call for me, and I got up thinking it was a good opportunity as the room was full of substantial yeomen both of explaining why all the clergy were with Ward and of striking while the iron of political excitement was hot and leaving an impression of Churchmanship thereafter.[25]

The handbooks of the period increasingly cautioned their readers against participation in party politics. Throughout this period the cry was often heard, 'the clergy have nothing to do with politics'. It was frequently raised by Whigs or radicals, who knew the extent of the clergy's influence over many rural freeholders, but after the Reform Bill these sentiments were increasingly uttered by the clergy themselves. Three principal reasons may be suggested for the decreasing participation of the clergy in party politics in the mid-nineteenth century.

First, influenced by the new conception of their role, the clergy came to regard such mundane matters as the activities of party politics as incompatible with their office. Men influenced by this new conception did not adopt the sectarian attitude towards politics found among the early Evangelicals, but they considered that, whereas a clergyman might have political views and exercise his right to vote, this was part of his civic role, and was not an element of his professional role. The development of the notion of 'private life' and the segmentation of a parson's various roles were a part of the social pattern which was slowly replacing the older order of traditional society. Second, the traditional ties between the Church, the aristocracy and the squirearchy which had given the clergy their political strength in the past were unable to meet the challenge of urbanization and industrialization. The nature of English political life changed rapidly at this time and foremost among these changes was the growing opposition to hereditary privilege, unrepresentative government, and mounting resentment against the whole prescriptive basis of traditional society.[26] In the nineteenth century political power was passing, albeit slowly, into the hands of the urban middle class. The period from the repeal of the Test and Corporation Acts to the reorganization of the Indian Civil Service in 1853 saw the landed interest, of which the clergy were an integral part, yielding place to the urban industrial and commercial classes. In the face of this situation it befitted the clergy to withdraw from party politics, particularly when the long Tory rule was broken in 1830. Third, although there was still a considerable disparity between the number of clergymen and the number of available livings, the new residence legislation together with the creation of many new parishes and districts in urban areas, brought about a situation in which it was no longer necessary for a clergyman to be an active politician to gain the attention of a prospective patron. Indeed, so far had opinions changed, that such activity might have been a disadvantage in seeking preferment.

Furthermore, in the mid-nineteenth century the nature of politics was also changing. Political issues which previously had been resolved at Westminster were increasingly being determined outside Parliament in the new committees and commissions, which were demanded by the scale and complexity of Victorian society and the attendant development of bureaucratization. In this way political decisions were arrived at by the interaction of interest groups who sought to influence these decision-making bodies by mounting campaigns on particular issues, using the new cheap newspapers and public meetings, and by direct lobbying. It is noticeable in the middle decades of the nineteenth century, when the clergy had largely abandoned direct involvement in politics, that a number became active campaigners on a wide range of social and humanitarian issues, such as Poor Law reform, sanitation and factory reform, the improvement of housing, and educational issues. In the previous decades there had been some examples of this non-party campaigning on specific issues. Dr Arthur Wade, the Vicar of Warwick, had led a procession of 50,000 people in protest against the transportation of the Tolpuddle 'martyrs'. The Revd George Bull sought to challenge the assumption that labour was a commodity to be bought at the cheapest price, and championed the Ten Hour Movement (1830–31), and factory reform. On the requisition calling for the meeting in the Castle Yard at York which terminated 'the pilgrimage of mercy' were the names of sixty-eight West Riding clergy.[27] J. C. Miller campaigned for social reform and municipal activity in Birmingham, and W. P. Hook in Coventry and Leeds was an active supporter of the Ten Hour Movement.[28] An illustration of the way in which the clergy as an interest group could bring pressure to bear on the legislature is afforded by the Poor Law Commission on the Employment of Women and Children in Agriculture in 1843. Among the people who gave evidence were a large number of rural clergy who regarded the employment of women working alongside men in the fields to be one of the major causes of rural immorality. They particularly deplored the gang system. On such an issue as this the clergy risked alienating the farmers of the parish. In *The Spectator* of 23 November 1872, a letter from a country clergyman recorded how his congregation had been deserted by many of the farmers because of his consistent campaign against women, especially when pregnant, working in the fields.[29]

Sanitation reform and bad housing conditions became something of a passion with the clergy of the 1850s and 1860s. The clergy knew that 'low fever' was almost constantly present in the areas of poor housing and no sanitation, and that infectious fatal diseases were common in such areas. The clergy of the eighteenth century largely disregarded such things – the laws of settlement and the attitude of the squirearchy did not encourage them to interfere in such matters. In the mid-nineteenth century, new professions had arisen, among which were the Poor Law officer and the sanitary inspector whose job it was to attend to these matters. The clergy gave such assistance as they could, but largely restricted their activities to agitation for the amelioration of the conditions of the poor. Archdeacon Fearon, in his Charge of 1865, encouraged the clergy to make representations to the landlord when they found cottages that were particularly bad and did not answer 'the requirements of health . . . self-respect and decorum'.[30] Henry Moule, Vicar of Fordington, wrote eight letters to Prince Albert between September 1854 and October 1855 about the insanitary state of many of the houses of the poor on property in the parish owned by the Duchy of Cornwall.[31] William Butler at Wantage was much concerned with such matters in the town and was a member of the sanitation committee. Furthermore, he purchased a row of cottages, had them demolished, and rebuilt them as model homes.[32]

A few of the clergy, influenced by Charles Kingsley and F. D. Maurice, took the part of the working people. Charles Kingsley campaigned on numerous social issues, and on one occasion he declared himself publicly to be a sympathizer with the chartists.[33] The Christian Socialist Movement was a demonstration of their concern with contemporary social issues, and its leaders helped start co-operative ventures in London. As a movement it was short-lived, for it met with comparatively little response from the working people, and the active opposition of a number of the clergy. Lord Sydney Godolphin Osborne, Rector of Durweston in Dorset, wrote many letters to *The Times* on behalf of the Dorset labourers; they form an interesting account of what many clergy knew at first hand about the countryside. The Revd Edward Girdlestone of Halberton in Devon was a campaigner for sanitary reform and a fairer wage for the rural labourer. He organized a mass migration of labourers from the area to counties where wages and conditions were better. Between 400 and 500 labourers and their families were said to have moved, and the Halberton farmers were forced to raise the wages from 7s or 8s to 17s to keep their remaining men.[34]

Some clergy were found among the early supporters of those who attempted to form a trade union for agricultural workers. An early union was helped by the vicar of Leintwardine; it claimed a membership of 30,000 and had twenty clergymen as vice-presidents.[35] However, Joseph Arch's National Agricultural Labourers' Union, established following his speech in Barford in Warwickshire in 1872, was strongly anti-clerical in many of its early pronouncements. It accused the clergy of being deeply implicated in agricultural capitalism and the changes in land tenure which had pressed so heavily on country people. No doubt some clergy would have agreed with Bishop Ellicott of Gloucester's suggestion that union leaders should be thrown in the duck pond. But Arch was not without supporters among the clergy, and these included Bishop Frazer of Manchester, and Dr Percival, President of Trinity College, Oxford (later Bishop of Hereford), and there is little doubt that many parochial clergy, from their intimate knowledge of the countryside, saw the justice of his demands. The Hon and Revd J. W. Leigh of Stoneleigh was a remarkable supporter of the strikes. He met Arch on several occasions and attended his meetings. Archdeacon Holbeche of Banbury proposed the workers' motion on their behalf at a meeting of landowners. The South Warwickshire Clerical Meeting formally recognized the right of combination put forward in Arch's manifesto of April 1872.[36] In the same year R. F. Lawrence, Vicar of Chalgrove in Oxfordshire, became secretary of the local branch. On 2 June 1874 he not only chaired a union meeting in the village but gave permission for it to be held on the vicarage lawn. At the meeting he expressed 'willingness to help in any way he possibly could'.[37] However, in 1874, the union suffered defeat over the strike in Suffolk and Norfolk, and the membership fell rapidly. Within two years agriculture began to enter a period of deep recession and the union lost much of the ground it had gained. Clearly the received view of the early period of the Agricultural Workers' Union that the clergy invariably sided with the farmers needs some qualification. It seems that a number of the clergy quite outspokenly supported the workers, and the justice of their claims, for they knew at first hand the hardships of the countryside.

But it may be assumed that for various reasons the majority of clergy were reluctant to take sides, whatever they might have felt. The Revd Mr Jenyns, Vicar of Hitcham, wrote: 'It is not every clergyman that will boldly stand up against a body of farmers, who have long had their own way in everything . . .'[38] Certainly, at Halberton and Chalgrove, the incumbents met implacable opposition not only in respect of their political activities but in every way. Though many clergy campaigned for better sanitary conditions and on other humanitarian issues, few at this time concerned themselves with wider political issues, and those who did were forced to face strong opposition. William Tuckwell, Vicar of Stockton, recorded the strong sanctions brought to bear by middle- and upper-class parishioners on those clergy who, like himself, deserted 'the class interest' and embraced radical political views.[39]

By the second half of the nineteenth century the involvement of the clergy in party politics had declined markedly. Some still actively supported the Tory cause. At a Tory meeting in Reading in February 1865, Archdeacon Christopher Wordsworth (shortly before he became Bishop of Lincoln) declared:

> What, gentlemen, is Conservatism? It is the application of Christianity to civil government. And what is English Conservatism? It is the adoption of the principles of the Church of England as the ground of legislation. Gentlemen, I say with reverence, the most Conservative book in the world is the Bible and the next most Conservative book in the world is the Book of Common Prayer.[40]

Following the election of 1868, Gladstone attributed the failure of the Liberal Party to the political endeavours of the country clergy. But following the second election in that year, Lord Malmesbury wrote to Disraeli attributing the Conservative loss of the Christchurch seat to the fact that 'the Church cannot hold its own with the new electors . . .'[41] However, in the main it would seem that the majority of the clergy, influenced by the new professional and spiritual conception of their role which left them little time for such activities, took a markedly less active part in the political life of the neighbourhood. Most clergymen realized, at a time when the clergy increasingly depended upon good will, that it was impossible to engage in politics without making enemies as well as friends. Bishop Hamilton wrote: 'We clergy have enough work to do in bringing men to know and love God against the bent and bias of their nature, without making our task more difficult by enlisting against ourselves many of the great sections of political feelings.'[42]

Thus it may be seen that throughout the nineteenth century the clergy dissociated themselves from participation in party politics. The new conception of their role caused them to extricate themselves from the mundane activity of party politics. But at the same time, many became aware that the gospel message could mean little to people living in the conditions which prevailed in nineteenth-century cities, towns, and villages. J. C. Miller said in a speech in 1853,

> It was a happy thing that the religious part of the community were now aware that they had been too neglectful of questions of this nature, which had no small influence on the moral and spiritual interests of masses. Where there were filthy lodging-houses, necessitating indecency and dirt, there the Minister, the Scripture Reader, or the Missionary might labour in vain.[43]

Politics as such became for the clergy a part of their civic role as electors and citizens rather than an element in their professional role. A clergyman's politics, like those of a civil servant, a doctor, or an architect, were increasingly regarded as 'his personal affair', and irrelevant to the practice and execution of his profession. This distinction, which came to be made in the late nineteenth century, illustrated the increasing significance of the professional ideal as the role model for the clergy. The notion that the clergyman is 'above politics' may be taken as a significant indicator of the degree to which the clergy had accepted this ideal; for the concept of neutrality – affective, emotional, and political – is of central importance in the professional model. The professional man is regarded as practising his skill and exercising his judgement in a way which is wholly independent of these considerations. However, the very term 'above politics' betrays something of the marginality and alienation from the mainstream of society which adopting such a posture necessarily involved, and which became such a significant feature of the role of the clergyman in the twentieth century.

PART THREE

The Clergyman's Role and Contemporary Society

16

The Late-nineteenth-century Clergyman as a Professional Man

We have argued that to understand the clergyman's role in contemporary society, it is essential to know how that role developed in its formative period, which, in the foregoing chapters, we have examined in some detail. Today, the clergyman's role differs little from what it had become at the end of the last century, certainly when compared to the changes that had occurred during that century. If, in the mid-eighteenth century, ordination had been seen mainly in terms of entry into a livelihood which was compatible with the status of a gentleman and whose duties were minimal, by the mid-nineteenth century, ordination had come to mean something very different. Both the Evangelicals and the Tractarians had sought to emphasize the spiritual and consecrated nature of the clergyman's role. No longer was the role legitimated principally by appeals to its social utility, but in terms of the spiritual and sacramental nature of the Church. If, in the eighteenth century, the clergyman had been a member of the leisured class free to indulge his interests in gentlemanly sports, the administration of the county, together with scholarly and social pursuits, the typical mid-nineteenth-century clergyman was a man without leisure. At a time when the tempo of life was quickening, the clergy were required to be energetically engaged in the sacred duties of their calling, which the handbook authors exhorted them to fulfil.

The process of professionalization, which affected all high-status roles in the nineteenth century, affected the clergyman's role principally in two ways. It emphasized the charter elements in the role, and it sharply contracted the range of the clergyman's functions. In the late eighteenth century, the clergyman's role approximated closely to that of the country gentleman, and the clergyman performed a range of functions which were legitimated not by his ordination, but by his status as a country gentleman: a man of integrity and some learning in a society where the majority were illiterate. As the previous chapters have recorded, the clergy were active as politicians, Poor Law administrators, and land tax commissioners, in many aspects of local government, in medicine, in the provision of such social welfare facilities as existed, in teaching, and pre-eminently on the magistrates' bench. Such secular responsibilities were regarded as compatible with the clerical office, and were in fact necessary for the administration of the county and the country. However, such was the growth and complexity of Victorian society that many of these activities outgrew the competence of the clergy, and there arose a number of new professional roles which were concerned exclusively with those spheres which the clergy had previously been content to perform in an amateur way. The accredited country doctor, the lay magistrate, the policeman, the party agent, the trained teacher, the country solicitor, the registrar, and the number of new local government officials were all in a sense new professional roles in the mid-nineteenth century. The effect of their emergence on the clergyman's role was to sharply contract the range of his functions. In some instances, this happened quickly and with resentment, as when the clergy ceased to be the registrars of births and deaths. In other instances, the clergy gradually disengaged themselves in the face of mounting public opinion as in the case of politics and the magistracy. The teachers were a new professional body initially created by the clergy, and the clergy were prominent in the movements which led to the appointment of the Medical Officers of Health and the improvements in the police service, particularly in rural areas.

The principal reason for the disengagement of the clergy from so many of these essentially secular duties was the new pre-eminence which was accorded to the charter elements of their role. In mid-Victorian society, all high-status roles acquired a new specificity, and centred around certain central and characteristic functions. The lawyer abandoned much of his general involvement in the management of estates, and became almost exclusively concerned with the law and litigation. If, in the mid-eighteenth century, the clergyman's performance of his liturgical function had been perfunctory and his pastoral endeavours limited, the mid-nineteenth-century clergyman saw these as the central and defining functions of his role which demanded his total attention. In a society which increasingly attached value and status to skill and expertise, no professional group could remain as a refuge for the unqualified and the incompetent. Liturgical and pastoral work, and the development of the appropriate knowledge and skills, were promoted to a position of unchallenged importance. As other professional men became skilled and technically competent (the middle decades of the nineteenth century saw great advances in the law and medicine), so the clergy developed a professional language and refined skills and expertise.

Perhaps the most noticeable effect of these changes was the growing tendency in Victorian society to regard the clergyman as a man apart. In the eighteenth century the clergyman's role had almost lost its distinctiveness so closely had it become identified with the behaviour, manners, culture, and recreations of the laity. First, the Evangelicals, and then the Tractarians, laid emphasis on the apartness of the clergyman, as a man consecrated and set apart for a particular and sacred duty. Ashley Oxenden wrote that 'the everyday life of a Christian pastor, instead of being as the life of men in general, should be sacred'.[1] Archdeacon Manning emphasized the same point when he told the clergy of the archdeaconry of Chichester in his Charge of July 1846: 'Relaxed habits – blameless in our lay brethren – are not innocent in us.'[2] This widespread rejection of the submergence of the clergy in the dominant lay culture, and the desire for distinctiveness and apartness was a principal manifestation of professionalization, and provoked accusations of 'priestcraft' which had been absent from English society for several generations.

By the last quarter of the nineteenth century, it was agreed on all sides that the clergy ought to be different, and they began to develop a distinctive professional sub-culture – 'the rectory culture'. Distinctive clerical dress, which, in the eighteenth century, had been abandoned except on formal occasions, was widely readopted. The clergy of the mid-nineteenth century customarily wore a black coat and a white necktie, but, by the 1880s, the 'Roman' collar was gaining popularity among high-church clergy, and was in a relatively short period of time universally adopted. At the same time, the clergy began to develop professional habits and mannerisms which made them immediately recognizable and which gave the late-nineteenth-century music halls a rich vein of humour to explore. Even the rectories themselves took on a particular form so that it is possible to speak of 'a typical Victorian rectory'. Their fittings and furnishings, the prints on the walls of the study all witnessed to the development of a distinctive professional sub-culture. The clergy's sense of apartness even extended to a desire to withdraw from the London clubs which they had so extensively patronized in previous decades. An exclusively clerical club operated for some years at 13 Henrietta Street in the 1840s, and, in the late 1860s, the 'Clergy Club and Hotel Company' was operating a London club. In the 1880s, there existed several hotels, including one at Mentone,[3] where clergy could take their holidays in the company of their professional colleagues.

It is perhaps in their recreations that the clergy most clearly demonstrated their disengagement from the lay culture and the desire of society at large that this should be so. In the eighteenth century and in the early decades of the nineteenth century, many clergy had been pre-eminent in the hunting field (hunting at that time being not so much a sport as the focus of all social life in rural society). A number of famous hunts were formed by clergymen, particularly in the West Country. However, in the middle decades of the nineteenth century, Bishop Phillpotts of Exeter conducted a long campaign against the hunting parsons of his diocese. A handbook author wrote in 1830:

> In my jealousy for the dignity of our office, I may err in my estimation of these things. But whether the racecourse, the sporting field, and the clubroom be proper theatres for

the exhibition of the clerical character; and whether the gamekeeper and the groom and the huntsman, the jockey and the boon companion be proper associates for a clergyman, are questions which I think well worthy of the consideration of every member of our profession who has been or may be tempted to appear in such scenes and to hold such communications.[4]

And F. E. Paget wrote in 1843:

You must remember that the tone of feeling which existed in the Church even five and twenty years ago, both with respect to duties and amusements, was very different from that which is to be found among us at present. At that time a person in Holy Orders might have been seen at Ascot or Newmarket without any very great scandal. But were a clergyman now to be seen on a racecourse he would, even by worldly people, be considered to have disgraced himself and his profession.[5]

This disengagement of the clergy from the amusements of their lay peers may be regarded as signifying a deeper separation of the clergy which was hinted at in a letter, written in 1903, by a man who revisited a country district south of the Trent, which he had not seen for thirty years. 'The clergy seem more equipped in technique, more earnest and willing and but somehow less easy in society less like ordinary gentlemen, more likely to go to a tennis party than to walk across the stubble with the farmer's shooting party.'[6]

Thus the clergyman's role emerged in its recognizably modern form from its long formative period as a distinctive role much influenced by the professionalization of high-status roles in the mid-nineteenth century and with its own sub-culture. The period that followed, the last decades of the nineteenth century and the years before the First World War, are often spoken of as a 'golden era' for the clergy, particularly those in rural areas. In some rectories, where the income was sufficient to allow the employment of many servants, the clergyman was able to sustain a style of life which approximated to that of the manor or the hall, to send his sons to public schools and professional careers in the

Army, the Empire, or the Church. But for the majority the long period of decline had already set in. The residence legislation earlier in the century, which had done so much to reawaken the clergy to their duties, had also settled many clergy in parishes that were too small and too poorly endowed. The decline in agricultural prices in the last two decades of the nineteenth century resulted in a sharp decline in clerical incomes. Those dependent on the letting of their glebe often had to face years when their fields were untenanted. The Revd E. B. Rutherfield recorded that the value of his benefice fell from £1500 per annum in the 'high-farming' years of the 1860s to £300 per annum in the depressed 1880s.[7] By 1905 the practice of making the Easter offering a gift to the incumbent was widespread throughout the Church. Less income led directly to the dismissal of the curate, less contributions to the village charities, to the school, and the work of the Church, and, ultimately, to a loss of status in the community in the eyes of some at least. But poverty may have been easier to bear than the vague presentiment of life passing one by, which many rural clergy were beginning to feel. Richard Jefferies provided a touching vignette of a country parson in the 1870s as seen through the eyes of his wife:

> But the work, the parish, the people, all seemed to have slipped out of her husband's hands . . . But surely his good intentions, his way of life, his gentle kindness should carry sway. Instead of which the parish seemed to have quite left the Church, and the parson was outside the real modern life of the village.[8]

In an age characterized by activity, achievement, success, and almost boundless opportunity for the energetic and determined, there was increasing concern for the loneliness and stagnation of clergy ministering in small country parishes, many no larger than hamlets. As early as the 1870s, a country doctor said that the great disease which afflicted the mass of the country clergy was want of work.[9] Such was the appointment and patronage system of the Church, that many clergy spent their lives in places where their new perception of the content and functions of their role only increased their frustration with their limited rural horizons. It is no coincidence that the first criticisms of the patronage and freehold system dated from this time, when it became generally realized that clergy, like other professional men, needed a periodic change of environment and task, as well as a rudimentary career structure.

THE CLERGY AS A PROFESSIONAL BODY

In the nineteenth century, the clergy gradually gained a greater sense of their own corporate identity as a body of professional men. Clerical meetings of all varieties played a prominent part in the life of the late-nineteenth-century clergyman, the railways having made travelling so much easier. The original Church House in Westminster was built to commemorate the Silver Jubilee of Queen Victoria in 1887. The re-establishment of rural deaneries, distinctive clerical dress, and the proliferation and wide circulation of church newspapers and journals all contributed to the clergy's growth sense of themselves as a professional body. It was characteristic of the emerging professions in the nineteenth century to attempt to gain control over such matters as recruitment, training, professional standards of competence, ethics, discipline, conditions of service, and remuneration. The extent to which the clergy failed to achieve some of these goals demonstrated the degree to which the nature of their occupation, and the nature of the Church as the institutional context of their work, prevented their complete professionalization.

However, the clergy came nearest to achieving the professional ideal in the degree of control that they were able to exercise over the training of new entrants into the profession. Previous generations had believed that the clergy received sufficient training at the universities where they shared in the generalized socialization of the country's élite. (Oxford and Cambridge did not have theology degree courses until the 1870s.) The establishment, in the middle decades of the nineteenth century, of residential training colleges, similar to those of other professions, provided the clergy with the means of regulating the training, and to a certain extent the recruitment, of ordinands. But the implementation of any comprehensive or uniform policy was thwarted by the operation of the church parties to which most colleges either owed their origins or had a strong allegiance. None the less, the development of a professional ideology and ethos was facilitated by the measure of control which the clergy as a professional body were able to exercise over the colleges, and their establishment was a significant factor in the professionalization of the clergy.

As with other professions, there was a desire among the clergy to encourage higher professional standards, and to discipline those whose dereliction of duty or sheer indifference brought the whole profession into disrepute. This matter exercised many clerical minds, particularly towards the end of the century, when the Church was becoming more conscious of the need of the general good will of society. There were, in the nineteenth century, many scandalous cases of clerical default, but the clergy as a body were inhibited from disciplining these defaulters by the fact that the benefice was the incumbent's property. The only effective means of discipline was to proceed against him in the courts on one of the counts on which a clergyman could be debarred from his living and defrocked (i.e. failure to read the services and certain moral and criminal offences). The expense and uncertainty of this procedure made the bishops and archdeacons cautious in their prosecutions. Effectively, professional discipline was in the hands of the bishops and archdeacons by whose public censure or subtle pressure for reform much was done to enforce higher standards. When Robert Wilberforce was appointed Archdeacon of the East Riding in 1841, he wrote to his brother Samuel:

> You can hardly fancy such louts as many of the clergy here. I am preparing next week for a commission on two drunken clergymen in this neighbourhood who have been a scandal about here for years. This is very shocking, but I have heard of two men, in the very next parish to my own, who I feel are habitual offenders in this way.

By the end of the year, he reported: 'I have already ejected or suspended five persons within the year, besides two others who are gone into temporary exile.'[10] The revival of the office of rural dean was not unconnected with the general desire among the bishops and archdeacons to achieve higher professional standards or, at least, to harass those whose neglect of duty or moral standards brought disgrace to their profession.

Richard Seymour, when Rural Dean of Alcester, sat on the commission to investigate the misdemeanours of a brother clergyman, and had the same duty to perform again in March 1847. In June 1867, he reported a clergyman to the Bishop for being intoxicated between 2 a.m. and 3 a.m. on a Monday.[11] Although the first diocesan synod was called by Bishop Phillpotts of Exeter principally to get a diocesan judgement on a disciplinary matter ('the Gorham Affair'), the fact remained that the structure of the Church and its legal framework made any effective and uniform enforcement of professional discipline impossible, though subsequently there were several notorious cases associated with the prosecution of the 'ritualist' clergy.

Like other professions, the clergy were particularly concerned not only with the quality of the clergy but also with the quantity. During the nineteenth century there was a dramatic increase in the number of professional men as the new technical and bureaucratic professions developed. The clergy also experienced a sharp rise in their numbers; in 1841, there were 14,613; by 1861 there were 19,195 clergymen. However, perhaps the most dramatic rise was in the number of assistant clergy engaged in parochial duties which more than doubled between 1835 and 1841, when it stood at 2032, and had risen to 3437 in 1853. This expansion of the profession in the mid-nineteenth century can be attributed in part to the Oxford Movement, the Pluralities Act of 1838, and the Church Extension movement. Throughout the rest of the century, clergy numbers continued to rise: in 1871 – 20,694; in 1881 – 21,663; and in 1891 – 24,232. The figures for one diocese indicate the local impact of this increase. In 1836, when the diocese of Ripon was created, there were 296 incumbents and 76 curates; by 1874, there were 462 incumbents and 245 curates.[12]

The figures for ordinations in each year indicate the number of new entrants into the profession, and during the

1840s the figure rose to an early peak of 632 in 1853. To the disappointment of contemporary observers the figure then steadied, and in some years markedly declined. The low figure of 489 in 1862 caused particular concern. But in the last quarter of the century increasing numbers of ordinands were recorded, culminating in the peak year of 1885 when 870 men entered the profession. But from that year a steady decline set in: 1889 – 777; 1890 – 746; 1896 – 704. In 1900 the number fell sharply to 650, and in the year which saw the start of the First World War 610 men were ordained.[13]

Despite the fact that between 1835 and 1900 the number of clergy active in English parishes more than doubled, only in the 1870s and 1880s did the rise in their number match the rise in the population, and in terms of the ratio of clergy to people, the profession lost ground steadily through the century.[14] But what appeared to concern contemporary observers more was the growing conviction, particularly after the 1860s, that the most able men were no longer seeking ordination. By 1862, the number of ordinands who had not graduated from a university was three times the figure for 1841. The number of men coming from Oxford and Cambridge was halved in the twenty years preceding 1862.[15] In that year, it was estimated that one in three of the ordinands were non-graduates; and in 1879, it was estimated that, of the total professional strength of 23,612, one in six had no degree.[16] The decline in graduates caused particular concern at a time when other professions were increasing their entry standards. Contemporary commentators regarded the challenges, opportunities, and remuneration of the new professions to be the chief cause for the decline in university graduates. The changing professional preferences of the Victorian upper middle class were demonstrated in the intended careers of the boys who left Winchester in 1836 and 1893:[17]

	1836	1893
Clergy	23	4
Barrister	5	9
Solicitor	2	6
Doctor	4	1

	1836	1893
Accountant	—	3
Engineer	—	6
Army	10	25
Civil Service	5	8
Business	1	9

Despite the seemingly large number of clergy, it is interesting to record that as early as the 1850s, Archdeacon W. M. Hale made proposals for an 'extended deaconate', which would provide for a temporary and part-time ministry for those, particularly in urban areas, who on account of their educational and social backgrounds could never aspire to enter the profession as ordained clergy.[18] The idea was taken up in convocation, but a committee of that body reported in 1857 that legal difficulties prevented a self-supporting ordained ministry in the Church of England. Such suggestions as those of Archdeacon Hale questioned by implication one of the central pillars of nineteenth-century professionalism that membership of a profession was compatible with gentlemanly status in society. If, in the eighteenth century, gentlemanly status had meant 'of the gentry', in the nineteenth century it took on a much wider meaning, partly because the former rigid stratification between the leisured and the labouring classes had been blurred by the emergence of the Victorian urban upper middle class, and partly because what constituted gentility had itself considerably changed. The Victorian upper middle class, from whose ranks the professions were principally recruited, regarded themselves as 'gentlemanly', even if their connection with the powerful role model of the country gentleman had become somewhat tenuous.

The Victorian church assumed that one of its main strengths was that its clergy were gentlemen, and Englishmen in every generation have been accustomed to speak derisively of the 'peasant priesthoods' of Ireland and continental Catholic countries. A ministry comprised of 'learned clerks' was regarded as a hallmark of the Church of England, and 'a gentleman in every parish' was the keystone of Victorian church strategy. Bishop Tait, whose unconventional attitudes to evangelism in his metropolitan diocese shocked many contemporaries, and who appeared ready to countenance any reasonable expedient to extend the outreach of the Church, nevertheless attacked, in his Charge of 1858, the notion that a more homely type of clergyman would benefit the Church.[19] Such suggestions had come from various quarters and included Hurrell Froude's attack on 'the gentleman heresy' in the 1830s. Particularly after the period of urban growth, it was widely believed that the social gulf between the university-educated clergyman and his artisan parishioners was too wide in an age when pastoral strategy was increasingly stressing the ability of the clergy to 'get alongside' their parishioners. As a correspondent of the *Guardian* wrote on 7 December 1864 of such parishioners, 'if they . . . could say of the clergyman sometimes, "He is one of us."'[20] However, the clergy as a profession were not willing to countenance widening the narrow band from which they and the other professions customarily drew their recruits. Indeed, at a time when other professions were rising in social status, and society at large was aware that entering into the professions was the most speedy path of upward social mobility, the clergy became particularly concerned to maintain the gentlemanly ideal. The defenders of the gentleman theory stressed the need for a highly educated and cultivated clergy in a time of intellectual and social unsettlement, and attached great value to the links which the clergy had, by family and education, with the leaders of public life. Certainly, one means by which the clergy and others guaranteed the exclusive nature of their professional bodies was by recruiting only those who could afford to pay for their own training. Most professions were, through the nineteenth century, expensive to enter and required the family of the aspirant to support him for a number of years both in training and after qualifying. Like many of the early theological colleges, those started by the religious orders sought to train men who had neither the educational background nor the financial resources to attend university. Gore (then Superior at Mirfield) described the situation which prevailed at that time as 'a new form of simony', and Father Bull told the Mirfield Chapter: 'We have invented a class priesthood with a money qualification.' In 1891, H. H. Kelly founded the Society of the Sacred Mission for the purpose of offering free training for ordinands 'with no half-baked gentility', but in the initial period those trained were all destined for dioceses in the colonies.[21] The Church remained a relatively expensive profession to enter, particularly in view of the poor remuneration of many clergy. It was not until after the First World War that the Church made grants available to those training for the ministry and it was only at that time (in accordance with a decision of 1909) that all ordinands were required to fulfil a period of residence at a theological college.

A further reason for the decline in the number of university graduate ordinands was the uncertainty of the career structure in the Church for all but the well-connected, and the disparity of income which the clergy received for the same work. Whilst all other professions in the nineteenth century were able to formulate a career structure and a promotional ladder based on merit and ability with a commensurate reward structure, the Church (alone after the abolition of the purchase of commissions) retained a pre-professional structure. Patronage as a system was an integral part of traditional society. In the nineteenth century, it was protected and defended by the laity, who saw it as an essential safeguard against the development of a priestly caste, and by many clergy who had either benefited by its operation, or who regarded it as a means of ensuring that no one church party was ever able to gain control of appointments. The clergy were not able to alter the system, but they were able to influence its operation in significant ways. As the relative value of advowsons began to fall steadily, the clergy (or their families) were able to purchase them on the open market. In the last quarter of the nineteenth century, £1000–£1500 would secure a benefice with a house and a modest but permanent income. By 1878, one-ninth (753) of the total livings in private patronage had clergy who were not only incumbents but also patrons; 599 more livings had incumbents with the same surname as the patron.[22] Promotion by merit had become the slogan of all professional reformers of the mid-ninetcenth century and

Victorian church reformers, such as Edward Bartrum (who wrote in 1866 a pamphlet entitled *Promotion by Merit Essential to the Progress of the Church*), counselled the adoption of the same principle. But the legal and institutional framework of the Church made it impossible without a thorough reshaping of the whole system of tenure and appointment. However, some slight progress was made in this direction, particularly in dioceses where the bishop was able to control a reasonable number of livings. Samuel Wilberforce, during his twenty-four-year tenure of the see of Oxford, managed to increase the bishop's patronage in that diocese from nine to thirty-nine livings and was thus able to promote energetic and competent clergymen to wider spheres of work and larger incomes. [23]

The size of the benefice income of an individual parish was determined by a number of historical factors, which included whether the parish had been impropriated, the generosity of ancient benefactors, and how the parish had fared during the enclosures. The benefice income of many parishes had been sharply increased by the enclosures. Henry Homer, Rector of Birdingbury (Warwickshire), a leading enclosure commissioner, had valued the tithe at as much as two-sevenths of the total land of the parish. Parliamentary Papers for 1867 showed that the clergy obtained 185,000 acres and almost £40,000 in lieu of their tithe rights. In Lincolnshire alone, 16 per cent of all the land allocated went to the clergy. [24] In the middle decades of the nineteenth century, the clergy as a profession were generally regarded as being well rewarded, although there was concern about the very poor benefices. H. Byerley Thompson in *The Choice of a Profession* (1854) regarded the clergy as better rewarded than other professional men, including barristers. In 1853, when four classes of Army chaplain were created, their salaries ranged from £241 15s to £511 10s 11d, whilst in the Church at large anything over £200 per annum was considered good. [25] However, the coincidence of inflation at the end of the century, and a decline in the value of many benefice incomes in the agricultural depression, made it increasingly difficult for the clergy to be regarded as anything other than poorly paid. It may also be suggested that the number of clergy who were entirely dependent on their benefice income increased. Whereas, in 1854, Conybeare had suggested that the private incomes of the clergy at least equalled their professional incomes, by the end of the century the Church was increasingly recruiting its clergy from those whose means were relatively more modest. [26] By the end of the century, livings which had been adequate by the standards of thirty years before had become distinctly unattractive, and patrons of such benefices in remote areas with a poor house were beginning to find it difficult to attract clergy.

As a profession, the clergy found themselves unable to deal with the problems of the aged and the chronically sick within their ranks. The most frequently advocated solution was that of building homes, but few were established. The Incumbents Resignation Acts (1871 and 1887), which allowed a clergyman to retire on a proportion of his former income, was basically the same as the medieval system which had been abolished in 1571, and worked on the principle that the retiring incumbent retained for life one-third of the benefice income. The scheme was satisfactory neither to those who retired nor to those newly appointed. As it did not apply to benefices under £200, its effect was further limited. [27] Advertisements in church papers of the period indicate that a number of companies specialized in providing annuities for the clergy and their families. But here also the less wealthy clergy were unlikely to be able to afford the premiums. The problem of elderly clergy, unable to perform their duties satisfactorily but also unable to retire, persisted into the inter-war years when a modern pensions scheme was introduced.

In conclusion, it may be seen that whilst the role of the clergyman underwent a process of professionalization, the clergy as a body were inhibited from closely approximating to the model of a profession because they were unable to gain control of a number of aspects of their professional life. Unlike other professions, the clergy did not have a professional institution which played such a critical role in the professionalization of other high-status occupational groups. The nature of the institutional context in which the clergy worked and, in particular, the Church's legal and constitutional status, together with the history of the role, which sanctioned certain pre-professional practices (particularly with regard to appointments and remuneration), were factors which prevented the clergy as a body achieving the degree of professionalization which other high-status occupational groups achieved in the nineteenth century.

THE CLERGY AND THE BEGINNINGS OF MARGINALITY

To complete the picture of the clergyman's role and position in English society at the end of the formative period, account must be taken of the profound changes which transformed society in the nineteenth century. The clergyman's role, as may be seen from the previous chapters, was shaped within the constraints of a paternalistic traditional society and its performance was dependent on a number of assumptions about the nature and workings of society which the clergy had formally shared with the gentry. Gradually, throughout the century, these assumptions were undermined as England became predominantly an urban and industrial nation with an economy which delivered most of its citizens from the poverty and insecurity of pre-industrial rural life. Whereas, previously, almost the whole population had lived within the constraints of a village, and its dependency system, in which the clergyman played such a significant role, by the end of the century over half the population lived in urban areas. Particularly in the new industrial areas, the disposition to challenge the assumptions of previous generations was strong, and there arose a new secular urban culture which owed little to the attitudes and values of the traditional rural society in which the clergyman's role had been shaped. The Church, so inextricably a part of the old order, found only a precarious foothold in these new communities.

Many nineteenth-century churchmen expressed the fear that the working classes were becoming alienated from the life of the Church, and the publication of Horace Mann's religious census statistics of 1851 revealed a situation which did nothing to quieten these fears. Though Victorians tended to blame themselves, the sympathies and attention of the working classes had been lost in the rural areas before the period of urbanization and industrialization. Such were the abuses and the neglect of the eighteenth-century Church, that attendance at church had gradually ceased to play a part in the life of the working man. Alick the Shepherd, in George Eliot's *Adam Bede* '. . . held the general impression that public worship and religious ceremonies like other non-productive employments were intended for people who had leisure'.[28] Even the remote rural areas felt the impact of these changes in English life, and the old establishment which had dominated the counties for so long began to give place to new men and new ideas. The smock, as Owen Chadwick has observed, which had been worn almost as a badge of servitude for generations, went out quite suddenly in the 1850s.[29]

The changes in society profoundly affected the position of the clergyman, who ceased to be typically the most educated man in the parish, and, by the late nineteenth century, he commonly found an increasing proportion of parishioners with an education that – certainly in practical affairs – matched or outmatched his own. Not only this, but the knowledge and values possessed by others frequently conflicted with the Church's view of the world. At this time a teacher might present to his pupils a set of values and a world-view basically at variance with that of the clergyman. His hour of 'religious instruction' was a last attempt to keep his foothold in an institution which the process of differentiation was gradually separating from the Church. The same may be said of social welfare and entertainment, both of which developed a degree of autonomy and professional personnel as well as standards of competence which exceeded the resources of energies of clerical amateurism. In an age of professionalism the clergyman became an amateur in all but the charter elements of his role.

However, the latter decades of the nineteenth century saw the Church gaining ground numerically, and on the eve of the First World War a higher percentage of Englishmen attended the services of the Church of England than had done in the 1830s. After the laxity of the eighteenth century, the Church of England was re-established as a ubiquitous institution, and it is part of the paradox of nineteenth-century history, that, although the Church received more popular support, at the same time, it was beginning to lose significance and centrality in English social life.[30] Society was gradually less inclined to accept its leadership, and educated men preferred to look elsewhere for the guidance and leadership which the Church and its clergy had traditionally provided. The vigour and the energy of the late-nineteenth-century parochial clergy in a sense masked their gradual removal from the mainstream of public life as, in an age of increasing scepticism and secularism, men looked elsewhere and to other institutions for those things the Church had formerly provided. The Church itself, in an increasingly differentiated society, progressively took on the nature of a voluntary, and in a sense optional or at least less socially prescribed, leisure activity. By the end of the nineteenth century, religion had become a commodity which had to be marketed (hence the late-Victorian concern for evangelism), in a society developing a wealth of alternative leisure activities. The clergy acknowledged, by implication, the competition of these leisure activities by their opposition to such things as the Sunday newspapers, the bioscope, and the bicycling and rambling clubs which all undermined old social habits. Bishop Randall Davidson devoted part of his Charge to his clergy in the diocese of Winchester in 1899 to observing that the bicycle was having a particularly deleterious effect on Sunday church attendance.[31]

In a work-oriented urban society, the clergy found themselves as the bearers of a traditional home-centred culture. Increasingly their ministry was concerned with women and children, and with the non-work areas of life, such as organizing entertainments and the uniformed organizations, which were then gaining popularity. The clergy had little contact with the work situation and many of the leisure activities of the men (the pubs and sport). The 'muscular Christianity' of the Edwardian period may be regarded in some respects as a bid by some clergy to remain in touch with ordinary people by taking part in their recreational and leisure activities. However, the very self-consciousness of the movement testifies to the growing marginality of the Church in everyday affairs. Thus, despite the transformation of English life in the nineteenth century, the Church remained essentially a part of the old order. Many clergy appeared to share with sensitive Victorians the view that the cities were a monstrous aberration, and that the countryside was where any man of consequence would naturally prefer to live. The ideal of the rural parish continued to dominate the thinking and the strategy of the Church of England well into the twentieth century.

The First World War was a critical time for the Church of England and marked, as in many spheres of life, a period of abrupt change. The popular unease created by the jingoistic attitude to the war of many prominent churchmen, coupled with the erosion of many of the social conventions which had previously sustained church attendance among the middle classes, notably 'the English Sunday', left the Church in the post-war years in a weakened situation. If the generality of the clergy could remain unaware of their growing marginality in the life of the nation, the 3030 clergy commissioned as chaplains in the First World War were forced to confront this reality. Perhaps nothing confirmed this in the popular mind so forcibly as the orders issued in the early stages of the war which forbade Church of England chaplains to go farther forward than brigade headquarters, unlike the Roman Catholic chaplains who went into the frontline trenches. Though some clergy quietly disregarded this order, only a few shared with the men the full horrors of living in the waterlogged trenches. These men discovered at firsthand the degree to which the bulk of the male population were estranged from the Church.[32]

By the end of the war many of the chaplains were committed to initiating far-reaching changes in the Church. Several reports were produced, and in *The Army and Religion*, it was recorded that in the popular mind the Church was almost wholly identified with its clergy, but that the clergy were almost completely out of touch with the lives and aspirations of ordinary men.[33] The more widespread realization of this estrangement and its implications caused at least some clergy in the next few decades to reflect on whether the alienation of the Church from working-class society was not in some way related to the particular form in which its ministry had been shaped throughout the previous century.

17

The Professions and Change in the Twentieth Century

It is necessary to place any consideration of the role of the clergyman as a professional man in contemporary society within the context of the changes which have affected the professions as a whole in recent years. The professions are still regarded as the occupational élite, and if they have not retained their relative economic advantages, they still occupy the position of high social status, privilege, and power which they attained in the nineteenth century. In the early decades of this century the widespread belief that the professional upper-middle classes were the backbone of the country, from whose ranks the ablest administrators, statesmen, colonial legislators, and military and ecclesiastical leaders were drawn, reached its zenith. Based on the common experience of public-school education, the professions developed behaviour patterns and social values which made them a homogeneous and identifiable unit in English society, whilst at the same time they retained the moral superiority and gentlemanly status which they inherited from the previous century. Thus a study of country doctors immediately after the introduction of the National Health Service revealed that they were still widely regarded as minor members of the local gentry.[1]

Perhaps the most noticeable changes in the professions in recent decades have been their expansion and the spread of some of the ideals of professionalism into almost all occupations. In the mid-nineteenth century, no more than a few thousand men could be regarded as professional men, and of these the overwhelming majority were clergymen. Today, 100 years later, one-sixth of the workforce is described as 'professional men' in the census return. Whilst, in the mid-nineteenth century, there were only a few thousand lawyers, today there are approximately 30,000

252

solicitors and nearly 5000 practising barristers. The Industrial Revolution and the subsequent developments in technology and bureaucracy have given rise to a large number of new administrative and technical professions. At the same time, not only has the number of recognized professions increased vastly, but professionalization as a process has affected almost all non-manual occupational roles. Spokesmen for many 'white-collar' occupational groups can be heard asserting that they are 'professionals', and entitled to the status and emoluments that such a claim implies.

The professions derive their authority and legitimacy from the possession of knowledge that is important in society, and therefore they are highly sensitive to changes in its nature and scope. In the nineteenth century, the form in which socially important knowledge had been cast, namely precedent, proverbial wisdom, and tradition, gradually gave place to empirical knowledge based on scientific discovery and to its dissemination and control in bureaucratic procedures. Whilst, in the nineteenth century, the ideal type of professional man had been characterized by classical learning, cultured tastes, gentlemanly manners, and a sound judgement on many topics, in the twentieth century, the ideal type of the professional man increasingly became that of the expert. A professional man in the twentieth century is characteristically a man of high and certificated competence in a defined area of knowledge in which he is an expert. However, this new ideal type did not completely eclipse the old, and there remains, in the older and learned professions pre-eminently, a preference for members who are able to combine characteristics of both. In 1958, the Royal College of Surgeons included these observations in their evidence to the Royal Commission on Doctors' and Dentists' Remuneration:

> . . . there has always been a nucleus in medical schools of students from cultured homes . . . This nucleus has been responsible for the continued high social prestige of the profession as a whole and for the maintenance of medicine as a learned profession. Medicine would lose

immeasurably if the proportions of such students in the future were to be reduced in favour of precocious children who qualify for subsidies from the local authorities and the state purely on examination results.[2]

In the nineteenth century, the professional man customarily worked on his own with the assistance of clerks and other non-professionals. The situation in which he worked was in some senses entrepreneurial in that the professional man 'put up his plate' and stood or fell by his own efforts in competition with others within the same area. (The regulation of this competition was one of the primary functions of the professional institutions.) Two changes in this century have radically altered the work situation of most professional men. First, such are the demands and complexity of contemporary society that few professional men are able to work on their own and provide a competent and comprehensive service to their clients. The need for complex and expensive back-up facilities has made single practice almost impossible in many professions. Second, the extent of professional knowledge, and the need to keep this up to date, has made it increasingly difficult for a professional man to be competent in more than a certain limited range of his professional concerns. This has led to the segmentation of professions and to increased specialization. The influence of these processes may be seen in their most developed form in American medicine where, currently, there are approximately eight doctors in specialist and consultant practice for every one in general practice.

These factors have determined that today few professional men work in individual practice and the vast majority are members of colleague teams. Initially such teams were comprised entirely of professional men, frequently with complementary specialisms, but increasingly today the team setting in which professional men work also includes non-professionals, whose role is increasingly seen as complementary rather than subservient. In a number of professions the characteristic work situation of the contemporary professional man is as the leader or consultant of a task-orientated team. Thus, the contemporary architect frequently works as a 'project director' leading and co-ordinating a team of specialists involved in a particular piece of construction. Since the 'charter' of 1965, there has been positive encouragement within the National Health Service for doctors to develop the team concept for primary medical care in purpose-built health centres (the team includes nurses, social workers, secretaries, receptionists, pharmacists, and other ancillary staff). Thus, in 1931, 34 per cent of professional men worked in individual practice, but by 1951, the figure had fallen to 10 per cent.[3] Today only a very small minority of professional men work outside a colleague group. The clergy form a major exception to this development, for the vast majority work in an individual practice. This proportion has fallen slightly in recent years, with the more extensive development of group and team ministries, but still the overwhelming majority of clergy, unlike other professional men, remain in individual practice.

If, in the nineteenth century, the professional man was typically an independent gentleman providing personal services for his social equals, in the twentieth century many professional men are the salaried employees of large corporations or bureaucracies. In modern society, many of the professions serve social rather than individual needs. The state has become a major employer of professional personnel, whose work situation is within the structural framework of a bureaucratic hierarchy. In this way institutional or corporate practice has arisen alongside colleague-group practice and individual practice. Some professions work almost wholly for the state, and most professions have some members employed by the state or local government (including the clergy). The classical dilemma, which has been much explored in the sociology of professions, is that faced by the professional man who is forced to choose between the ideals of his profession and the dictates of the bureaucracy or business corporation for which he works.[4] (The military chaplain is a much quoted example.) However, institutional or corporate practice is often attractive to modern professional men, as they are offered the possibility of advancing in a career structure which colleague-group and individual practice does not offer. It is noticeable that those in the Church who advocate a change to institutional or corporate practice (such as the authors of the Morley Report who suggested that a clergyman should be an employee of the diocese) usually base part of their case on the difficulties and tensions arising in a profession which lacks a formal career structure.

This shift from individual practice to colleague-group or institutional practice has resulted in a number of changes in the performance of the role of the professional man. Perhaps the most significant of these is that the reference group, which has such a powerful effect on the way the role is performed, is no longer composed of clients but of colleagues. There is a sense in which professional men in a team perform their role before a role-audience comprised of co-professionals. By any index such a performance tends to become more professional (in the sense that it conforms more closely to the role models and behaviour patterns currently sanctioned by the professions). The effect of this, and of colleague-group practice as a whole is to distance the professional man from the demands, expectations, and sanctions of his clients. Among the criticisms which are levelled at team and group ministry in the Church is that it leads to the development of a 'neo-clericalism' based on the fact that the clergyman's clerical colleagues, rather than the members of the congregation, become his principal role-audience and reference group.

Professional men in every age have been alert to the possibilities of encroachment by other occupational roles into areas of work which they previously regarded as their monopoly. The standardization of some aspects of professional work, and the impact of new technology on certain procedures, has created the conditions in which encroachment has become a major issue. The legal profession is particularly susceptible to encroachment by those who gain sufficient knowledge and competence to perform a particular legal act and are able to offer their services to the public at significantly cheaper rates. Recently, the legal profession has been attempting, both in the courts and in Parliament, to prevent non-professionals dealing with such matters as divorce procedure and property conveyancing. Since its inception, the Royal College of Psychiatrists has been concerned to restrict the encroachment of untrained therapists. At the same time many professions have found it necessary in the face of technical developments and increasing demands to sanction the rise of sub-professional groups within their area of competence. These occupational roles are frequently of a technical nature, such as the architectural technician. In some professions, principally medicine, the professional man is heavily dependent on the work of a number of sub-professionals. The sub-professions have developed autonomous professional institutions, though many of their practitioners are also members of a trade union. Many professions have become particularly sensitive to encroachment and also anxious for the sake of their own standing to require the sub-professions to maintain the highest standards. (Thus, the Department of Industry has recently set up an inquiry into the professional standards among technicians and draughtsmen.) It is possible to see the recent development of the Auxiliary Pastoral Ministry as an example of the emergence of such a group. In this instance the parent professional body has been successful in demanding similar standards with regard to entry qualifications.

A further feature of the development of the professions in recent years has been the admission of women. The professional bodies which have historically been self-governing bodies of men have only recently overcome their reluctance to admit women. Many factors concerning the status of women in society have contributed to this reluctance, not least the lingering belief among the upper middle classes that women should be leisured (in the way that gentlemen were leisured in the eighteenth century). During this century, women have gained admission into almost all professions, but their ability to reach high office within the professions is often hampered by the traditions and workings of the professional body. The clerical and military professions were alone in gaining exemption from the Sex Discrimination Act of 1975.

However, it is the social and attitudinal changes of the last few decades which have had the most far-reaching effect on the professions. Today, the professions find themselves culturally estranged and socially isolated from the mainstream of society, which is dominated, both in political and cultural terms, by egalitarian and proletarian attitudes. This is a part of the decline in the significance of middle-class value patterns which has occurred since the 1950s. Thus, today, it is not uncommon for the professions to be described, at least by implication, as socially exclusive, self-perpetuating monopolies. In the evidence of the Trade Unions Congress to the Royal Commission on Legal Services,[5] the legal profession are criticized for being socially exclusive (guaranteed by the system of premiums), monopolistic, and involving excessive costs. Recent criticisms of the Civil Service, and in particular its failure to implement the reforms outlined in the Fulton Committee Report (1968); and of the Diplomatic Service (by the Central Policy Review Committee of the Labour Party) have concerned themselves with the appropriateness of the lifestyle, manners, and social attitudes of professional men recruited predominantly from Oxford and Cambridge to represent the nation overseas in countries with very different lifestyles and value systems. (The professions are, broadly speaking, culturally specific to European and American society, and are not found in recognizably the same form in Communist or Third World countries.)

Largely because of the persistence of the older ideal type, the learned professions continue to recruit from a relatively narrow social band, despite attempts at widening the range of new entrants. The Royal Commission on Doctors' and Dentists' Remuneration found that just under 70 per cent of medical students in their final year in 1961 (and now in early mid-career) had fathers in social categories 1 and 2 (compared with the Robbins Committee findings, that of all undergraduates in 1961, 59 per cent had fathers in these two categories). At the same time, the professions tend to be self-recruiting. The Royal Commission on Medical Education 1965–8 showed that the number of medical students who had fathers who were doctors had increased, from 17 per cent in 1955–6, to 20 per cent in ten years. The corresponding figures are slightly higher for the clergy. It is still the practice that before being accepted for the bar, a student must obtain a letter from a responsible person stating that he is 'a gentle-man of respectability'. Of those externally recruited to administrative grades in the Civil Service in 1975–7, 63 per cent were Oxford or Cambridge graduates.[6]

As well as being regarded as socially and culturally isolated, the professions are further alienated from society as a whole by being regarded as a part of the governing establishment at a time when most social groups are aware of their relative powerlessness. In the main, the professions have access to the centres of political power, and most professions have members in the legislature. This is pre-eminently true of the legal profession; at present 22 per cent of all Members of Parliament are lawyers.

At a more pragmatic level, it is suggested that the professions in their traditional form are becoming too costly a way of ensuring the provision of certain services within society. The cost of professional services in almost every case is controlled by an agreed scale of fees. Mandatory minima are enforced to prevent competition on the basis of price, as professional men are regarded as competing for clients only on the basis of the quality of the services offered. (The parochial system is at one level an early device for preventing competition between professional men.) In the public mind, there has always been a disposition to believe that the practices of professional men and their altruistic statements are a disguise for monopolistic practices, which are based on self-interest and personal aggrandizement. In 1970, the professions were the subject of a major investigation by the Monopolies Commission, and, in 1978, the Monopolies and Mergers Commission recommended that the professional fees of architects and surveyors should be abandoned in favour of a system of free competition. The argument that the traditional auditing of accounts, as required by law, is both too costly (it is estimated that it costs British industry in excess of £250 million a year) and is irrelevant to contemporary needs has recently gained considerable prominence.

In these and many other ways, the professions, despite their considerable efforts to adapt to contemporary circumstances, find themselves forced on to the defensive in an increasingly hostile climate. In some professions members who have become aware of the gulf which separates them from the attitudes, values, and lifestyles of the mainstream of society have taken steps to bridge this gulf by making the services of the profession and professional personnel more accessible in less formal surroundings than is normally the case. The drug abuse centres and the law centres are examples of this movement. The first law centre was opened in Kensington in 1971, and there are now thirty-five in England and Wales mainly in inner city areas. They are financed partly by doing work under the Legal Aid fund, partly by the Lord Chancellor's Department but pre-dominantly (and in some cases entirely) from local authority grants. Some professions, such as the Association of University Teachers, have themselves found it necessary to acknowledge the proletarianization of society by adopting attitudes and methods previously associated with trade unions. It is suggested that one of the reasons why relatively large numbers of professional men work abroad at some stage in their career (particularly in medicine, veterinary science, and accountancy) is their desire to work in a country which has not developed similar attitudes towards the professions. The subsequent examination of the role of the clergyman in contemporary society, and the situation of the clerical profession, needs to be placed within the context of these changes which have affected all professions in recent decades.

18

The Clergyman's Role in Contemporary Society

THE IMPACT OF SOCIAL CHANGE

The social and intellectual changes which have transformed English society in this century have profoundly altered the context in which the clergyman exercises his ministry. Today, the clergyman's role is performed within a society which no longer accepts the Christian framework of transcendental order within which Western European society and culture were formed, or the moral universe in which all acts both personal and social were once evaluated.[1] In advanced societies, religion has ceased to fulfil those integrating and regulating functions which it fulfilled in traditional society. The processes of change, initiated in the nineteenth century, have gathered momentum and contemporary society is characterized by rapid technological innovation, democratic and egalitarian political movements, humanist and secular social philosophies, cultural pluralism, and the growth of bureaucratization, urbanization, mobility, and affluence. In modern society, it is increasingly the case that the dominant behaviour patterns and values are those propagated by the entertainment industry and these are themselves subject to rapid and constant changes. Such is the society in which the contemporary clergy perform their historic role.

Whereas, in the nineteenth century, the Church's place in society was accepted, understood, and for the most part unquestioned, today the Church is regarded as an ambivalent institution, the role and function of which are far from clear. By many, religious institutions are seen as a part of the pre-technical, agrarian, paternalistic past, and in consequence are thought of as largely anachronistic in modern society. The word which is constantly employed to describe the situation of the contemporary Church is 'irrelevant', for the processes of social change have robbed the Church in this century of much of its former social, political, and cultural significance. As the representative figure of the Church, the clergyman feels in his own person the frustrations and dilemmas which these altered circumstances and the constant questioning of the Church's relevance in contemporary society have occasioned. Whereas, in the nineteenth century, the clergyman's role received widespread social support and was accorded a commensurate significance, in the twentieth century the clergy are seen predominantly as the bearers of a cultural inheritance and the exemplars of a moral and social tradition which is regarded as increasingly outmoded and unwanted at least in its traditional form.

Above all else, in contemporary society the clergyman's role is characterized by marginality to the mainstream concerns of ordinary people. The knowledge to which the clergyman has access and which he seeks to impart is seen as irrelevant to the day-to-day decisions which people and groups face. Modern man now turns to other experts for advice and counsel. For the overwhelming majority in contemporary Britain, whose connection with formal religion is either extremely tenuous or non-existent, the clergyman's role is seen as one which has little contemporary significance and belongs essentially to the past. In such a situation it is hardly surprising that the clergy have suffered from a deep sense of bewilderment and disorientation, and are inclined to hold fast to the old certainties. At all levels in the Church there is an awareness that the ministry is passing through not just a period of temporary uncertainty but a profound crisis.

THE CLERGY AS A PROFESSIONAL BODY

Most professions, as we noted in the previous chapter, have expanded at a considerable rate in this century. By contrast, the clergy who, at the turn of the century, were more numerous than all other professions combined, have experienced a marked contraction in their numbers. This phenomenon has been the central concern of the clergy as a professional body in recent decades and it is commented on frequently at some length, in almost every preface to *Crockford's Clerical Directory* in this century. In 1841, there were 14,613 clergymen (total number in England and Wales), and the number rose to 25,235 in 1901. However, by 1911 the total number had fallen back to 23,918; and by 1931 to 19,147 (England only). The 1940s marked a period of more rapid decline, and despite a slight upturn in the late 1950s, by 1961 there were only 13,429 members of the clerical profession, and in 1968 the number of beneficed clergy dropped below 10,000 for the first time. There were 12,905 clergy in 1971; 12,056 in 1976; and the most recent statistics indicate that there are currently 11,782 clergymen in the forty-three dioceses of the Church of England. Recent planning in the Church has been based on the assumption that there will be 11,000 in 1981; this figure has already been revised downwards to 10,700 in 1981 and 10,500 in 1982. [2]

The decline in the number of clergy, as the *Crockford's* prefaces constantly emphasized, particularly in recent years, has been caused by the low levels of recruitment into the clerical profession. In order to maintain the profession at a strength of 20,000, it is calculated that an annual recruitment of 600 is necessary and in the 1890s this figure was on average exceeded. However, in the period 1948–52, the yearly average had fallen to approximately 400. In the mid- and late 1950s, following demobilization (and the vast evangelistic meetings of the Billy Graham London Crusade in Harringay Arena in 1954) the figures began to rise (1955 – 455; 1957 – 480; 1959 – 534; and 1961 – 605). In 1963, when 636 men were ordained, a peak was reached and since that year there has been a steady decline in the number of those entering the clerical profession (1962 – 633; 1965 – 592; 1967 – 496; 1969 – 436; and 1971 – 393). In 1972, 340 men were ordained to the stipendiary ministry but the total number of those ordained was increased by the first group of twenty-one men ordained under the Auxiliary Pastoral Ministry scheme. A slight increase in 1973, 350 + 23* encouraged the belief that the decade of declining recruitment had ended. However, the figures for subsequent years (1974 – 345 + 44; 1975 – 321 + 52; 1976 – 281 + 81; and 1977 – 301 + 82) indicate that recruitment into the clerical profession remains at a comparatively low level.

*The second figure refers to those ordained under the APM scheme which should be added to the previous figure to give the total number of those ordained in each year. (Source – ACCM statistics.)

Whilst the inability of the profession to attract sufficient new members was one cause of its contraction, another was the accelerating rate of retirements. In previous generations, retirement had been impossible for many clergy for financial reasons, and, as has been mentioned above, it was a mark of the clergy's growing professional self-consciousness that, in 1871, a rudimentary pension scheme was introduced. Between 1928 and 1936, measures were introduced which shaped a more modern pensions scheme. In 1971, the present scheme came into operation, whereby clergy who have completed forty years' service, or are over seventy years old, qualify for a full pension. The retirement age for clergy is sixty-five, but, at the bishop's discretion, clergy may continue to serve until they are seventy. After the age of seventy, a clergyman may continue to serve only in a voluntary capacity.

Among those who were ordained in the 1950s, when the post-war peak years were reached, were many former servicemen. Thus, the rate of retirements has recently risen sharply, and at approximately 505 per year has considerably exceeded, and in some years nearly doubled, the rate of recruitment. The average age of Church of England clergy is fifty-three and there were, in 1976, only 2792 clergy under forty years of age, which is almost equal to the number of clergy who were sixty or over (2685). Thus, the clerical profession has an age structure heavily weighted towards the older age groups, a fact which has a number of ramifications in the life of the Church, for age is customarily regarded as one of the most significant variables in accounting attitudinal differences. It is usual to regard the older age groups as generally more conservative in their attitudes and less likely to initiate or encourage changes.[3] Furthermore, it may be said that high levels of retirement will continue well into the 1980s, further decreasing the total number of clergy unless recruitment levels reach an average of 600 per year.

But inadequate recruitment and retirements are not the only causes of the contemporary contraction in the profession; for resignations and those who 'opt out' also constitute a significant loss. The Church of England does not publish figures of those who resign their orders and sever all connections with the clerical profession. But their number must be relatively small. Far more significant are those who 'opt out' and take up employment outside the Church without formally resigning their orders. (The number of worker-priests in the Church of England after the French model is extremely small.) The situation may be judged from a survey undertaken in 1973–4 to discover what had happened to the 2131 theological students who had entered four colleges between 1951 and 1965. Of the entry group (2131), the number subsequently ordained was 1823; of these 1278 were in parochial work in 1973–4. Of the remaining 545 (more than a quarter of the ordained group), 307 were known to hold specialist non-parochial posts within the Church, and twenty had died or retired. The remaining 218 (approximately 11 per cent of those ordained) were all employed outside the Church – 89 had formally resigned their orders, the rest had 'opted out'. Among the 'opting out' group, it was noticed that few had left because of a crisis of faith; the majority had left either for financial or marital reasons, or because of the tensions and frustrations associated with the Church in general and the clerical role in particular.[4] Among those who opted out were some of the recruits with the highest academic and intellectual qualifications, and the failure of any professional body to hold within its ranks men of this calibre must be of particular concern. The level of resignations and 'opting out' has almost certainly been rising in recent years.

The effect of this contraction has become more marked at the local level as the decline in numbers has accelerated. In 1974, the diocese of Norwich had 340 clergy, whilst in 1982 it is scheduled to have 228. In 1976, the Gloucester diocese had 240 clergy, whereas in 1982 it is scheduled to have 168. The Coventry diocese had 201 clergy in 1973 and is scheduled to have 166 in 1982. The implications of the ageing of the profession may be judged from the fact that one-third of the clergy in the Warwick Archdeaconry are currently sixty years of age or over. Diminishing number has a direct effect on the way in which the clergyman conceives of and performs his role, as each clergyman is required to be responsible for a larger area (and in rural areas more churches).

In the face of declining numbers, the clerical profession has been under constant pressure both to widen the catchment area from which it recruits, and to alter the entry requirements to accommodate those who formerly would not have qualified. The clerical profession has never had an absolute entry requirement, and a bishop is free to ordain whom he chooses, having been assured by his Examining Chaplains that the candidate is fit for ordination. In the early decades of the nineteenth century, almost all ordinands attended Oxford or Cambridge (91 per cent of those ordained in 1827–8)[5] and, in the final decades of the nineteenth century and the years before the First World War, approximately half the ordinands attended Oxford or Cambridge, a quarter some other university, principally Durham, and a quarter were non-graduates. In the period after the First World War, the number of men who had not been to university began to rise, and in the immediate post-war years the Church established a special college at Knutsford which prepared servicemen for ordination. Though Knutsford was closed in 1922, the college which fulfilled the same function after the Second World War, Brasted Place, remained in operation until 1976, preparing men, many of whom had had the minimum of formal education, for a place in a theological college, and for subsequent ordination. Through the century, the percentage of graduate ordinands has continued to decline, and in 1976 42 per cent of those ordained were not university graduates. Alongside the 'less scholarly candidates', the Church was increasingly willing to ordain men embarking on a second career, many of them coming from the services after an early retirement. A number of theological colleges provided sandwich or shorter courses for 'mature students', whose numbers reached a peak in the late 1960s.

The number of theological colleges has been reduced from over forty to fourteen, and these offer 900 places of which 672 in 1978 were occupied by ordinands in residential training. The high cost of such training coupled with changes in local authority educational grant payments resulted in the Church recommending, in 1977, that the normal length of training be reduced from three to two years (two to one year for graduates). However, these regulations have since been cancelled as a general rule. As in other professions, there can be little doubt that those qualifying now are better equipped than previous generations and that the theological colleges have greatly altered and updated their courses; none the less, in the clerical profession the percentage of graduates continues to fall (whereas many other professions are greatly increasing their graduate intake, and some will not now accept non-graduates) and the requirements of entry appear both in relative and actual terms to be falling. An ACCM working party on training courses (which reported in January 1978) has questioned whether many of the ordinands are now sufficiently able to make use of the form and type of training which theological colleges have traditionally offered.[6] Statements about the declining academic standards of those seeking ordination may sometimes be regarded as the only measurable and acceptable way in which to make more fundamental assessments of the new recruits to the profession. Changes in the quality of men coming forward are much less accessible. But in recent years concern that the quality of men offering themselves for ordination may also be falling has been occasionally expressed. Certainly, at a time when residential training is so costly, questions about quality which have not previously been asked, at least in public, are more widely heard.

Like most professions, the clergy have been concerned to maintain their relative position in society with regard to their remuneration. The amount of money which a role can command may be regarded as an indication of the significance that society accords it. Today, pay is increasingly related to status as is implied in the current use of the word 'differentials'. In the mid-nineteenth century, the stipends of the clergy were in general regarded as providing a reasonable living for a professional man, although it is difficult to generalize, considering the minority of very poor benefices. However, in the early decades of this century, when the remuneration of other professions advanced considerably, clerical incomes failed to keep their comparative value, and often actually fell in real terms. At the end of the Second World War, men were inducted into country livings with incomes below £200 per annum, and the Church was obliged to initiate a more widespread policy of augmenting the incomes of poorer benefices. In 1957, the average clerical income was £582 per annum, whilst at the same time the average income of other professional men (barristers, solicitors, doctors, and dentists) was approximately five times as much. In 1948, the Church Commissioners were established, through the amalgamation of Queen Anne's Bounty and the Ecclesiastical Commissioners, to hold, invest, and administer the ancient endowments of the Church. The Commissioners have been successful in considerably increasing the income of the clergy relative to other professions. In 1978, a clergyman of incumbent status received a stipend within the range of £2900 to £3250 (as recommended by the Central Stipends Authority), together with a house, rent- and rate-free. However, a part of the clergy's inability to approximate closely to the professional model lies in the fact that the profession's finances are almost entirely in the hands of the Church Commissioners, a body which draws its authority not from the profession but from Parliament, and which submits its annual report to the Home Secretary. The Church Commissioners are not responsible to the General Synod and rank as a Department of State. The effective management of the Church's finances is in the hands of the three Church Estates Commissioners (one of whom must be a Member of Parliament).

The parsonage house represents a large proportion of the clergyman's remuneration, and is currently calculated to be worth the equivalent of £1700 per annum. Recently, the Commissioners have disposed of many of the older and larger parsonages which belonged to the era of cheap fuel and many servants. However, despite the recent increases effected by the Church Commissioners, the cash salary which the clergy receive remains modest when compared with other professions, and is currently below the government definition of 'low paid'. A clerical family with no other income than the stipend and with two children qualifies to receive Family Income Supplement and other benefits; and in some parishes both the vicar and assistant priest are dependent on social security for some part of their total income. The situation can be further exacerbated by the fact that as previous chapters have indicated, the clergyman has traditionally met all the costs incurred in exercising his ministry out of his own stipend. In recent years, the clergy have campaigned vigorously for these to be met by the parish. Clerical families, like many families, are increasingly dependent on the incomes of two salary earners; and today, the majority of younger clergy wives work. This new pattern has altered the traditional expectations of the role of the clergyman's wife and not a few clergy wives have sought jobs in part to escape these expectations.

There is among the clergy a small and vocal group which believes that 'the clergy are being grossly exploited'. Currently a body (The Association of Clergy) which claims to act as a professional association for the clergy has a membership of 130, and approximately forty clergy have become members of a trade union (the Association of Scientific, Technical, and Managerial Staffs). An advertisement in 1978 in a church newspaper for a diocesan training officer indicated that if a clergyman were appointed, he would receive the diocesan minimum stipend (£2900 and a house), whilst if a layman were appointed he would receive £7000 per annum. This reveals something of the gap between the clerical stipend and the comparable professional salary.

In the 1960s, it was widely recognized that profound changes were taking place in every area of national life and that it was necessary to adapt and alter existing institutions to take account of these changes. Dr Beeching radically restructured the railway network; Lord Fulton proposed extensive reforms in the Civil Service, as did Lord Franks at Oxford University. In the same way the Church of England commissioned Dr Leslie Paul to conduct a detailed analysis of the institution and to propose such reforms as might be considered necessary. The Paul Report was received in 1964 and proposed a variety of changes aimed at rationalizing the deployment of the clergy and altering the institutional context in which the clergyman was employed and worked. The report proposed the transformation of the parson's freehold into a limited tenure leasehold; the abolition of patronage in favour of an appointments system based on national and regional staff boards; the pooling of benefice incomes; and a number of alterations to the parochial system including the setting up of group and team ministries. A number of these later recommendations have since been implemented in the Pastoral Measure, 1968. However, little progress was made with many of the central propositions, as the clergy rallied to defend the ancient system of the benefice and the parson's freehold. Despite the commonly admitted dysfunctions of both these ancient systems, the clergy were unwilling to contemplate even minor changes to the legal framework which they regarded as guaranteeing their status as independent professional men. So much was this the case that, when the report of the Morley Commission, which was set up to consider these aspects of the Paul Report, was found to be even more drastic in its recommendations, it was defeated in the Church Assembly's final session (July 1970). The committee which was asked to examine these issues a third time (The Terms of Ministry Committee, which first reported in 1972) was requested to do so without bringing in recommendations which interfered with either patronage or freehold.

The strength of the clergy's adherence to the traditional understanding of their role, as self-employed, independent professional men precluded any alteration to those arrangements on which professional status appeared to depend. Whilst many of the subsidiary recommendations in the Paul Report have now been implemented, the failure of the clergy as a profession to confront the central recommendations concerning patronage and freehold have meant that the process of change initiated by the Report has been by no means as drastic and far-reaching as its author clearly hoped it would be. Since the defeat of the Morley Commission's proposals, the clergy have constantly indicated that they are unwilling to consider changes in the area of the institutional context of their role, as was demonstrated by the failure of the Parsonage Amendment Measure in July 1977, which involved only a very slight erosion of the incumbent's rights.

In 1957, a clergyman wrote to *The Times* regretting that 'the parochial clergy of the Church of England are becoming transformed into the salaried members of a diocesan staff, living in houses provided and maintained for them on incomes fixed and guaranteed by diocesan stipend funds'.[7] It is a measure of the strength of the traditional role image that the clergy have been particularly sensitive to changes which undermine their independent status. Whereas other professional men have come to terms with the idea that, in an advanced society, they must necessarily be employed within bureaucratic structures, the clergy have consistently indicated that they are unwilling to change in this way, despite the inadequacies of the present system. Much of the breadth of the opposition to the Morley Report stemmed from the particular recommendation that on ordination a man should be placed 'on the strength' of a diocese which would be responsible for paying and employing him. Although the creation of the Central Stipends Authority (in November 1972), the payment of clergy centrally (from April 1978), the transference of the ownership of glebe land and endowment (from April 1978), and the treatment of the clergy for National Insurance purposes as employees, all marked steps in the direction which other professions have followed, none of these changes have been brought about without clerical opposition and the need for constant reassurance that such measures in no way undermine the independence of the clergyman. Whilst observers have tended to see the clergy's opposition to organizational changes as merely a preference for historic modes of procedure and a distrust of centralized administration, it may be seen that this opposition stems in large measure from the clergy's image of their role as that of independent professional men.

Two further areas of concern which professions seeking to adapt to contemporary circumstances have had to confront are the development of a suitable career structure and the problems associated with the distribution of professional services. A recent career pamphlet issued by the Church of England stated: 'Unlike most secular organizations, the Church has no defined pay or promotion structure.'[8] Within three to eight years of his entry to the profession, a clergyman may be appointed as an incumbent of a parish (or to a position of incumbent status) and his subsequent career will involve a number of moves to different parishes, none of which is likely to involve an increase in his salary. Like many of the older professions, the clerical profession has a wide base and is narrow at the apex. There was, in 1976, a ratio of approximately 100 clergy to every bishop (there were 117 bishops and 11,565 other clergy in that year). Most other professions, conscious of the tensions and problems caused by such a situation, have taken steps to create a rudimentary career structure. It was one of the grievances of the junior hospital doctors, in their strike of 1977, that the opportunities to become a consultant were very limited. However, as has been noted, the clergy's adherence to the ancient patronage system has prevented the emergence of a formal career structure.

As professions recruit predominantly from the middle classes, there is a tendency for professional men to wish to live in middle-class areas, with the result that the provision of professional services in certain areas is limited, whilst other areas are relatively well served. Many professions, particularly those with strong central organizations, have taken steps in recent years – usually by a system of incentive payments – to ensure professional services in those areas least attractive to middle-class professional men. The clerical profession, because of the vocational nature of its work and the positive attraction of working in areas such as inner-city and slum parishes, has not had to face such a severe problem. However, the diminishing number of clergy has served to emphasize the uneven nature of the profession's distribution. Clergy have, as a whole, always preferred to work in the more accessible rural and market town parishes in the Midlands, south-west and south-east England (the Province of Canterbury). Many clergy expect to spend the last years of their active ministry in a rural parish, and the ageing of the profession has meant that there is much competition to work in certain favoured rural areas (such as Somerset, Gloucester, Worcester, Hereford, Dorset, and the West Country). On the other hand, vacancies have become increasingly difficult to fill in some northern and midland industrial towns. The reasons for this are varied, but prominent among them is the fact that clergy wives do not find it easy to secure jobs in such areas, and increasingly the movement of clergy depends upon the clergyman's wife being able to find a suitable job in the new area, as well as the availability of suitable schools. The Morley Report proposal for national and regional appointments boards was turned down, and more recently a system of maximum recommended numbers for each diocese has been accepted. This system operates as a check on over-recruiting by the favoured dioceses, but does not provide an incentive for a clergyman to work in some of the least attractive areas. It is suggested by some that just as priority areas are recognised by the medical and teaching professions, so the clerical profession may have to devise positive incentives to encourage members of the profession to work in deprived and less attractive areas if a reasonable spread of professional services is to be ensured – a matter of some significance for a national Church.

Finally, many professional bodies have recently been concerned with matters of discipline and professional standards. The clerical profession inherited a complex system of archidiaconal, diocesan, and provincial courts, which was rationalized by legislation of 1963. All matters concerning doctrine, ritual, and ceremony are now referred to the Court of Ecclesiastical Causes Reserved. Matters regarding the conduct of clergy are tried in diocesan Consistory Courts (with appeal to Provincial Courts). In practice, the clerical profession has only a rudimentary discipline procedure, and with the exception of cases of gross dereliction of duty or immorality for which a clergyman can be deprived of office, status, and livelihood – a process known as 'defrocking' – the profession is unable to deal with members who bring it into disrepute. The recent Incumbents (Vacation of Benefice) Measure enacted in 1977 has made it possible for a clergyman to be removed from a benefice, despite his freehold, where there has been a serious breakdown of pastoral relations. The first case was not brought until 1979, as such matters do not easily submit themselves to the examination of the bishop's court of inquiry and the expense and attendant publicity is enough to deter diocesan authorities from proceeding. The clerical profession is, therefore, without any effective official disciplinary procedures and a clergyman cannot be dismissed for either incompetence or inactivity. In fact, the general lack of accountability is a feature of the clerical profession and a point of significant dissimilarity from other professions. This is not to deny that the episcopate is in a position to exercise disciplinary influences informally and generally prefers, for obvious reasons, to act by such means.

Thus, whereas the clerical profession continues to exhibit many characteristics which are shared with other professions in contemporary society, these are derived in the main from their common history and particularly from the changes which reshaped high-status occupational roles in the mid- and late nineteenth century. In contemporary society, the clerical profession has found itself unable to embrace many of the changes which have altered other professions in recent years and remains, in many significant aspects, in the form which it assumed in the mid-nineteenth century.

CHANGES IN THE ROLE OF THE CONTEMPORARY CLERGYMAN

In any comparison of the handbooks written for the clergy today, such as *The Office and Work of a Priest* by Robert Martineau (1972) and *A Handbook of Pastoral Work* by Michael Hocking (1977), with those written in the mid-nineteenth century, it is the similarities rather than the changes that are most striking. Though the detailed advice takes account of differing circumstances, the headings under which it is given, and the assumptions on which it is based, are largely unchanged. However, there have been changes despite the overall similarities, not least those caused by the contraction of the profession and changed attitudes in society as a whole. These changes may be grouped under four general headings: the increased concentration on the defining functions of the role; the contraction in the range of functions; the decline in community-orientated functions; and the increased significance of administration.

In many professions, there has been a tendency in this century for the range of functions to contract, and for the professional man to devote the vast majority of his time to those functions which are the irreducible core of his role, and from which his role derives its legitimacy and authority. For the clergymen, these central and defining functions are those of leading public worship and celebrating the sacraments, together with the other charter roles, of which that of pastor is pre-eminent. The decline in the number of clergy has further accelerated this process, as those who remain are compelled to fulfil these functions over a larger area and for a greater number of people. In the countryside, it is inevitable that a clergyman with seven or eight (and in some cases twelve to fourteen parishes) will spend a much higher proportion of his time on these functions than did his predecessors. It follows that the contemporary clergyman has much less time to involve himself in those other functions which occupied so much of the time of his Victorian predecessors. In urban areas, the reduction of clergy coupled with the increase in the population makes this process of change even more demonstrable. Surplice duties, and especially funerals, have now come to occupy a position of prominence in the clergyman's role which they did not have in the nineteenth century. The parish of St Andrew's, Rugby, had a staff of ten in the years immediately after the First World War serving a population of 26,000. Today, the parish has a staff of three serving the same population (a staffing ratio which is high by contemporary standards). In the parish of Stoke St Michael, in East Coventry, in the winter of 1976, a single clergyman conducted an average of fourteen funerals per week and there are many urban areas in which, in the winter, this weekly figure is exceeded. Many clergy are troubled by being obliged to provide this service for people, the vast majority of whom have no connection with the Church, and they feel that their role has become merely that of an adjunct to the funeral director. Various solutions to this problem are currently being canvassed in the Church and there is some support for laymen taking funeral services in certain instances (particularly the short committal service at a crematorium and to this there is no legal objection). However, what is clear at present is that the clergy spend a much higher proportion of their time on these central and charter functions than was formally the case.

This contraction in the range and scope of functions which the clergyman is able to perform means that the contemporary clergyman, particularly in urban areas, increasingly finds that he has little time to allocate to those extra-ecclesial functions with which the Victorian clergyman concerned himself. The clergy often speak of the Church's ministry as the 'pastoral ministry', and recent surveys of the attitude of clergy to their work demonstrate the dominance of this understanding.[9] In M. G. Daniel's research into the attitudes of ninety-six Anglican clergy in Greater London in 1967, he found (using Blizzard's role sector categorization) that 53 per cent of the clergy regarded 'pastor' as the most important role sector; 17 per cent 'priest'; 8 per cent 'preacher'; 6 per cent 'teacher'; and 0 per cent 'organizer/administrator'.[10] The more recent research of Ransom, Bryman, and Hining (1977), using different, but broadly similar role sectors, confirms the dominance of the pastor.[11]

Role sector	Rank order	Average placing
Pastor	1	1.9
Celebrant	2	2.7
Preacher	3	3.1
Counsellor	4	3.4
Leader	5	4.6
Administrator	6	5.2
Official/representative	7	6.5

Both these and other surveys, together with the general literature of the profession, accord to the pastoral functions of the clergyman's role an overarching precedence, and the majority of clergy see their role principally in terms of this function. Yet it may be observed that the reduction in the number of the clergy and other changes in the clergyman's role (particularly the increased significance of administration) has reduced markedly the amount of time which they are able to give to this function. Such is the demand made on the clergyman's time by leading worship and preaching (and preparing for these functions), visiting the sick, the 'surplice duties', and various administrative commitments, that in many parishes the proportion of the clergyman's week that can be given to more general pastoral functions is relatively small. General parish visiting by the clergyman is no longer possible in all but some rural areas, and house-to-house visiting is now often undertaken by members of the congregation. In many areas of the clergyman's pastoral functions, the clergy are increasingly having to depute specific functions to members of the congregation. Most dioceses now organize training schemes for lay pastors. The awareness that the clergy have little time to perform those functions to which they accord overarching significance is a major cause of contemporary unease in the clerical profession. Increasingly, the amount of pastoral work which a clergyman is able to do is being curtailed, and as a result the clergy feel estranged from the role for which they were trained.

Bryan Wilson has identified the eroding of the traditional functions of the clergyman's role as one of the chief causes of uncertainty and confusion.[12] In this century, the emergence and development of the 'caring' professions and of the Welfare State has continued a process begun in the second half of the nineteenth century, whereby the clergy have been obliged to concede functions which they previously performed to new occupational roles. At the same time, the many recreational and leisure activities which the clergy organized in the early decades of this century (especially the uniformed youth organizations) are an area of activity from which they have now largely withdrawn. Similarly, the involvement of the clergy in politics, the administration of law and order, and the social and welfare services has now diminished to very small proportions. These alterations in the clergyman's role reflect wider changes in society and particularly the decline in community in recent decades.

Among all the processes of change which have altered society since the Second World War, the atrophy of community has had the most far-reaching effects for the Church.

This decline, for which the causes are complex and varied, has meant that areas of social activity which were once characterized by public activity have become essentially private. All voluntary associational activities have suffered declining levels of support and the Church has been among them. The recent suggestion, that those viewing a Holy Communion service on television should place bread and wine before them and take part in the Communion, represents the extreme privatization of what is essentially a public act. In the nineteenth century, the Church was a focus, and in a sense a sacralized expression, of community, and the clergyman (as previous chapters have indicated) fulfilled many functions which derived from the community-orientation of his role. In this century, in a predominantly urban society, the Church is no longer seen as a focus of community and the clergy are no longer expected to perform those focal and representative functions which were revived from the clergyman's former position in a traditional rural society.

This is not the only area in which the range of the clergyman's functions has contracted, for there has been a growing tendency for those needing spiritual counsel to seek the advice and guidance of gurus, poets, commune leaders, proponents of self-sufficiency and alternative lifestyles, experts in yoga, and the expositors of other world faiths. At the same time, those seeking guidance in more pragmatic matters increasingly tend to seek the advice of marriage guidance counsellors, psychiatrists, social workers, schools' counsellors, and the personnel of Citizens' Advice Bureaux, and other voluntary organizations which offer counselling such as Alcoholics Anonymous and the Samaritans, all of which are regarded as specialist agencies that have effectively taken over areas in which the clergyman formerly worked in an essentially amateur and untrained capacity. Many clergy have acknowledged this change by becoming trained counsellors in these organizations, particularly in marriage guidance and the Samaritans.

Finally, there has been a marked increase in the significance of administrative functions in the clergyman's role in recent decades. Like all large institutions, the Church has developed a sophisticated bureaucratic structure which places administrative demands on its local officials. Indicative of this change is the subtle way in which the furnishings of the clergyman's study have altered so that the room today commonly resembles an administrator's office. On the clergyman's desk are forms and returns of many sorts, agendas for meetings in the diocese, the deanery, the local council of churches, and numerous parish committees, together with the accounts and reports which relate to the clergyman's responsibility for the finances of the parish and the fabric of its church. In all the surveys recently made of the clergyman's attitude to his work, it is consistently recorded that the clergy accord very low levels of significance to administrative and organizational activities. Clergy customarily regard such functions as burdensome and mundane and a distraction from the more highly regarded elements of their role. Yet in contemporary society the clergyman, like all officials of large bureaucratic institutions, is compelled to devote an increasing proportion of his time to administrative functions.

In the previous chapter it was noted that two complementary processes of change have radically reshaped the professions in this century; these are the change from individual to corporate practice and the development of specialization. Individual practice in the clerical profession has been institutionalized in the form of the parochial system, and although a number of clergy may work in one parish, they have not until recently worked as equals at a common task, but rather in an employer-employee relationship. The movement towards corporate practice in the clerical profession is older than is usually supposed, and, in 1894, a scheme was drawn up for a new form of ministry in the country area around Andover.[13] It was proposed that a number of clergy would be corporately responsible for a number of parishes, but legal impediments prevented this scheme becoming a reality. As we have seen (page 270), it was argued in the Paul Report that the legal objections to the development of corporate practice among the clergy should be set aside, and in the Pastoral Measure of 1968 provision was made for the formation of group and team ministries.

Currently there are approximately 400 group and team ministries in the Church of England, served by approximately 1000 clergy. The distribution of these corporate practices is by no means even, with the majority being found in rural areas (especially in Norfolk where they were pioneered) and in new towns and industrial areas. [14]

Specialization has become almost the predominant feature of the professions in this century. In the clerical profession, as a result of its history and diffuse functions, there has always been an element of specialization. The clerical schoolmaster, and those clergymen who ministered to specialist pastoral charges, such as a hospital, a ship, a university, a regiment, or a prison provide examples of some degree of specialization. In this century, the Church has appointed specialist clergy to work in industry, in social work, and community relations, in adult education, and evangelism, in youth work, in the arts and leisure activities. These men are appointed from the parochial clergy and customarily receive no specialist training. The majority of them are seen as providing specialist support for the parochial clergy. Their numbers are relatively small; in 1976 there were only 229 full-time specialist clergy (though a number of parochial clergy devote a part of their time to specialist activities). The fact that so few clergy are involved in this form of ministry reflects the resistance of the Church (which has increased with the reduction in manpower) to such appointments and may be regarded as further evidence of the strong adherence of the clerical professional to the traditional role image.

THE CHANGED SOCIAL POSITION OF THE CLERGY

Whereas the changes in the functions of the clergyman's role have been limited, so that in many aspects it still closely resembles the form that it assumed in the mid-nineteenth century, the changes which have resulted from the altered social position of the role have been of a more radical and far-reaching nature. In the late nineteenth century, the role occupied a position of high social status, and there was in society at large a broad consensus concerning its duties, functions, and appropriate behaviour pattern. Not only did the role have high social status, but it possessed a central position in the social and cultural life of the nation, and, if in the intellectual and political arenas the involvement of the clergy was less significant, none the less they retained an acknowledged place.

In contemporary society, the clergy still occupy a prominent position in the vertical hierarchy of prestige accorded to occupational roles, and in surveys the clergy consistently receive high ratings.[15] It is on the horizontal plane that the altered position of the clergyman's role can be clearly seen. In contemporary society, the clergy no longer occupy a position of prominence or centrality in the social, cultural, intellectual, political, or any other aspect of national life. Just as, in advanced society religion has lost the position of centrality which it formerly held, so the social position of the clergyman's role has changed in a similar manner. Through the decades of this century, the clergyman's role has increasingly come to be regarded as marginal to the mainstream life of English society, principally because the knowledge to which the role has access is no longer seen by most people as having any direct relevance to their day-to-day concerns. In many cases, the clergy are characterized as the bearers of an old and respected cultural tradition but one which has become increasingly irrelevant to contemporary social conditions. It is perhaps only in the area of ritual that the clergy retains a residual centrality, for the clergy are still required to solemnize and sanctify significant events in the national, civic, local, and family life of the nation.

This developing marginality is reinforced by changes which have taken place in society. In modern society, occupation has acquired a new significance as the pre-eminent indicator of both a person's identity and general social position. Part of the crisis which the clerical profession faces (and which many clergy must weather individually) derives from the fact that the clergyman's role is no longer seen as part of the division of labour in a modern society. In a sense, it has become 'non-work'. The clergyman does not possess skills in the sense in which the term is used in modern society, and his theological insights and pastoral experience have no market value. It is the prerequisite of an occupation that it should be able to make a definite statement about the functions and content of the role. Beyond their liturgical functions, the clergy find it particularly difficult to make statements about the content of their role in terms to which the rest of society can readily relate. The popular view that Sunday is the clergyman's busy day (whereas in fact many clergy are less busy on Sunday than on other days) relates to the fact that people only understand the clergyman's liturgical functions as 'work'. Contemporary English society is predominantly work-centred and work-orientated, so that the dominant view of the clergyman's role as 'non-work' seems to emphasize further its marginality.

This view is reinforced by various aspects of the clergyman's lifestyle. The clergyman customarily works from his home and does not have a separate place of work (a situation characteristic of traditional society, where home and workshop were under the same roof, and where occupational and familial roles overlapped). The clergyman may be found at home during working hours, and in many residential parishes he may be the only ablebodied man of working age left in the parish. Furthermore, many aspects of the clergyman's role involve him with women and children in the home, and with men in their familial and 'non-work' situation. At the same time, many aspects of his role involve the clergyman in activities which are principally associated with those hours in the day, and those parts of the week (especially Sunday) when people are not working. Attending the meetings of voluntary organizations (including church meetings), visiting elderly people in the community, attending a school or a hospital as a visitor, are all activities which people do (or choose not to do) in their leisure time. Thus, there is an increasing tendency for many of the most time-consuming functions of the clergyman's role to be classified as 'non-work'. Part of the current crisis in the clergyman's role is related to the fact that for the majority of the population, the functions of the role are regarded as 'non-work', and therefore as having no place in the work life which is at the centre of contemporary society.

If the nature of the clergyman's role reinforces its marginality in contemporary society so does the social composition of the clerical profession. Like other professions in the nineteenth century, the clergy were recruited predominantly from the upper middle class. Though attempts were made, as in other professions, to widen the social band from which recruits were drawn, the clergy continued to come predominantly from professional and middle-class homes. When the number of ordinands started to decline seriously in the inter-war years, the authors of the *Crockford* prefaces in that period constantly deplored the rising levels of taxation which inclined those social groups, from which the profession customarily drew its recruits, to seek more lucrative careers. Today, the situation remains almost unaltered, and the clergy are predominantly drawn from a fairly distinct social background in the middle to upper reaches of the social hierarchy. In Hining's recent survey, only 5.5 per cent of the fathers of the Church of England clergy did not come from the first three social categories (as used by the Registrar-General).[16] This is confirmed by a recent survey of the membership of the General Synod, which revealed that among the clerical members only 3.9 per cent had not been to a grammar or public school.[17] Leslie Paul has written that the general tone of the clergy is middle to upper class and their overall background, especially of those who have risen to senior positions, is that of the public school and ancient university.[18]

In the 1950s, it was often asserted that there was a growing convergence in English society, that the historic class divisions were being eroded, and that there would emerge a single-class society in which almost everyone would embrace the values and behaviour patterns of the middle classes. If such a society had emerged, it might be suggested that the professions would have been in a significantly less alienated situation than that in which they now find themselves. However, the 1960s saw dramatic changes in English society which included the emergence of the youth culture; the growing influence of proletarian and egalitarian philosophies; the emergence of new essentially working-class rather than élitist value patterns and behavioural codes, created and propagated by the media; and perhaps most significant of all, the marked shift of political power away from the professions and middle classes. In addition these can now be seen as causes and symptoms of more deep-seated changes in the structure, economy, and polity of society. The clergy were profoundly affected by the changes of the 1960s, and find themselves in this decade in a position of social isolation and marginality. Their origin, their education, their training, the nature of their role, and the institutional nature of the Church all serve to distance the clergyman from the lifestyle, the work situation, and the aspirations of those who now represent the mainstream of English society. It is possible to suggest that the changes of the 1960s have had the most dramatic effect on the clergy since their role was influenced by professionalization in the mid-nineteenth century.

THE AUXILIARY PASTORAL MINISTRY

Perhaps the most significant development within the clerical profession itself in this decade has been the emergence of a new role model, which marks a divergence from the dominant model of the clergyman as a professional man. Although numerically this new group is still relatively small, its existence has of itself caused the clergy to re-examine their own role and functions. This new group are customarily (though not now officially) known as Auxiliary Pastoral Ministers (APMs), and are comprised of men who, having been selected by the same procedure as the clerical profession, are trained (by evening classes and occasional residential weekends) whilst remaining in full-time employment. After ordination, the APMs function as priests in the Church on an unpaid voluntary basis, whilst remaining still in their full-time employment. The proposition that the clerical profession has needed some form of supplementary assistance, particularly in its pastoral functions, has been discussed in the Church for many generations. Proposals have been placed before the Church in almost every decade in the last 120 years. They usually took the form of suggesting the establishment of a voluntary or stipendiary diaconate (this was debated in the 1850s, and most recently in the General Synod meeting of November 1977). In the Anglican Communion overseas, a similar idea (though with significant differences) was developed by Roland Allen, principally in his book *The Case for Voluntary Clergy* (1930), and it has been overseas dioceses that have been prominent in creating supplementary ministries. In the diocese of Alaska, for instance, men in the small remote Indian and Eskimo communities are currently given a modest training and ordained to the priesthood, to perform the role of 'sacramentalist' in communities which would otherwise receive a visit from a priest only at infrequent intervals. (In the diocese of Vermont similar men are called 'eucharistizers'.) In many African dioceses, it is envisaged that in the next decade almost the total ministry will be performed by 'supplementary' indigenous priests.

In this country, in the late 1960s, a number of changing circumstances caused the Church of England to translate long-discussed proposals into action. First, by this time, it was becoming clear that the total number of clergy was now contracting sharply; second, there was widespread concern that in a situation of rapid inflation, the Church would be unable to pay for full-time clergy on anything like the scale it had formerly done; and third, the success of the Parish and People Movement, which sought to make the Holy Communion the central act of the Church's worship, increased the demand for this charter function of the clergyman's role (and at the same time made the existing lay supplementaries, the readers, of less assistance). Following a report in 1968, the bishops approved 'The Regulations for the Selection and Training of Candidates for Auxiliary Pastoral Ministry' in 1970.[19] In 1977 there were 183 such priests in the Church and some predictions indicate that there may be as many as 1000 by 1986. A recent survey, by W. H. Saumarez Smith, has shown that of the contemporary APMs, approximately one-third are teachers; of the remainder he writes: 'They are nearly all, in a broad sense, professional; there are very few "artisans" indeed.'[20]

The reaction of the clerical profession to the emergence of this new group of priests has been varied. Some clergy believe that the Auxiliary Pastoral Ministry results from a mistaken theology of the priesthood; others that it is misguided as a matter of policy; others that it is merely a response to inflation and its alleged biblical legitimation is merely making a virtue out of a necessity. However, there are others who regard this new form as heralding a radical reshaping of the Church's ministry which will eventually lead to its indigenization in working-class areas and its penetration of areas of society, particularly those concerned with work, from which the Church now realizes itself to be alienated. In so far as a generalization is possible, there appears to be a disposition among parochial clergy to treat the Auxiliary Pastoral Ministry as a sub-profession. Thus, APM may be seen in some respects (although by no means all) as a part of the emergence of the sub-professions, which have been such a marked feature of the recent history of professionalization. It is noticeable that the term 'Auxiliary Pastoral Ministry' does of itself denote sub-professional status and that the clergy appear reluctant to respond to the official injunction to call this new form of ministry the Non-Stipendiary Ministry (the term now used in official documents). Furthermore, the clerical profession have insisted upon certain safeguards which emphasize the sub-professional status of the APMs. APMs are not permitted to hold a benefice (which means that, in the parochial sphere, they can never operate independently of a beneficed clergyman). Should they wish to transfer to the stipendiary ministry, they are obliged to submit themselves for further training. At the parochial level, most APM candidates continue after their ordination to serve in the parish in which they have previously given long service as laymen, and they act as voluntary assistants to the incumbent. In functional terms, their assistance is now more extensive since they are able to celebrate the sacraments and to fulfil those functions which only a priest can fulfil. At the same time the clerical profession, like other professions, has insisted on the highest academic standards (comparable to their own) in the sub-profession, since lower standards would reflect adversely on the profession.

The ambivalent, and uncertain attitude of the clerical profession to the Auxiliary Pastoral Ministry is in part related to the fact that no professional can view with equanimity the implication that its functions can be adequately performed either on a part-time basis or as a hobby. However, the principal cause of this unease would appear to lie in the dominant understanding of the clergyman's role as a professional role comparable with other professions in society. It is central to a profession that the prolonged socialization and training that the aspirant receives should form in him professional attitudes and behaviour patterns, and acquaint him with the ethos and the codes of conduct of the profession. Because a profession involves the totality of a man, part-time membership of a profession (after part-time training) is almost by definition impossible. A man either is or is not a member of the profession. There is a sense in which the Augustinian and medieval doctrine of the indelibility of the priestly character is a theological statement of this aspect of a professional role, and in some form this doctrine is held by many clergy in the contemporary Church as part of their view of themselves. In consequence the experience of the first decade of the Auxiliary Pastoral Ministry has served, among other things, to demonstrate the strength with which the majority of the clergy retain, in modern society, the traditional understanding of the nature of their role. Despite the intentions of those who framed this new form of ministry, it was perhaps inevitable that many members of the clerical profession should have been inclined to regard it as a sub-profession. However, *Auxiliary Pastoral Ministry is not so much a sub-profession but more a re-interpretation of the whole nature of ministry*, and as such it has been the means of opening up new understandings of the way in which the Church's ministry may be performed in the much altered social conditions of the last quarter of the twentieth century.

THE INCLUSION OF WOMEN IN THE CLERICAL PROFESSION

Finally, given the present debate concerning the ordination of women it is impossible to discuss the clerical profession without some reference to a possibility which the Church has under active discussion. In a sense most of the modern professions have their origin in the role of the clergyman, which has been historically an exclusively male role in both Eastern and Western Christendom. Thus, all professions have been reluctant to admit women into full membership. In part, this derives from the lingering belief that the admission of women would affect adversely the status of the profession; in part, from the belief that women do not engage in occupational roles with the same degree of commitment as men. The ordination of a woman as a member of the clerical profession first occurred within the Anglican Communion in the diocese of Hong Kong and Macao in 1944. Since then an increasing number of overseas provinces of the Anglican Communion have begun to ordain women. It is not possible to consider this issue at any length since complex emotional, symbolic, and ecumenical considerations are at stake. But it may be suggested that part of the reluctance among members of the clerical profession to admit women priests, as evidenced by the recent vote in the General Synod (November 1978), stems from their adherence to historic ideas concerning the nature of the profession and traditional models of the clergyman's role.

19

The Future of the Clergyman's Role and the Church's Ministry

It can be seen from the previous chapter that the evidence for asserting that the ministry of the Church is currently undergoing a profound crisis is extensive. On the one hand there are the verifiable indices of crisis (the decline in recruitment, the increase in opting out, the high level of retirements, the ageing and contraction of the profession), and, on the other hand, there are the less accessible dimensions of the crisis, of which the marginality of the profession is probably the most significant. John Bowden has recently written that the clergyman 'is more often than not an odd man out, involved in great personal tension over what he should or should not do, puzzled over his status and above all isolated and removed from the general life of society, following a completely different lifestyle and being robbed by virtue of his status of the involvement with others which he so much needs'.[1] For many clergy these dimensions of the crisis are all the more problematic because the Church as a whole appears not to recognize their existence. Thus, when a country clergyman with many parishes dies of a stress disease at an early age; when an urban clergyman spends a fortnight doing nothing else but conducting funerals; when a team-vicar 'opts out' for a job in industry out of sheer frustration; when the marriage of a clergyman proves unequal to the demands of his double job as a parish priest and a diocesan official; when a West Midland urban parish is turned down by thirteen prospective incumbents, there is in each case compassion and concern at the human level. However, such occurrences are not usually followed by any attempt at sustained analysis and change. In recent years, at both the national and the local level, only modest changes have been made in the clergyman's situation.

The many contemporary books about the ministry of the

Church tend to be dominated by a consideration of the development of the theology of priesthood and its ramifications in the life of the contemporary Church. As a consequence of the nature of theological debate, with its long-standing preoccupation with history, attention is focused on detailed studies of the development of the Church's ministry in the first three centuries of its life. The New Testament and patristic texts are closely analysed in the search for dominant models and verifications of contemporary practices. The questions asked of the ministry are whether contemporary practices conform to those found in the early Church, whether contemporary practices and suggested alterations are congruent with the Church's historic understanding of the development of its ministry, and whether from a sacramental point of view they may be regarded as 'valid'. Clearly, no one within the Christian tradition can ignore these issues or deny their importance, but what is of significance is the way in which these considerations obscure that other question which everyone else asks of every other human institution, namely, 'do the present arrangements actually work?'; or to ask the same question in the language of sociology, 'are these arrangements functional or dysfunctional?'[2]

It might be suggested that the act of formulating such a question of itself betrays a lack of understanding of the essential nature of religious institutions. Certainly, from a theological standpoint this is not a question of primary significance, and the effectiveness of a religious institution is not a criterion on which judgements are based. The objectives of religious institutions are such (in so far as 'salvation' may be regarded as the principal objective) that the canon of rationality cannot be applied in the same way that it can be applied to other organizations in order to determine their effectiveness. However, this does not mean that the question is wholly inapplicable to religious institutions. It is observable from the sociological standpoint that society tends to discard those roles and institutions for which it has no further functional use. In part, the increasing marginality of the Church and the clergyman's role is occasioned by the operation of this process. However, an institution which has the incarnation as a central part of its authorization and believes the world to be the creation of God and the object of his love, must regard marginality as in some sense an abnegation of its charter, and must seek at all times to remain with the mainstream of the society in which it is set. Such considerations of a theological and sociological nature imply that the question 'does it work?' must be pressed.

Historically, the ministry of the Church of England has been exercised by its clergy, whose role in the nineteenth century approximated increasingly to that of the professional man, though for various historical, legal, and constitutional reasons, the clergy were inhibited from identifying totally with the professional model. In this century, the professions have continued to develop, in response to changes in many aspects of society, but the clerical profession has remained in a largely unaltered form. Thus, the clergy in contemporary society occupy a role which principally reflects attitudes, methods, and practices which were current in the mid-nineteenth century, rather than those of contemporary professional roles. In many respects this role has served the Church's ministry well, and it has certainly facilitated many deeply effective and notable ministries. Indeed, the hesitant and ambivalent attitude of the profession towards proposed changes stems in part from a reluctance to dismantle arrangements which produced such notable ministries as those of John Keble, Charles Kingsley, and the many humble and godly clergy who have brought honour and dignity to their profession. But just as certain religious symbols, which were an aid to belief in former generations, have in our generation become a barrier, so the shape and structure of the clergyman's role are in danger of becoming less a means of facilitating the Church's ministry, and more a problem and a barrier. In any institution, the growing awareness that the deficiencies are beginning to outweigh the merits will cause more radical questions to be asked of the shape and structure of those agencies which are designed to achieve the institution's goals. Therefore, it may be regarded as legitimate to question whether the dysfunctions of the clerical profession and the clergyman's role as traditionally conceived and structured have not now reached a point where they are beginning to outweigh the undoubted advantages.

The areas in which the clergyman's role dysfunctions and in which the clergyman himself experiences conflict and tension may be summarized under seven headings. The first area of dysfunction is the marginality of the role. In the previous chapter it has been noted that the clergyman today is increasingly isolated from the mainstream of the community. Declining numbers and the demand that those who remain should serve in larger areas, more churches, and more people – these things in themselves tend to cocoon the clergyman within an ecclesial world. The nature of his role and the demands made upon him (particularly with regard to funerals and administration) structure his life in such a way that his engagement with the mainstream life of the community can be minimal.

The élitism of the profession in a popularist culture reinforces its marginality, and forms a second area of dysfunction. The clergy's strong attachment to the image of their role as that of a professional man has resulted, in practice, in the restriction of recruitment to that narrow band in the middle and upper middle class from which the other professions predominantly recruit. Despite constant pressure from a small minority within the profession for a widening of this catchment area, only slight changes have been made in the last 120 years. The clergy share the thought-forms, opinions, and culture of the professional middle classes, which are those of the public and grammar school and the ancient universities. Thus, to many, the Church of England appears to be a part of the social and cultural expression of being middle class in England, a fact which alienates it from the dominant social and cultural forces in contemporary society. It was only in 1880, more than two centuries after the first missionaries were sent overseas, that English missionary colleges began to teach native languages and as a consequence missionaries went out equipped to preach in the language and thought-forms of their hearers. Previously, missionaries learned the local dialect if they could, or more commonly preached through an interpreter. The parallels with the contemporary English experience are obvious; in all but a few cases the clergy are unaware of the language and thought-forms of working-class culture.[3]

Third, the professions in contemporary society find themselves in an increasingly ambivalent and exposed position and the clergy, as members of this occupational category, find themselves a part of this developing situation. Whilst the professions are still accorded high levels of prestige, there is an increasingly significant minority who regard the professions in a less favourable light, and are inclined to portray them as monopolistic organizations and to question their values, judgements, and, in some instances, their motives. Recent legislation has been aimed at curbing restrictive practices, and many professions have begun to respond to the changed public attitudes. Whilst this may have affected the clergy less than other professions, the recent conclusions of an American conference of the laity 'that religion is too important to be left in the hands of the clergy' indicates the same process at work. Certainly, the professions find it hard to avoid being regarded as part of the powerful governing establishment in a society where most people are becoming increasingly aware of their relative powerlessness. There is a tendency in working-class areas to regard religion, like other professional services, exclusively as something which is done to and for the individual by professional personnel.

This leads to the fourth area of dysfunction – that which is most significant from the organizational viewpoint. It arises from a consideration of the appropriateness of a profession as the vehicle of leadership for an institution such as the Church. Though a recent ACCM publication states that the professional form of the Church's ministry is sanctioned neither by Scripture nor the early history of the Church, this question is rarely considered within the Church.[4] For historical reasons there is a tendency to regard the Church in institutional terms principally as a legal and constitutional entity. The Church of England is inter-related closely with the monarchy and the constitution and plays an important role in the civic life of the nation. Furthermore, all its activities at every level are prescribed within a legal framework. Yet from a different standpoint, the Church in contemporary society may be regarded as a voluntary associational organization, and as one of the many forms of organized leisure. Like other leisure organizations, those who are involved in the Church are involved on a voluntary basis. The Church operates in that area in which people make their own decisions about how they will employ their leisure time and the energy and wealth that they wish to devote to it.

However, when in reflecting upon its own organization, the Church seeks to draw parallels with other bodies, it is observable that these are not drawn from comparable voluntary associational organizations, but, either directly or indirectly, they are usually sought in the structures of industrial management or the armed forces. The influence of military models and the military mind-set has been particularly dominant among the leadership of the Church. The use of such models involves making assumptions about the nature of the institution, which, whilst they may be true for industry or the armed services, are not true for voluntary associational organizations. An examination of the structure of comparable national voluntary associational organizations reveals a pattern of leadership which is almost entirely different from that of the Church. Such organizations have a relatively small number of full-time professional personnel at national and area levels, and leadership at the local level is exercised by those who emerge from the local membership. As the Church increasingly takes on the nature of a voluntary associational organization in contemporary society, so the appropriateness of professional leadership to the structure of the institution may be regarded as increasingly questionable.

Furthermore, the dynamism of an institution is in some way related to the form in which its leadership is structured. This is the fifth area in which dysfunctions may be observed in the contemporary situation. It may be suggested that the notorious passivity of the laity of the Church of England is in some way a consequence of the form in which the Church's leadership has been traditionally exercised. The presence of a highly trained man, whose role it is to promote the goals of the organization, encourages those around him to leave matters entirely in his hands. When the leader is a professional man, this disposition is reinforced by the fact that professional roles of all types encourage in their clients attitudes of deference and dependence. In former generations, the professional clergyman with time to devote to the smallest details of parish life created attitudes of dependence, and these have persisted. It can be argued that the presence of a professional man inhibits the growth of a shared and corporate ministry even in those places where the professional clergyman is willing and able to share with his congregation functions which were previously a part of his role. This situation must be contrasted with other voluntary associational organizations where leadership is exercised not by professional personnel but by local volunteers who emerge out of the ranks of the organization and assume leadership roles. Such leaders have a considerable local investment as well as identification with the aims and goals of the organization. They are usually skilled at activating a group of local volunteers and their style of leadership encourages participation and corporate responsibility. It is suggested that the strength of many voluntary associational organizations derives in part from the nature of their leadership, which is particularly appropriate to their organizational form. The Church on the other hand faces the double problem that its traditional leadership model is not well-suited to a voluntary associational organization, and that its highly fragmented organizational form is not a structure in which the services of professional men can be employed to best advantage.

A sixth dysfunction of the present system is that it has proved to be peculiarly inflexible as a mode of leadership. The form of the Church's leadership has proved impervious to the impress of social change and has not responded to the new conditions of the twentieth century. Despite the considerable changes that have transformed other aspects of society and other occupational roles, the clergyman's role in many respects remains in the form which it assumed in the mid-nineteenth century. An inability to respond quickly to altered social circumstances is a facet of heavily institutionalized organizations and roles which develop high levels of resistance and inertia.

The final dysfunction is of a lesser order of importance and concerns the expense of professionalized leadership. All professional roles in contemporary society are coming under pressure because of the high cost of professional services. Even in the clerical profession, where costs are significantly lower, none the less it costs approximately £6000 a year to keep a clergyman in a parish. The cost of maintaining a stipendiary ministry has been one of the factors which has led to the recent consideration of alternative models of ministry. At the same time, a few lay members of the Church are beginning to suggest that in some cases, if £6000 per annum were actually available to a local church for financing its ministry, they might not wish to spend it in employing a professional man. What is clear is that there are relatively few churches which can finance professional leadership out of their annual income. The endowments of the Church of England, administered by the Church Commissioners, have allowed the continuance of a form of leadership which the local church has long been unable to finance. In a time of inflation, the cost of maintaining the ministry is beginning to influence and determine almost every aspect of church life, and so expensive and financially demanding is this form of ministry, that a large proportion of the Church's energies are of necessity channelled into its maintenance.

THE FUTURE OF THE CHURCH'S MINISTRY

The range and extent of these dysfunctions have suggested to some analysts of the contemporary dilemmas of the Church that the clergyman's role will disappear, and to others to demand that it should disappear. Some sociologists, noting that society evidently discards roles which technological or social change has made irrelevant, have suggested that the clergyman's role, as traditionally conceived, will eventually disappear from English society. The contraction in the clerical profession, and particularly the high levels of 'opting out', together with the development of APM, and the suggestion by some bishops that this will be the normative ministry of the Church in the next generation, are seen as evidence of this process already at work. At the same time, many radical theologians have suggested amidst their many criticisms of the contemporary Church that the role of 'the professional paid Christian' ought to be abandoned. Pre-eminently in the 1960s, calls for the immediate abolition of the full-time professional ministry formed part of the manifesto of radical Christians, who tended to see almost all institutional forms as imprisoning the gospel in an ecclesial world.

However, the Church of England, despite all the statistics of decline, remains a very large organization, and is far larger both in terms of membership and assets than any other non-governmental agency in this country. Clearly such a large and complex institution cannot function without full-time officials working at both the central and the local level. As the Anglican and Roman Catholic International Commission states, 'like any human community the Church requires a focus of leadership and unity'. The Church has traditionally found this focus of leadership and unity in its ordained priesthood, and its continuance is not in question. However, what is at issue is the form which this leadership will take in the future. It is not the role of a historian or a sociologist to proffer suggestions concerning the likely future of the clergyman's role, but it is to the future of that role that those concerned for the life and witness of the Church must necessarily look. At a time of rapid social change it is particularly difficult to plan for the future because uncertainty surrounds so many factors. Most large commercial companies and governmental agencies have 'forward planning' departments, which attempt on the basis of current practice and likely trends and developments, to extrapolate into the future and to analyse the environment in which the company or agency will have to operate. A part of the work of such departments involves the construction of alternative scenarios of the future, which depict the range of options that seem to be open on the basis of present experience. If this methodology is applied to the Church, three principal scenarios may be outlined which contemporary practices are already anticipating.

THE CHURCH OF THE TRADITIONALIST FUTURE

Among social institutions, churches are notable for their

ability to persist in essentially unaltered forms despite profound changes in all other aspects of social life. Indeed, the very pace of change creates a need in many people for a sense of historical continuity and for a point of connection with the unchanging past. The past is attractive not merely to those of a nostalgic disposition, but also to those, especially the elderly, who find themselves disorientated by rapid technical and social change. Thus, in the Soviet Union the Orthodox Church is the principal vehicle of the 'Russian movement', which acts as a cultural focus for those with a feeling for Russian history, culture, and nationality. In the Church of the traditionalist future, there is a strong sense of keeping faith with the past, so that changes which occasion a break with what has gone before are not readily countenanced. Such churches, which tend to have an essentially static view of society and the Church, regard all change as threatening, but particularly where it carries with it the implication that former generations were mistaken or misguided.

In the Church of the traditionalist future, much contemporary and historic practice continues essentially unchanged. The institution meets threats to its organization or value patterns by emphasizing distinctive and traditionalist attitudes and methods. This is complemented by a tendency to emphasize fundamentalist forms of legitimation for these attitudes and practices. The Church of the traditionalist future is smaller in overall membership, and losses occur principally because people are increasingly unable to regard the Church and its concerns as relevant to the day-to-day issues which they face. This contracted Church tends to see itself as a faithful remnant keeping faith with the past and with former generations in an essentially secular and hostile world. The theological and ethical stance of the Church of the traditionalist future is conservative and ecclesial, and it tends to deny rather than affirm the central values and concerns of society. The Church of the traditionalist future does not welcome theological speculation and believes that it is the role of the Church to defend the faith of the simple believer. In institutional terms, such a Church may be regarded as increasingly sectarian in nature. Indeed, its marginality and separateness from the mainstream concerns of society and its preoccupation with domestic issues (principally the problems of allocating diminishing resources) are the characteristic features of the Church of the traditionalist future.

In the Church of the traditionalist future, the clerical profession continues to contract, and increasing difficulty is experienced in maintaining the strength of the full-time ministry at anything like former levels. The number of those entering the profession remains substantially less than those leaving or retiring, and among those entering, the percentage of university graduates continues to decline. 'Opting out' remains a prominent feature with the consequent loss of experienced men in mid-career. In an attempt to widen the entry to the profession, older men (many of whom are seeking post-retirement employment in their mid-fifties) are recruited more extensively and these form a 'local priesthood' able to maintain the sacramental life of small churches unable to have a stipendiary priest. Despite the constrained financial situation and the example of other professions, the Church of the traditionalist future continues to devote a large proportion of its resources to providing residential training for the clerical profession, in the belief that it is in such colleges that new entrants are socialized with the traditionalist ethos and attitudes. Perhaps the most severe organizational problem to face the clerical profession in the traditionalist future is that of its distribution and the maintenance of a national system of ministry. The declining number of clergy and their preference to live and work in middle-class, urban, suburban, and certain accessible rural areas results in many inner-city, industrial, urban, and remote rural areas being almost devoid of the professional ministry.

The clergyman's role in the Church of the traditionalist future continues largely unchanged and at its centre remain those elements which form the charter role. There is a tendency among some members of the profession to regard liturgical functions in general, and the celebration of the sacraments in particular, as the irreducible and defining core of the role. The contraction in the number of clergy inevitably means that individual clergy have to spend a high proportion of their time engaged in these functions, and funerals come to constitute a major part of the clergyman's workload. Despite the difficulties associated with this, the clergy do not look favourably on the suggested employment of authorized laymen to conduct funerals, and are inclined to see all liturgical functions as integral to their role and its status. Although the clerical profession still regards pastoral care as the overall frame of reference for its work, in practice the amount of pastoral work which the clergy can perform in the Church of the traditionalist future is severely limited. On the one hand, the proliferation of counselling and therapy agencies provides a service which is increasingly preferred to the amateur abilities of the clergyman; on the other hand, the demands on the clergyman's time are such that pastoral work (in the specific sense of the term) occupies a relatively small part of his week's work.

Thus the clergyman's role in the Church of the traditionalist future remains largely unchanged, although declining numbers and financial and organizational problems effect some alteration to its historic mode. Above all, the clergy continue to see themselves as members of a professional body; it is this understanding of their role which determines those changes which are encouraged and those which are resisted.

THE CHURCH OF THE ADAPTIONIST FUTURE

The Church of the adaptionist future seeks to maintain the organizational forms which are sanctioned by tradition in altered social circumstances. Unlike the Church of the traditionalist future, it is willing to effect changes and modifications which will safeguard and strengthen its position whilst maintaining the principal elements of the known order. The Church of the adaptionist future values the positive opportunities which are offered by the Church's position in the national and civic life of the country and is anxious not to jeopardize this relationship. However, the approach of the Church of the adaptionist future to the problems of the institution is characteristically pragmatic and organizational, rather than ideological. The manner in which Auxiliary Pastoral Ministry was developed in the 1960s may be regarded as an example of this approach. Such an approach facilitates the continuity of much of the inherited organizational pattern, and represents a modification of the old order rather than a radical change.

The Church of the adaptionist future is in many central respects not markedly dissimilar from the Church of the traditionalist future, although a greater degree of flexibility and change may be observed. The clerical profession as traditionally conceived, continues to occupy a position of prominence, although it experiences contraction in its overall size. The worsening financial situation dictates that the profession has to alter its training arrangements, and residential training forms only a part of an ordinand's total training, much of it being done on a non-residential basis. Declining numbers incline the profession to widen the area of its recruitment and women are admitted into the clerical profession after prolonged debate. However, the adherence to the old order remains strong and the admission of women does not significantly change the nature of the clergyman's role.

In the Church of the adaptionist future, there is considerable enthusiasm for the use of assistants, in order that the Church may maintain its position in and service to the community despite the decline in the clerical profession. In the first instance, APM schemes are widely developed, and a significant number of the priests serving the Church do so in a non-stipendiary capacity, though their status as a sub-profession continues to be evident. At the same time 'lay training' forms a prominent feature of the Church of the adaptionist future. Members of the laity are encouraged to take responsibility for various administrative, pastoral, and liturgical activities, which have previously formed part of the role of the clergyman. The problem of funerals is partially resolved by authorizing laymen to read the short service at the crematorium, a practice which relieves the clergy of much travelling. The essential pragmatism of this solution is indicative of the general approach of the Church of the adaptionist future to such problems. However, on account of the clericalist origins of the 'theology of the laity' and the fear of congregationalism, the situation of lay assistants remains subordinate and ambivalent.

The provision of sufficient celebrations of Holy Communion at a time when the number of clergy remains at a low level is a problem which affords the Church of the adaptionist future one of its most contentious and potentially divisive problems. Those of a traditionalist inclination cannot countenance the possibility of lay celebration, in the belief that presiding at the Eucharist is the irreducible, and, in a sense, the definitive priestly act. Others are inclined to regard the fact that a number of congregations are only rarely able to receive the Eucharist as constituting a more serious offence. The solution adopted by the Church of the adaptionist future, whereby celebration alone remains a priestly function, but administration becomes a lay function (so that consecrated elements can be taken to a church by a lay person and administered to the congregation by him or her), again demonstrates the organizational rather than ideological approach of the Church of the adaptionist future.

Thus, the Church of the adaptionist scenario is willing to make gradual changes in order to accommodate itself to altered circumstances. Such a Church seeks to hold in tension those of a traditionalist stance and those who favour the adoption of more reformist policies. This tension is difficult to contain in practice because traditionalists tend to despise adaptionists, whom they regard as willing to compromise principles for pragmatic reasons, whilst reformists are equally critical of adaptionists because they embrace change in a less than thoroughgoing manner, not from conviction but in order to maintain the known order in altered circumstances. Thus, the Church of the adaptionist future is characterized by conflict and vigorous debate.

THE CHURCH OF THE REFORMIST FUTURE

The Church of the reformist future is essentially a movement in society rather than an institution, and as such has experienced a considerable measure of de-institutionalization. In its structure, the Church of the reformist future is much more pluriform than the contemporary Church, and it is comprised in many areas of small groups or cells which interrelate and come together to form large units for certain purposes. A principal feature of the Church of the reformist future is its lower 'visibility' in society, for the Church sees itself as hidden within society as a popularist movement rather than set over against society in an institutional form. The clergy of the reformist future are increasingly reluctant to perform the civic and 'folk religion' functions which the Church formerly fulfilled in the life of the nation. The Church is less willing to accept the role of the guardianship of the nation's cultural tradition and ethical norms, and is, in a sense, a less public institution. Essentially the Church of the reformist future sees itself as community-orientated, and believes that one of its principal functions is to act as a model of community in a society increasingly affected by alienation, privatization, and social atomization.

The manner in which ministry is exercised in the Church of the reformist future is significantly changed from contemporary experience. Of central significance is the understanding that priesthood is the calling, and ministry is the function, of the whole Church under Christ. The Church of the reformist future believes that elements of the contemporary situation have prevented the development of a shared and corporate ministry in the Church, and a sense of the ministry as the common task of the whole Church. Although this has been talked about for many decades, it has made little impact on the Church's organization, and even less on the ordering of its budgetary priorities. In the Church of the reformist future, the priesthood is seen as the servant of the Church, and as something which does not have an existence in its own right outside or beyond its ecclesial setting. Whilst there is a tendency in the Church of the traditionalist future to believe that the priesthood validates the Church, in the Church of the reformist future it is the Church which validates the priesthood.

Thus, in the Church of the reformist future, the local congregation, Eucharist group or Christian cell assumes a major responsibility for its own ministry within the overall framework of the Church's authorization. At the centre of these local church groups is a 'focal person' who occupies a role which involves responsibility for the life and leadership of the local church. (The existence and calibre of 'focal persons' is critical to the dynamics of voluntary associational groups.) Such leadership is not clericalized, though it is legitimate to apply the term 'priestly' to such leadership both in the formal theological sense and in that it articulates, actualizes, 'energizes' and epitomizes the ministry and life of the local church. The Church of the reformist future resists the distinction between the consecration and administration of Holy Communion made by the Church of the adaptionist future, and believes that the celebration of the Eucharist is the focal act of the local church. Thus, the local leadership of the Church, duly authorized by the bishop, is empowered to preside at the Eucharist.

However, such local groups and their leaders do not exist in isolation in the Church of the reformist future, for the stipendiary ministry provides the means of maintaining the coherence of small separate units, whilst at the same time it does not constitute a separate order of ministry. The role of the religious functionary in the Church of the reformist future is significantly altered from contemporary practice and is principally seen as that of providing resources, skills, and knowledge with which to support the local churches and their leaders. The stipendiary ministry forms a closely knit team, centred on the leadership and authority of the bishop, for the support of the local churches within the diocese. There is a marked tendency to recruit to this team those with particular skills in motivating and animating local groups of church members to pursue the objectives of the organization, as well as skills in training, communication, spirituality, and pastoral and liturgical matters. Many of them have learned these skills in the exercise of local leadership roles. Thus, the functions of the stipendiary ministry are principally those of teaching and training the local churches, and particularly their leadership. Pastoral work, for so long the dominant element in the role, is predominantly a function of the local church. The stipendiary ministry of the Church of the reformist future is a ministry of support and leadership.

CONCLUSION

Such scenarios merely indicate, in highly speculative and generalized terms, the range of futures which are before the contemporary Church. In the future situation and thinking of the Church, elements from all three scenarios are likely to be found, as indeed they may be found in the Church today. However, the changes in the clergyman's role in general, and the degree to which the clergy determine to retain its historic form in particular, will be critical in determining the balance which is struck between these differing understandings of the nature of the Church and the clergyman's role. For the present it is the case that the problems surrounding the clergyman's role are some of the most critical which the Church of England has to confront, both internally and ecumenically.

This study has been an attempt to show that the clergyman's role, as it is currently structured, resulted from processes of change in English society in the late eighteenth century and the nineteenth century, and in particular that of professionalization. This formative period ended in the last quarter of the nineteenth century, and the clergyman's role in contemporary society resembles in many of its principal aspects that of a nineteenth-century professional man. In the dramatically altered social circumstances of the last quarter of the twentieth century, the Church is being called to re-examine the vehicle of its priestly ministry and to discover whether there is not much in the received pattern which, having been taken for granted for so long, merely serves to reinforce the marginality of the contemporary Church. For it is ironic that a part of the reason that the Church is now less able to exercise the priesthood of Christ in English society is because its own ministry has become trapped in an increasingly problematic institutional form.

A Norfolk parish decided to hang a framed list of former incumbents in the church. When it was hung, the list contained forty-seven names, ending with that of the present clergyman. There was no space for adding to the list. By our actions, we demonstrate that the parish ministry has a long and honourable past, but our respect for the past must never be so great that it sets a limit to the future. For it is by changing and adapting inherited practices that we are better able to keep faith with the past and fulfil ancient intentions in changed circumstances.

The old order changeth, yielding place to new,
And God fulfils himself in many ways.

Notes
Bibliography
Index

Notes

1 Introduction

1 R. W. Church, *The Oxford Movement* (1891), p. 3
2 See Bibliography, section 1

2 The Emergence of the Professions in English Society

1 A. M. Carr Saunders and P. A. Wilson, *The Professions* (1933), p. 2
2 J. A. Jackson, ed., *Professions and Professionalization* (1970), p. 155
3 Herbert Spencer, *The Principles of Sociology* (1896), vol. III, pt. vii
4 H. M. Vollmer and D. L. Miles, eds., *Professionalization* (New Jersey 1966), p. 11
5 T. J. Jackson, *Professions and Power* (1972), p. 43
6 G. B. Shaw, *The Doctor's Dilemma* (1906), Act 1
7 T. M. Marshall, *Sociology at the Crossroads* (1963), p. 151
8 Talcott Parsons, 'The Professions and Social Structure', in *Social Force* (May 1939), vol. 17, no. 4; pp. 457ff; see also J. Ben-David, 'Professions in the Class System of Present-day Societies', in *Current Sociology* (1963–4), vol. 12, pp. 247ff.
9 A. M. Carr Saunders and P. A. Wilson, op. cit., p. 12
10 J. A. Jackson, ed., op. cit., pp. 155ff.
11 G. Millerson, *The Qualifying Associations: a Study in Professionalization* (1964)
12 H. L. Wilensky, 'The Professionalization of Everyone', in *American Journal of Sociology* (1964), vol. 70, pp. 137ff.
13 J. A. Jackson, ed., op. cit., p. 77
14 E. Goffman, *Asylums* (New York 1961)
15 Peter Laslett, *The World We Have Lost* (1965), p. 30
16 W. J. Reader, *Professional Men* (1966), p. 28
17 Ibid., p. 3
18 Edward Hughes, 'The Professions in the Eighteenth Century', in *Durham University Journal* (March 1952), vol. 44, p. 52
19 Ibid., p. 50
20 Ibid., p. 54
21 Philip Elliot, *The Sociology of Professions* (1972), p. 50
22 W. J. Reader, op. cit., p. 75
23 James Boswell, *Life of Dr Johnson* (Everyman edition 1958), vol. I, p. 393, quoted by W. J. Reader, op. cit., p. 25
24 W. J. Reader, op. cit., p. 148

25   H. Byerley Thomas, *The Choice of a Profession* (1857), p. 5
26   T. J. Johnson, op. cit., p. 52
27   Philip Elliot, op. cit., p. 48
28   W. J. Reader, op. cit., p. 149
29   H. M. Vollmer and D. L. Miles, op. cit., p. 3
30   *Annual Register* 1832, quoted by Philip Elliot, op. cit., p. 36
31   W. J. Reader, op. cit., p. 64
32   Ibid., pp. 51ff.
33   Philip Elliot, op. cit., p. 46
34   W. J. Reader, op. cit., pp. 98ff.
35   Anthony Trollope, *The Vicar of Bullhampton* (1870), (World Classics
      edition 1924), pp. 60–61

3   The Clergyman's Role and Professionalization

1   A. D. Gilbert, *Religion and Society in Industrial England* (1976), p. 5
2   Ibid., pp. 10–11
3   Alan Smith, *The Established Church and Popular Religion* (1970),
     p. 10
4   B. Williams, *The Whig Supremacy* (1962), p. 168
5   W. R. Ward, *Religion and Society in England 1710–1850* (1972), p. 11
6   William Paley, *A Sermon preached in the Castle Chapel of Dublin, 21
     September 1782* (Works ed. E. Lynam 1828, vol. v, p. 261)
7   W. R. Ward, 'The Tithe Question in England in the Early Nineteenth
     Century', in *Journal of Ecclesiastical History* (1965), vol. XVI, pp. 69ff.
8   G. E. Mingay, *English Landed Gentry in the Eighteenth Century*
     (1963), p. 3
9   The Values of the Tithe at Long Melford, Suffolk, between 1735 and
     1817 indicate the improvement in the financial position of the clergy:
     1735 – £303 9s 6d; 1754 – £339 4s 0d; 1789 – £460 11s 8d; 1801 – £787
     13s 3d; 1807 – £855 10s 6d; 1811 – £950 17s 2d; 1817 – £1217 15s 0d.
     Quoted by A. Tindal Hart, *The Eighteenth-century Country Parson*
     (1955), p. 105
10   *The Letters of Lord Chesterfield*, ed. Bradshaw, vol. III, pp. 1151–2,
     quoted by Edward Hughes, op. cit., p. 47
11   Compare the one-storeyed thatched cottage of the Vicar of Wakefield
     with Edmund Bertram's parsonage at Thornton. Oliver Goldsmith,
     The Vicar of Wakefield (1766), ch. IV; Jane Austen, *Mansfield Park*
     (1814), ch. XXV
12   G. Kitson Clark, *Churchmen and the Condition of England
     1832–1885* (1973), p. 31
13   G. F. A. Best, *Temporal Pillars* (1964), p. 68
14   C. P. Fendall and E. A. Crutchley, *The Diary of Benjamin Newton
     1816–1818* (1933), p. 51
15   O. F. Christie, *The Diary of the Revd William Jones of Broxbourne
     1777–1821* (1929), p. 148

16 H. Coombs and A. N. Bax, *Journal of a Somerset Rector, John Skinner* (1930), p. 112
17 Giles Hunt, 'A Real-life Jane Austen Clergyman', in *Theology* (May 1976), pp. 151ff.
18 A. Blomfield, *A Memoir of C. J. Blomfield (1863)*, vol. I, p. 59
19 A. D. Gilbert, op. cit., p. 14
20 William Cobbett, *Rural Rides*, ed. G. Woodcock (1967), p. 106, quoted by A. D. Gilbert, op. cit., p. 81
21 A. D. Gilbert, op. cit., p. 132
22 Philip Elliot, op. cit., p. 42
23 Anon., *The Views of a Church of England Layman* . . . (1866), p. 19
24 Robert Wilberforce, Charge (1851), pp. 10–11
25 K. A. Thompson, *The Organizational Response of the Church of England to Social Change* (Oxford D.Phil. thesis 1976), p. vii
26 H. B. J. Armstrong, ed., *A Norfolk Diary* (1949), p. 156
27 When the Moules arrived at Fordington in 1829: 'For a long time no one called at the Vicarage. In due season this was explained. At a meet of the hounds it transpired Mr. Moule was discussed and presumed to be a Methodist; as such he was a person to whom normal courtesies were scarcely due.' H. C. G. Moule, *Memories of a Vicarage* (1913), p. 55
28 Bishop Kaye, Charge (1846), p. 4
29 Anon., *Clerical Recreations* (1853), pp. 11–12
30 J. D. Walsh, *The Yorkshire Evangelicals* (Cambridge Ph.D. thesis 1956), pp. 252ff; A. Warne, *Church and Society in Eighteenth-century Devon* (1969), p. 117; G. F. A. Best, op. cit., p. 76; Charles Smyth, *Simeon and Church Order* (1941), p. 243; John Pratt, ed., *Eclectic Notes* (1865)
31 Revd Sir John Stonhouse, *Hints from a Minister to his Curate* . . . (1774), p. 41
32 H. C. G. Moule, op. cit., p. 40
33 C. J. Vaughan, *Addresses to Young Clergymen* (1875), p. 78
34 R. Seymour and J. F. Mackarness, *Eighteen Years of a Clerical Meeting* (1862), p. xi
35 D. Newsome, *The Parting of Friends* (1966), p. 230
36 These included: *The British Critic* (1827); *The Record* (1828); *The British Magazine* (1828); *The Ecclesiologist* (1841); *The English Churchman* (1843); *The Surplice* (1845); *The Church Times* (1863); and *The Church Quarterly Review* (1878)
37 F. W. B. Bullock, *A History of Training for the Ministry of the Church of England and Wales from 1800 to 1874* (1955), p. 245
38 Ibid., pp. 53, 84
39 A. Blomfield, op. cit., vol. I, p. 56
40 W. E. Gladstone, *Gleanings of Past Years* (1879), vol. VII, p. 220
41 Hon and Revd S. Best, *Parochial Ministrations* (1839), p. 13. Also see Harry Jones, *Priest and Parish* (1866), p. 10. For a recent attempt to use the professions as a model, see: G. R. Dunstan, 'The Sacred

Ministry as a Learned Profession', G. R. Dunstan, ed., *The Sacred Ministry* (1970), pp. 1ff.
42 A. R. Ashwell and R. G. Wilberforce, *Life of Samuel Wilberforce* (1881), vol. III, p. 155
43 Owen Chadwick, *The Victorian Church* (1970), pt. II, p. 169

4 Leader of Public Worship – Sunday Worship

1 R. Mant, *The Clergyman's Obligations Considered* (1830), p. 1
2 57 Geo. III, c. 99
3 J. J. Blunt, *The Parish Priest: His Achievements, Principal Obligations, and Duties* (1856), p. 140
4 A. Blomfield, op. cit., p. 57
5 Anon., *Medicina Clerica* (1828), p. 12. This handbook stressed the importance of having a lavatory in the vestry, which gives an indication of the time spent in church by the clergy.
6 G. R. Balleine, *A History of the Evangelical Party in the Church of England* (1937), p. 18
7 D. McClatchey, *Oxfordshire Clergy 1777–1869* (1960), p. 80
8 Ibid., p. 80
9 A. Warne, op. cit., p. 44
10 John Beresford, ed., *The Diary of a Country Parson, the Revd James Woodforde*, vol. V, pp. 34, 99, 125, 127, 145
11 James Woodforde did not take a service in church in his last seven years at Weston Longville.
12 John Beresford, ed., op. cit., vol. I, pp. 31, 236, 266
13 Ibid., vol. I, p. 173
14 Charlotte M. Yonge, *John Keble's Parishes* (1898), p. 88
15 Dr George Horne, *Olla Podrida*, No. 33 (1788), Saturday 27 October 1787, p. 194; quoted by J. Wickham Legg, *English Church Life* (1914), p. 124. Perhaps the most exotic example is that of the non-resident incumbent who had as his curate 'a harmless maniac'. 'He used to be fastened to the altar or the reading desk. When once there, he was quite sane enough to go through the services perfectly. On weekday evenings he earned his subsistence by playing the fiddle at village taverns but he continued to be the officiating clergyman at St Buryan's till his death in 1808.' A. J. C. Hare, *The Story of My Life* (1896), vol. VI, p. 177
16 R. A. Soloway, *Prelates and People. Ecclesiastical Thought in England 1783–1852* (1969), p. 50
17 *Report from the Clergy of a District of the Diocese of Lincoln convened for the purpose of considering the state of religion in the several parishes in the said district . . .* (1800), p. 6
18 William Addison, *The English Country Parson* (1947), p. 131
19 John Napleton, *Advice to a Minister of the Gospel* (1801), p. 25
20 R. B. Walker, op. cit., p. 13
21 C. Smyth, op. cit., p. 56n

22 G. W. E. Russell, *Collections and Recollections* (1898), p. 77
23 C. Smyth, op. cit., p. 78
24 G. R. Balleine, op. cit., p. 147
25 Ibid., p. 197
26 R. Mant, op. cit., p. 3
27 D. McClatchey, op. cit., pp. 81–2
28 A. Tindal Hart and E. Carpenter, *The Nineteenth-century Parson* (1954), p. 86
29 A. J. C. Hare, *Memorials of a Quiet Life* (1872), vol. I, p. 336
30 P. H. Ditchfield, *The Old-time Parson* (1908), p. 295
31 A. Blomfield, op. cit., vol. I, p. 54
32 G. A. Selwyn, *The Work of Christ in the World* (1855), p. 7
33 D. McClatchey, op. cit., pp. 81–3
34 C. F. Lowder, *Twenty-one Years in St George's Mission* (1877), p. 148
35 Ashley Oxenden, *The History of My Life* (1891), p. 86
36 D. E. H. Mole, 'John Cale Miller: a Victorian Rector of Birmingham', in *Journal of Ecclesiastical History* (1966), vol. XVII, p. 98
37 W. R. W. Stephens, *The Life and Letters of W. F. Hook* (1880), p. 465
38 Alfred Gatty, *The Vicar and his Duties* (1853), p. 58
39 *Life and Letters of W. J. Butler* (1897), p. 72
40 Harry Jones, op. cit., p. 95
41 C. P. Fendall and E. A. Crutchley, op. cit., p. 214
42 Robert Gregory, *The Difficulties and the Organization of a Poor Metropolitan Parish*. Two Lectures delivered at Cuddesdon (1866), p. 19
43 R. T. Davidson and W. Benham, *Life of A. C. Tait* (1891), vol. I, p. 256
44 Anon., *The Pastor or Scenes from the Life of a Clergyman* (1866), p. 22
45 S. L. Ollard and P. C. Walker, *Archbishop Herring's Visitation Returns York 1743*, Yorkshire Archaeological Society (1928), vol. LXXI, p. xv
46 A. Warne, op. cit., p. 44
47 D. McClatchey, op. cit., p. 84
48 F. G. Stokes, op. cit., p. 242; also cf. pp. 17, 46, 264, 288
49 E. Middleton, *Biographia Evangelica*, vol. IV, p. 404; quoted by J. Walsh, op. cit., p. 100
50 *Works*, ed. Whittingham, p. 491; quoted by C. Smyth, op. cit., p. 25
51 J. Walsh, op. cit., p. 150
52 G. R. Balleine, op. cit., p. 105
53 *Evangelical Magazine* 1794, vol. II, p. 402; quoted by C. Smyth, op. cit., p. 25
54 *Evangelical Magazine* 1798, vol. VI, p. 11; quoted by C. Smyth, op. cit., p. 25
55 Sir George Gilbert Scott, *Personal and Professional Recollections*

(1879), p. 28; quoted by C. Smyth, op. cit., p. 24
56   D. McClatchey, op. cit., p. 85
57   Anon., *A Letter to His Grace The Archbishop of Canterbury* (1824), pp. 8–10
58   John Sandford, *Parochialia* (1843), p. 18
59   Charlotte M. Yonge, op. cit., p. 103
60   David Newsome, *The Parting of Friends* (1966), pp. 127, 283
61   Brian Taylor, 'Bishop Hamilton', in *Church Quarterly Review* (1954), vol. CLV, p. 237
62   Isaac Williams, *A Short Memoir of the Rev. P. A. Suckling* (1852), p. 12
63   William Butler, op. cit., pp. 71, 144
64   W. R. W. Stephens, op. cit., p. 121; and Michael Reynolds, *Martyr of Ritualism* (1965), p. 66
65   J. F. Briscoe and M. F. B. Mackay, *A Tractarian at Work. A Memoir of Dean Randall* (1932), p. 74
66   A. Blomfield, op. cit., vol. I, p. 110
67   A. Oxenden, *The History of My Life* (1891), p. 43
68   G. R. Balleine, op. cit., p. 246
69   H. C. Ridley, *Parochial Duties* (1829), p. 15
70   W. R. W. Stephens, op. cit., p. 45
71   A. Oxenden, op. cit., p. 51
72   Owen Chadwick, *Victorian Miniature* (1960), p. 79
73   A. J. C. Hare, op. cit., p. 112
74   A. R. Ashwell and R. G. Wilberforce, op. cit., vol. I, p. 49
75   R. W. Evans, *The Bishopric of Souls* (1842), p. 144
76   *British Magazine* (November 1838), vol. XIV, p. 548
77   T. A. Methuen, *A Memoir of the Rev. R. P. Beachcroft* (1832), p. 110
78   H. G. C. Moule, op. cit., p. 55
79   H. C. Ridley, op. cit., p. 15
80   J. C. Gill, *Parson Bull of Byerley* (1963), p. 55
81   E. G. Sandford, ed., *Memoir of Archbishop Temple by Seven Friends* (1906), vol. I, p. 27
82   A. R. Ashfield and R. G. Wilberforce, op. cit., vol. I, p. 57
83   J. Bryan, op. cit., p. 172
84   E. Monro, *Pastoral Work* (1850), pp. 36ff; cf. E. Monro, *Pastoral Life* (1862), pp. 47ff.
85   J. H. Blunt, *Directorum Pastorale* (1864), p. 47; and J. J. Blunt, *The Parish Priest* (1856), p. 220
86   *British Magazine* (April 1841), vol. XVIII, p. 457
87   E. Monro, *Pastoral Work* (1850), p. 41
88   H. B. J. Armstrong, op. cit., p. 35
89   *Memoir of Dean Hole* (1892), p. 173
90   C. F. Lowndes, op. cit., p. 148
91   R. Seymour and J. F. Mackarness, op. cit., p. 274
92   J. R. Woodforde, *Ordination Lectures in the Chapel of Cuddesdon College* (1861), p. 16
93   E. Monro, *Pastoral Life* (1862), p. 93

94 J. H. Blunt, op. cit., p. 387
95 J. Beresford, ed., op. cit., vol. III, p. 292
96 A. Oxenden, op. cit., p. 41
97 W. H. Hutchings, op. cit., p. 14
98 Thomas Hardy, *Under the Greenwood Tree*, 1872 (Macmillan edn 1914), p. v
99 J. H. Blunt, op. cit., p. 383
100 H. B. J. Armstrong, op. cit., p. 114

5 Leader of Public Worship – Surplice Duties

1 L. P. Fendall and E. A. Crutchley, op. cit., p. ix
2 J. Beresford, op. cit., vol. I, p. 24
3 F. H. West, *Sparrows of the Spirit* (1961), p. 65
4 R. Seymour and J. F. Mackarness, op. cit., p. 34
5 J. Beresford, op. cit., vol. II, p. 299
6 *British Magazine*, vol. XIII, p. 534
7 Peter Hammond, *The Parson and the Victorian Parish* (1977), p. 98
8 F. H. West, op. cit., p. 95
9 Owen Chadwick, op. cit., vol. II, pp. 220–21
10 P. G. Stokes, ed., op. cit., p. 27
11 John Clubbe, 'A Letter of Free Advice to a Young Clergyman', in *Miscellaneous Tracts* (1770), vol. II, p. 26
12 W. R. W. Stephens, op. cit., p. 87
13 J. Walsh, op. cit., p. 124
14 W. H. Hutton, ed., *Robert Gregory 1819–1911* (1912), p. 53
15 F. H. West, op. cit., p. 95
16 M. Reynolds, op. cit., p. 43
17 J. Burgon, op. cit., p. 370
18 H. Coombes and H. N. Bax, op. cit., p. 108
19 L. P. Fendall and E. A. Crutchley, op. cit., p. 223
20 H. R. Moody, *Hints to Younger Clergymen . . .* (1835), p. 38
21 *British Magazine* (1839), vol. XV, p. 199
22 Anon., *Pastoral Recollections* (1837), p. 63
23 J. R. Briscoe and H. F. Mackay, op. cit., p. 80
24 W. R. W. Stephens, op. cit., pp. 222, 379
25 R. Gregory, op. cit., p. 20
26 W. R. Ward, op. cit., p. 221

6 Preacher

1 William Jesse, *Parochialia* (1785), p. 107
2 George Herbert, op. cit., p. 232; Simon Patrick, *The Work of the Ministry* (1692), p. 67; Thomas Wilson, *Parochialia* (1708), p. 383; William Paley, *Advice to a Young Clergyman* (1781), p. 20; William Jesse, op. cit., p. 85

3   Anon., *A Discourse of a Great and Solemn Charge* . . . (1722), p. 28
4   Job Orton, op. cit., p. 52; William Jesse, op. cit., p. 76; and F. K. Brown, *Fathers of the Victorians* (1961), p. 72
5   G. M. Trevelyan, *English Social History* (1944), p. 361; and N. Sykes, *Church and State in England in the Eighteenth Century* (1934), p. 251
6   Anon., *Advice to a Young Clergyman* (1741), p. 12
7   Quoted at length and with approval in William Jesse, op. cit., p. 30. Also see Bishop Horsley, *Primary Charge* (1790), pp. 1ff.
8   A. Tindal Hart, op. cit., p. 41
9   William Addison, op. cit., p. 147
10 John Walsh, op. cit., p. 109
11 G. W. E. Russell, *A Short History of the Evangelical Movement* (1915), p. 63
12 Job Orton, op. cit., p. 1
13 John Walsh, op. cit., pp. 197ff.
14 Charles Smyth, op. cit., pp. 226, 229
15 John Walsh, op. cit., p. 140
16 William Addison, op. cit., p. 120
17 J. Wickham Legg, op. cit., p. 262
18 C. P. Fendall and E. A. Crutchley, op. cit., p. 243
19 R. A. Soloway, op. cit., p. 58
20 Charles Bridges, *The Christian Ministry* (1830), and Henry Thompson, *Pastoralia* (1830) which included 200 pages of sermon outlines.
21 T. A. Methuen, op. cit., p. 110
22 A. R. Ashwell and R. G. Wilberforce, op. cit., vol. I, pp. 48, 56
23 R. Whately, *Letter to a Clergyman* (1836), p. 4
24 H. C. Ridley, *Parochial Duties* (1829), p. 19
25 Isaac Williams, op. cit., p. 152
26 O. Chadwick, *Victorian Miniature* (1960), pp. 52–3
27 A. Tindal Hart and E. Carpenter, op. cit., p. 103; W. R. W. Stephens, op. cit., p. 123
28 Charles Bridges, op. cit., p. 245
29 E. Monro, *Parochial Work* (1850), p. 97
30 *British Magazine*, vol. XXII (1842), p. 13
31 J. R. Miller, Sermon 'Preaching' (1847), p. 15
32 John Skinner, op. cit., p. 8
33 R. A. Soloway, op. cit., p. 341
34 J. R. Miller, Sermon 'Home-Heathen' (1854), p. 47
35 *The Christian Observer* (1856), no. 228, p. 833
36 R. T. Davidson and W. Benham, op. cit., vol. I, pp. 255ff.
37 W. R. W. Stephens, op. cit., p. 465
38 H. C. G. Moule, op. cit., p. 57
39 C. F. Lowndes, op. cit., p. 63
40 William Butler, op. cit., p. 115
41 R. T. Davidson and W. Benham, op. cit., vol. I, p. 255
42 Ibid., vol. I, p. 261
43 John Burgon, op. cit., p. 198
44 Samuel Best, *On Catechising* (1849), p. 46

45 John Burgon, op. cit., pp. 289–90
46 E. Monro, *Parochial Work* (1850), p. 58
47 B. Heeney, *A Different Kind of Gentleman* (1976), p. 136
48 Ibid., p. 97
49 Ibid., p. 41
50 John Burgon, op. cit., p. 168
51 George Herbert, op. cit., p. 232

7 Celebrant of the Sacraments

1 B. Colloms, *Victorian Country Parsons* (1977), p. 253
2 W. Addison, op. cit., p. 113
3 D. McClatchey, op. cit., p. 36
4 A. Warne, op. cit., p. 45
5 C. P. Fendall and E. A. Crutchley, op. cit., p. 70
6 S. C. Carpenter, op. cit., p. 255
7 B. Porteus and G. Stinton, *Eight Charges . . . by Thomas Secker* (1771), p. 60
8 J. Wickham Legg, op. cit., p. 33. The survival of a weekly communion at Christ Church, Oxford afforded them this opportunity.
9 J. Walsh, op. cit., p. 103
10 A. Tindal Hart, op. cit., p. 78
11 J. Walsh, op. cit., p. 174
12 G. W. E. Russell, *A Short History of the Evangelical Movement* (1914), p. 19
13 C. Smyth, op. cit., p. 228
14 D. McClatchey, op. cit., p. 87
15 James Coleridge, *Practical Advice to a Young Parish Priest* (1834), p. 110
16 H. C. Ridley, op. cit., p. 23
17 A. J. C. Hare, *Memorials of a Quiet Life* (1862), p. 400
18 R. Mant, op. cit., p. 41
19 E. B. Ellman, *Recollections of a Sussex Parson* (1912), p. 159
20 G. M. Young, *Victorian England* (1936), p. 68
21 W. H. Hutchings, op. cit., p. 28
22 David Newsome, op. cit., p. 283; A. R. Ashwell and R. G. Wilberforce, op. cit., vol. I, p. 172
23 Isaac Williams, op. cit., p. 16
24 William Butler, op. cit., pp. 107, 116
25 Anon., *A Clergyman's Companion to the Celebration of the Divine Service* (1847), p. 12
26 S. R. Hole, *More Memories* (1894), p. 27
27 D. McClatchey, op. cit., p. 87
28 Brian Taylor, 'Bishop Hamilton', in *Church Quarterly Review* (1954), vol. CLV, pp. 243–4
29 E. B. Pusey, *Spiritual Letters* (1878), p. xii
30 C. P. S. Clarke, *The Oxford Movement and After* (1932), p. 143

31 C. F. Lowder, op. cit., p. 143
32 Owen Chadwick, op. cit., vol. II, p. 179
33 J. Bateman, *The Life of Daniel Wilson* (1860), vol. I, p. 226
34 W. R. W. Stephens, op. cit., p. 465; Michael Hennell, 'Evening Communion in the Church of England in the Nineteenth Century', in *Theology* (1959), vol. LVII, pp. 7ff.
35 D. E. M. Mole, 'J. C. Miller', in *Journal of Ecclesiastical History* (1966), vol. XVII, p. 99; Michael Hennell, op. cit., p. 7
36 Michael Hennell, op. cit., p. 8; Owen Chadwick, op. cit., vol. II, p. 308
37 P. J. Welsh, 'Bishop Blomfield and the Development of Tractarianism in London', in *Church Quarterly Review* (1954), vol. CLV, p. 334
38 S. L. Ollard, op. cit., p. 172
39 Marcus Donovan, *After the Tractarians: Recollections of Athelstan Riley* (1932), p. 16
40 Bryan Wilson, *Religion in Secular Society* (1966), p. 137
41 H. B. J. Armstrong, ed., op. cit., p. 10
42 Anon., *Medicina Clerica* (1821), p. 133
43 John Beresford, op. cit., vol. I, p. 327
44 John Walsh, op. cit., p. 260
45 J. H. Newman, *Certain Difficulties felt by Anglicans in Catholic Teaching Considered* (1888), vol. I, p. 22
46 E. Monro, *Parochial Work* (1850), p. 21
47 J. H. Blunt, op. cit., pp. 164, 166
48 W. M. Hutton, op. cit., p. 53
49 Frank West, op. cit., p. 95
50 J. H. Blunt, op. cit., p. 164
51 J. W. Burgon, op. cit., p. 350

8 Pastor

1   A. Gerard, *Sermons* (1760), p. 31
2   George Herbert, op. cit., p. 247
3   A. Tindal Hart and E. Carpenter, op. cit., p. 37
4   John Beresford, op. cit., vol. I, p. 83
5   William Paley, *Charge* (1785), p. 15
6   J. D. Walsh, op. cit., p. 104
7   Ibid., p. 150
8   Ibid., p. 280
9   C. Smyth, op. cit., p. 225
10 William Jesse, op. cit., p. 182
11 J. Pratt, op. cit., p. 337
12 J. Stonhouse, op. cit., p. 21
13 W. R. W. Stephens, *A Memoir of Richard Durnford D.D.* (1899), p. 92
14 W. H. Hutton, op. cit., p. 35; E. B. Ellman, op. cit., p. 167

15   William Butler, op. cit., p. 118
16   Harry Jones, op. cit., pp. 40, 46
17   E. Monro, *Pastoral Work* (1850), p. 157
18   C. Smyth, op. cit., p. 289; John Pratt, op. cit., p. 412
19   F. K. Brown, op. cit., p. 238
20   R. A. Soloway, op. cit., p. 324
21   Samuel Best, *Parochial Ministrations* (1839), p. 95
22   *The Christian Remembrancer* (1829), vol. XI, p. 356
23   R. Whately, op. cit., pp. 34–5; also see J. H. Blunt, op. cit., p. 318; H. Wilberforce, op. cit., p. 37 and *British Magazine* (1835), vol. VII, p. 297
24   C. Bridges, op. cit., p. 604
25   C. H. Simpkinson, *The Life and Work of Bishop Thorold* (1896), p. 40
26   R. W. Evans, op. cit., p. 26
27   Anon., *Pastoral Duties* (1818), p. 49
28   S. L. Ollard, op. cit., p. 109
29   William Addison, op. cit., p. 131
30   J. J. Blunt, op. cit., p. 224
31   J. Walsh, op. cit., p. 210
32   A. Gerard, op. cit., p. 147
33   D. Newsome, op. cit., p. 231; William Butler, op. cit., p. 36
34   R. Seymour and J. F. Mackarness, op. cit., p. 62
35   J. H. Blunt, op. cit., p. 211
36   T. W. Allies, *Journal in France in 1845 and 1848* . . . (1849), p. 337
37   E. Monro, *Pastoral Work* (1850), pp. 53–5. Also see J. H. Blunt, op. cit., p. 253; J. W. Burgon, op. cit., p. 220; C. J. Vaughan, op. cit., p. 34
38   E. Monro, op. cit., p. 45
39   M. Reynolds, op. cit., p. 231
40   W. R. Ward, 'The Last Chronicle of Barset', in *Journal of Ecclesiastical History* (1967), vol. XVII, p. 69
41   S. Baring Gould, *The Church Revival* (1914), p. 302
42   S. C. Carpenter, op. cit., p. 407
43   E. Monro, op. cit., p. 35
44   J. Skinner, op. cit., p. 148
45   G. M. Sumner, *Life of Charles Richard Sumner* (1876), p. 166
46   D. McClatchey, op. cit., p. 97
47   A. R. Ashwell and W. G. Wilberforce, op. cit., vol. II, p. 139
48   E. Monro, op. cit., p. 160
49   J. H. Blunt, op. cit., p. 227

9   Catechist

1   George Herbert, op. cit., p. 255
2   T. Secker, Charge (1741), p. 48
3   J. H. Overton and F. Relton, *The English Church 1714–1800* (1906), p. 294

4   A. Warne, op. cit., p. 48
5   R. B. Walker, 'Religious Changes in Cheshire 1750–1850', in *Journal of Ecclesiastical History* (1966), vol. XVII, p. 81
6   D. McClatchey, op. cit., p. 146; T. Secker, op. cit., p. 48
7   J. Beresford, op. cit., vol. I, p. 255
8   F. G. Stokes, op. cit., pp. 196, 198, 200, 201
9   A. Tindal Hart, op. cit., p. 39
10 W. K. Lowther Clarke, *Eighteenth-century Piety* (1944), p. 8
11 A. Hartshorne, ed., *Memoirs of a Royal Chaplain 1729–1763* (1905), p. 88. In 1722, Bishop White Kennett confirmed 1700 persons at Uppingham in Rutland. There had been no confirmation in that county for forty years. N. Sykes, *Church and State in England in the Eighteenth Century* (1934), p. 93
12 J. Beresford, op. cit., vol. II, p. 325
13 William Jesse, op. cit., p. 155
14 J. S. Reynolds, *The Evangelicals at Oxford* (1953), p. 27; J. Walsh, op. cit., p. 27
15 J. Walsh, op. cit., p. 206
16 J. Stonhouse, *Hints from a Minister to His Curate* (1774), p. 6. Also *The Religious Instruction of Children Recommended* (1774) and *Material for Talking Familiarly with Children* (1795)
17 J. Orton, op. cit., p. 4
18 C. Smyth, op. cit., p. 219
19 J. Pratt, ed., op. cit., pp. 6, 72, 358
20 G. R. Balleine, op. cit., p. 139
21 *Report from the Clergy of a District in the Diocese of Lincoln . . .* (1800), p. 18
22 G. Arden, *A Manual of Catechetical Instruction* (1847); E. Bather, *Hints on the Art of Catechising* (1848)
23 S. Best, *On Catechising* (1849), p. 5
24 *British Magazine* (1846), vols. XXIX and following
25 J. Sandford, op. cit., p. 269
26 J. Skinner, op. cit., p. 56
27 T. Methuen, op. cit., p. 68
28 S. L. Ollard, op. cit., p. 82
29 A. R. Ashwell and R. G. Wilberforce, op. cit., vol. I, p. 171
30 W. R. W. Stephens, op. cit., pp. 127, 349
31 A. Tindal Hart and E. Carpenter, op. cit., p. 91
32 E. B. Ellman, op. cit., p. 158
33 A. Tindal Hart and E. Carpenter, op. cit., p. 22
34 Ibid., p. 60
35 C. J. Vaughan, op. cit., p. 103
36 J. C. Miller, op. cit., p. 185
37 Anon., *More Disclosures about St Barnabas and the Tractarians* (1857), p. 8
38 W. Addison, op. cit., p. 153
39 H. J. B. Armstrong, op. cit., p. 56
40 J. F. Briscoe and H. F. B. Mackay, op. cit., pp. 56, 71

41 E. Monro, *Parochial Work* (1850), p. 145
42 J. H. Blunt, op. cit., p. 279
43 J. C. Miller, op. cit., p. 192
44 C. F. Lowder, op. cit., p. 104
45 A. Oxenden, op. cit., p. 224
46 E. Monro, *Parochial Papers* (1856), p. 84 and *Parochial Work* (1850), p. 153

10 Clerk

1   F. G. Stokes, op. cit., p. 94. Also see J. Beresford, op. cit., vol. I, p. 311; vol. IV, p. 118; vol. III, p. 36. It appears that the charge for searching the register and giving a certificate was 2s 6d.
2   32 Geo. III, c. 34. See J. Beresford, op. cit., vol. III, p. 303
3   T. E. Thiselton Dyer, op. cit., p. 3
4   Owen Chadwick, op. cit., vol. I, p. 144
5   T. E. Thiselton Dyer, op. cit., p. 3
6   A. Tindal Hart and E. Carpenter, op. cit., p. 59
7   *British Magazine* (1836), vol. X, p. 569
8   J. W. Burgon, op. cit., p. 236
9   W. W. Champneys, *Parish Work* (1866), pp. 99, 103; R. Gregory, op. cit., p. 20
10 E. Spooner, *Parson and Parish* (1864), p. 54

11 Officer of Law and Order

1   B. R. Wilson, *Contemporary Transformations of Religion* (1976), p. 4; A. D. Gilbert, op. cit., p. 12
2   Richard Watson, *Anecdotes of his own Life* (1818), vol. II, p. 127 quoted by G. F. A. Best, op. cit., p. 151
3   E. Gibson, *Directions given to the Clergy of the Diocese of London* (1724), p. 322
4   Their decline was not uniform and resulted in large measure from the fact that an appeal lay from this court to the bishop's court, to which suitors preferred to resort in the first instance. A case concerning the subtraction of a legacy was brought before the Archdeacon of Barnstaple's court in 1812. A. Warne, op. cit., p. 84
5   William Grimshaw at Haworth directed his congregation to sing Psalm 119, whilst he patrolled the streets and public houses to seek out non-attenders. J. Walsh, op. cit., p. 104
6   J. Beresford, op. cit., vol. I, p. 69
7   J. W. Burgon, op. cit., p. 410
8   C. Wordsworth, ed., *Memories of William Wordsworth* (1851), vol. I, p. 8 quoted by J. Wickham Legg, op. cit., p. 259
9   G. R. Balleine, op. cit., p. 134
10 *Proceedings of the Ecclesiastical Courts Commission* (1832), pp. 568–9
11 A. D. Gilbert, op. cit., p. 13

12 The statutory qualification was an income of £100 per annum from land (raised from £50 in 1774).

13 D. McClatchey, op. cit., pp. 179ff.

14 C. P. Fendall and E. A. Crutchley, op. cit., p. 168

15 A. Blomfield, op. cit., vol. I, p. 38. The author comments: 'The farmers of this parish long remember how his union of magisterial and ministerial authority kept them in order.'

16 Anon., *An Admonition to the Younger Clergy* (1764), p. 18

17 A. W. Brown, *Recollections of the Conversation Parties of the Rev. Charles Simeon* (1863), p. 129

18 O. F. Christie, op. cit., p. 258

19 Lewis Melville, *The Life and Letters of William Cobbett in England and America* (1913), vol. I, p. 156

20 G. B. Hill, ed., *Boswell's Life of Johnson* (1934), vol. III, p. 437. For a similar observation see Anon., *The Pastoral Care* (1808), p. 126

21 George Herbert, op. cit., p. 254

22 Anon., An Admonition to the Younger Clergy (1764), pp. 7–8

23 Richard Watson, *Christianity Consistent with Social Duty* (1769), p. 15 quoted by R. A. Soloway, op. cit., p. 21

24 J. Beresford, op. cit., vol. I, p. 95

25 Ibid., vol. I, p. 316

26 J. Skinner, op. cit., pp. 134, 141, 292

27 J. Beresford, op. cit., vol. II, p. 324. Also see A. Blomfield, op. cit., p. 53; P. H. Ditchfield, op. cit., p. 205; J. Skinner, op. cit., p. 45

28 For an eyewitness account, see Richard Twining, ed., *Recreation and Studies of a Country Clergyman in the Eighteenth Century* (1882), pp. 80ff.

29 G. F. A. Best, op. cit., p. 71

30 R. A. Soloway, op. cit. p. 33

31 Anon., *A Country Parson's Address to his Flock* (1799), p. 38

32 John Napleton, *Advice to a Minister of the Gospel* (1801), p. 23. Also see John Randolph, Primary Charge (1802), p. 7

33 D. Newsome, op. cit., p. 12

34 A. J. C. Hare, *Memorials of a Quiet Life* (1872), vol. I, p. 290

35 R. B. Walker, op. cit., p. 92

36 D. Newsome, op. cit., p. 126

37 A. J. Peacock, *Bread and Blood* (1965), p. 111. Bate Dudley's career was unusual even by the standards of the day. He was involved in the famous Vauxhall Affray and numerous other scandals and several duels. He was imprisoned for a year for libelling the Duke of Richmond. He paid £28,000 for the living of Bradwell but the Bishop refused to institute him on the grounds of simony.

38 H. C. G. Moule, op. cit., p. 67

39 *Report of the Select Committee on the Sale of Beer* (1833), p. 7

40 E. J. Hobsbawn and G. Rode, *Captain Swing* (1969), p. 120

41 Ibid., pp. 136ff.

42 R. Quinault and J. Stevenson, *Popular Protest and Public Order 1790–1920* (1974), pp. 187ff.

43 B. Heeney, op. cit., p. 65
44 R. W. Evans, op. cit., p. 233. Also see R. Mant, op. cit., p. 284
45 D. McClatchey, op. cit., p. 182
46 A. Blomfield, op. cit., vol. I, p. 39
47 *Hansard Parliamentary Debates*, 3rd series, vol. XXXVI, col. 419
    quoted by D. McClatchey, op. cit., p. 181
48 G. Kitson Clark, op. cit., p. 35
49 *Hansard Parliamentary Debates*, 3rd series, vol. XLVIII, cols.
    1298–1301 quoted by O. Brose, *Church and Parliament* (1959), p. 191
50 See S. Best, *Village Libraries and Reading Rooms* (1854); Anon., *The
    Priest and the Parish* (1858), p. 184
51 J. Sandford, op. cit., p. 212
52 H. Jones, op. cit., p. 214. Also see E. Munro, *Parochial Work* (1850),
    p. 41
53 Anon., *Entries or Stray Leaves from a Clergyman's Notebook* (1853),
    p. 17
54 G. Kitson Clark, op. cit., p. 146
55 R. Quinault and J. Stevenson, op. cit., p. 188
56 A. Tindal Hart and E. Carpenter, op. cit., p. 38
57 J. B. Sumner, *Apostolic Preaching* (1850), p. 364
58 H. Jones, op. cit., p. 214
59 *Quarterly Review*, 'The Church and the Landlords', vol. XLIX (1833),
    p. 211 quoted by G. F. A. Best, op. cit., p. 153
60 J. H. Blunt, op. cit., p. 289
61 J. R. Woodforde, *Ordination Lectures* (1861), p. 9
62 Charles Kingsley, *Politics for the People* (1848), p. 58

12 Almoner

1   George Herbert, op. cit., p. 224
2   Gilbert Burnet, op. cit., p. 207
3   A. Gerard, op. cit., p. 207
4   A. Redford, *The Economic History of England 1760–1860* (1960),
    p. 117
5   Thomas Gisborne, *An Inquiry into the Duties of Men . . .* (1795),
    vol. II, p. 61
6   C. P. Fendall and E. A. Crutchley, op. cit., p. 240
7   J. Beresford, op. cit., vol. III, p. 382
8   Thomas Gisborne, op. cit., vol. II, p. 62
9   C. P. Fendall and E. A. Crutchley, op. cit., p. 124
10 W. H. Hutchings, op. cit., p. 27
11 Beilby Porteus and George Stanton, op. cit., p. 190
12 D. McClatchey, op. cit., pp. 123–4
13 A. Warne, op. cit., p. 149
14 J. D. Walsh, op. cit., p. 175
15 Charles Smyth, op. cit., p. 225
16 R. A. Soloway, op. cit., p. 196

17 D. Owen, *English Philanthropy 1660–1960* (1965), p. 97
18 R. A. Soloway, op. cit., p. 161
19 N. Sykes, op. cit., p. 114
20 G. M. Trevelyan, *English Social History* (1944), p. 474
21 R. A. Soloway, op. cit., p. 184
22 A. Tindal Hart and E. Carpenter, op. cit., p. 90
23 W. R. W. Stephens, op. cit., p. 98
24 A. J. C. Hare, *The Story of My Life* (1896), vol. I, p. 155
25 J. Sandford, *Parochialia* (1845), pp. 189, 348. Also see Anon., *Hints to a Clergyman's Wife* (1832), pp. 178, 190; H. C. Ridley, op. cit., p. 32; C. Bridges, op. cit., pp. 471ff; S. Best, *A Manual of Parochial Ministrations* (1849), pp. 625ff; R. Simpson, *The Clergyman's Manual* (1842), p. 200
26 G. Kitson Clark, op. cit., pp. 186, 192
27 Joseph Arch, *The Story of His Life told by Himself* (1898), p. 7
28 S. Best, op. cit., p. 56
29 Ibid., p. 142
30 *Parliamentary Papers* (1834), vol. XXVIII, pt. 1, appendix A, p. 410 quoted by G. Kitson Clark, op. cit., p. 170
31 R. Seymour and J. F. Mackarness, op. cit., p. 92
32 R. W. Evans, op. cit., p. 270; John Kaye, *Charge to the Clergy of the Diocese of Lincoln* (1846), reprinted in Anon., *The Clergyman's Instructor* (1855), p. 471
33 Anon., *A Churchman's Appeal to his Brother Clergymen in Defence of the Clergy of the Church of England* (1835), p. 10
34 H. B. J. Armstrong, ed., op. cit., pp. 54, 87
35 J. C. Miller, *Letter to a Young Clergyman* (1878), p. 173
36 J. C. Talbot, *Parochial Mission Women* (1862), p. 8
37 W. H. Hutton, op. cit., p. 60
38 H. B. J. Armstrong, ed., op. cit., p. 27
39 D. McClatchey, op. cit., p. 152
40 R. Simpson, op. cit., p. 206
41 W. W. Champneys, op. cit., p. 29
42 J. W. Burgon, op. cit., p. 225
43 A. Oxenden, op. cit., p. 182

13   Teacher

1 R. Twining, op. cit., p. 2
2 C. Thornton and F. McLaughlin, *The Fothergills of Ravenstonedale* (1905), p. 71
3 A. Warne, op. cit., pp. 64ff.
4 C. Smyth, op. cit., p. 224
5 N. Sykes, op. cit., pp. 162–6. See also Anon., *How to rise in the Church* (1837), pp. 2ff.
6 J. D. Walsh, op. cit., p. 292
7 J. Beresford, op. cit., vol. I, p. 194

8   W. Addison, op. cit., p. 127
9   J. Orton, *Letters to a Young Clergyman* (1791), p. 98
10 Anon., *A Discourse . . .* (1722), p. 49
11 Quoted by A. Warne, op. cit., p. 138
12 G. R. Balleine, op. cit., p. 139
13 J. D. Walsh, op. cit., p. 323
14 *Anti-Jacobin Review and Magazine* (1799), vol. III, pp. 180, 321
15 Bishop Horsley, *Charge* (1800), quoted by G. R. Balleine, op. cit., p. 142
16 F. Wollaston, *A Country Parson's Address to his Flock* (1799), p. 27
17 Quoted by R. A. Soloway, op. cit., p. 352
18 Hannah More, *Stories* (1818), vol. I, p. 178
19 M. G. Jones, *The Charity School Movement* (1938), p. 148
20 Ibid., p. 153
21 *Report from the Clergy of a District in the Diocese of Lincoln . . .* (1800), p. 7
22 Anon., *A Manual for a Parish Priest* (1818), p. 114
23 A. Blomfield, op. cit., vol. I, p. 16
24 A. Oxenden, op. cit., p. 7
25 R. B. Walker, op. cit., p. 86
26 G. F. A. Best, op. cit., p. 153
27 R. A. Soloway, op. cit., p. 374
28 W. F. Hook, *On the Means of Rendering more Efficient the Education of the Poor* (1846); W. R. Ward, op. cit., p. 234
29 J. D. Coleridge, op. cit., p. 46
30 J. Sandford, op. cit., p. 67
31 I. Williams, op. cit., p. 85
32 W. H. Hutton, op. cit., p. 34
33 J. Skinner, op. cit., pp. 58ff.
34 E. B. Ellman, op. cit., p. 167
35 J. C. Atkinson, *Forty Years in a Moorland Parish* (1871), p. 46
36 D. Newsome, op. cit., pp. 236–7
37 A. Tindal Hart and E. Carpenter, op. cit., p. 83
38 See *Report of the Special Assistant Poor Law Commissioners on the Employment of Women and Children in Agriculture* (1843), pp. 249, 258
39 C. K. Francis Brown, *The Church's Part in Education* (1942), p. 11
40 E. B. Ellman, op. cit., p. 284
41 Pamela Horn, 'Problems of a Nineteenth-century Vicar 1832–1885', in *Oxford Diocesan Magazine*, Oct. 1969, pp. 16ff. and Nov. 1969, pp. 18ff.
42 O. J. Brose, op. cit., p. 191
43 G. Kitson Clark, op. cit., p. 102
44 J. Sandford, op. cit., p. 69
45 J. Skinner, op. cit., p. 39
46 R. Simpson, op. cit., p. 82
47 E. Monro, *Parochial Work* (1850), p. 256
48 Anon., *More Discourses about St Barnabas Pimlico* (1857), pp. 8ff.

49 William Butler, op. cit. (1897), pp. 128, 158
50 Thomas Dale, *Five Years of Church Extension in St Pancras* (1852), p. 46
51 A. Blomfield, op. cit., vol. I, p. 242
52 C. M. Simpkinson, op. cit., p. 34
53 D. McClatchey, op. cit., pp. 155ff.
54 J. J. Blunt, op. cit., p. 209
55 J. C. Miller, *Letters to a Young Clergyman* (1878), p. 20
56 S. Wilberforce, *Charge* (1848), p. 32
57 R. A. Soloway, op. cit., p. 426

14 Officer of Health

1 George Herbert, op. cit., p. 260
2 Anon., *A Letter of Advice to a Young Clergyman* (1709), p. 5
3 A. Gerard, op. cit., p. 237
4 C. D. Linnell, ed., *The Diary of Benjamin Rogers 1720–1771*, Bedfordshire Historical Records Society, Luton (1950), vol. XXV, p. xi
5 J. Beresford, op. cit., vol. I, pp. 110, 192ff, 212 and vol. III, p. 168
6 Hesketh Pearson, *The Smith of Smiths* (1934), p. 196
7 C. P. Fendall and E. A. Crutchley, op. cit., p. 129
8 J. Beresford, op. cit., vol. III, p. 255
9 J. Skinner, op. cit., pp. 26, 43
10 D. McClatchey, op. cit., pp. 168ff.
11 E. B. Ellman, op. cit., p. 281
12 Owen Chadwick, *Victorian Miniature* (1960), p. 53
13 A. Tindal Hart and E. Carpenter, op. cit., p. 54
14 A. Jessop, *Arcady, for better or worse* (1887), p. 5
15 Anon., *Hints to a Clergyman's Wife* (1832), p. 77
16 H. C. Ridley, op. cit., p. 37
17 A. Newsome, op. cit., p. 103
18 Richard Marks, *The Village Pastor* (1827), vol. II, p. 57
19 *British Magazine* (1842), vol. LXXI, p. 451
20 J. Sandford, op. cit., p. 342
21 S. Best, *Village Libraries and Reading Rooms* (1854), p. 9
22 A. Newsome, op. cit., p. 144
23 D. McClatchey, op. cit., p. 168
24 H. C. Ridley, op. cit., p. 31
25 G. Kitson Clark, op. cit., p. 204
26 Charles Kingsley, *His Letters and Memories of his Life*, edited by his wife (1876), vol. I, p. 318
27 G. Kitson Clark, op. cit., p. 143
28 Charles Kingsley, op. cit., vol. I, pp. 177, 186
29 William Butler, op. cit., pp. 72–3, 120, 219
30 D. McClatchey, op. cit., p. 167
31 C. Girdlestone, *Sanitary Reform: a lecture* . . . (1853). Also see *Seven Sermons preached during the Prevalence of Cholera in the Parish of Sedgley* (1833)

32 D. McClatchey, op. cit., p. 166
33 H. B. J. Armstrong, ed., op. cit., p. 23
34 J. H. Blunt, op. cit., p. 397
35 *British Magazine* (1847), vol. XXXII, p. 331
36 J. Sandford, op. cit., p. 382
37 W. J. E. Bennett, *The Old Church Porch* (1854–62), vol. I, pp. 44ff.
38 A. Tindal Hart and E. Carpenter, op. cit., p. 125
39 C. F. Lowder, op. cit., p. 199; W. J. Butler, op. cit., p. 128; W. H. Hutchings, op. cit., pp. 99ff; J. Sandford, op. cit., p. 382; T. W. Allies, op. cit., p. 119
40 W. J. E. Bennett, op. cit., vol. I, p. 44
41 D. McClatchey, op. cit., p. 77
42 D. Reynolds, op. cit., p. 199

15 Politician

1 Quoted by D. Nicholls, ed., *Church and State in Britain since 1820* (1967), p. 29
2 B. Porteus and G. Stanton, op. cit., p. 87
3 G. V. Bennett and J. D. Walsh, *Essays in English Church History* (1966), p. 175
4 N. Sykes, op. cit., p. 168
5 J. Dixey, *Sermons* (1781), p. 11
6 Anon., *A Discourse of the great and solemn charge and office of the Minister of the Gospel* (1772), p. 71
7 O. F. Christie, op. cit., p. 192
8 C. K. Francis Brown, op. cit., p. 138
9 J. Beresford, op. cit., vol. IV, p. 281
10 C. C. Brookes, *History of Steeple Aston* (1929), p. 154 quoted by D. McClatchey, op. cit., p. 207
11 C. J. Abbey and J. H. Overton, *The English Church* (1878), vol. II, p. 33
12 Job Orton, op. cit., p. 134
13 G. F. A. Best, 'The Evangelicals and the Established Church in the Early Nineteenth Century', in *Journal of Theological Studies* (April 1959), new series, vol. X, pt. 1, p. 76
14 J. D. Walsh, op. cit., p. 351
15 F. K. Brown, op. cit., p. 134
16 E. R. Norman, *Church and Society in England 1770–1970* (1976), p. 21
17 M. J. Quinlan, op. cit., p. 71
18 C. Smyth, op. cit., p. 297
19 A. D. Gilbert, op. cit., p. 57
20 Sydney Smith, *Letters on the Subject of Catholics . . .* (1807), Letter V, p. 37
21 W. R. Ward, op. cit., p. 121
22 Owen Chadwick, op. cit., vol. I, p. 26

23   *British Magazine* (April 1832), vol. I, p. 172
24   R. L. Hill, *Toryism and the People 1831–1846* (1929), p. 57
25   A. R. Ashwell and R. G. Wilberforce, op. cit., vol. I, p. 79
26   A. D. Gilbert, op. cit., p. 77
27   J. C. Gill, *Parson Bull of Byerley* (1963), pp. 62ff.
28   D. E. H. Mole, op. cit., p. 102; W. R. W. Stephens, op. cit., p. 385
29   *Report of Special Assistant Poor Law Commissioners on the Employment of Women and Children in Agriculture* (1843). Also see G. Kitson Clark, op. cit., p. 258
30   Quoted by G. Kitson Clark, op. cit., p. 219
31   H. C. G. Moule, op. cit., p. 60
32   William Butler, op. cit., p. 120
33   Charles Kingsley, op. cit., vol. I, pp. 111ff.
34   A. Tindal Hart, op. cit., p. 60
35   Owen Chadwick, op. cit., vol. I, p. 155
36   G. Kitson Clark, op. cit., pp. 255ff.
37   Pamela Horn, op. cit., p. 18
38   G. Kitson Clark, op. cit., p. 175
39   W. Tuckwell, *Reminiscences of a Radical Parson* (1905), p. 128
40   Owen Chadwick, *The Secularization of the European Mind in the Nineteenth Century* (1975), p. 108
41   Owen Chadwick, *The Victorian Church* (1970), vol. II, p. 246
42   B. Taylor, op. cit., p. 239
43   D. E. H. Mole, op. cit., p. 102

16   The Late-Nineteenth-Century Clergyman as a Professional Man

1   A. Oxenden, op. cit., p. 31
2   Archdeacon Manning, Charge (1846), quoted by B. Heeney, op. cit., p. 11
3   B. Heeney, op. cit., p. 14
4   R. Mant, op. cit., p. 307
5   Anon. [F. E. Paget], *The Warden of Berkingholt* (1843), p. 215
6   Owen Chadwick, op. cit., vol. II, p. 170
7   B. Colloms, op. cit., p. 30
8   Richard Jefferies, *Hodge and His Master* (1946), p. 269
9   O. Chadwick, op. cit., vol. II, p. 166
10   D. Newsome, op. cit., p. 279
11   A. Tindal Hart and E. Carpenter, op. cit., p. 96 and p. 118
12   O. Chadwick, op. cit., vol. II, p. 244
13   See B. Heeney, op. cit., p. 126; O. Chadwick, op. cit., vol. II, p. 249; *Crockford Prefaces* (1947), p. 118
14   A. D. Gilbert, op. cit., p. 131
15   Ibid., p. 133
16   O. Chadwick, op. cit., p. 247
17   W. J. Reader, op. cit., p. 157
18   B. Heeney, op. cit., p. 16

19 O. Chadwick, op. cit., vol. II, p. 245
20 B. Heeney, op. cit., p. 25
21 O. Chadwick, op. cit., vol. II, p. 251 and Alan Wilkinson, *The Church of England and the First World War* (1978), p. 65
22 Ibid., vol. II, p. 207
23 P. C. Hammond, op. cit., p. 17
24 Eric J. Evans, 'Some Reasons for the Growth of English Rural Anti-Clericalism 1750–1830', in *Past and Present*, vol. LXVI (1975), pp. 84ff.
25 Olive Anderson, 'The Growth of Christian Militarism', in *English Historical Review*, vol. LXXXVI (1971), p. 65
26 B. Heeney, op. cit., p. 31
27 Ibid., p. 116
28 George Eliot, *Adam Bede* (1858; Everyman edition 1966), p. 132
29 O. Chadwick, op. cit., vol. II, p. 154
30 A. D. Gilbert, op. cit., pp. 138, 174
31 P. C. Hammond, op. cit., p. 104
32 Alan Wilkinson, op. cit., pp. 111, 129, 215
33 *The Army and Religion. An Inquiry and its Bearing upon the Religious Life of the Nation* (1919); see Alan Wilkinson, op. cit., p. 163

17   The Professions and Change in the Twentieth Century

1 P. Elliot, op. cit., p. 109
2 Quoted by P. Elliot, op. cit., p. 67
3 Ibid., p. 60
4 J. A. Jackson, ed., op. cit., pp. 53ff.
5 Currently taking evidence (1978)
6 P. Elliot, op. cit., pp. 67ff.

18   The Clergyman's Role in Contemporary Society

1 B. R. Wilson, op. cit., p. 97
2 See R. Currie, A. Gilbert and L. Horsley, *Churches and Churchgoers* (1977); and *Statistical Supplement to the Church of England Yearbook* (1978)
3 S. Rawson, A. Bryman and B. Hinings, *Clergy, Ministers and Priest* (1977), p. 12
4 Research undertaken for ACCM by Professor Alec Rodger and John Barker
5 A. Gilbert, op. cit., p. 133
6 *The Second Report of the Working Party on Courses* (GS 359). See also Trevor Kerry, 'Quality in the Ministry', in *Church Times* (5 Jan. 1979), p. 5
7 *The Times* (19 June 1957)

8 *A Life of Service* (ACCM 1973), p. 2

9 S. Rawson, A. Bryman and B. Hinings, op. cit., pp. 65ff.

10 Ibid., p. 15. See also S. Blizzard, *The Minister's Dilemma: The Christian Century* (1973), pp. 508–9

11 Ibid., p. 63

12 B. R. Wilson, *Religion in Secular Society* (1966), p. 84

13 O. Chadwick, op. cit., vol. II, p. 214

14 See *The State of the Teams* (1977), an annual report compiled by Peter Croft, published by ONE for Christian Renewal; also see Anthony Russell, ed., *Groups and Teams in the Countryside* (1975)

15 N. Lash and J. Rhymer, *The Christian Priesthood* (1970), p. 168

16 S. Rawson, A. Bryman and B. Hinings, op. cit., pp. 28ff.

17 Survey undertaken by Dr Kathleen Jones

18 Leslie Paul, *The Deployment and Payment of the Clergy* (1964), pp. 111–14, 275

19 *A Supporting Ministry.* A report of the Ministry Committee of ACCM (1968)

20 W. H. Saumarez Smith, *An Honorary Ministry* (ACCM occasional paper no. 8, 1977), p. 11

19 The Future of the Clergyman's Role and the Church's Ministry

1 John Bowden, *Voices in the Wilderness* (1977), p. 67

2 R. K. Merton defined 'function' as '. . . those observed consequences which make for the adaption or adjustment of a given system', and 'dysfunction' as '. . . those observed consequences which lessen the adaption or adjustment of the system'. R. K. Merton, *Social Theory and Social Structure* (rev. edn 1957), p. 51

3 I am indebted to Canon Peter Hinchliff for this example.

4 *A Supporting Ministry.* A report of the Ministry Committee of ACCM (1968), p. 7

Bibliography

The Bibliography is divided into three sections; in the first works are listed in chronological order. Books are published in London except where otherwise stated.

1 THE HANDBOOKS
Manuals of advice written for the clergy

Herbert, George, *A Priest to the Temple or the Country Parson. His Character and Rule of Holy Life* (1652), ed. P. E. Hutchinson. *The Work of George Herbert* (Oxford 1941), pp. 223ff.

Baxter, Richard, *The Reformed Pastor* (1656).

Taylor, Jeremy,* *Rules and Advices of the Clergy of the Diocese of Down and Connor* (1661).

Patrick, Simon,* *A Letter of the Bishop of Chichester to his Clergy* (1690)

Patrick, Simon,* *The Work of the Ministry represented to his Clergy of the Diocese of Ely* (1692).

Burnet, Gilbert,** *A Discourse on the Pastoral Care* (1692).

Sprat, Thomas,** *A Discourse made by the Lord Bishop of Rochester to the Clergy of his Diocese* (1695).

Watson, Thomas, *The Clergyman's Law or the Complete Incumbent* (1701).

Wilson, Thomas,** *Parochialia, or Instructions to the Clergy in the discharge of their parochial duty* (1708).

Anon., *A Letter of Advice to a young clergyman entering upon a cure of souls* (1709).

Anon., *The Parochial Clergyman's Duty* (1711).

Bull, George,** *A Companion for the Candidates of Holy*

---

*Titles marked thus are included in Moorman, J. R. H., *The Curate of Souls* (1958), to which book the page numbers in the notes refer.
**Titles marked thus are included in *The Clergyman's Instructor* (Oxford 1807), to which book the page numbers in the notes refer.

Orders; or the great importance and principal duties of the priestly office (1714).

Gibson, Edmund,** *Directions given to the Clergy of the Diocese of London* (1724).[1]

Anon. [by a Presbyter of the Church of England], *A Discourse of the Great and Solemn Charge and Office of the Minister of the Gospel* (1722).

Anon., *The Country Parson's Companion or Young Clergyman's Lawyer* (1725).

Wesley, Samuel, *Advice to a Young Clergyman . . .* (1737). Thomas Jackson. *The Life of the Rev. Charles Wesley* (1841), vol. II, pp. 503ff.

Secker, Thomas, *Eight Charges delivered to the Clergy of the dioceses of Oxford and Canterbury*, ed. Beilby Porteus and George Stinton (2nd edn 1771).[2]

Gibson, Edmund,** *Charge to the Clergy of his diocese* (1741).

Anon., *Advice to a young clergyman how to conduct himself in the common offices of life in a letter from a late Rt. Rev. prelate* (1741).[3]

Hart, Josiah,** *Instructions to the Clergy of the Diocese of Tuam* (Primary Visitation Charge) (1742).

Mason, John, *The Student and Pastor* (1755).

Wesley, John, *An Address to the Clergy* (1756).

Anon., *Advice from a Bishop in a series of letters to a younger clergyman* (1757).

Newton, John,* *Letter to the Rev. Mr. N—* (1757).

Venn, Henry, *Sermon*: 'The Duty of a Parish Priest; His Obligations to perform it; and the incomparable pleasure of a life devoted to the care of souls' (1760).

Anon., *An Admonition to the younger clergy, shewing the expediency of propriety, temperance, assiduity, and candour* (1764)

---

[1] Gibson's *Primary Visitation Charge* to the clergy of the diocese of Lincoln of 1717 was reprinted in 1724 under this title.
[2] Containing Secker's *Charge* of 1738, 1741, 1747, 1750, and 1753 in the diocese of Oxford, and 1758, 1762, and 1766 in that of Canterbury.
[3] J. R. H. Moorman, op. cit., p. 171. This pamphlet was originally published in 1730.

Clubbe, John, *A Letter of free advice to a young clergyman. Miscellaneous Tracts*, vol. II (Ipswich 1770).

Owen, Henry, *Directions for Young Students in Divinity, with regard to those attainments which are necessary to qualify them for Holy Orders* (2nd edn 1773).

Stonhouse, Sir James, *Hints from a minister to his curate for the management of his parish* (1774).

Paley, William, *Advice addressed to the young clergy of the diocese of Carlisle in a sermon* (1781).

Jesse, William, *Parochialia, or observations on the discharge of parochial duties . . .* (1785).

Orton, Job, *Letters of a Young Clergyman*, ed. Rev. Thomas Stedman (1791).

Gisborne, Thomas, *An Inquiry into the Duties of Men in the Higher and Middle Classes of Society* (vol. II), *The Clerical Profession*, (1795).

Anon., [William Gilpin], *Three Dialogues on the Amusements of Clergymen* (1796).[1]

Gerard, Alexander, *The Pastoral Care* (1799).

Napleton, John, *Advice to a Minister of the Gospel* (Hereford 1801).

Anon., *The Clergyman's Assistant* (Oxford 1806).[2]

Anon., *The Clergyman's Instructor, or a collection of tracts on the ministerial duties* (Oxford 1807).[3]

Anon., *The Pastoral Care* (1808).

Jebb, *A letter from the Right Rev. Bishop Jebb to the clergymen in his diocese, February 1808. On Fashionable Amusements.*

Anon., *The Duties of the Clerical Profession selected from various authors* (1810).

Anon., *A Manual for the Parish Priest, being a few hints on*

[1] R. Mant, *The Clergyman's Obligations Considered* (Oxford 1831) gives the author of this work as William Gilpin, Vicar of Boldre.

[2] A collection of the Acts of Parliament which concern the clergy and a digest of the writings of ecclesiastical lawyers. Subsequent editions: 2nd – 1808; 3rd – 1808; 4th – 1822; 5th – 1825.

[3] R. Mant, op. cit., p. xx gives the compiler as Dr Randolph. Subsequent editions appeared as follows: 3rd – 1824; 4th – 1827; 5th – 1843; 6th – 1855.

the pastoral care, to the younger clergy of the Church of England (2nd edn 1822). [1]

Mant, Richard, *The Order for the Visitation of the Sick . . .* (3rd edn 1816).

Anon., *Pastoral Duties* (1818).

Anon., *The Gentleman's and Clergyman's Companion for Visiting the Sick* (1818).

Anon., *Medical Hints, designed for the use of the clergy* (1820).

Anon., *Medicina Clerica, or Hints to the Clergy for the healthful discharge of their ministerial duties* (1821).

Anon. [Revd George Hughes], *The Clerical Portrait; a study for the Young Divine* (1824).

Anon. [H. C. Ridley], *Parochial Duties*, practically illustrated (2nd ed. Henley on Thames 1829).

Anon., *Parochial Letters from a Beneficed Clergyman to his curate* (1829).

Thompson, Henry, *Pastoralia. A Manual of Helps for the Parochial Clergy* (1830).

Mant, Richard, *The Clergyman's Obligations Considered* (Oxford 1830).

Bridges, Charles, *The Christian Ministry* (3rd edn 1830).

Kaye, John, *A Charge delivered in 1831 to the clergy of the diocese of Lincoln.* [2]

Anon., *A Letter to a Young Clergyman on the consistency of his employments and amusements with his professional character and office* (1832).

Coleridge, James Duke, *Practical Advice to the Young Parish Priest* (1834).

Anon. [Henry R. Moody], *Hints to younger clergymen on various matters of form and duty* (1835).

Gresley, W., *Ecclesiastes Anglicanus, being A Treatise on the Art of Preaching* (1835).

Whately, Richard, *Letter to a Clergyman* (1836).

Anon., *The Clergyman's Private Register and Assistant in his Ministerial Visits* (1838).

---

[1] W. H. Cope and H. Stretton. *Visitatio Infirmorum* (1848), p. XXVII and R. Mant, op. cit., p. 338 both list this work as by the Revd Mr Sawbridge. 1st edn 1815.

[2] Only in 6th edn (1855) of *The Clergyman's Instructor.*

Anon. [Robert Hussey], *A Help to Young Clergymen in reading and preaching in the congregation of the Church* (1839).

Best, Hon and Revd Samuel, *Parochial Ministrations* (1839).

Cull, Richard, *Garrick's Mode of Reading the Liturgy of the Church of England* (1840)

Simpson, Robert, *The Clergyman's Manual of Ministerial Duties* (1842).

Evans, R., *The Bishopric of Souls* (1842).

Sandford, John, *Parochialia; or Church, School, and Parish* (1845).

Arden, G., *A Manual of Catechetical Instruction* (1847).

Bather, Edward, *Hints on the Art of Catechising, edited by his widow* (1848).

Best, Hon and Revd Samuel, *A Manual of Parochial Institutions . . .* (2nd edn 1849).[1]

Best, Hon and Revd Samuel, *On Catechising* (1849).

Cripps, Henry William, *A Practical Treatise on the Law relating to the Church and the clergy* (1850).

Monro, Edward, *Parochial Work* (1850).

Cope, William H. and Stretton, Henry, *Visitatio Infirmorum* (2nd edn 1850).

Gatty, Alfred, *The Vicar and his Duties* (1853).

Pinnock, W. H., *Clerical Papers on the Ministerial Duties and the Management of a Parish*, 3 vols. (Cambridge 1855–63).

Blunt, J. J., *The Parish Priest. His Acquirements, Principal Obligations, and Duties* (1856).

Oxenden, Ashton, *The Pastoral Office: its duties, difficulties, privileges, and prospects* (1857).

Dale, James Murray, *The Clergyman's Legal Handbook* (1858).

Arden, G., *The Cure of Souls* (Oxford 1858).

Anon., *The Parish and the Priest: colloquies on the pastoral care and parochial institutions of a country village* (1858).

---

[1] It is possible that Best's earlier book *Parochial Ministrations* is the first edition of this work; although there are many differences, the content is similar. Neither the Bodleian Library nor the British Museum lists a first edition of this popular work.

Wilberforce, Samuel, *Addresses to Candidates for Ordination* (1859).

Anon. [A. K. H. Boyd], *The Recreations of a Country Parson* (1859).

Sweet, J. B., *Speculum Parochiale* (1859).

Browning, Henry B., *Aids to Pastoral Visitation* (1860).

Whately, Richard, *The Parish Pastor* (1860).

Monro, Edward, *Pastoral Life* (1862).

Anon., *Hints to Clergymen on Visiting the Sick* (1863).

Anon., *Clerical Recreations; thoughts for the clergy* (1863).

Burgon, John W., *A Treatise on the Pastoral Office* (1864).

Blunt, J. H., *Directorium Pastorale. Principles and Practice of Pastoral Work in the Church of England* (1864).

Champneys, W. W., *Parish Work* (1866).

Jones, Harry, *Priest and Parish* (1866).

How, William Walsham, *Pastor in Parochia* (1868).

Anon., *A Manual of Pastoral Visitation* . . . (1868).

Blunt, J. H., *The Book of Church Law*, revised by W. G. F. Phillimore (1872).

Anon., *Hints to Young Clergymen* (1874).

Parnell, Frank, *Ars Pastoria* (1875).

Vaughan, C. J., *Addresses to Young Clergymen* (1875).

Miller, John C., *Letters to a Young Clergyman* (1878).

James, Herbert, *The Country Clergyman and His Work* (1890).

Liddon, H. P., *Clerical Life and Work* (1895).

2 GENERAL

Abbey, C. J., and Overton, J. H., *The English Church in the Eighteenth Century*, 2 vols. (1878).

Adair, John, *The Becoming Church* (1977).

Adamson, J. W., *English Education 1789–1902* (Cambridge 1930).

Addison, William, *The English Country Parson* (1947).

Allies, Thomas William, *Journal in France in 1845 and 1848 with letters from Italy in 1847 on things and persons concerning the Church and Education* (1849).

Anderson, Olive, 'The Growth of Christian Militarism', in *English Historical Review*, vol. LXXXVI (1971).

Andrews, J. H. B., 'The Country Parson, 1969', in *Theology*, vol. LXXII, March 1969, p. 103.

Anon., *A Handy Guide to the obtaining of Holy Orders in the United Church of England and Ireland* (n.d., *c.* 1863).

Anon., *The Clergyman's Advocate* (1711).

Anon., *A Letter from a Gentleman in Town to his friend in the Country* . . . (1753).

Anon., *The Curate* (1810).

Anon., *Hints for bettering the condition of the clergy, likewise some proposals respecting the poor* (1812).

Anon. [J. W. Cunningham], *The Velvet Cushion* (1814).

Anon., *Observations on the new Residence Bill and on objections which have been made to it* (1817).

Anon., *The Curate's Appeal to the equity and Christian principles of the British legislature* . . . (1819).

Anon., *The Sufferings of the Clergy* (1819).

Anon., *A Letter to His Grace the Archbishop of Canterbury* . . . (1824).

Anon., *A Layman's Charge to the Clergy of the Church of England* (1828).

Anon., *The Constitutional Assemblies of the clergy, the proper and only effectual security of the Established Church* (1829).

Anon. [Edward Field], *Machine Breaking and the changes occasioned by it in the village of Turvey Down* (Oxford 1830).

Anon. [G. R. Gleig], *The Country Curate*, 2 vols. (1830).

Anon., *A Country Rector's Address to his Parishioners* (2nd edn 1830).

Anon., *A Pastoral Letter in the time of alarm occasioned by the cholera morbus* (1832).

Anon., *Hints for a Clergyman's Wife; or female parochial duties practically illustrated* (1832).

Anon. [Samuel Wilberforce], *The Note Book of a Country Clergyman* (1833).

Anon., *The Churchman's appeal to his brother churchmen in defence of the clergy of the Church of England* (1835).

Anon., *Hints to District Visiting Societies* (1836).

Anon. [E. Thompson], *The Rector of Auburn*, 2 vols. (1837).

Anon., *How to rise in the Church* (4th edn 1837).

Anon., *Pastoral Recollections* (1837).

Anon., *The Life Book of a labourer by a working clergyman* (1839).

Anon., *Sermon on behalf of the Society for Promoting the Enlarging, Building, and Repairing of Churches* (1840).

Anon. [F. E. Paget], *St Antholins or Old Churches and New* (1841).

Anon., *Humbling Recollections of my Ministry* (1842).

Anon. [W. F. Wilkinson], *The Rector in Search of a Curate* (1843).

Anon., *The Whole Case of the Unbeneficed Clergy* (1843).

Anon., *Difficulties of a Young Clergyman in times of division* (1844).

Anon., *The Diaconate and the Poor* (1849).

Anon., *Entries or Stray Leaves from a clergyman's notebook* (1853).

Anon., *The Handbook for Magistrates and Quarter Sessions* (1855).

Anon. [F. E. Paget], *The Owlet of Owlstone Edge* (1855).

Anon., *Parson-ography* (1857).

Anon., *Hints and Prayers designed for District Visitors* (1858).

Anon. [F. E. Paget], *The Curate of Cumberworth and the Vicar of Roost* (1859).

Anon., *The Curate's Wife* (1860).

Anon., *Clerical Papers* (1861).

Anon., *The Clerical Question* (1862).

Anon. [Mrs Mary Grylls], *The Parsonage and the Park* (1863).

Anon. [Revd Austin Leigh], *Recollections of the early days of the Vine Hunt . . .* (1865).

Anon., *'Tekel', the views of a Church of England Layman relative to the Church of England clergy . . .* (1866).

Anon. [James Hollis], *The Pastor, a scene from the life of a clergyman* (1866).

Anon. *The Rector's Homestead*, 2 vols. (1868).

Anon. [T. W. M. Marshall], *My Clerical Friends* (1873).

Anon. [Josiah Bateman], *Clerical Reminiscences* (1880).

Arch, Joseph, *The Story of his Life told by himself* (1898).

Armstrong, H. B. J., ed., *A Norfolk Diary* (1949).

Armstrong, H. B. J., ed., *Armstrong's Norfolk Diary* (1963).

Ashwell, A. R. and Wilberforce, R. G. *Life of Samuel Wilberforce*, 3 vols. (1880–82).

Atkinson, J. C., *Forty Years in a Moorland Parish* (1891).

Balleine, G. R., *A History of the Evangelical Party in the Church of England* (1933).

Baring-Gould, S., *The Church Revival* (1914).

Barnard, H. C., *A History of English Education from 1760* (2nd edn 1961).

Battiscombe, G., *John Keble* (1963).

Bennett, G. V. and Walsh, J. D., eds., *Essays in Modern English Church History* (1966).

Bennett, W. J. E., *The Old Church Porch* (1854–62).

Berens, Edward, *Sermon*: 'Pastoral Watchfulness and Zeal' (1826).

Berens, Edward, *Sermon*: 'The Claim of Destitute Clergymen to Assistance' (1836).

Beresford, John, ed., *The Diary of a Country Parson. The Revd James Woodforde*, 5 vols. (1924–31).

Best, G. F. A., *Temporal Pillars* (Cambridge 1964).

Best, G. F. A., 'The Evangelicals and the Established Church in the early nineteenth century', in *Journal of Theological Studies* [n.s.], vol. x, pt. i, April 1959, p. 63.

Best, G. F. A., 'The Constitutional Revolution 1828–1832' in *Theology*, LXII, June 1959, p. 226.

Best, Hon and Revd Samuel, *Thoughts on Prudence; or the means of improving the condition of a family offered in Savings Banks and Friendly Societies* (1850).

Best, Hon and Revd Samuel, *Village Libraries and Reading Rooms* (1854).

Bickersteth, Edward, *The Christian Student* (1832).

Blomfield, Alfred, *A Memoir of Charles James Blomfield*, 2 vols. (1863).

Bowden, John, *Voices in the Wilderness* (1977).

Brilioth, Y. T., *The Anglican Revival* (1925).

Briscoe, J. F. and Mackay, H. F. B., *A Tractarian at Work. Memoir of Dean Randall* (1932).

Brose, Olive, *Church and Parliament* (Oxford 1959).

Brown, C. K. Francis, *The Church's Part in Education: 1833-1941* (1942).

Brown, C. K. Francis, *A History of the English Clergy 1800-1900* (1953).

Brown, Ford K., *Fathers of the Victorians* (Cambridge 1961).

Bullock, F. W. B., *The History of the Training for the Ministry of the Church of England 1800-1874* (St Leonard's-on-Sea 1955).

Burfield, H. J., *Sermon: 'The Ministry and its Hindrances'* (1857).

Burgess, George, *An Address to the Misguided Poor of the disturbed districts throughout the Kingdom* (1830).

Burgess, H. J., *Enterprise of Education* (1958).

Burgon, J., *Lives of Twelve Good Men,* 2 vols. (2nd edn 1891).

Butler, W. J., *The Life and Letters of Dean Butler* (1897).

Byerley, Thomas H., *The Choice of a Profession* (1857).

Carpenter, S. C., *Church and People 1789-1889* (1933).

Chadwick, Owen, *The Mind of the Oxford Movement* (1960).

Chadwick, Owen, *Victorian Miniature* (1960).

Chadwick, Owen, *The Victorian Church,* 2 vols. (1966 and 1970).

Chadwick, Owen, *The Secularization of the European Mind in the Nineteenth Century* (1975).

Christie, O. F., ed., *The Diary of the Revd William Jones of Broxbourne 1777-1821* (1929).

Church, R. W., *The Oxford Movement* (1891).

Clark, C. P. S., *The Oxford Movement and After* (1932).

Clark, W. K. Lowther, *Eighteenth-century Piety* (1944).

Coleridge, J. T. A., *A Memoir of John Keble* (3rd edn 1870).

Colloms, B., *Victorian Country Parsons* (1977).

Conrad, Charles O. P., 'The Origins of the Parish Mission in England and the Early Passionist Apostolate 1840-1850', in *Journal of Ecclesiastical History*, vol. xiv, 1964, p. 60.

Cook, William, *Weekly Communion, the clergy's duty* . . . (1851).

Coombes, H. and Bax, H. N., eds., *Journal of a Somerset Rector* (1930).

Cope, Sir William H., Bart., *History of the Parish of Eversley* (1886).

Cornish, F. Ware, *The English Church in the Nineteenth Century*, 2 vols. (1910).

Crockford Prefaces, The Editor Looks Back (1947).

Cunningham, J. W., *Sermon*: 'The Political Duties of the Minister of Religion in times of great National Excitement' (1831).

Currie, R., Gilbert A., and Horsley, L., *Churches and Churchgoers* (1977).

Dale, Henry, *Hints on Clerical Reading* (1869).

Dale, Thomas, *Five Years of Church Extension in St Pancras* (1852).

Darvall, F. O., *Popular Disturbances and Public Order in Regency England* (Oxford 1934).

Davidson, R. T. and Benham, W., *Life of A. C. Tait, Archbishop of Canterbury*, 2 vols. (1891).

Davies, G. C. B., 'The Early Evangelicals', in *Church Quarterly Review*, vol. CLV, 1954, p. 121.

Davies, John, *The Subdivision and Rearrangement of Parishes* (1849).

Dibden, Sir Lewis, *Establishment in England . . . essays on Church and State* (1932).

Ditchfield, P. H., *The Parish Clerk* (1907).

Ditchfield, P. H., *Old-time Parson* (1908).

Dunbabin, J. P. D., *Rural Discontent in Nineteenth-century Britain* (1974).

Dunstan, G. R., ed., *The Sacred Ministry* (1970).

Dyer, T. F. Thiselton-, *Old English Social Life, as told by Parish Registers* (1898).

Ecclestone, Alan, 'The Town Parson', in *Theology*, vol. LXXII, February 1969, p. 65.

Ellman, Edward Boys, *Recollections of a Sussex Parson* (1912).

Espin, T. E., *Our Want of Clergy. Its causes and suggestions for its cure* (Oxford 1863).

Evans, E. J., 'Some Reasons for the Growth of English Rural Anti-clericalism 1750–1830', in *Past and Present*, vol. LXVI (1975).

Evans, R. W., *The Rectory of Valehead* (1831).

Faber, F. W., *Sights and Thoughts in Foreign Churches and among Foreign People* (1842).

Fendall, C. P. and Crutchley, E. A., *The Diary of Benjamin Newton 1816–1818* (Cambridge 1933).

Figgis, J. H. and Laski, H. J., *Studies in the Problem of Sovereignty* (Newhaven 1917).

Finer, S. E., *The Man on Horseback* (1962).

Gilbert, A. D., *Religion and Society in Industrial England* (1976).

Gill, J. C., *Parson Bull of Byerley* (1963).

Girdlestone, Charles, *Seven Sermons, preached during the prevalence of cholera in the parish of Sedgley* (1833).

Girdlestone, Charles, *Sanitary Reform* (1853).

Greaves, R. W., 'Golightly and Newman, 1824–45', in *Journal of Ecclesiastical History*, vol. ix, 1958, p. 209.

Gregory, Robert, *A Plea on behalf of small parishes with particular reference to the County of Lincoln* (1849).

Gregory, Robert, *The Difficulties and the Organisation of a Poor Metropolitan Parish*. Two lectures delivered at the Theological College, Cuddesdon (1866).

Goodridge, R. M., 'The Religious Condition of the West Country in 1851', *Social Compass* 1967, p. 285.

Guttsman, W. L., *The British Political Élite* (1963).

Hammond, J. B. and B., *The Village Labourer 1760–1832* (1911).

Hammond, J. B. and B., *The Town Labourer 1760–1832* (1917).

Hammond, J. B. and B., *The Age of the Chartists 1832–1854* (1930).

Hammond, Peter, *The Parson and the Victorian Parish* (1977).

Hare, A., *Memorials of a Quiet Life*, 3 vols. (1872).

Hare, A., *Story of My Life,* 6. vols. (1896–1900).

Hart, A. Tindal and Carpenter, E., *The Nineteenth-century Country Parson* (Shrewsbury 1954).

Hart, A. Tindal, *The Eighteenth-century Country Parson* (Shrewsbury 1955).

Hart, A. Tindal, *The Country Priest in English History* (1959).

Hart, J. M., *The British Police* (1951).

Hartshorne, A., ed., *Edmund Pyle. Memoir of a Royal Chaplain 1729–1763*, annotated and edited (1905).

Hatchard, Mrs Goodwin, *Eight Years' Experience of Mothers' Meetings* (1871).

Heeney, B., 'Tractarian Pastor: Edward Monro of Harrow Weald', in *Canadian Journal of Theology*, vol. XII, 1967, pp. 241–53 and vol. XIV, 1968, pp. 13–27.

Heeney, B., *A Different Kind of Gentleman* (Connecticut, 1976).

Hennell, Michael, 'Evening Communion in the Church of England in the Nineteenth Century', in *Theology*, vol. LXII, January 1959, p. 3.

Hill, R. L., *Toryism and the People 1831–1846* (1929).

Hobsbawn, E. J. and Rule, George, *Captain Swing* (1969).

Hocking, Michael, *A Handbook of Pastoral Work* (1977).

Hodgson, John, *Proposed Improvements in Friendly Societies* (1830).

Hole, Dean S. Reynold, *The Memories of Dean Hole* (3rd edn 1892).

Hole, Dean S. Reynold, *More Memories* (1894).

Horn, Pamela, 'Problems of a Nineteenth Century Vicar 1832–1885', in *Oxford Diocesan Magazine*, October 1968, p. 16, and November 1968, p. 18.

Hughes, Edward, 'The Professions in the Eighteenth Century', in *Durham University Journal* (March 1952).

Humphreys, A. R., 'Literature and Religion in Eighteenth Century England', in *Journal of Ecclesiastical History*, vol. III, 1952, p. 159.

Hunt, Giles, 'A Real-Life Jane Austen Clergyman', in *Theology* (May 1976).

Hutchings, W. H., *Life of T. T. Carter* (2nd edn 1904).

Hutton, W. H., ed., *Robert Gregory Autobiography* (1912).

Inglis, K. S., *Churches and the Working Class in Victorian England* (1963).

Inglis, K. S., 'Patterns of Religious Worship in 1851', in *Journal of Ecclesiastical History*, vol. XI, 1960, p. 74.

Jefferies, Richard, *Hodge and His Master* (1946).

Jessop, Augustus, *Arcady for better or worse* (1887).

Johnson, A. H., *The Disappearance of the Small Landowner* (Oxford 1909).

Jones, M. G., *The Charity School Movement* (Cambridge 1938).

Kerr, Eleanor, *Hunting Parson. The Life and Times of Rev. John Russell* (1963).

Kingsley, Charles, *His Letters and Memories of His Life*, ed. by his wife, 2 vols. (1877).

Kitson Clark, G., *The Making of Victorian England* (1962).

Kitson Clark, G., *Churchmen and the Condition of England 1832–1885* (1973).

Lash, N. and Rhymer, J., *The Christian Priesthood* (1970).

Laskett, Peter, *The World We Have Lost* (1965).

Legg, J. Wickham, *English Church Life from the Restoration to the Tractarian Movement* (1914).

Linnell, C. D., ed., 'The Diary of Benjamin Rogers 1720–1771', in *Bedfordshire Historical Record Society*, vol. xxv (Luton 1950).

Lloyd, H. R., *Sermon*: 'The Responsibilities and Requirements of the Clergy' (1857).

Lowder, C. F., *Twenty-one Years in St George's Mission* (1877).

Macaulay, T. B., *History of England,* ed. C. H. Firth, 6 vols. (1913).

McClatchey, D., *Oxfordshire Clergy 1777–1869* (Oxford 1960).

Macdermott, K. H., *Sussex Church Music in the Past* (Chichester 1922).

Macdermott, K. H., *The Old Church Gallery Minstrels* (1948).

Mackenzie, Henry, *On the Parochial System as a means of alleviating temporal distress in the metropolis* (1850).

Mackenzie, Henry, *Sermon:* 'The Parochial System: Its development and results' (1858).

McNeill, J. T., *A History of the Cure of Souls* (New York 1965).

Marks, Richard, *The Village Pastor*, 2 vols. (1827).

Marshall, J. D., *The Old Poor Law 1795–1834* (1968).

Martineau, Robert, *The Office and Work of a Priest* (1972).

Mathieson, W. L., *English Church Reform, 1815–1840* (1923).

Methuen, T. A., *A Memoir of the Rev. Robert P. Beachcroft* (1832).

Miller, J. C., *Sermon*: 'Preaching' (1847).

Miller, J. C., *Sermon*: 'Neglect of the Holy Spirit a main hindrance of Ministerial Success' (1848).

Miller, J. C., *Sermon*: 'The Defective Ministerial Training of our Universities, a main hindrance to the efficiency of the Church of England' (1851).

Miller, J. C., *Sermon*: 'Our Office – Our Work – Our Master' (1853).

Mingay, G. F., *English Landed Gentry in the Eighteenth Century* (1963).

Mole, D. E. H., 'John Cole Miller: a Victorian Rector of Birmingham', in *Journal of Ecclesiastical History*, vol. XVII, 1966, p. 95.

Molesworth, J. E. N., *Tales from the Scrapbook of a Country Clergyman* (1831).

Monro, Edward, *Agricultural Colleges and their Working* (1850).

Monro, Edward, *Parochial Papers for the clergyman, the schoolmaster, and the family* (1856).

Moorman, J. R. H., *A History of the Church of England* (1953).

Moss, C. B., *The Orthodox Revival 1833–1933* (1933).

Mosley, Thomas, *Reminiscences chiefly of Oriel College and the Oxford Movement*, 2 vols. (2nd edn 1882).

Moule, H. C. G., *Memories of a Vicarage* (1913).

Naylor, F. W., *Continuous Education or Practical Suggestions about libraries, discussion meetings, lectures* . . . (2nd edn 1858).

Nevine, William, *Sermon:* 'The clergy's privilege and the duty of daily intercession' (1846).

Newsome, D. H., *Godliness and Good Learning* (1961).

Newsome, D. H., *The Parting of Friends* (1966).

Norman, E. R., *Church and Society in England 1770–1970* (1976).

Obelkevich, J., *Religion and Rural Society. South Lindsey 1825–1875* (Oxford 1976).

Ollard, S. L., *A Short History of the Oxford Movement* (1915).

Overton, J. H. and Relton, F., *The English Church 1714–1800* (1906).

Owen, David, *English Philanthropy 1660–1960* (Harvard 1965).

Oxenden, Ashton, *The History of My Life* (1891).

Paget, F. E., *The Warden of Berkingholt* (1843).

Paton, D. M., ed., *Reform of the Ministry: a study of the work of Roland Allen* (1968).

Paul, Leslie, *The Deployment and Payment of the Clergy* (1964).

Paul, Leslie, *A Church by Daylight* (1973).

Peacock, A. J., *Bread and Blood. A Study of the Agrarian Riots in East Anglia 1816* (1965).

Pearson, J. G., *Sermon to Electors . . .* (1857).

Pellow, Hon and Revd Edward, *Sermon*: 'Preach the Word' (1847).

Phillott, H. W., *Sermon*: 'Watchfulness – the Duty of the Clergy' (1853).

Plomer, W., ed., *Diary of the Rev. Francis Kilvert*, 3 vols. (1938–40).

Pratt, John, *Eclectic Notes: or, notes of discussions on religious topics at the meetings of the Eclectic Society, London, 1798–1814* (2nd edn 1865).

Prevost, Sir George, *The Autobiography of Isaac Williams* (1892).

Purcell, W. H., *Onward, Christian Soldier* (Autobiography of Sabine Baring-Gould) (1957).

Quinault, R. and Stevenson, J., *Popular Protest and Social Order 1790–1920* (1974).

Quinlan, M. J., *Victorian Prelude. A History of English Manners 1700–1830* (New York 1941).

Redford, Arthur, *The Economic History of England 1760–1860* (2nd edn 1960).

Report from the clergy of a district in the diocese of Lincoln convened for the purpose of considering the state of religion . . . (1800).

Report of the Select Committee on the Sale of Beer 1833. Parliament Reports 1833, vol. xv, p. 7.

Report of the Poor Law Commissioners . . . (1840).

Report of the Special Assistant Poor Law Commissioners on the Employment of Women and Children in Agriculture (1843).

Report of the Medical Poor Relief Committee 1844, Parliamentary Papers 1844, vol. IX.

Report of the Proceedings of Church Congress (1861–70).

Reynolds, J. S., *The Evangelicals in Oxford 1735–1871* (Oxford 1953).

Reynolds, M., *Martyr of Ritualism; Father Mackonochie of St Alban's, Holborn* (1965).

Robinson, William, *The Magistrate's Pocket-Book* (1825).

Robinson, William, *Lex Parochialis* (1827).

Robson, Robert, *An Attorney in Eighteen-century England* (Cambridge 1959).

Royds, T. F., *Haughton Rectory* (Shrewsbury 1953).

Russell, Anthony, ed., *Group and Teams in the Countryside* (1975).

Russell, G. W. E., *A Short History of the Evangelical Movement* (1915).

Sandford, John, *Sermon*: 'Clerical Training' (1857).

Sandford, John, *The Mission and Extension of the Church at Home. Bampton Lectures* (1862).

Saumarez Smith, W. H., *An Honorary Ministry* (ACCM Occasional Paper no. 8, 1977).

Selwyn, G. A., *Sermon:* 'The Work of Christ in the World' (Cambridge 1855).

Sewell, William, *Christian Politics* (1844).

Seymour, Richard and Mackarness, J. F., *Eighteen Years of a Clerical Meeting;* minutes of the Alcester Clerical Association from June 1842 to August 1860 (1862).

Simpkinson, C. H., *The Life and Work of Bishop Thorold* (1896).

Sinclair, John, *Sermon*: 'On Preaching' (1855).

Sinclair, John, *Sermon*: 'The Parochial System of England' (1859).

Smith, Alan, *The Established Church and Popular Religion* (1970).

Smyth, Charles, *Simeon and Church Order* (Cambridge 1940).

Soloway, R. A., *Prelates and People. Ecclesiastical Social Thought in England 1783–1852* (1969).

Spooner, Edward, *Parson and People; or incidents in the everyday life of a clergyman* (1964).

Stephens, W. R. W., *The Life and Letters of W. F. Hook* (1880).

Stephens, W. R. W., *A Memoir of Richard Durnford* (1899).

Steward, J. H. and Bickersteth, E., *Addresses and Sermons delivered on the occasion of a meeting of two clerical associations at Weston-super-Mare* (1849).

Stillingfleet, E. W., *Sermon*: 'Clerical Qualifications and Restless Times' (1847).

Stokes, F. G., ed., *The Bletchley Diary of the Rev. William Cole, M.A., F.S.A., 1765-7* (1931).

Sumner, G. H., *Life of Charles Richard Sumner* (1876).

Sumner, J. B., *Apostolic Preaching Considered* (1815).

Sykes, N., *Church and State in England in the Eighteenth Century* (Cambridge 1934).

Talbot, Hon Mrs J. C., *Parochial Mission Women* (1862).

Tavard, G. H., *The Quest for Catholicity. A Study of Anglicanism* (New York 1964).

Taylor, Brian, 'Bishop Hamilton', in *Church Quarterly Review*, vol. CLV, 1954, p. 235.

Thompson, F. M. L., *English Landed Society in the Nineteenth Century* (1962).

Thompson, Henry, *The Sunday School* (1858).

Thompson, R. H. T., 'The Church and the Proletariat', in *Theology,* vol. LXI, May 1958, p. 179.

Thornton, C. and McLaughlin, P., *The Fothergills of Ravenstonedale* (1905).

Trevelyan, G. M., *English Social History* (1946).

Trollope, Anthony, *Clergymen of the Church of England* (1866).

Twining, Richard, *Recreations and Studies of a Country Clergyman in the Eighteenth Century* (1882).

Twining, Richard, *Selections from Papers of the Twining Family* (1887).

Twopenny, R., *Lectures for a Village Night-School* (1863).

Walker, R. B., 'Religious Changes in Cheshire 1750–1850', in *Journal of Ecclesiastical History,* vol. XVII, 1966, p. 77.

Ward, Mrs Humphrey, *Robert Elsmere* (1888).

Ward, W. R., 'The Tithe Question in England in the Early Nineteenth Century', in *Journal of Ecclesiastical History*, vol. XVI, 1965, p. 67.

Ward, W. R., *Religion and Society in England 1710–1850* (1972).

Warne, Arthur, *Church and Society in Eighteenth-century Devon* (Newton Abbot 1969).

Watson, E. W., 'An Eighteenth-century Clergyman', in *Church Quarterly Review*, vol. cv, January 1928, p. 255.

Webb, E. D., ed., *Notes on the Parishes of Fyfield, Kimpton . . . by Rev. R. H. Clutterbuck*, revised and edited (Salisbury 1898).

Welch, P. J., 'Bishop Blomfield and Church Extension in London', in *Journal of Ecclesiastical History*, vol. iv, 1953, p. 203.

Welch, P. J., 'Bishop Blomfield and the Development of Tractarianism in London', in *Church Quarterly Review*, vol. clv, 1954, p. 332.

Welch, P. J., 'The Revival of an Active Convocation of Canterbury (1852–1855)', in *Journal of Ecclesiastical History*, vol. x, 1958, p. 188.

Welch, P. J., 'Blomfield and Peel: a study in co-operation between Church and State, 1841–1846', in *Journal of Ecclesiastical History*, vol. xii, 1961, p. 71.

West, F., *The Country Parish Today and Tomorrow* (1960).

West, F., *Sparrows of the Spirit* (rev. edn 1961).

Whately, R., *Charge*: 'The Parochial System' (1859).

Wickham, E. R., *Church and People in an Industrial City* (1957).

Wilberforce, H. W., *The Parochial System. An Appeal to English Churchmen* (1838).

Wilkinson, Alan, *The Church of England and the First World War* (1978).

Willey, Basil, *Nineteenth century Studies* (1949).

Williams, Isaac, *A Short Memoir of the Rev. Robert Alfred Suckling* (1852).

Wilson, E., *Observations of the Present State of the Poor* (1795).

Wollaston, Francis, *A Country Parson's Address to his flock . . .* (1799).

Wood, A. Skevington, *Thomas Haweis 1734–1820* (1957).

Woodforde, J. R., *Ordination Lectures delivered in the Chapel of Cuddesdon College . . .* (1861).

Wray, Cecil, *Four Years of Pastoral Work . . .* (1854).
Wray, Cecil, *The Church's Work in our Large Towns* (Liverpool 1869).
Yates, Richard, *Patronage of the Church of England* (1823).
Yeo, S., *Religion and Voluntary Organisations in Crisis* (1976).
Yonge, C. M., *John Keble's Parishes* (1898).
Young, C. M., *Victorian England* (2nd edn 1953).

UNPUBLISHED WORKS

Blunt, J. H., *Essays, Reviews, etc., 1855–1858*. (A collection of Blunt's articles and printed papers, bound in two volumes and deposited in the Bodleian Library.)
Walsh, J. D., *The Yorkshire Evangelicals in the Eighteenth Century* (Cambridge Ph.D. thesis, 1956).

3 BACKGROUND WORKS ON THE SOCIOLOGY OF PROFESSIONS AND THE CLERGYMAN'S ROLE

Banton, Michael, *Roles: an introduction to the study of social relations* (1965).
Ben-David, J., 'Professions in the Class System of Present-day Societies', in *Current Sociology* (1963–4).
Bendix, Reinhard, *Max Weber: an intellectual portrait* (1966).
Berkes, N., 'Religious and Secular Institutions in Comparative Perspective', in *Archives de Sociologie des Religions* 8 (16), 1963, p. 65.
Blizzard, S. W., 'The Minister's Dilemma', in *Christian Century,* 25 April 1956, p. 508.
Blizzard, S. W., 'Role Conflicts of the Urban Protestant Parish Minister', in *City Church* VII (4), September 1956, p. 13.
Blizzard, S. W., 'The Protestant Minister's Integrating Roles', in *Religious Education*, July-August 1958, p. 1.
Blizzard, S. W., 'The Parish Minister's Self-Image of his Master Role', in *Pastoral Psychology*, December 1958.
Blizzard, S. W., 'The Parish Minister's Self-Image and Variability in Community Culture', in *Pastoral Psychology*, October 1959.

Brothers, Joan, 'Social Change and the Role of the Priest', in *Social Compass* 10 (6), 1963, p. 477.

Bunnik, R. J., 'The Ecclesiastical Minister and Marriage', in *Social Compass* 12 (1-2), 1965, p. 93.

Carr Saunders, A. M. and Wilson, P. A., *The Professions* (1933).

Coates, C. H. and Kistler, R. C., 'Role Dilemmas of Protestant Clergymen in a Metropolitan Community', in *Review of Religious Research* 6 (3), 1964-5, p. 147.

Coxon, A. P. M., 'Patterns of Occupational Recruitment: the Anglican Ministry', in *Sociology*, vol. 1, January 1967, p. 73.

Currie, Robert, *Methodism Divided* (1968).

Ehrenstom, N. and Muelder, W. G., *Institutionalism and Church Unity* (1963).

Elliott, Philip, *The Sociology of Professions* (1972).

Emmet, D., *Rules, Roles and Relations* (1966).

Etzoni, Amitai, *The Semi-Professions and their organization* (New York 1969).

Fichter, J. H., *Religion as an Occupation* (Notre Dame, Ind. 1961).

Fletcher, J. H., 'A Comparative view of the Parish Priest', in *Archives de Sociologie des Religions* 8 (16), 1963, p. 44.

Glasse, J. D., *Profession: Minister* (New York 1968).

Gross, Neal, ed., *Explorations in Role Analysis; studies of the School Superintendency* (New York 1958).

Gustafson, J. M., 'The Clergy in the United States', in *Social Compass* 12 (1-2), 1965, p. 35.

Hall, R. M., *Occupations and Social Structure* (New Jersey 1969).

Harrison, P. M., *Authority and Power in the Free Church Tradition* (Princeton 1959).

Hickson, D. J. and Thomas, M. W., 'Professionalization in Britain: a preliminary measurement', in *Sociology,* vol. 3 (1969).

Jackson, J. A., ed., *Professions and Professionalization* (Cambridge 1970).

Jackson, T. J., *Professions and Power* (1972).

Jarvis, Peter, 'The Ministry: Occupation, Profession or Status?' in *The Expository Times* (June 1975).

Jarvis, Peter, 'The Parish Ministry as a Semi-Profession', in *The Sociological Review*, vol. 23 (1975).

Jarvis, Peter, 'A Profession in Process; a theoretical model for the ministry', in *The Sociological Review*, vol. 24 (1976).

Jarvis, Peter, 'The Ministry-Laity Relationship: a case of potential conflict', *Social Analysis,* vol. 37 (1976).

Lee, Robert, *The Social Sources of Church Unity* (New York 1960).

Maclear, J. F., 'The Making of the Lay Tradition', in *Journal of Religion*, vol. XXXIII (2), 1953, p. 113.

Marshall, T. H., *Sociology at the Crossroads* (1963).

Martin, David, *A Sociology of English Religion* (1967).

Martin, David, *A General Theory of Secularization* (1978).

Merton, R. K., *Social Theory and Social Structure* (Glencoe, Ill., rev. edn 1957).

Mertz, David, *New Congregations* (Philadelphia 1967).

Millerson, G., *The Qualifying Associations: a study in professionalization* (1964).

Moberg, D. O., *The Church as a Social Institution* (New Jersey 1962).

Morgan, D. M. J., 'The Social and Educational Background of Anglican Bishops', in *British Journal of Sociology*, vol. 20 (1969).

Neagele, K. D., 'Clergy, Psychiatrists and Teachers, a study in Roles and Socialization', in *Canadian Journal of Economics and Political Science,* vol. XXII, 1956, p. 46.

Niebuhr, H. R. and Williams, D. D., eds., *The Ministry in Historical Perspective* (New York 1956).

O'Dea, T., *The Sociology of Religion* (Englewood Cliff 1966).

Parsons, Talcott, 'The Professions and Social Structure', in *Social Force* (May 1939).

Parsons, Talcott, *The Structure of Social Action* (Glencoe, Ill., 1949).

Parsons, Talcott, *The Social System* (1951).

Rawson, S., Bryman, A., and Hining, B., *Clergy, Ministers and Priests* (1977).

Reader, W. J., *Professional Men: the Rise of the Professional Classes in the Nineteenth Century* (1966).

Spencer, H., *The Principles of Sociology* (1896).

Steward, C. W., *Person and Profession: career development in the ministry* (New York 1974).

Tonna, B., 'The Allocation of Time among Clerical Activities', in *Social Compass*, vol. x, 1963, p. 125.

Tonnies, F., *Community and Association*, trans. Charles P. Loomis (1955).

Towler, Robert, 'The Changing Status of the Ministry', in *Crucible* (May 1968).

Vollmer, H. M. and Miles, D. L., eds., *Professionalization* (New Jersey 1966).

Wilensky, H. L., 'The Professionalization of Everyone', in *American Journal of Society* (1964).

Wilson, B. R., 'The Paul Report Examined', in *Theology*, vol. LXVIII, 1965, p. 89.

Wilson, B. R., *Religion in Secular Society* (1966).

Wilson, B. R., *Patterns of Sectarianism* (1967).

Wilson, B. R., *Contemporary Transformation of Religion* (1976).

Yinger, J. Milton, *Religion in the Struggle for Power* (Durham, N.C. 1946).

Yinger, J. Milton, *Religion, Society and the Individual* (New York 1957).

UNPUBLISHED WORKS

Coxon, A. P. M., *A Sociological Study of the Social Recruitment, Selection and Professional Socialization of Anglican Ordinands* (University of Leeds, Ph.D. 1965).

Thompson, K. A., *The Organizational response of the Church of England to Social Change with particular reference to developments associated with the Church Assembly* (Oxford University, D.Phil. 1967). [1]

Woolgar, M. J., *The Development of the Anglican and Roman Catholic Clergy as a Profession* (Leicester University, Ph.D. 1960).

[1] The material of this thesis has been published:
K. A. Thompson, *Bureaucracy and Church Reform. The Organizational Response of the Church of England to Social Change 1800–1965* (Oxford 1970).

Index

absenteeism, 29
administration, 117, 121, 144, 177, 201–2, 208, 276–7, 278–9, 292; see also clerk
Agricultural Workers Union, 226
Alcester Clerical Association, 43, 70, 77, 124, 180; see also Seymour, Richard
Allen, Roland, 285
allotments, 179–80
almoner, clergyman as, 169–83, 277
anti-clericalism, 104, 128, 156
Apostolic Succession, 39
Arch, Joseph, 178–9, 226
Armstrong, Benjamin John, 41, 70, 74, 139, 164, 181–2, 211
army officer, role of, 18, 20, 24, 26, 45, 243
Austen, Jane, 35
Auxiliary Pastoral Ministry, 243, 256–7, 263, 284–7, 296, 301

baptism, 110–12
Best, Samuel, 47, 96, 120, 135, 179
Blomfield, C. J. (Bishop of London 1828–56), 35, 47, 54, 59, 61–2, 68, 83, 108, 120, 152, 161–2, 190, 196, 210
Blunt, John Henry, 70, 72, 73, 112, 124, 129, 139, 168, 211
Blunt, John James, 53–4, 70, 122–3, 199
Book of Common Prayer, 53, 63, 76, 79, 100, 113, 123, 130, 148, 169, 203
Bridges, Charles, 121
Bull, George, 69, 224
Butler, William, 67, 95, 105, 117–18, 124, 210–11, 225
Burgon, John William, 69, 96–7, 98, 112, 144, 150, 183
burial, 79–81, 82, 275, 300

career, 15, 34, 151–2, 215–6, 239, 245–6, 255–6, 271–2
Carter, T. T., 73, 105, 172
Catechist, clergyman as, 130–45, 249

Celebrant of sacraments, clergyman as, 100–12, 276, 302
Central Stipends Authority, 268, 271
ceremonial, 108–10, 235
charter role, of the clergyman, 38, 63, 85, 100, 130, 148, 185, 203, 214, 233, 234–5, 249, 275–6, 285, 299
Chesterfield, Lord, 32
children, clergy's involvement with, 130–41, 250; special services for, 139
church, attendance, 4–5, 55–6, 60, 250
church, building, 62, 83–4, 221–2
church, restoration, 41
Church Association, 45, 108
Church Commissioners, 268
Church Congress, 45
Church, Dean R. W., 6
churching of women, 81–4
civil servants, role of, 18–19, 22, 26, 38, 234, 243
clerical dress, 235–6, 239
clerical directories, 45
clerical journals, 45, 239
clerical meetings, 43–5, 239
clericalism, 5, 256
clergy, numbers, 241–2, 262–6
clergyman,
   as a professional man, 9–27, 28–49
clerk, clergyman as, 142–5; see also administration
Cobbett, William, 36, 153
Cole, William, 80, 88, 114, 142
Commission on the Employment of Women and Children in Agriculture (1843), 224
community, atrophy of, 74, 277–8
confession, sacramental, 124
confirmation, 133–4, 139–40
Convocation, 44–5
corporate practice, 255–6, 279–80
cottage meetings, 67–70
Counselling, 123–9
curates, 19, 36–7, 87, 103, 115, 133, 162, 186, 238, 241

355